START HERE:
DRAW

LET'S GO

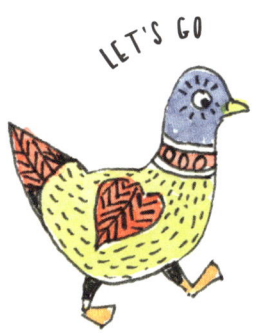

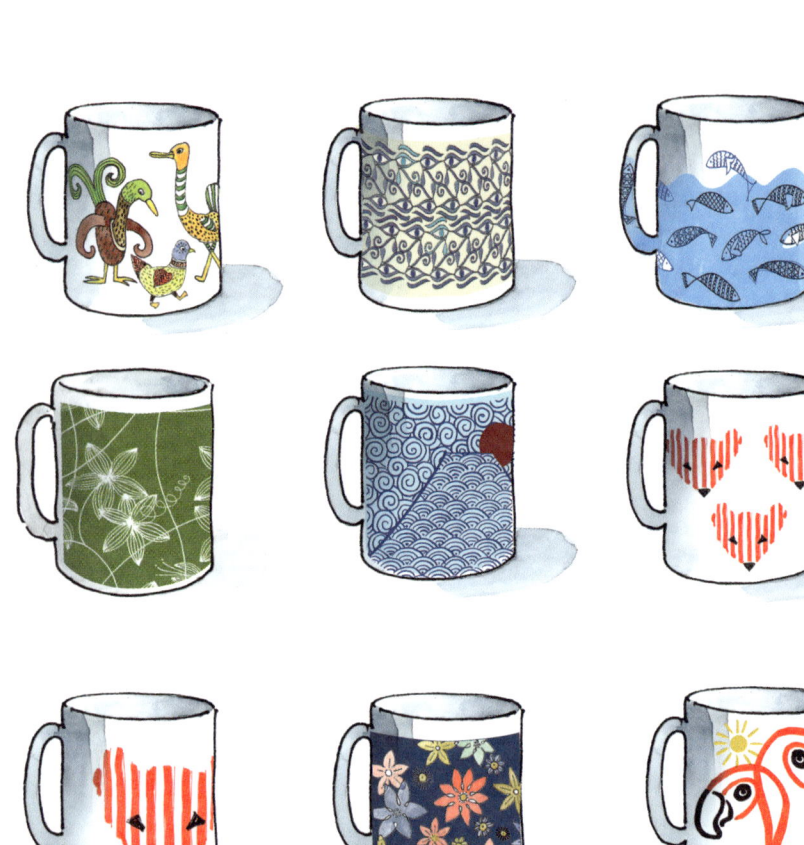
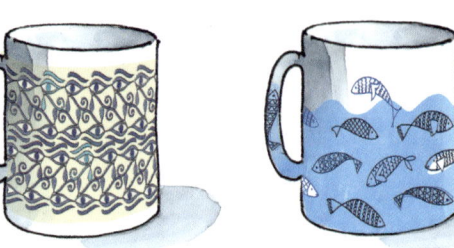
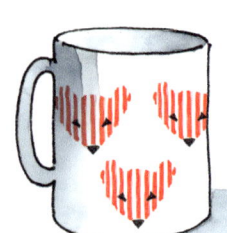
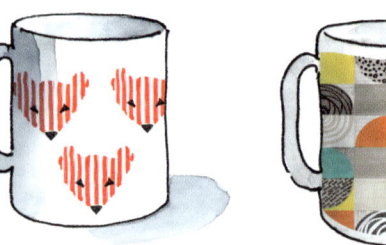
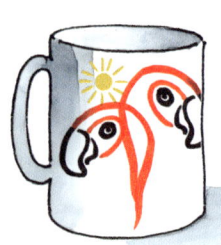
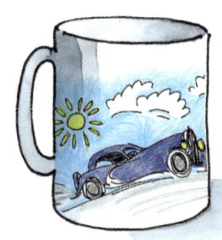
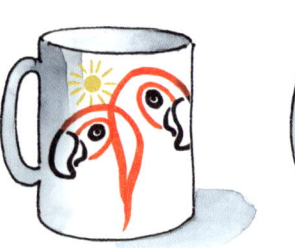
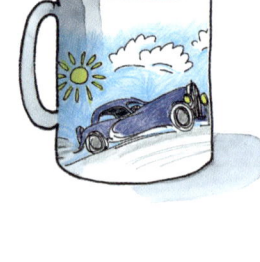
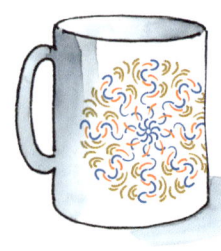
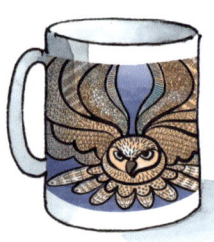
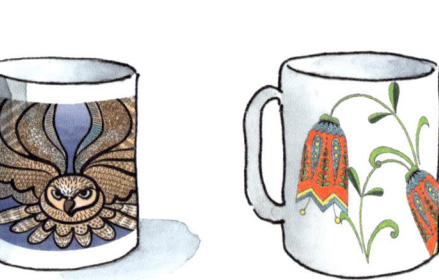
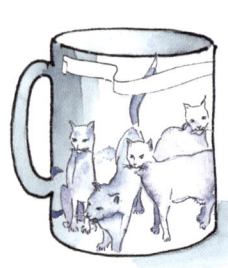
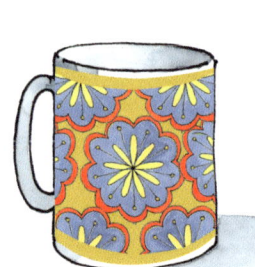
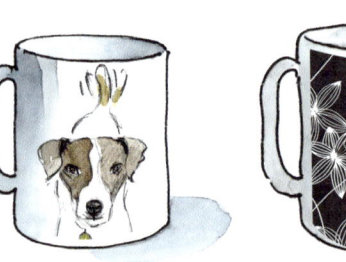

START HERE:
DRAW

50 Ways to Be an Artist Without Trying

MOIRA CLINCH

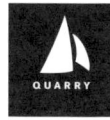

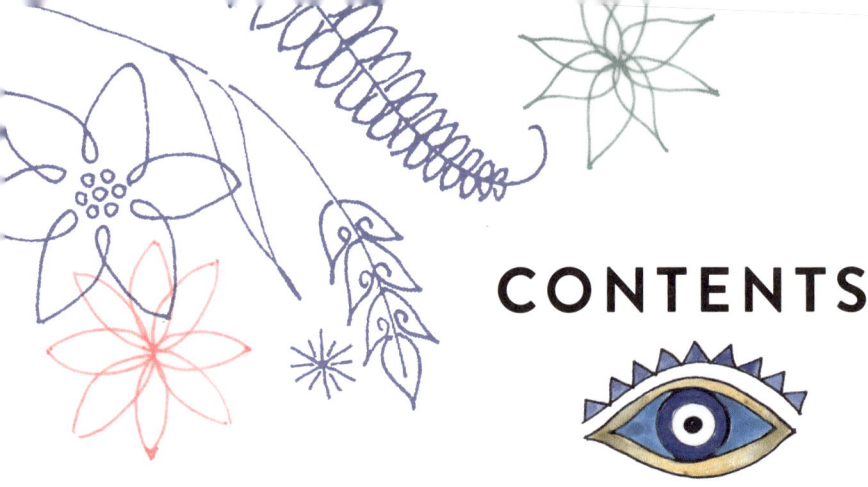

CONTENTS

HELLO!   6
Let's get started

1. START HERE   8
Here are some fearless "daily" mark-making ideas, using a variety of media. From the simplest single line drawings to cute repeated and built-up motifs. Most can be drawn in a few minutes to an hour or so, but can be adjusted by doing more or less.

2. GET A SKETCHBOOK   64
Get into the sketching habit. Your sketchbook is a great place to experiment without worry. Treat it as a journal of your art journey or draw things from everyday life and make it a personal journal.

3. PRACTICE MAKES PERFECT   108
Repeating anything is a way of honing your skills. It is no different with drawing and sketching, with the added advantage of creating patterns as you practice. It doesn't have to be perfect but it will help you make progress.

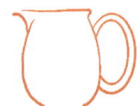
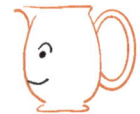
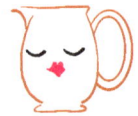
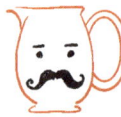

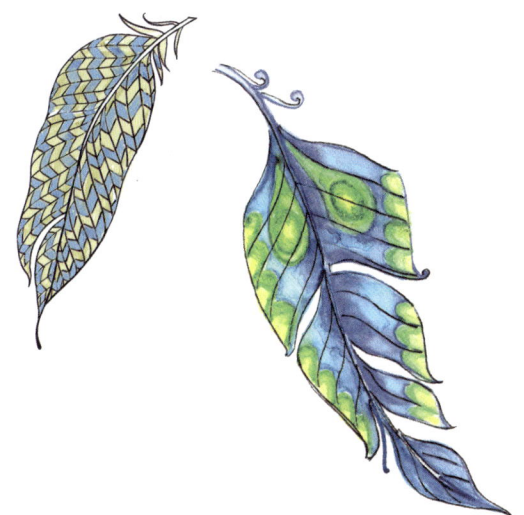

4. MAKE IT YOUR OWN   142

Building on the ideas and techniques from the first three sections, you will develop your own creative approach—from patternmaking with stylized motifs to more realistic drawings.

RESOURCES   182

Here are the few essential pieces of equipment you will need, or that you can add to your growing toolkit. You'll find a complete guide to the world of art supplies including the types of pens, pencils, and paper to build your starter kit.

Finally, some information on how to prepare your work if you want to reproduce it digitally.

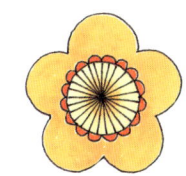

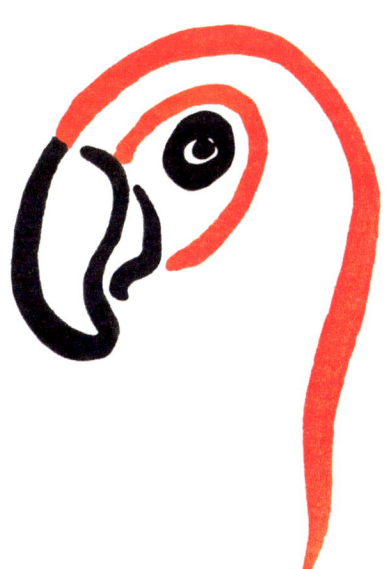

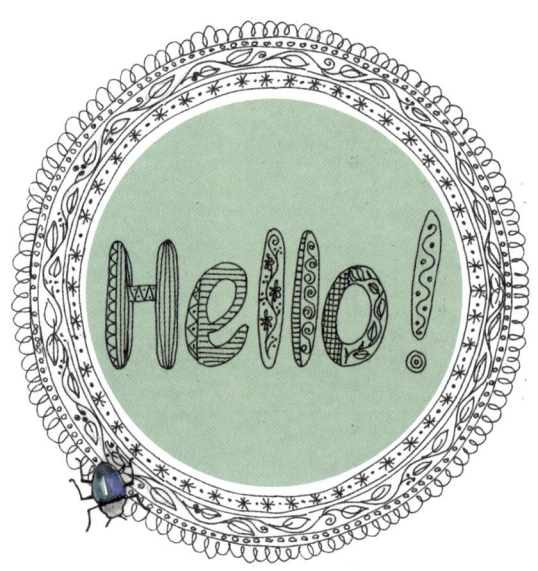

LET'S GET STARTED

I know you are eager to start, and reading an introduction slows you down,
but here are a few words of encouragement.

Drawing is both fun and relaxing, and you can create fun pieces of art in your first few
days. It does not have to be complicated—pick up a sketchbook or a piece of paper and
a pencil as your basic tools. Art can be something for yourself or something to share via
social media or as a gift, and by getting into the habit of drawing, the world around you will
become a source of inspiration and enjoyment.

Like anything, art takes practice. The more time you invest, the more you get
back, and the more you want to do it. Although it is difficult to set aside time, try making
a routine and doing one exercise a week. You will soon get in the habit of drawing
and see your skills improve.

This book is broken into units representing the stages of drawing, introducing different approaches and prompts. If you are new to drawing or returning after a number of years, begin with the ideas in the early chapters to help build up your confidence—if you feel more adventurous then just jump in anywhere. It's your book!

Take your time and enjoy each exercise—don't be afraid to experiment as you go along; a mistake can turn into a happy accident and give you a personal style. Sometimes it helps to refer back to the basics, since the styles and techniques you learn will be tools for more complex drawings. Remember to display your work around you for inspiration as you progress.

There are Takeaways indicated throughout the book, where you can follow projects to make for yourself or to offer as gifts to friends and family.

If you need advice on equipment, trying new media, or just tips on what is the best pen for a certain approach, then turn to page 182. However, most of the drawings can be done anywhere using any tool, so don't be afraid to simply pick up a pencil and begin. A majority of the art in this book is done with traditional media, although most of the ideas can also be done using digital drawing apps.

Creating this book through the difficult times of the past few years has kept me happy and optimistic, and I hope that drawing can do the same for you.

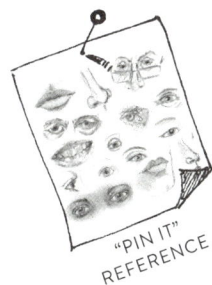

"PIN IT"
REFERENCE

"Pin" the things you may want to refer back to, such as:
Mark effects, p.29
Tone swatches, p.42
Eye shapes, p.92
Border patterns, p.120

QUICK START
If you are unsure of which media to use, try any of the items to the right; or go to Resources (page 182) for some more advice. Occasionally the unit will require a specific material, which will be mentioned.

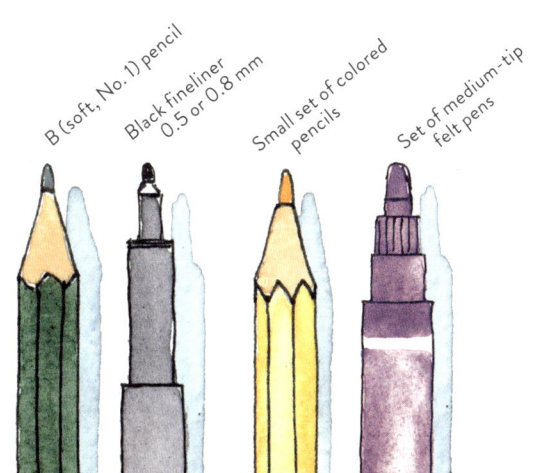

B (soft, No. 1) pencil

Black fineliner 0.5 or 0.8 mm

Small set of colored pencils

Set of medium-tip felt pens

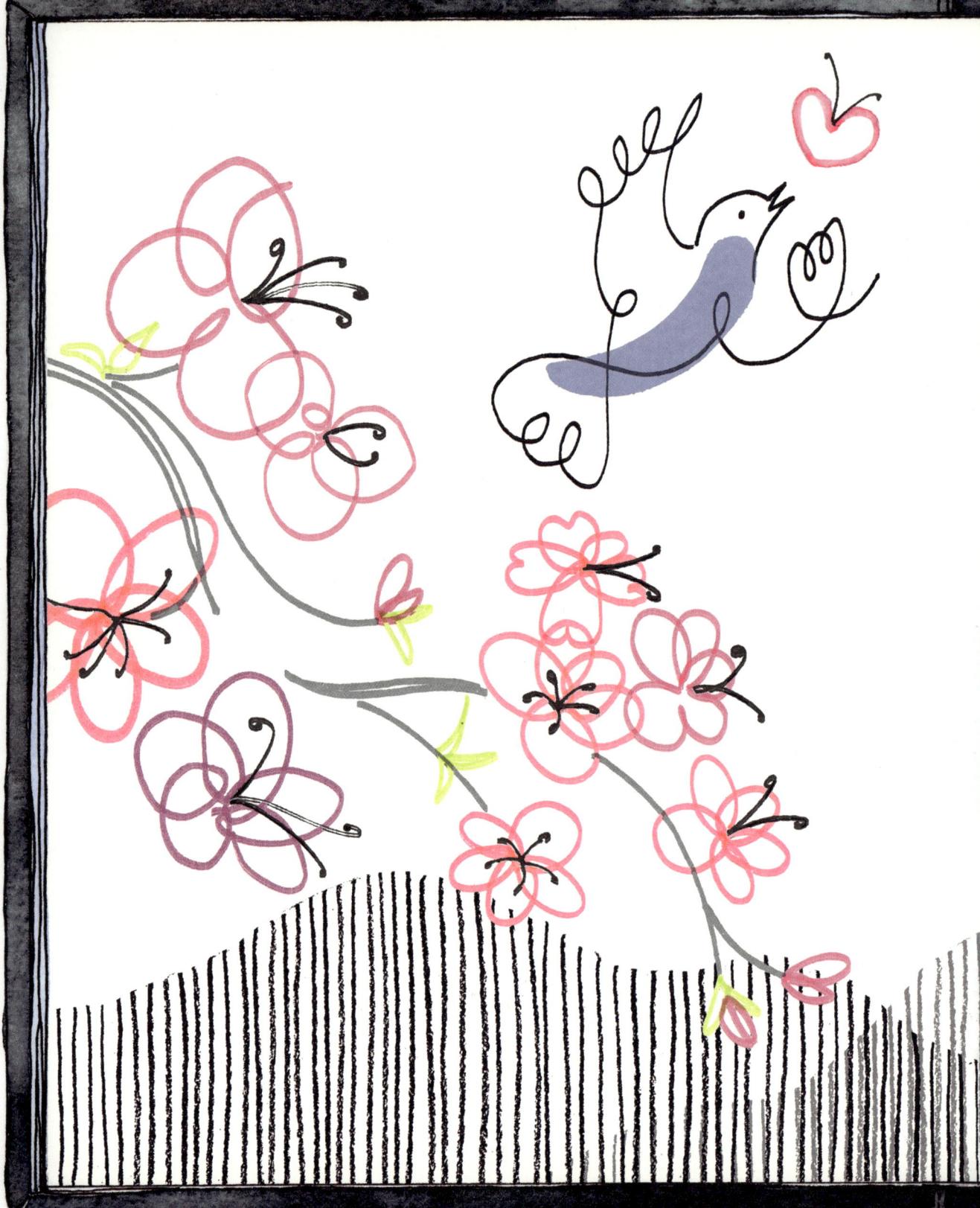

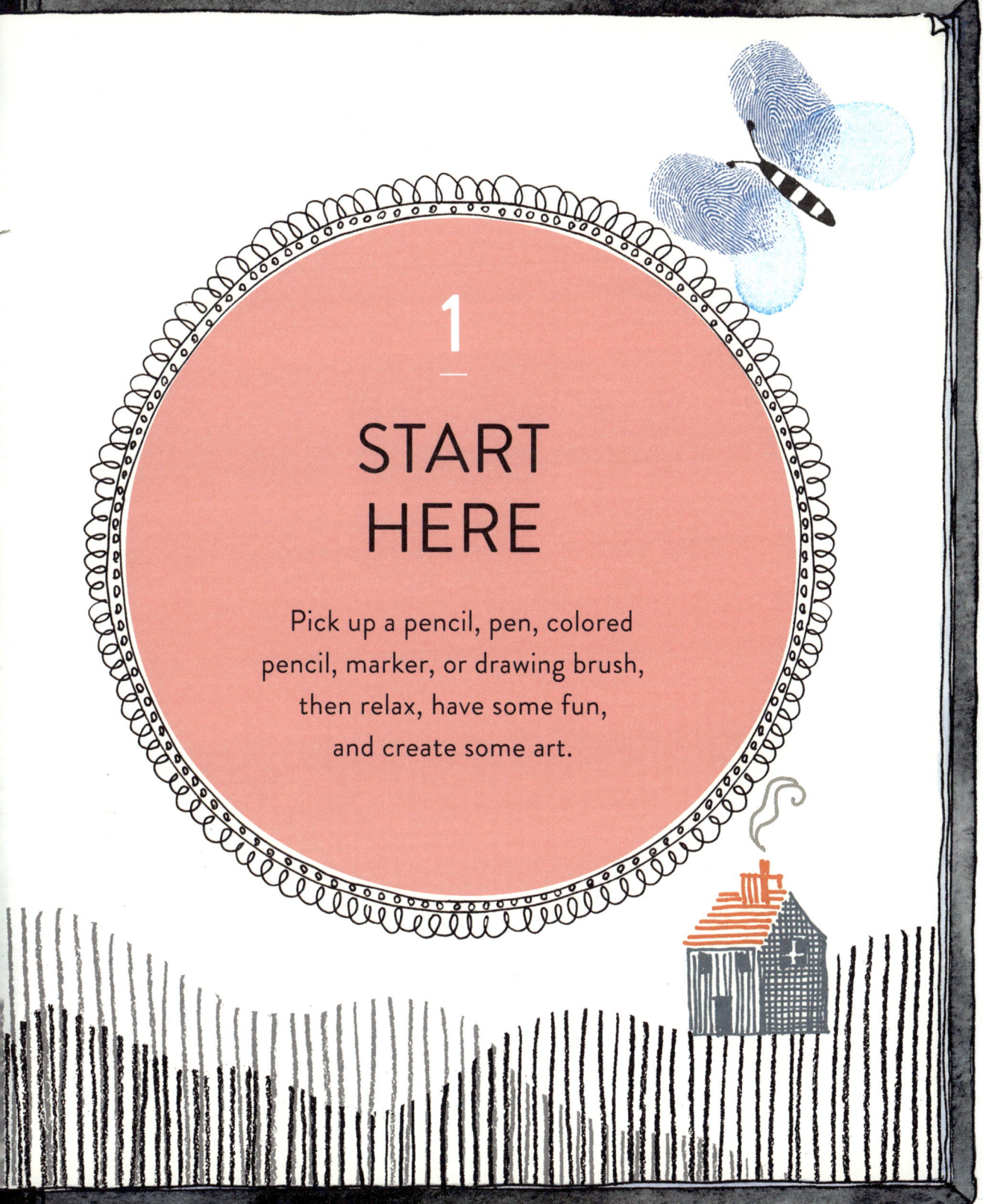

1

START HERE

Pick up a pencil, pen, colored
pencil, marker, or drawing brush,
then relax, have some fun,
and create some art.

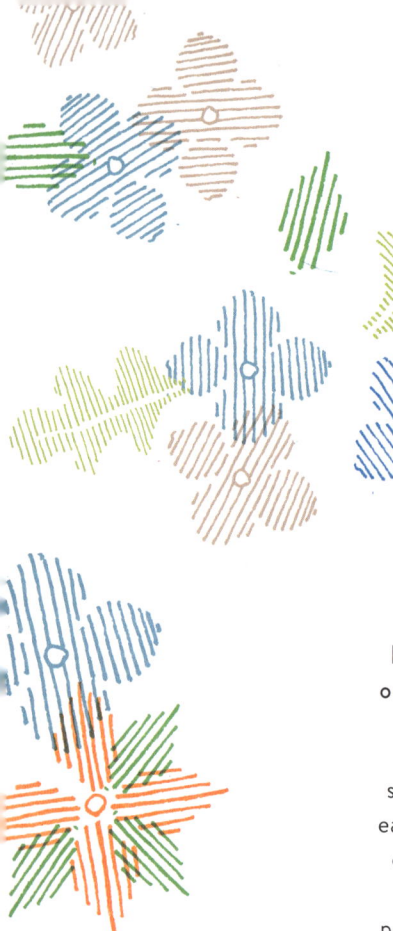

DRAW A FEW STRAIGHT LINES

It's amazing what you can do with a simple line. The line is one of the fundamental marks used in drawing or sketching.

Try practicing a few little areas of parallel lines to create shapes. Different tones can be made by the space between each line, or by overlapping them as in the circles below. You can experiment with a range of tools, such as using pencil, fineliner pens, colored pencils, or non-alcohol-based felt pens. I generally use a 0.5 mm to a 0.8 mm fineliner pen on heavyweight (90 lb, 200 gsm) paper.

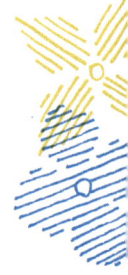

Hold your pencil or pen at about 45° to the paper, and don't tense up! Your grip should be relaxed. Try not to press too hard on the paper.

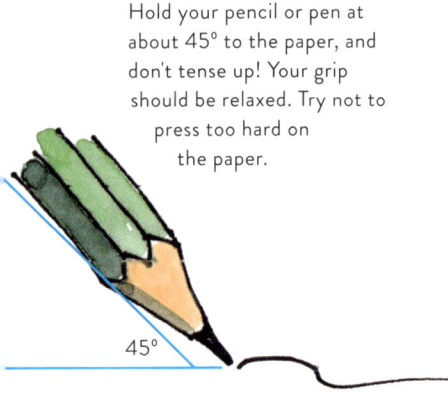

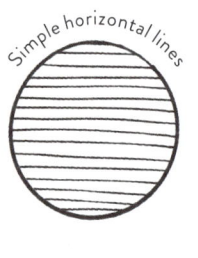

Simple horizontal lines

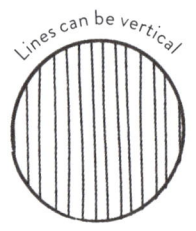

Lines can be vertical

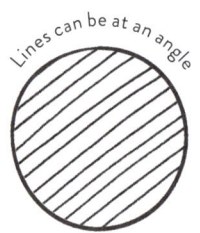

Lines can be at an angle

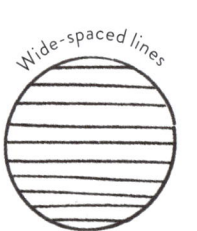

Wide-spaced lines

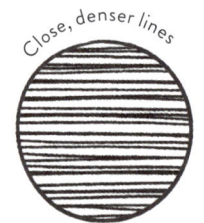

Close, denser lines

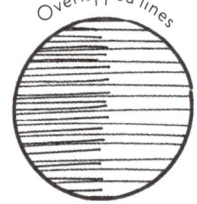

Overlapped lines

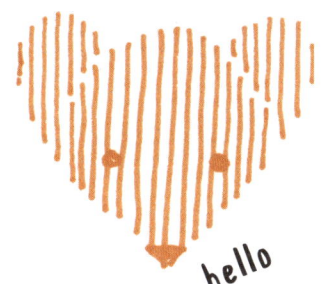

hello

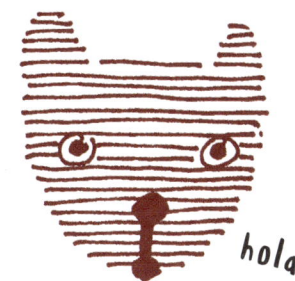

hola

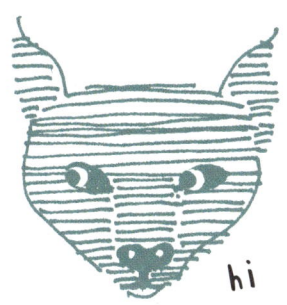

hi

. . . add some eyes and a nose

Make faces and objects by drawing the lines within a shape. Add some dots for eyes and a nose, more lines for whiskers, and even the ears can be defined.

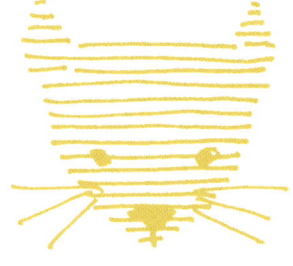

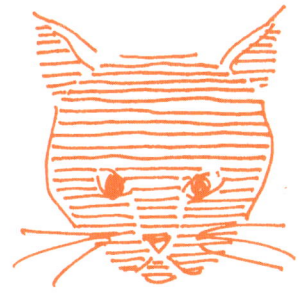

Different line directions

Try putting blocks of lines together, matching alternative angles to define different objects such as the horizontal and vertical lines in the trees. Or create three-dimensional objects, such as the house or the cubes. Copy these examples, then see what other subjects you can create.

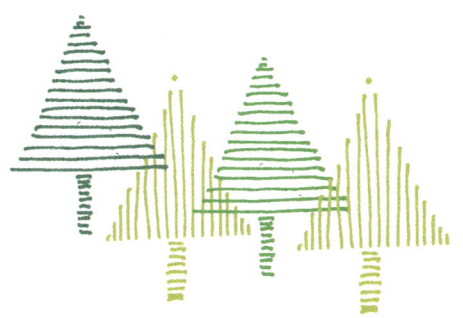

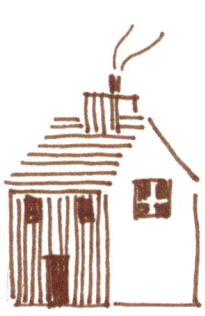

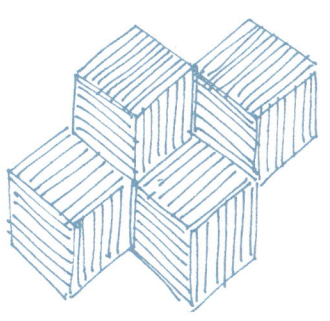

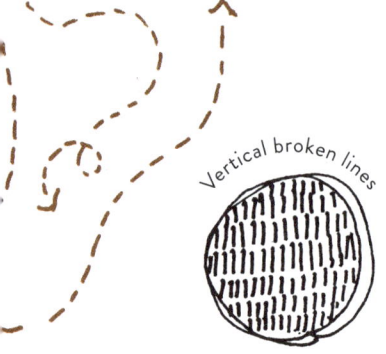

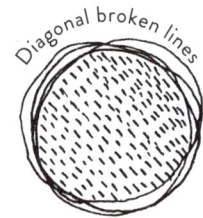

Vertical broken lines

Diagonal broken lines

Overlapping diagonal broken lines

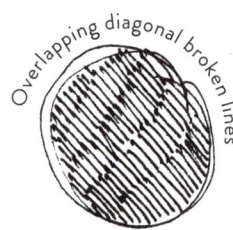

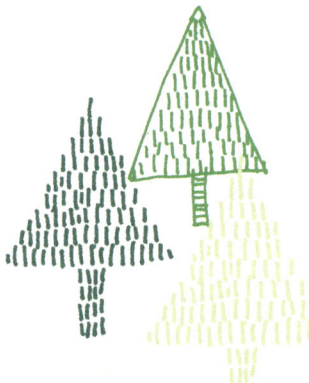

Lines can be dashed or broken . . .

Lines can be broken into small marks, put together in rows, drawn at any angle, or arranged into random patterns. Sometimes the direction of the lines can explain the shape of the subject, such as the face of the brown animal below where the lines radiate out from the nose. The lines also imply the direction of the fur. The squirrel has dashed lines for the fur in different directions and colors.

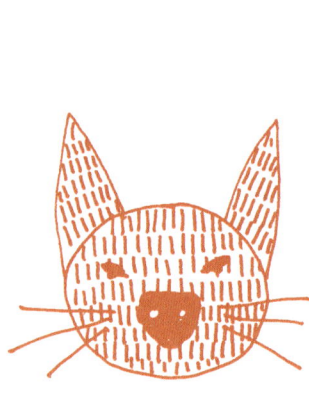

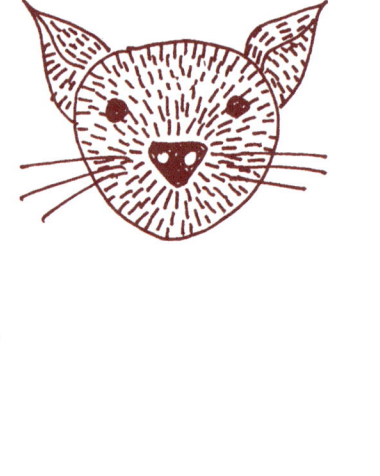

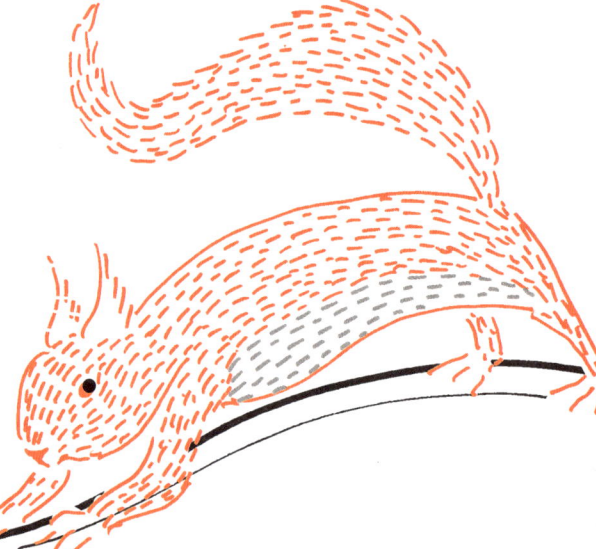

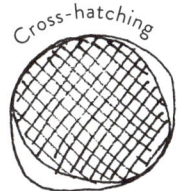

Cross-hatching

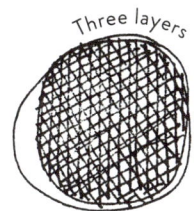

Three layers

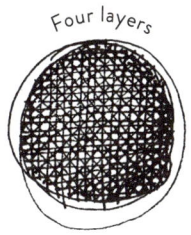

Four layers

. . . or crossed

The drawn lines can cross over each other at different angles.
Draw one set at one angle, then turn the paper and draw
another set to create dark tones and different shapes. This
technique is called cross-hatching and has been used since
medieval times in drawings and engravings.

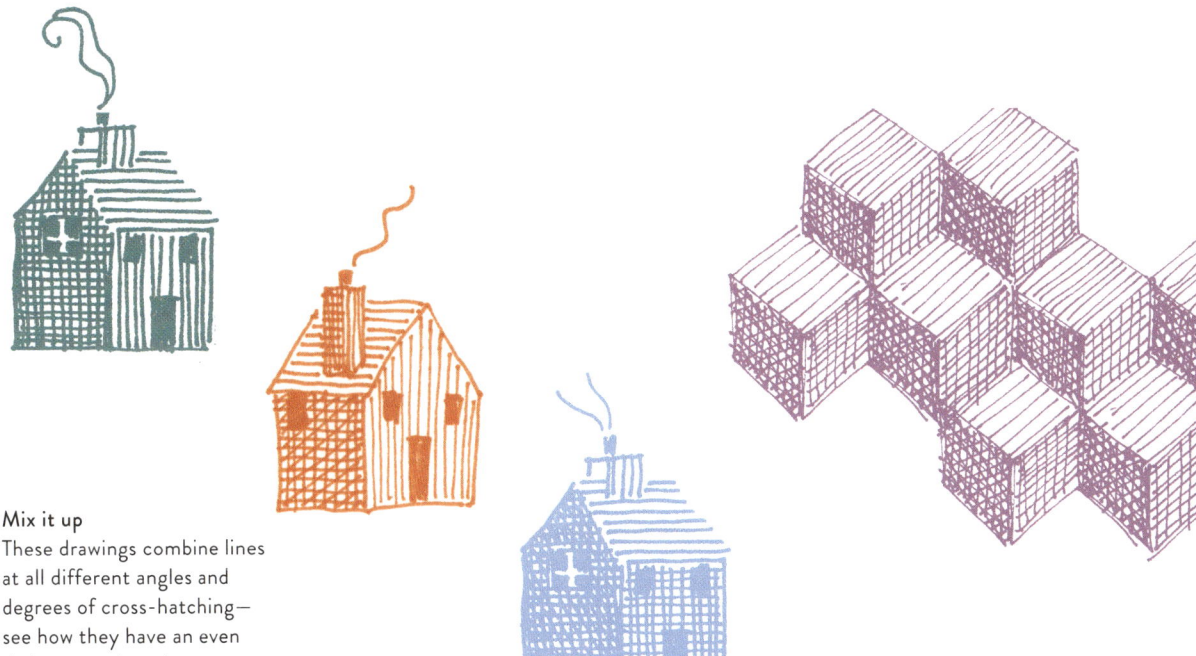

Mix it up
These drawings combine lines
at all different angles and
degrees of cross-hatching—
see how they have an even
darker area than the ones on
the previous page?

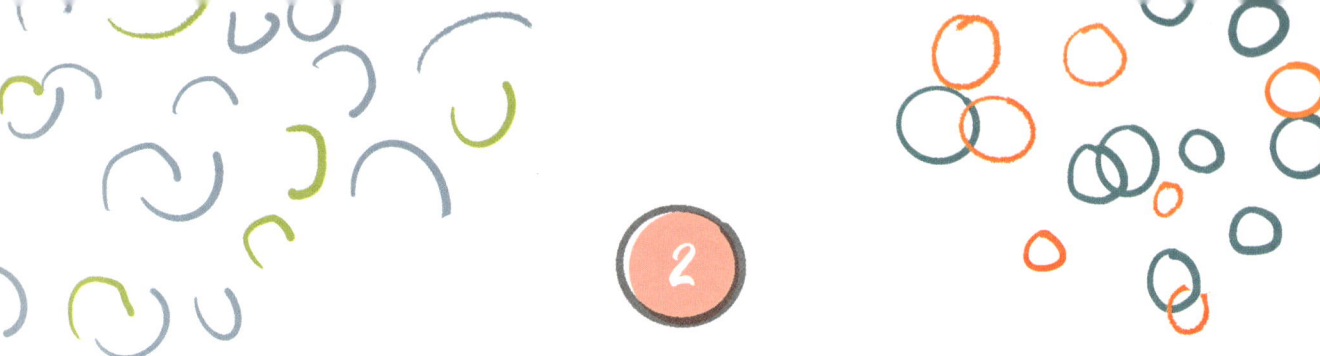

2

ADD SMALL CURVES
AND CIRCLES

You've tried lines, now draw some different marks like these curves and circles. Repeat each mark to see how closely you can make them match to create a pattern, or mix the different shapes and sizes to make a more varied pattern.

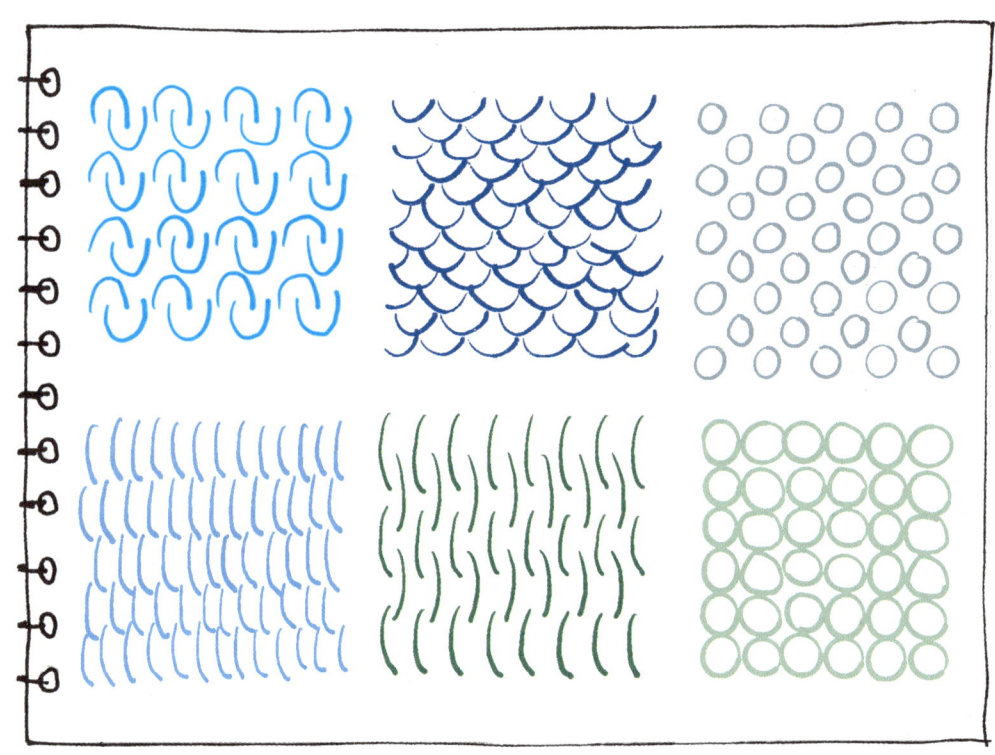

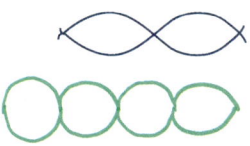

Try adding different marks together to give different patterns.

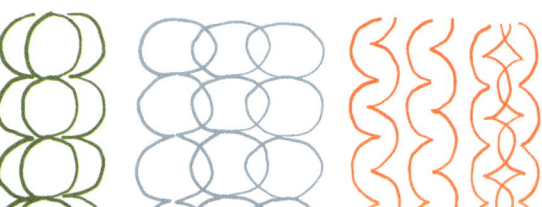

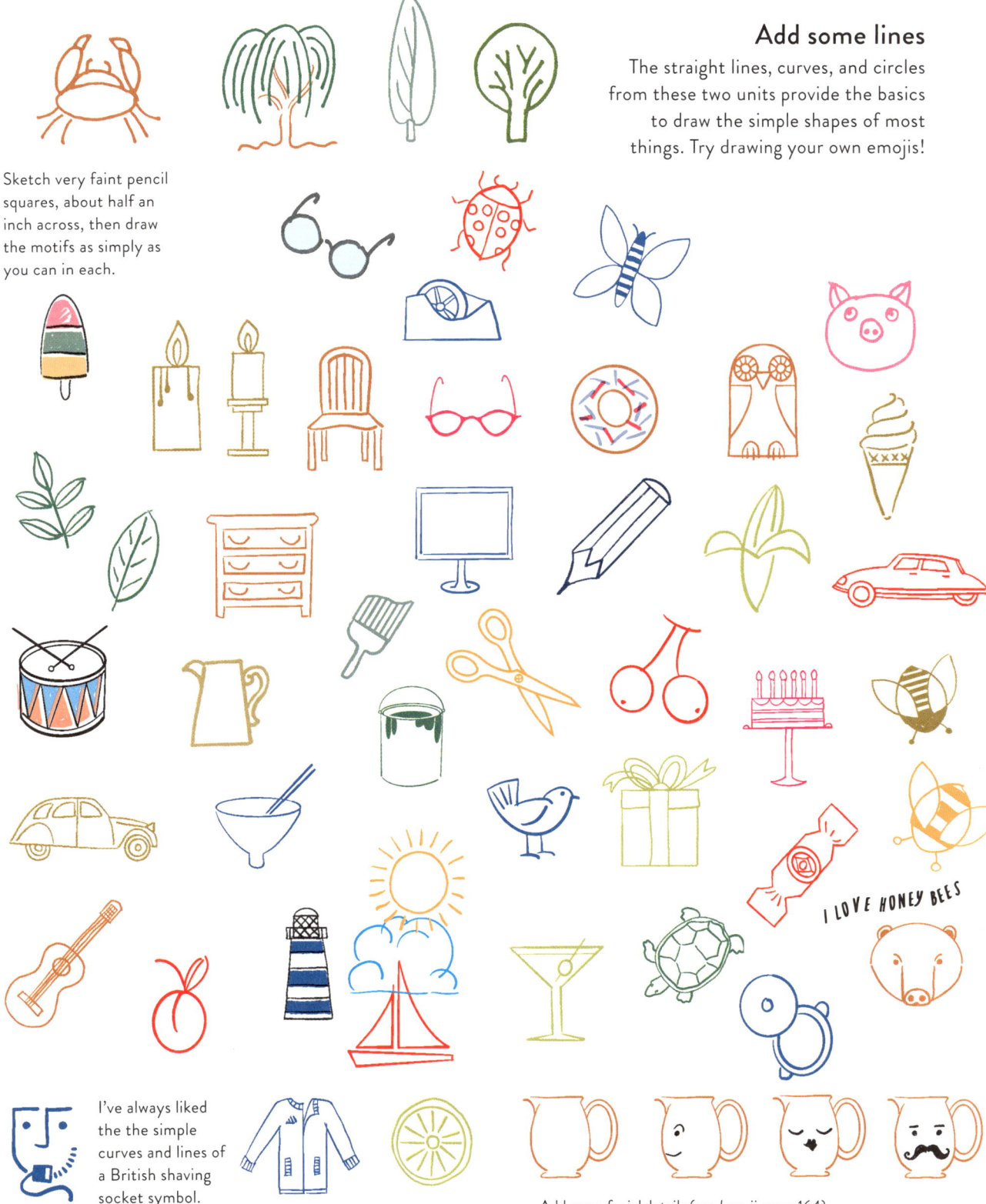

Add some lines

The straight lines, curves, and circles from these two units provide the basics to draw the simple shapes of most things. Try drawing your own emojis!

Sketch very faint pencil squares, about half an inch across, then draw the motifs as simply as you can in each.

I've always liked the the simple curves and lines of a British shaving socket symbol.

I LOVE HONEY BEES

Add some facial details (see *kawaii*, page 164).

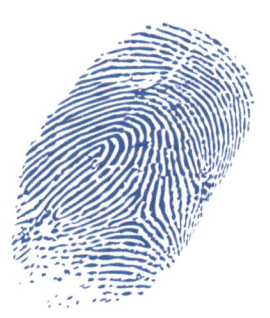

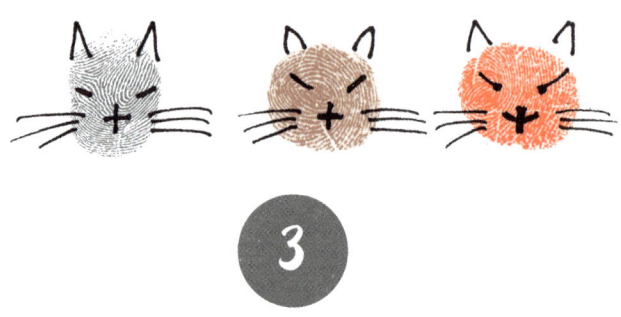

3

FINGERPRINT CHARACTERS

Make a fingerprint and add little arms and legs. Draw some whiskers and other details using curves and lines.

Ideally use stamp inks, which have the right consistency and come in lovely colors. Dab ink on a paper towel or sponge, then lightly press on your finger. Test your prints on paper—normally the first one will be too dense. Practice using different fingers and positioning the marks to create different characters. Then add some features, drawing eyes, legs, arms, ears, and more. . .

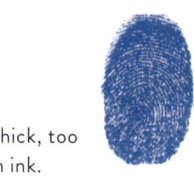
Too thick, too much ink.

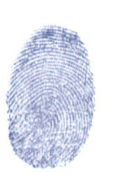
Just right.

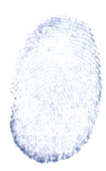
Too thin (unless it's for a fairy or butterfly wings).

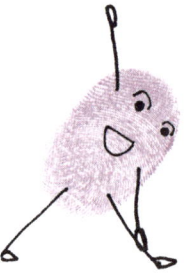

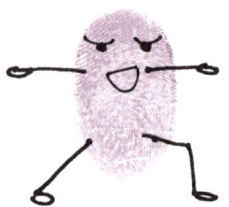

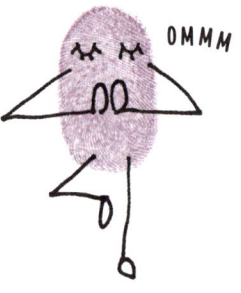
OMMM

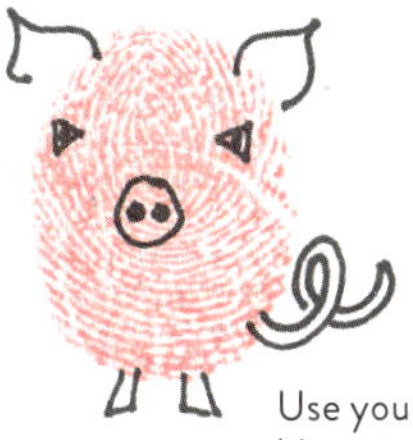

Use your thumb for the biggest mark.

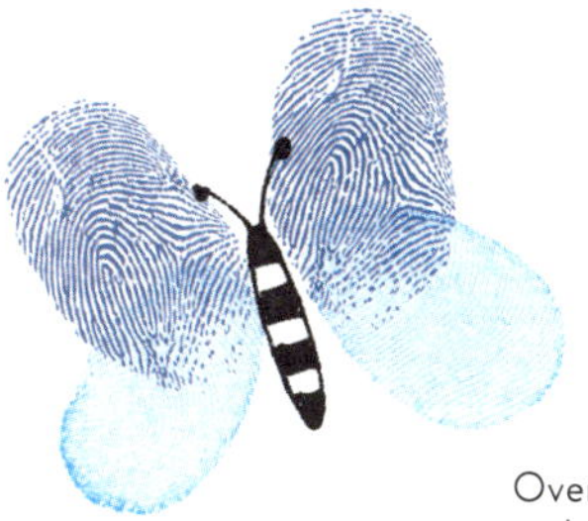

Overlap prints to make more complex finger pictures.

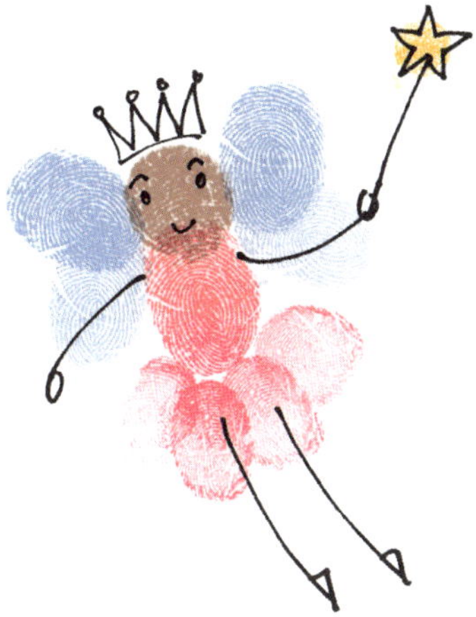

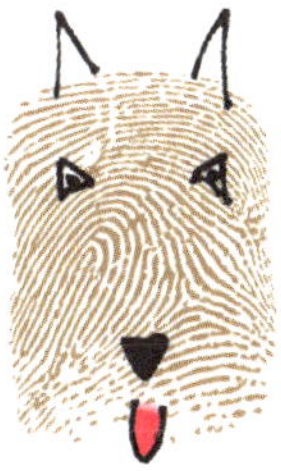

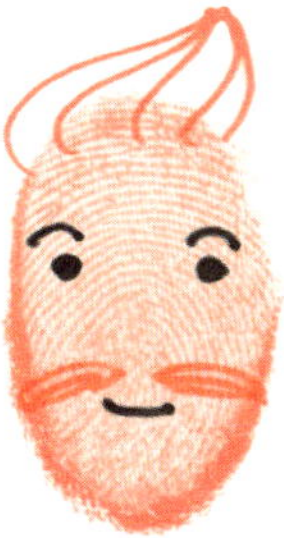

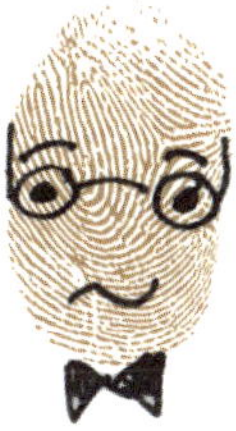

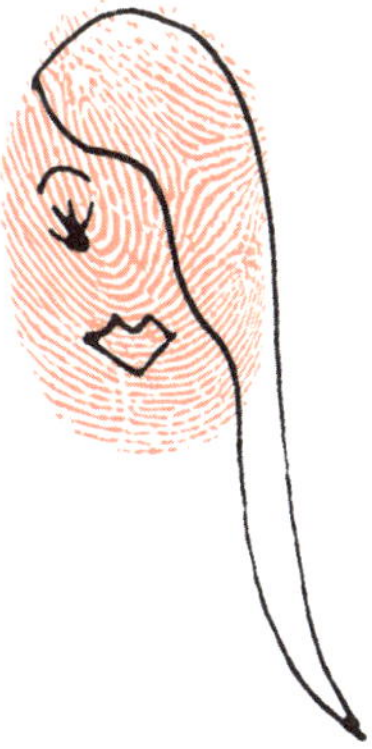

Excess ink at the edge? Great for a beard.

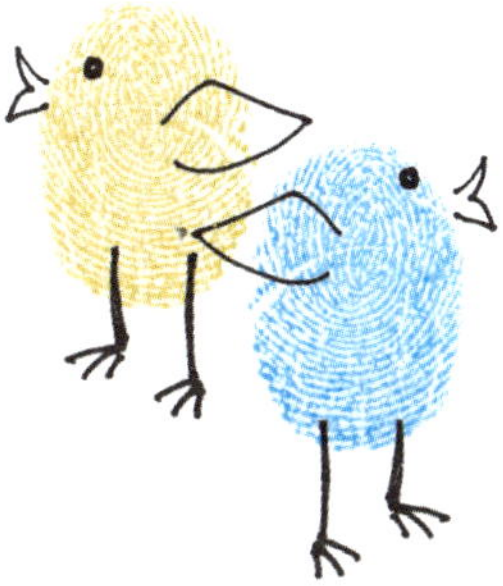

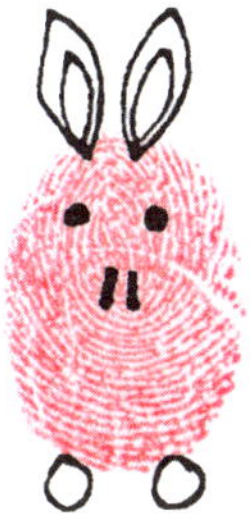

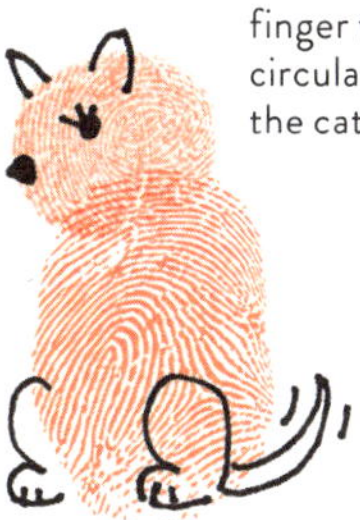

Use the top of your finger to create more circular marks such as the cat's head.

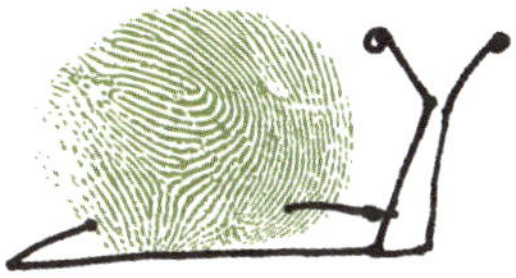

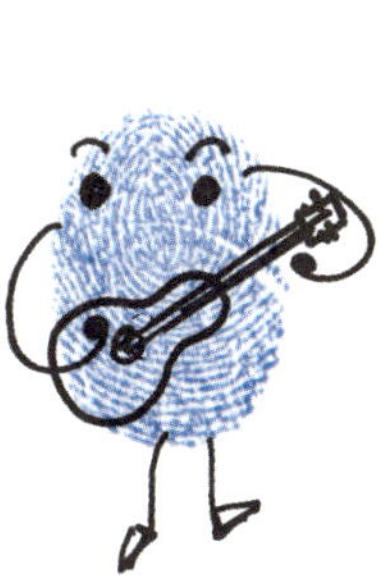

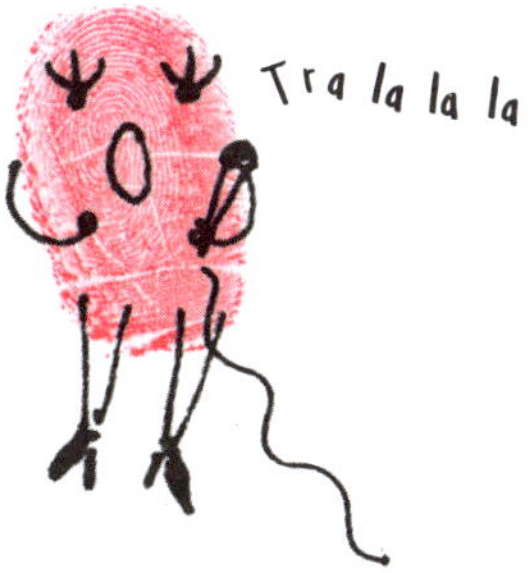

Tra la la la

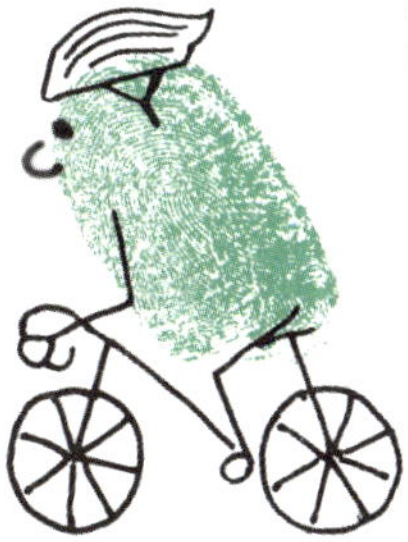

Roll your finger for wider marks.

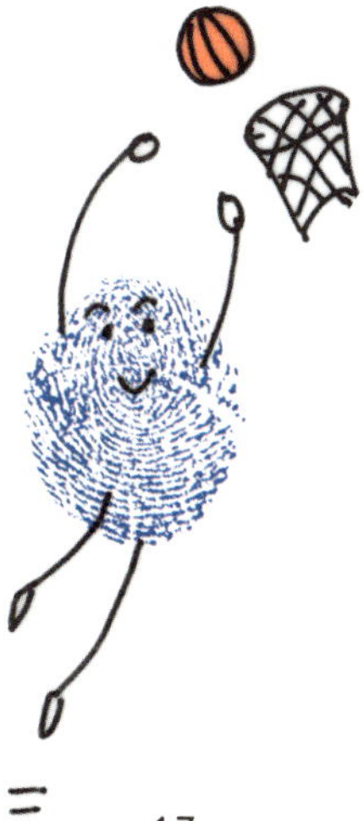

17

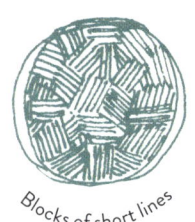

Blocks of short lines

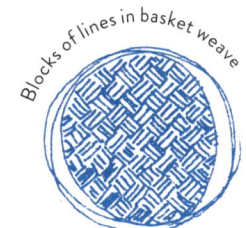

Blocks of lines in basket weave

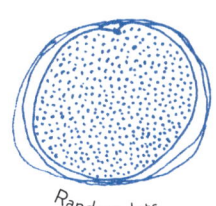

Random dots

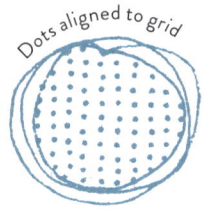

Dots aligned to grid

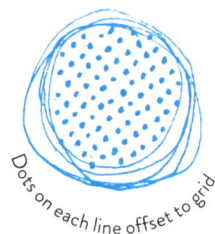

Dots on each line offset to grid

Dots make great
backgrounds
to motifs.

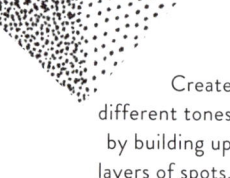

Create
different tones
by building up
layers of spots.

OTHER MARKS AND MEDIA

Find some scrap pieces of paper to see how many different marks you can create, or experiment in other media.

Dots, spots, or scribbles

Tiny dots can be used to create a simple texture or for filling in areas behind a motif. This dot method is called *stippling*, and can be used in layers to build up different tones. It is a labor-intensive process but can create a very delicate drawing. You can use other marks too, such as blocks of short hatched lines arranged randomly or in parallel blocks to form a basket weave.

Try another medium

Most of the samples in units 1 to 3 were drawn in a fineliner pen between 0.5 mm to 0.8 mm. Try drawing with a thicker felt tip to make bolder marks, or use colored pencils to see how the softer edges of the pencil lines alter the effect. You can use both soluble and non-water-soluble (waterproof) pencils, and keep the point sharp for the crispest lines.

Draw circles in water-soluble colored pencils then "tickle" the line with a brush and clean water.

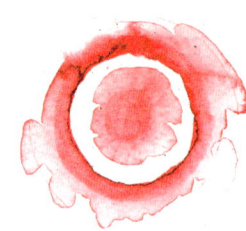

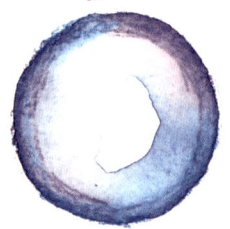

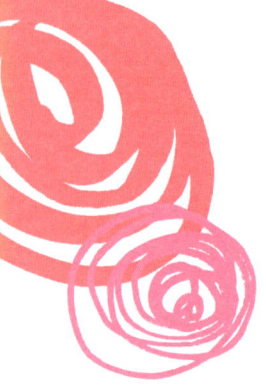

Thicker markers

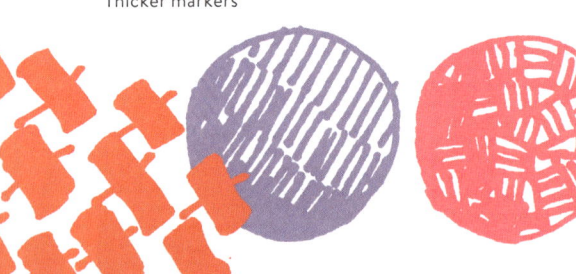

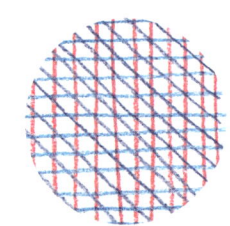

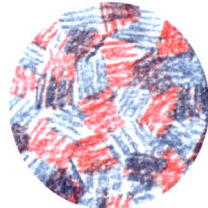

Waterproof colored pencils

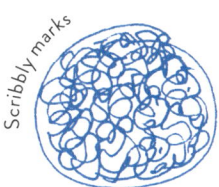
Scribbly marks

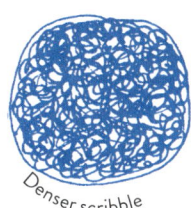
Denser scribble

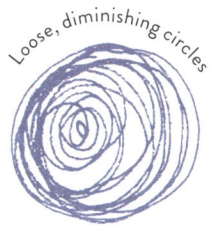
Loose, diminishing circles

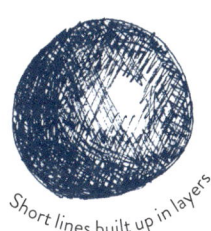
Short lines built up in layers

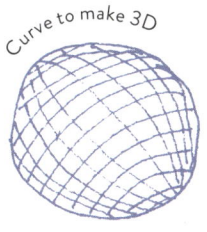
Curve to make 3D

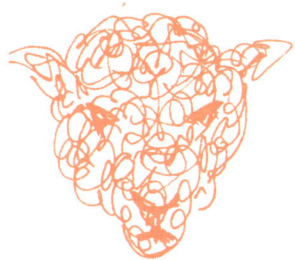

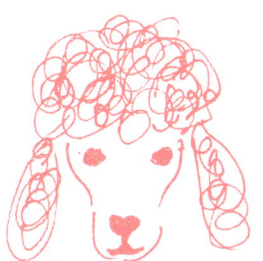

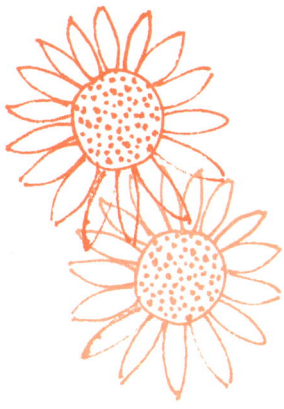

Make a sketch

Scribbles, curves, and groups of short lines
are just some of the marks you can make.
See what pictures you can create; little
landscapes, flower heads, woolly animals
or textures on clothing.

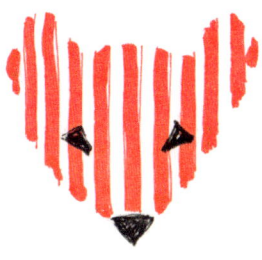

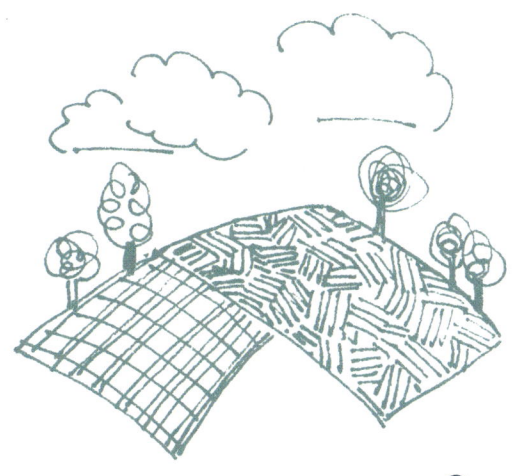

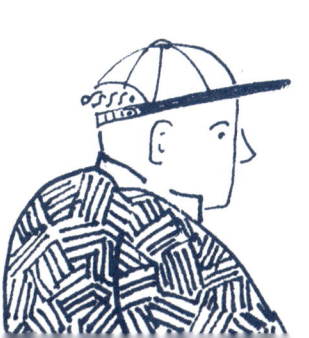

5

DRAWING PIXEL PETS

Drawing with squares is a good way to really think about the shapes you are making. Prior to this book, I hadn't worked on graph paper since I was a child, but it won me over. It is fun thinking about the position of each pixel and seeing how different results emerge. Take a look online at pixel art to find lots of inspiration. There are venerable traditions of thinking in pixels or squares, like mosaics or tile artists, as well as embroiderers creating cross-stitch.

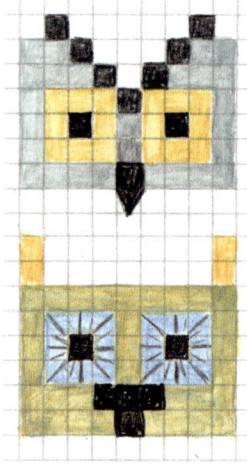

Keep it simple

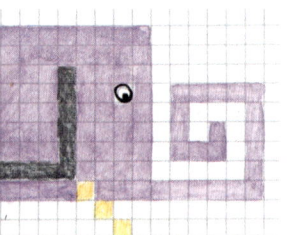

The attractive feature is keeping the individual pixel shapes while explaining the overall motif. If you work with too tiny a grid you might as well just paint freehand. Straight-sided objects such as houses are the easiest but simplifying other shapes, like animals, can create characterful motifs.

Purchase some graph paper or download a template to print. You can then color in the pixels with colored pencils. With thick 100 lb (160 gsm) drawing paper you can use watercolor pencils.

Colored squares can be aligned horizontally/ vertically with some diagonal squares for emphasis (top). You can add some linear details for eyes (bottom).

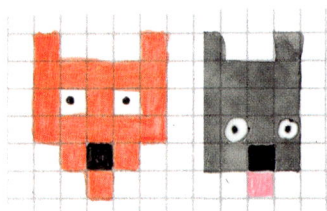

Five squares   Four squares

Faces
An odd number of squares on the horizontal row will allow you to place noses and eyes centrally; with an even number the facial features will be off-center and the head will look slightly turned to one side.

Placement of eyes and ears
Positioning makes all the difference—from mouse to hound to koala.

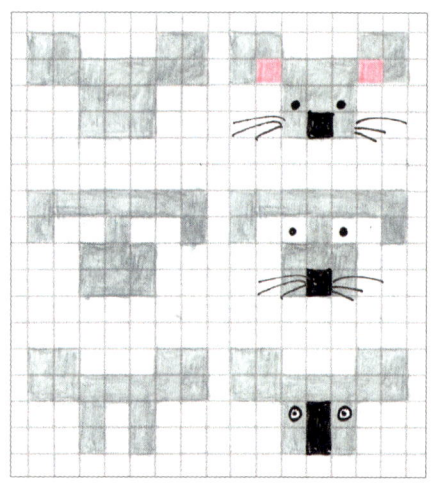

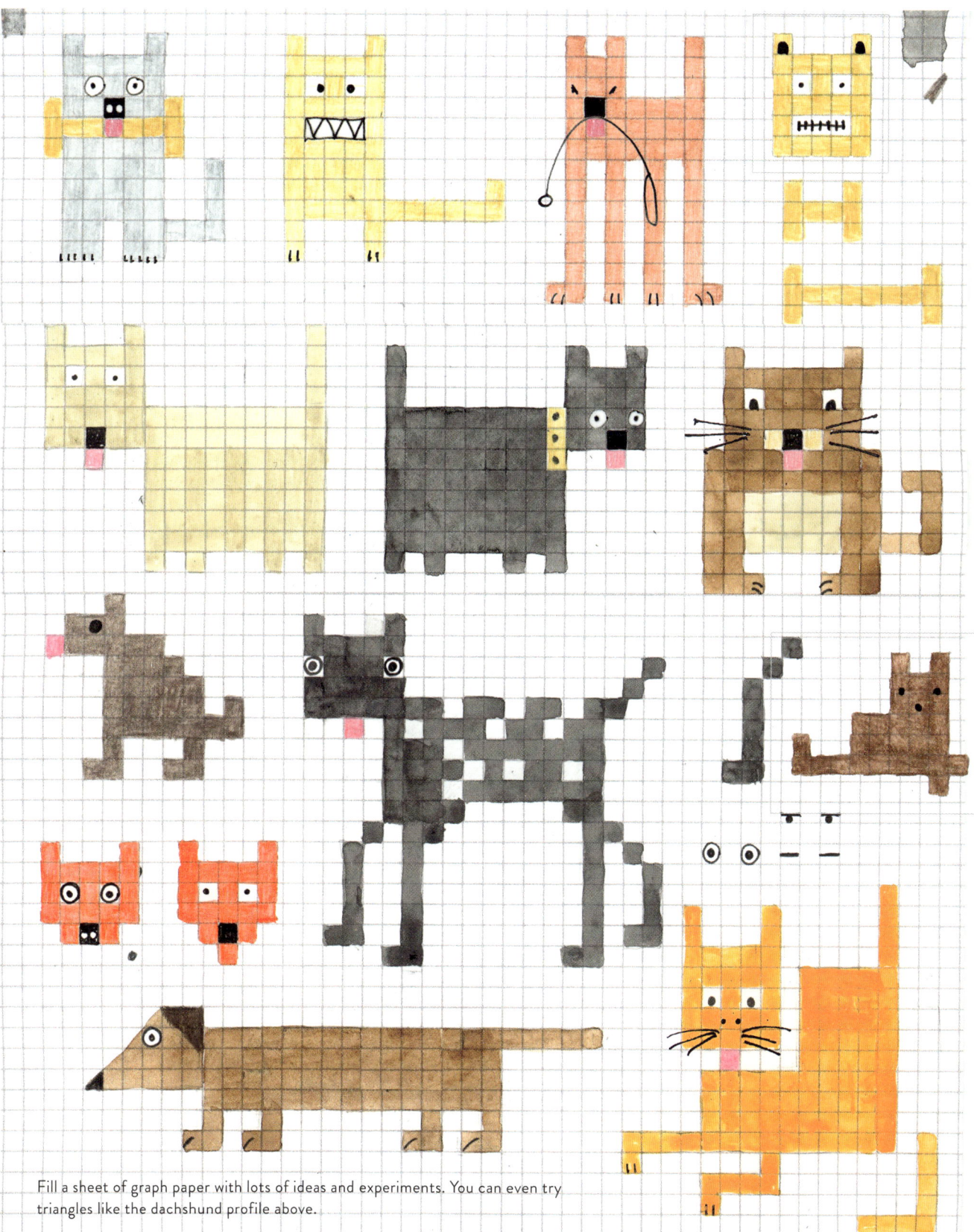

Fill a sheet of graph paper with lots of ideas and experiments. You can even try triangles like the dachshund profile above.

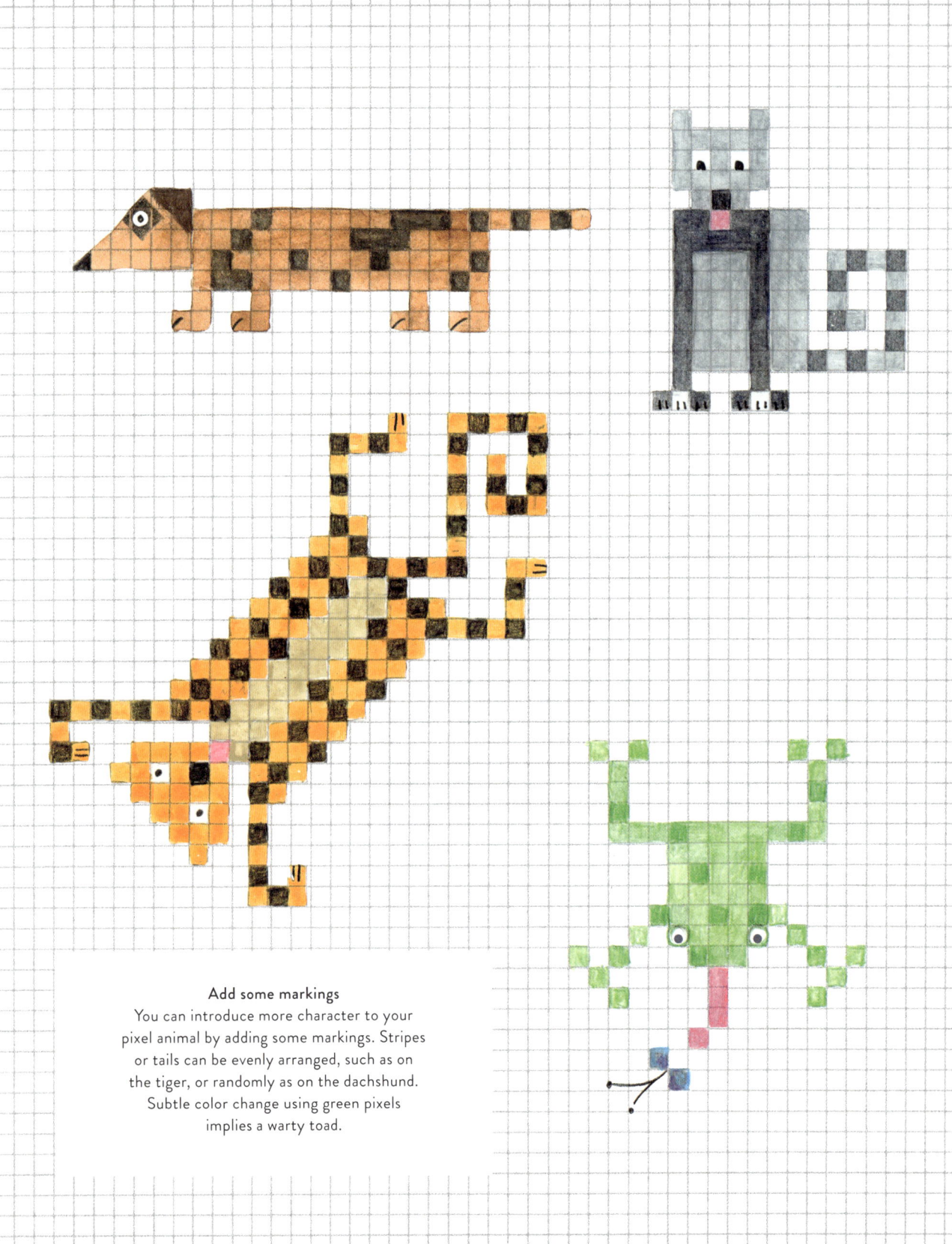

Add some markings
You can introduce more character to your
pixel animal by adding some markings. Stripes
or tails can be evenly arranged, such as on
the tiger, or randomly as on the dachshund.
Subtle color change using green pixels
implies a warty toad.

Try something different

Work on the diagonal. Turning the graph paper 45 degrees gives the faces a completely different set of options. The diamond shape for each face here contained only nine or sixteen pixels. Adding in the different features means 1,000s of possibilities!

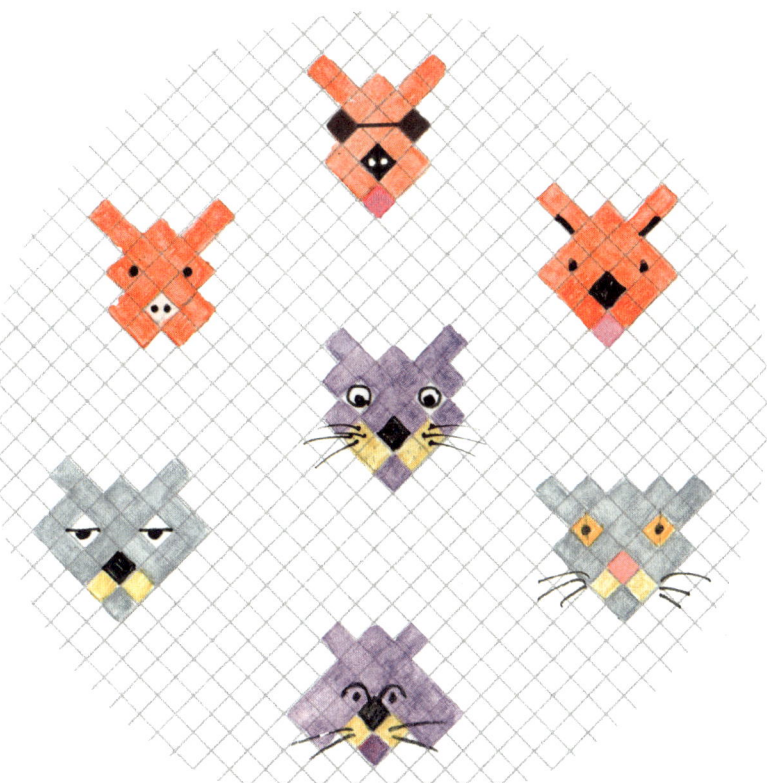

Try other subjects: folk art houses, trees, clouds . . .

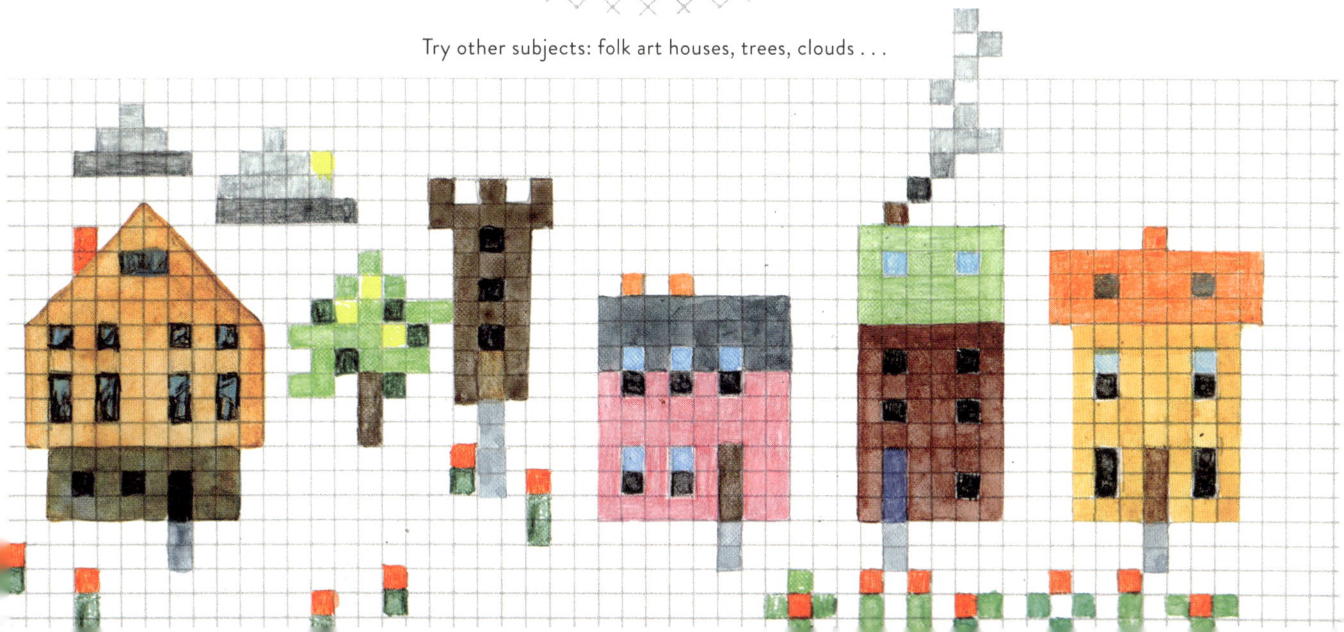

6

NOW FOR SOME LONGER LINES

Drawing relatively straight lines of an even weight and spacing is useful for all sorts of future drawing subjects.

Rest your hand on the paper for support, then move your hand along the page applying a gentle pressure. Practice working from side to side, top to bottom, or diagonally. Generally the pencil will flow more easily if you are not pushing. Try a slight dragging action because it will be a smoother action and you will wobble less (although sometimes wobbly lines are good!) You can experiment with pencil, pens, crayons, and markers.

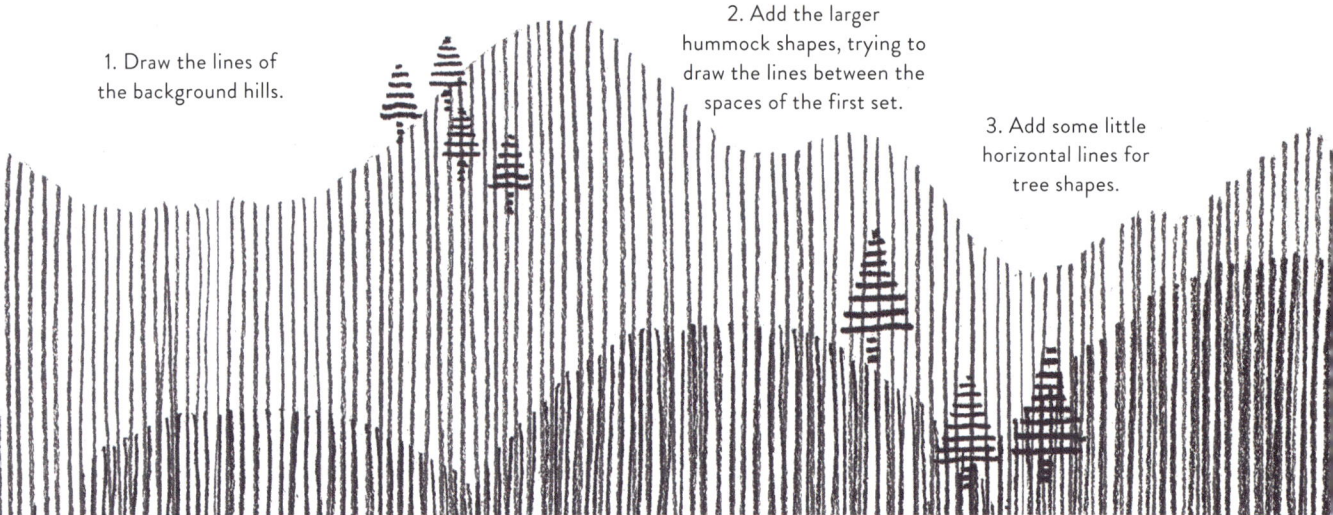

1. Draw the lines of the background hills.

2. Add the larger hummock shapes, trying to draw the lines between the spaces of the first set.

3. Add some little horizontal lines for tree shapes.

Try with monochrome pencil or pen first. Don't worry too much if the lines are not perfectly straight. It isn't a technical drawing!

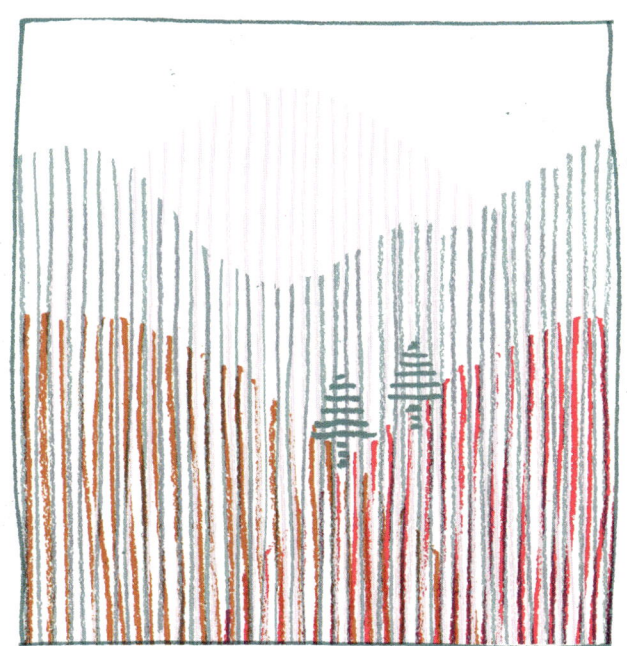

Line landscapes
See the effect that different colors have. Try paler colors for the distant mountains and stronger colors for the foreground hills, such as orange and red, or you could use strong greens (as below) if you want a more natural image.

You can create an even more realistic drawing, with sun rays and reflections. Any image composed of layers would work. Try a seascape with cliffs and clouds, or a cityscape with low buildings and bridges in the foreground, and skyscrapers and clouds in the background.

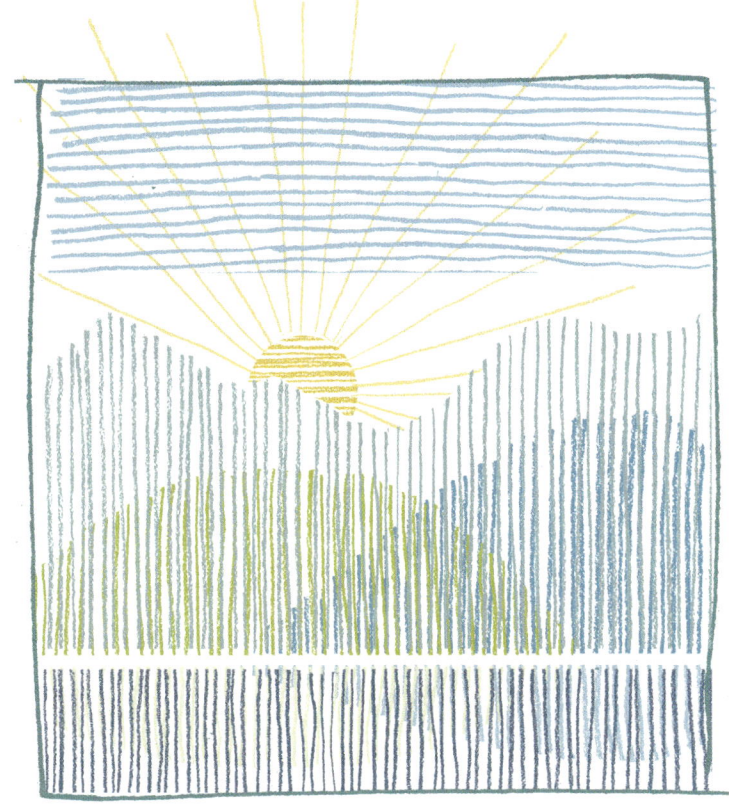

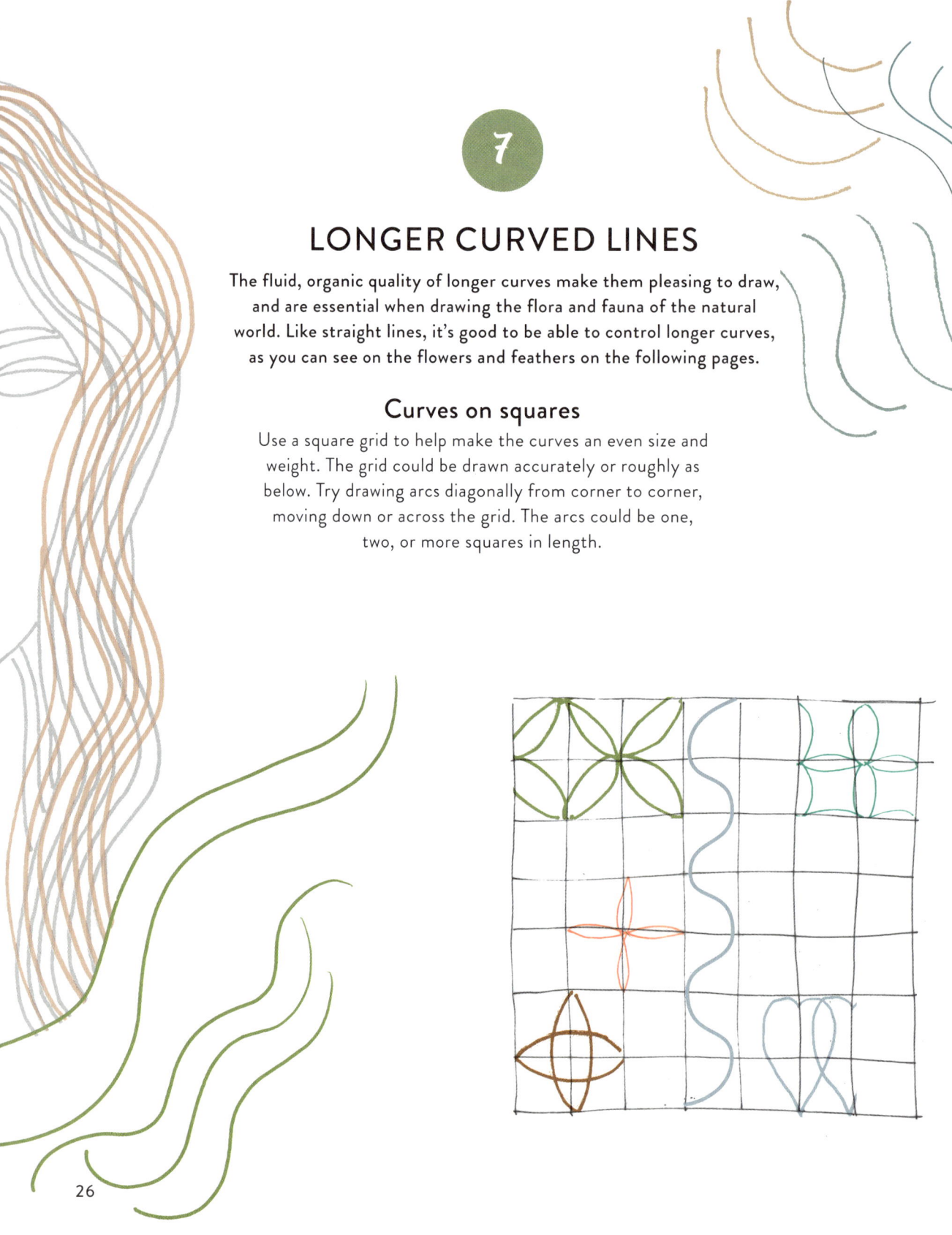

7

LONGER CURVED LINES

The fluid, organic quality of longer curves make them pleasing to draw, and are essential when drawing the flora and fauna of the natural world. Like straight lines, it's good to be able to control longer curves, as you can see on the flowers and feathers on the following pages.

Curves on squares

Use a square grid to help make the curves an even size and weight. The grid could be drawn accurately or roughly as below. Try drawing arcs diagonally from corner to corner, moving down or across the grid. The arcs could be one, two, or more squares in length.

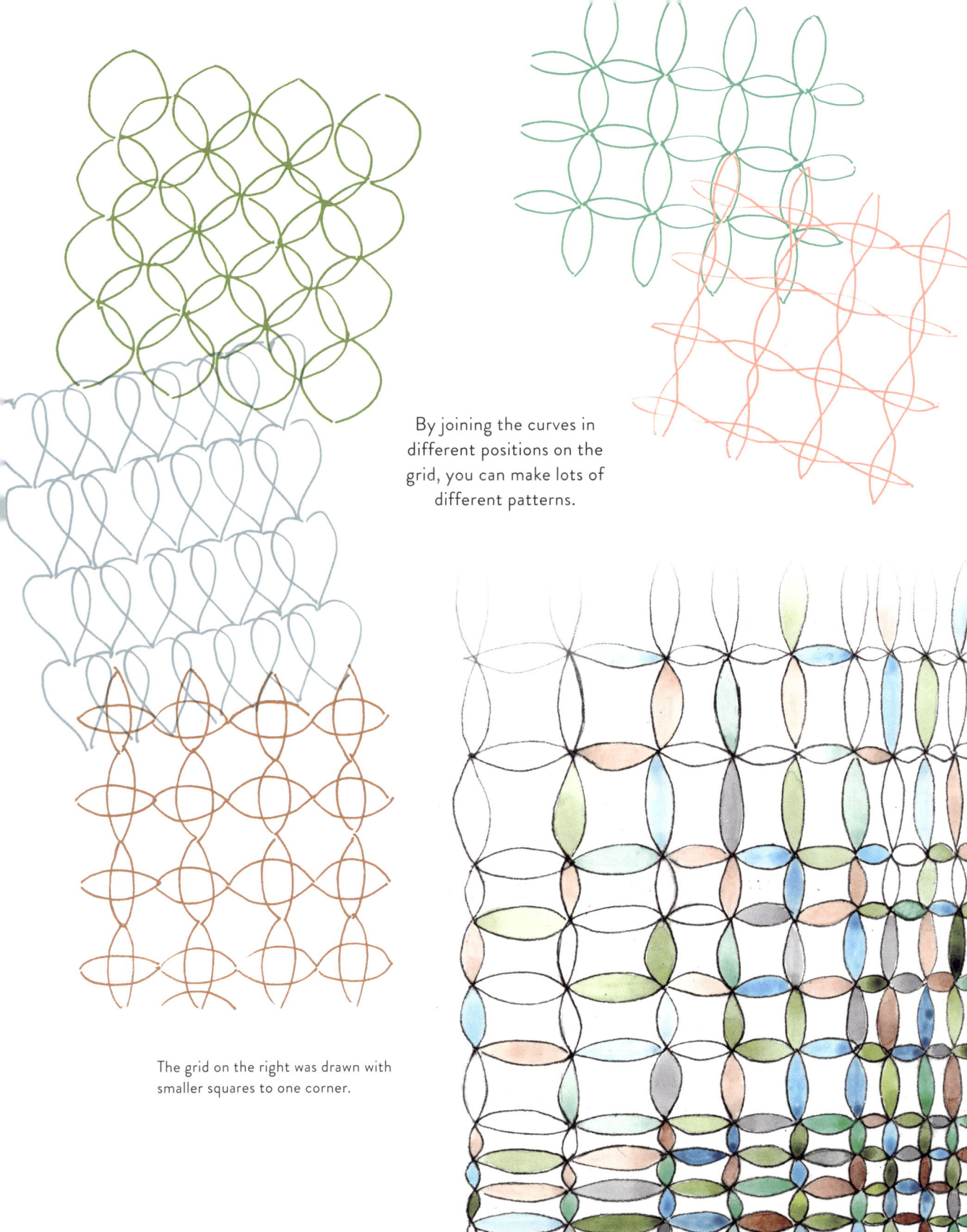

By joining the curves in different positions on the grid, you can make lots of different patterns.

The grid on the right was drawn with smaller squares to one corner.

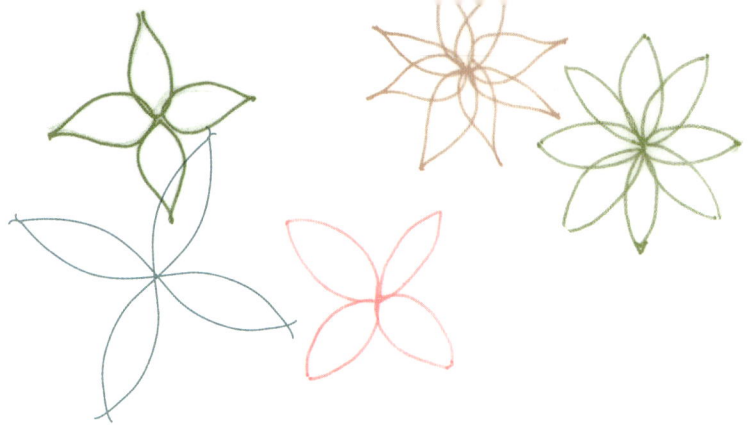
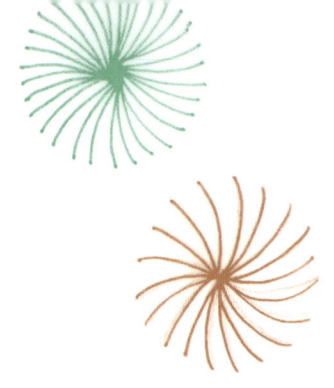

Organic curves

The curves can be put together in many ways to make simple flower, foliage, fruit, and even insect shapes. You may have to draw a few to achieve equal petal sizes and spacing, however irregularities add to the uniqueness of hand-drawn artwork. Most of these were drawn with an 0.8 mm fineliner pen. The image on the following page has been enlarged so the pen line looks a little thicker.

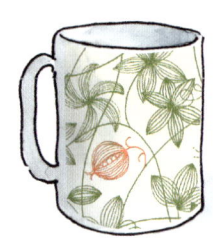

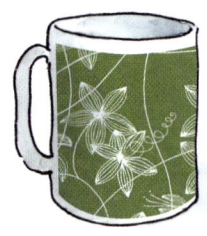

TAKEAWAY

Decorate a mug
You can have your drawing printed onto a mug—a great option for a present. Check the mug dimensions, or print a template showing the ratio of height and width, and then draw your image within those proportions. If you have a scanner you can create a digital file yourself, or take your drawing to a print shop and they will do it for you. They can then print your creation onto the side of a mug, so you can enjoy your artwork while having a cup of tea or coffee.

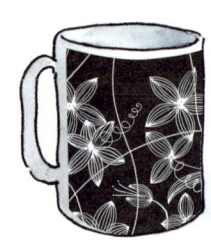

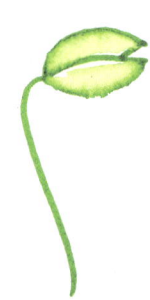

If you use watercolor marker pens, draw a line first, then with a brush gently stroke the edges to release the color. See page 186 for the best paper choice.

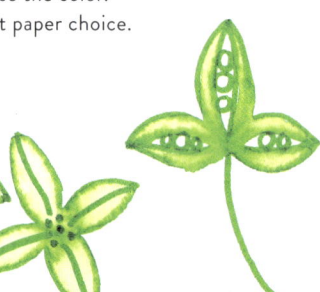

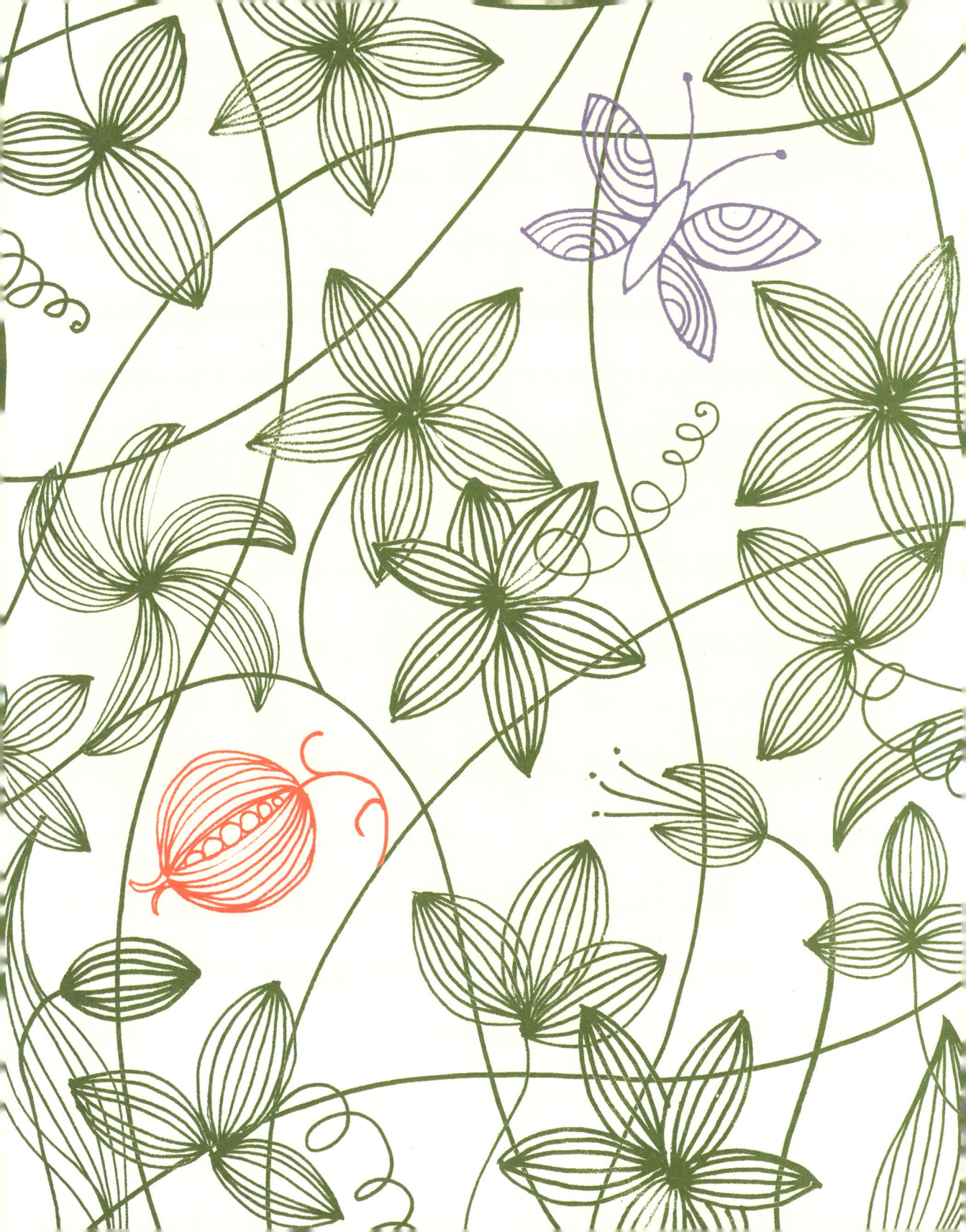

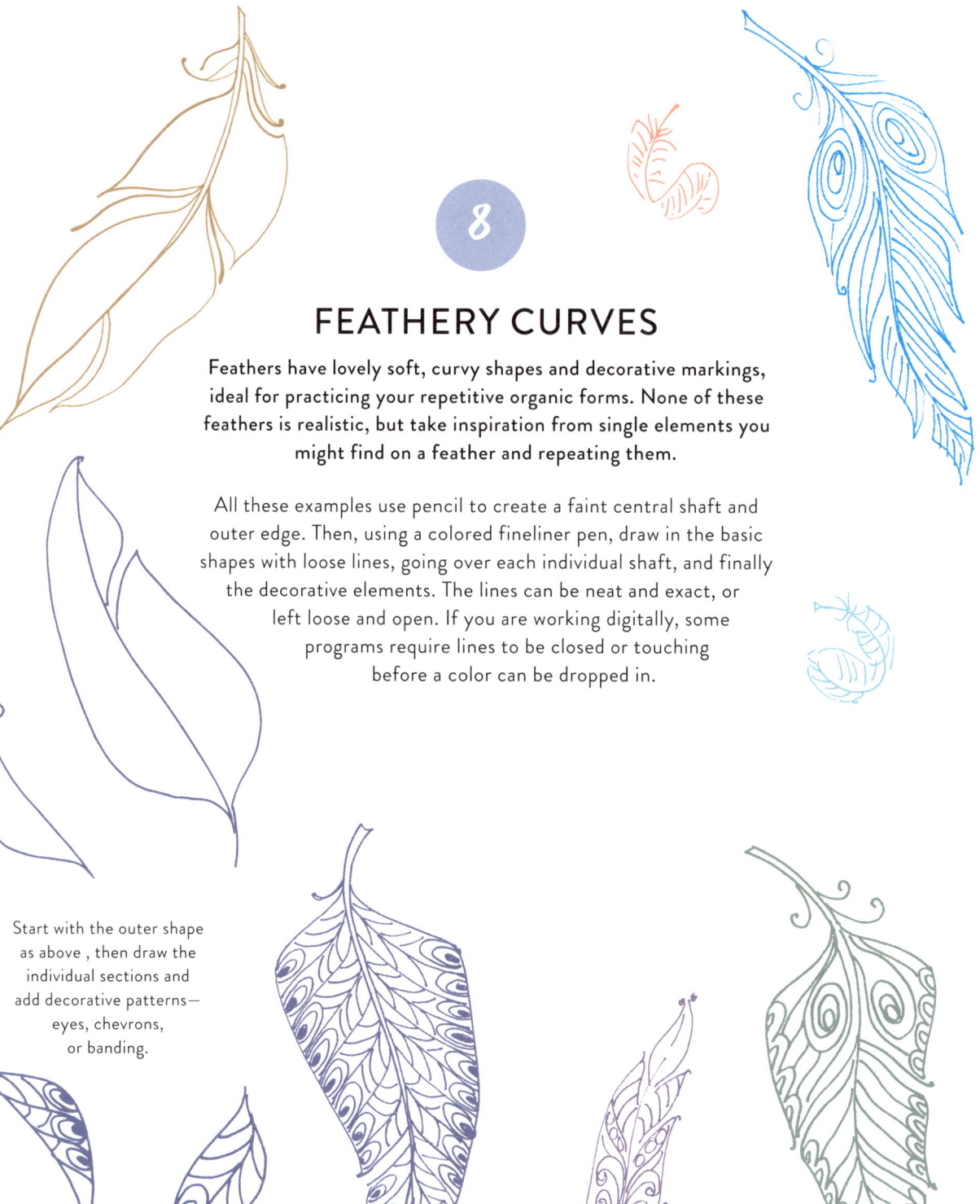

8

FEATHERY CURVES

Feathers have lovely soft, curvy shapes and decorative markings, ideal for practicing your repetitive organic forms. None of these feathers is realistic, but take inspiration from single elements you might find on a feather and repeating them.

All these examples use pencil to create a faint central shaft and outer edge. Then, using a colored fineliner pen, draw in the basic shapes with loose lines, going over each individual shaft, and finally the decorative elements. The lines can be neat and exact, or left loose and open. If you are working digitally, some programs require lines to be closed or touching before a color can be dropped in.

Start with the outer shape as above , then draw the individual sections and add decorative patterns— eyes, chevrons, or banding.

30

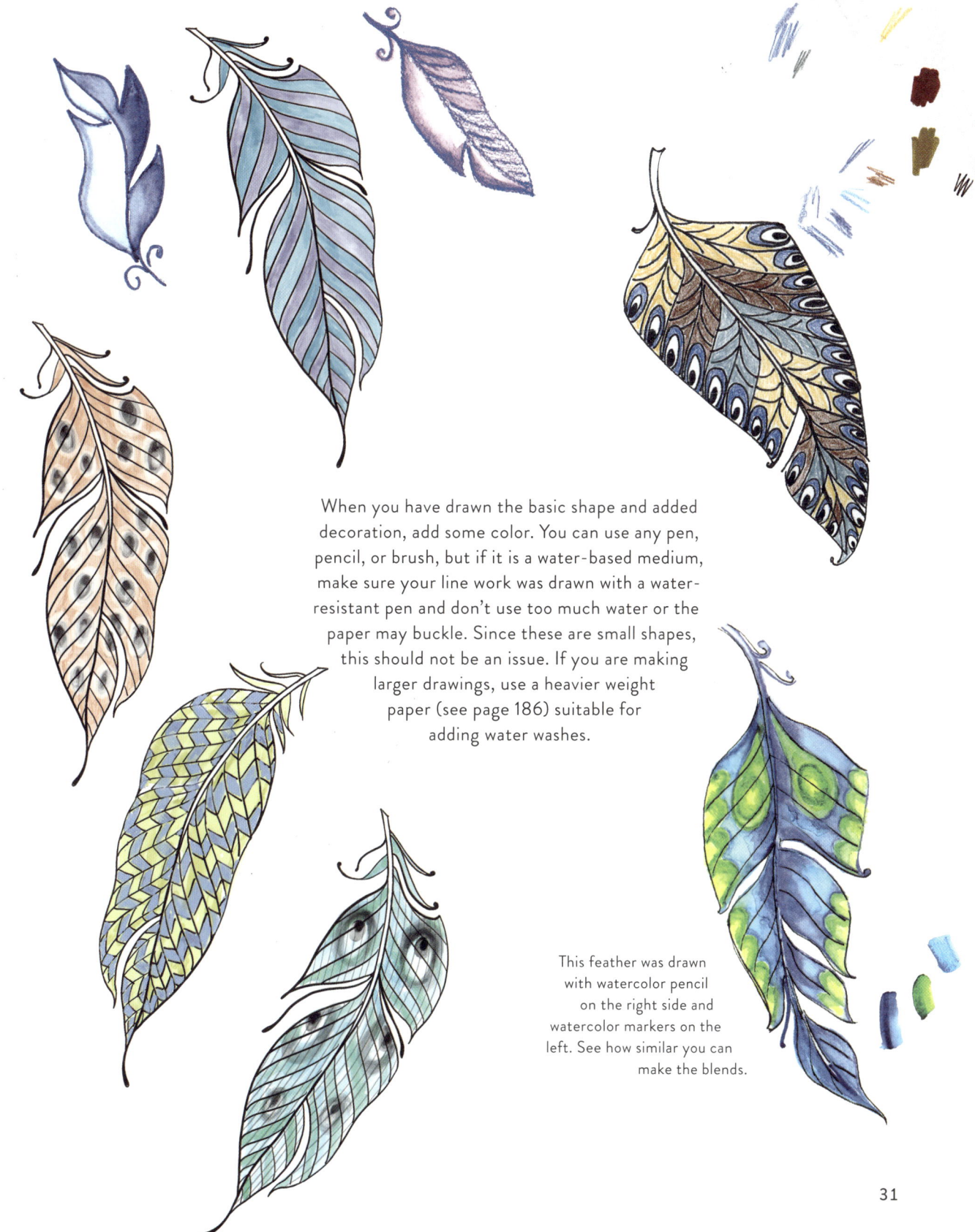

When you have drawn the basic shape and added decoration, add some color. You can use any pen, pencil, or brush, but if it is a water-based medium, make sure your line work was drawn with a water-resistant pen and don't use too much water or the paper may buckle. Since these are small shapes, this should not be an issue. If you are making larger drawings, use a heavier weight paper (see page 186) suitable for adding water washes.

This feather was drawn with watercolor pencil on the right side and watercolor markers on the left. See how similar you can make the blends.

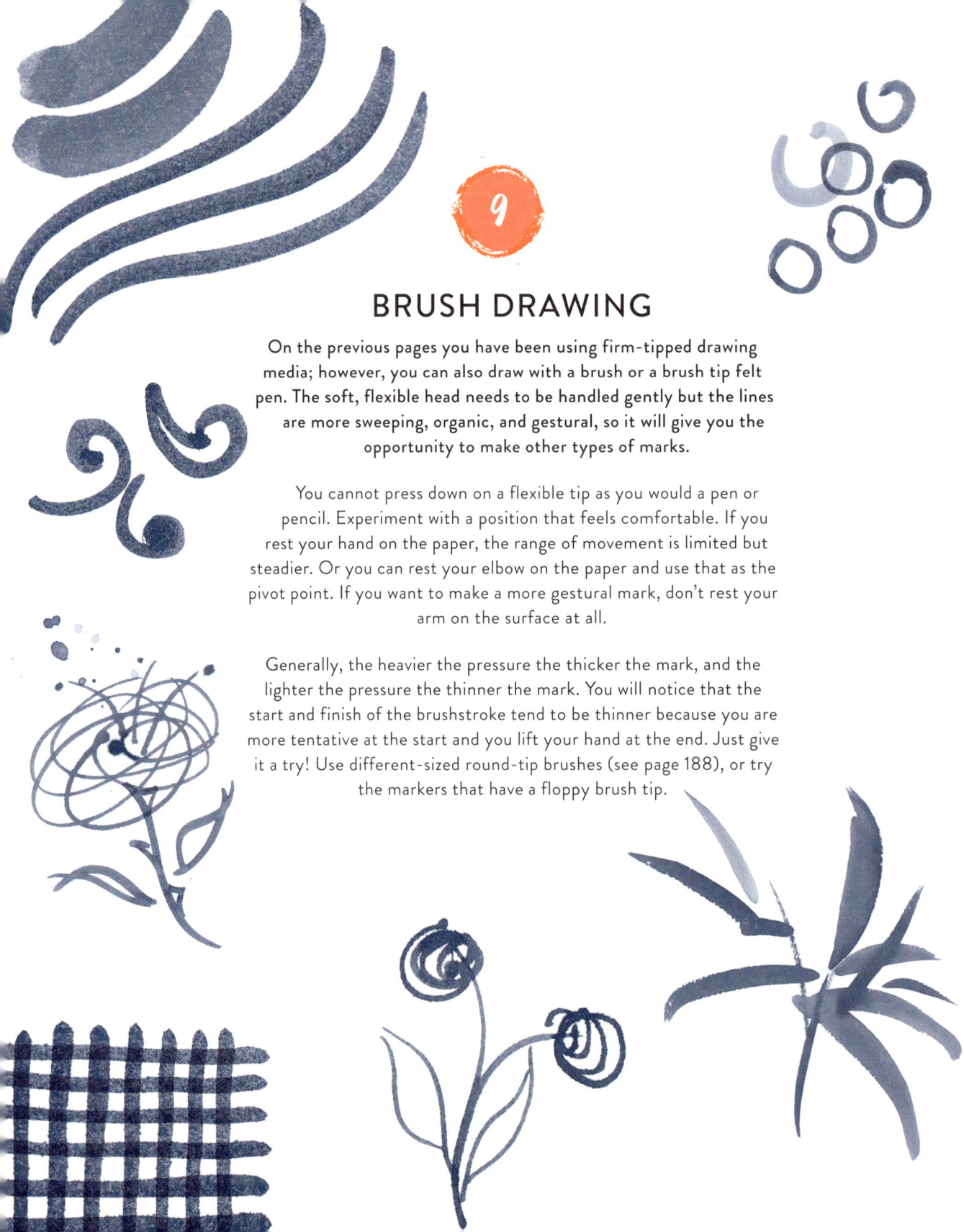

BRUSH DRAWING

On the previous pages you have been using firm-tipped drawing media; however, you can also draw with a brush or a brush tip felt pen. The soft, flexible head needs to be handled gently but the lines are more sweeping, organic, and gestural, so it will give you the opportunity to make other types of marks.

You cannot press down on a flexible tip as you would a pen or pencil. Experiment with a position that feels comfortable. If you rest your hand on the paper, the range of movement is limited but steadier. Or you can rest your elbow on the paper and use that as the pivot point. If you want to make a more gestural mark, don't rest your arm on the surface at all.

Generally, the heavier the pressure the thicker the mark, and the lighter the pressure the thinner the mark. You will notice that the start and finish of the brushstroke tend to be thinner because you are more tentative at the start and you lift your hand at the end. Just give it a try! Use different-sized round-tip brushes (see page 188), or try the markers that have a floppy brush tip.

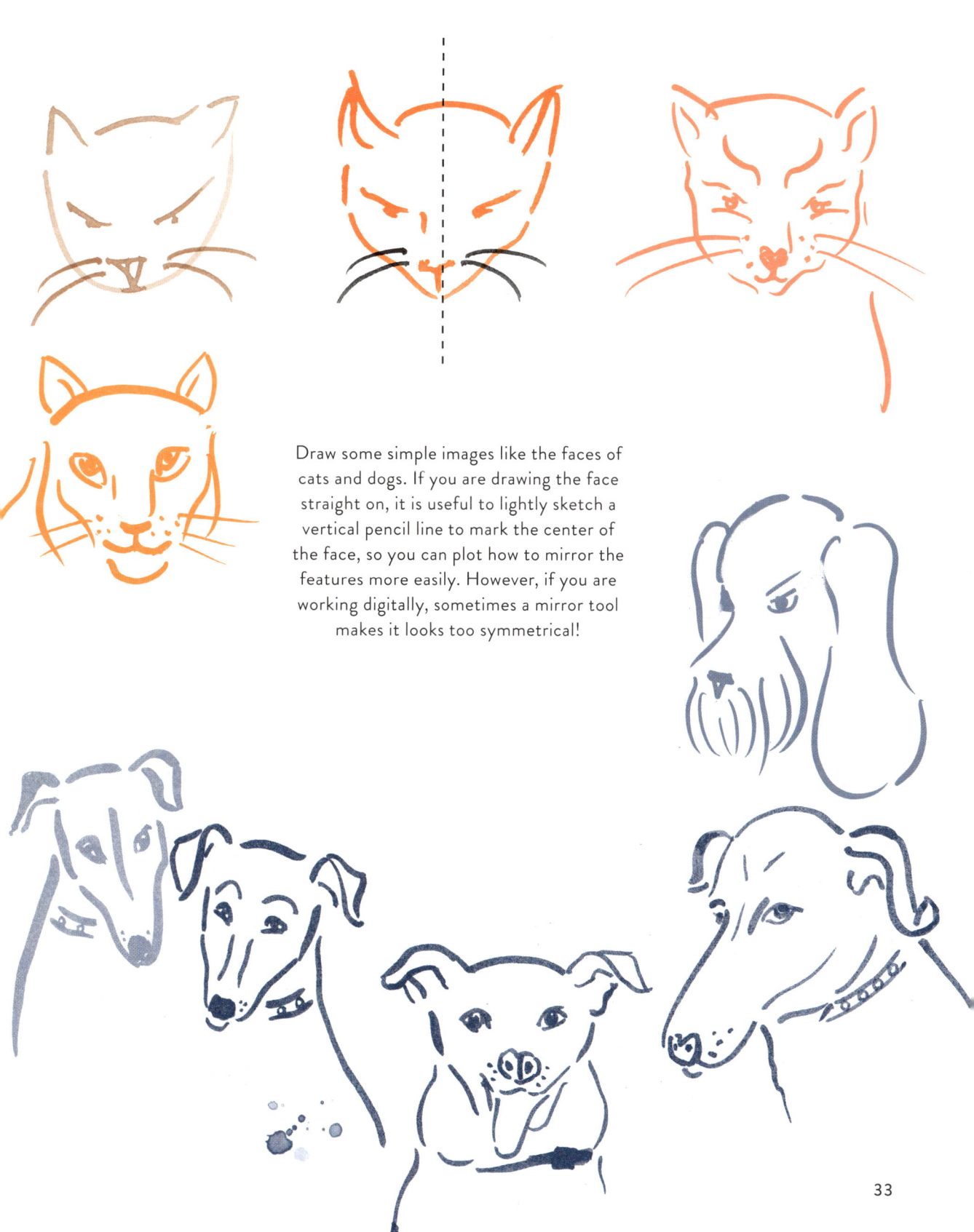

Draw some simple images like the faces of cats and dogs. If you are drawing the face straight on, it is useful to lightly sketch a vertical pencil line to mark the center of the face, so you can plot how to mirror the features more easily. However, if you are working digitally, sometimes a mirror tool makes it looks too symmetrical!

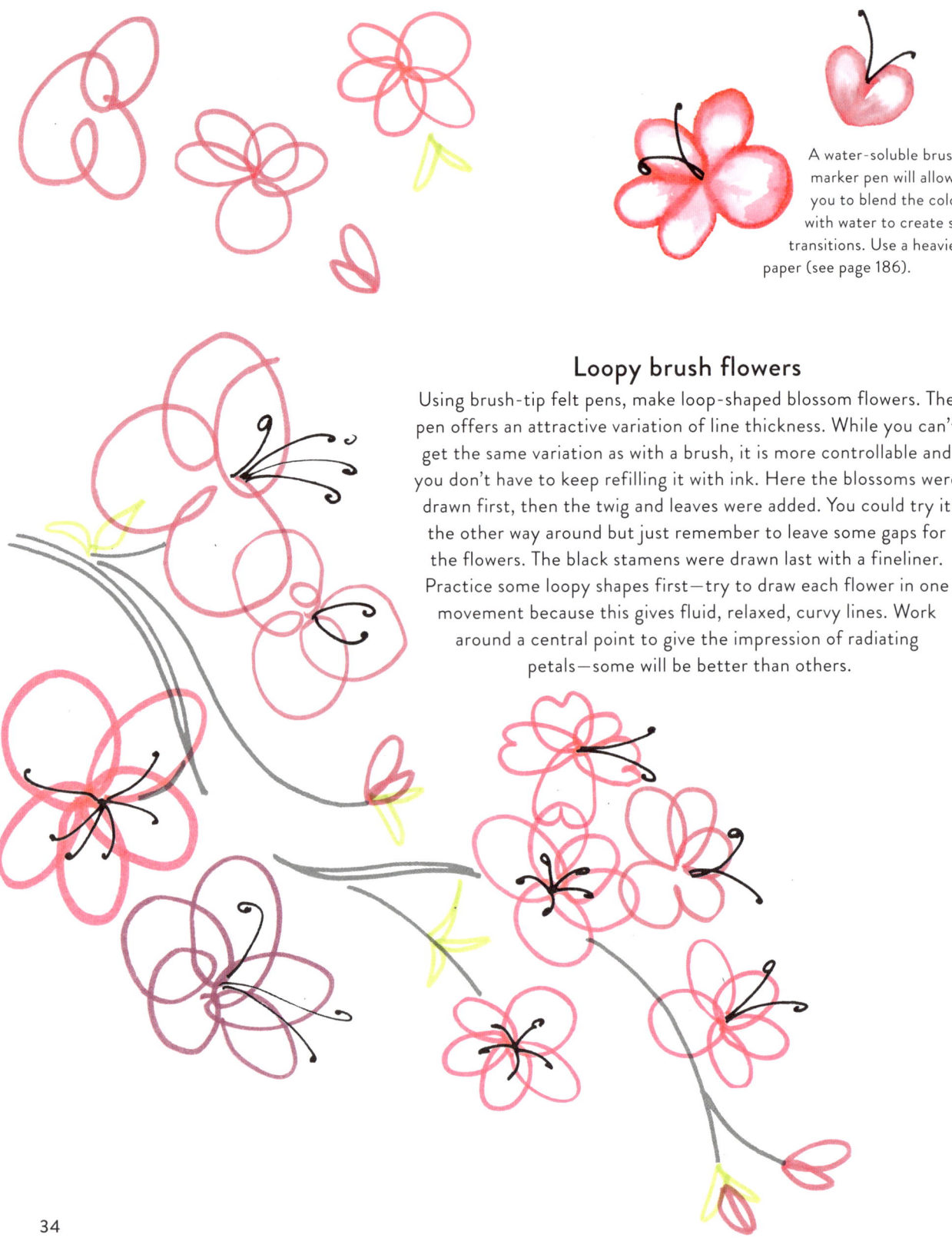

A water-soluble brush marker pen will allow you to blend the color with water to create soft transitions. Use a heavier paper (see page 186).

Loopy brush flowers

Using brush-tip felt pens, make loop-shaped blossom flowers. The pen offers an attractive variation of line thickness. While you can't get the same variation as with a brush, it is more controllable and you don't have to keep refilling it with ink. Here the blossoms were drawn first, then the twig and leaves were added. You could try it the other way around but just remember to leave some gaps for the flowers. The black stamens were drawn last with a fineliner. Practice some loopy shapes first—try to draw each flower in one movement because this gives fluid, relaxed, curvy lines. Work around a central point to give the impression of radiating petals—some will be better than others.

Daisy shapes

Draw more loops around a yellow center and you make daisies. The uneven nature of the petals adds to the hand-drawn quality, but you could make them more even-sized and spaced if you wish. They would make an attractive simple border or frame for a card.

Try creating the loops facing in and then out of the center: they look quite different.

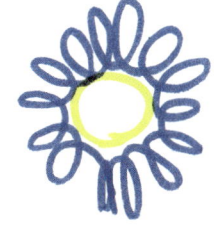

Bird of paradise

By lifting the brush pen lightly off the paper at the start and finish of each stroke, you can create the organic curve of the lines of a flower.

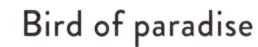

Frog

Draw thick green brush pen strokes for the body and thin circles for eyelids, then add some spindly legs and feet with a fine-tip pen or pencil.

Small brush, large brush

If you have a variety of brush sizes, try drawing quick sketches such as the figures below. I did these with a no. 4 brush (see page 188) while watching TV, noting down the main iconic shapes of the figures engaged in various sports. They are not very accurate, but when seen small they capture the movement. The circular marks on the right were drawn with a no.12 brush and watercolor paint. You don't always have to complete the circle since the way the brush hairs show at the end of the stroke can be attractive. To add more interest, you could draw a wobbly circle with a felt-tip pen over the top of the dry paint.

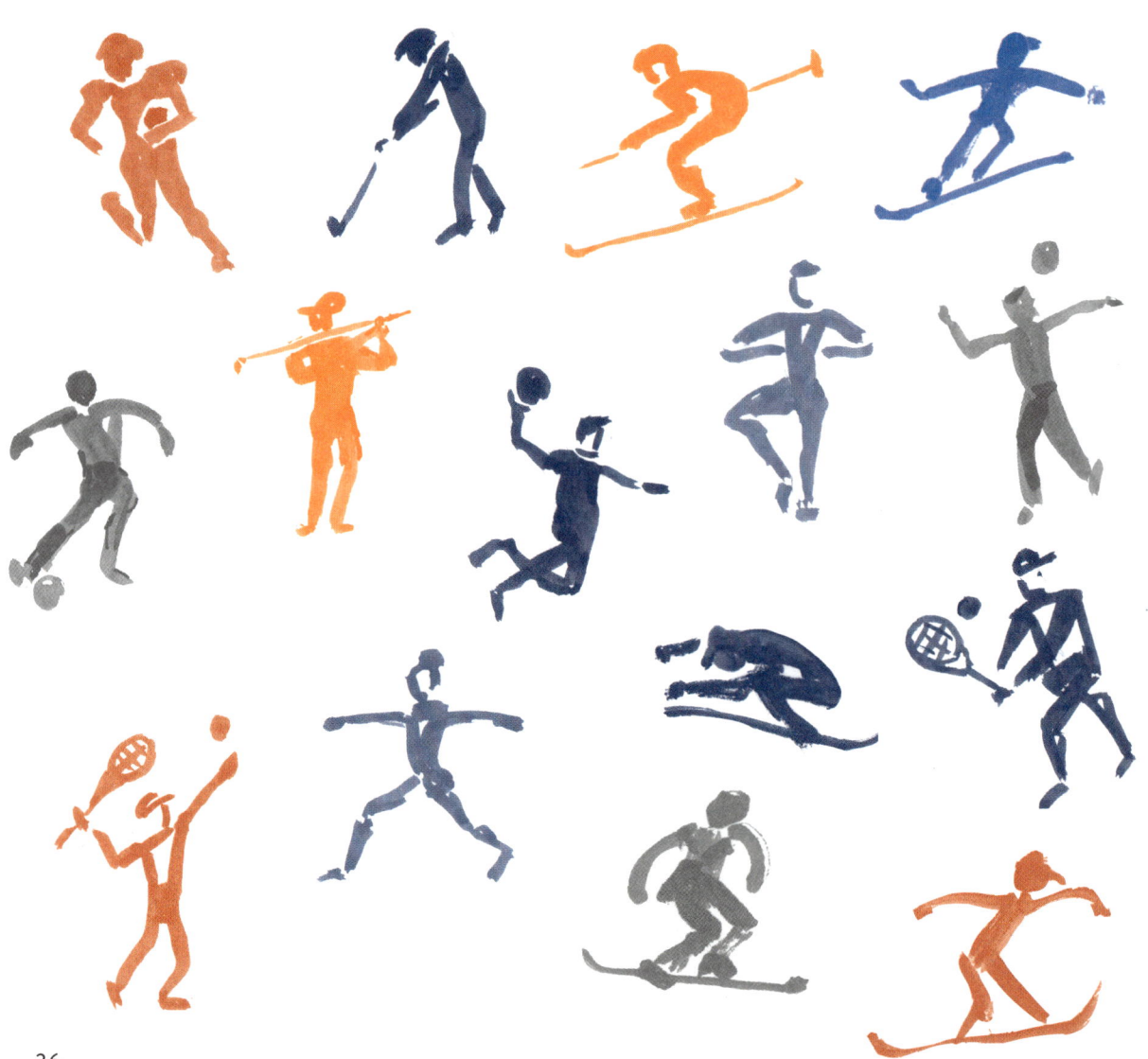

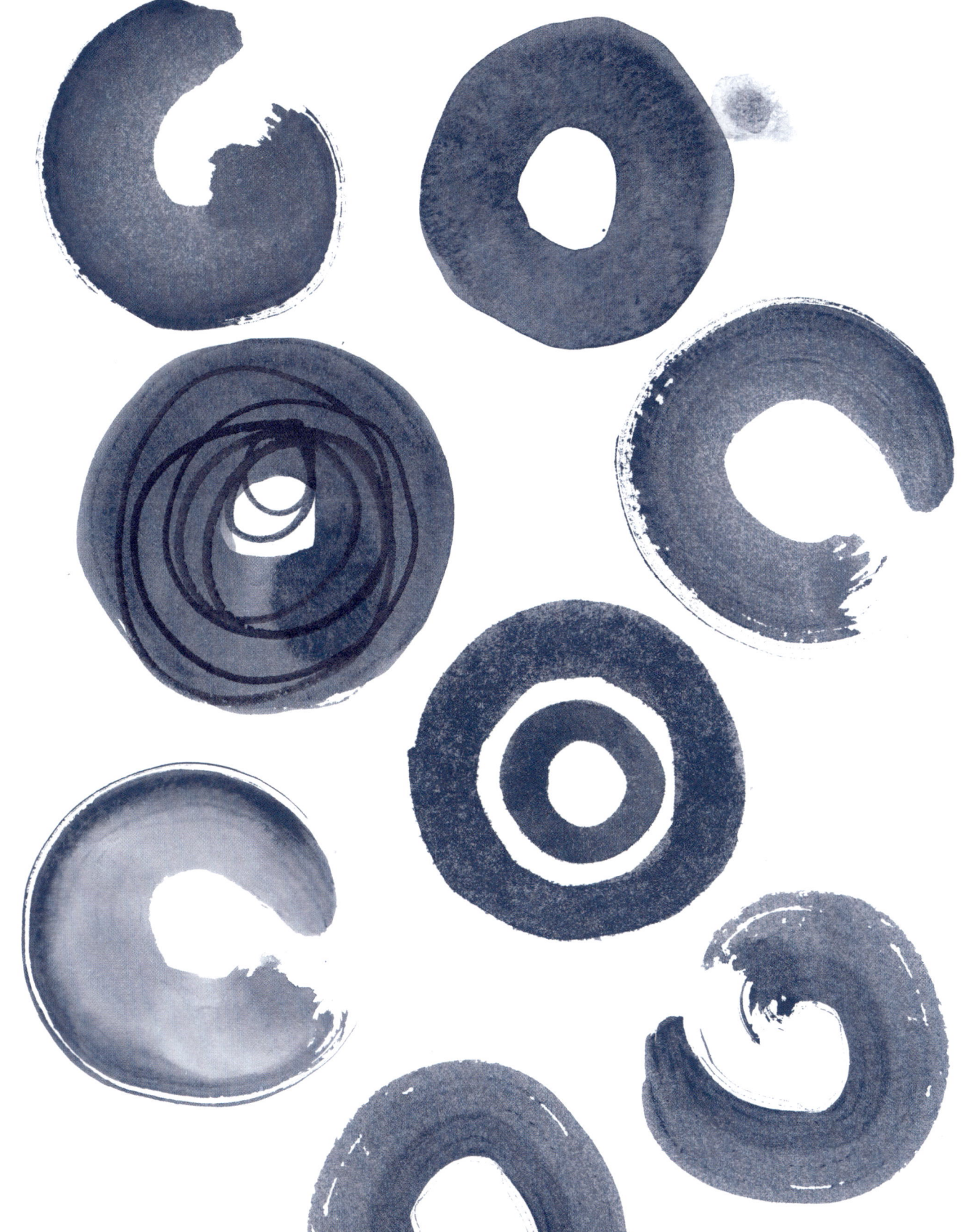

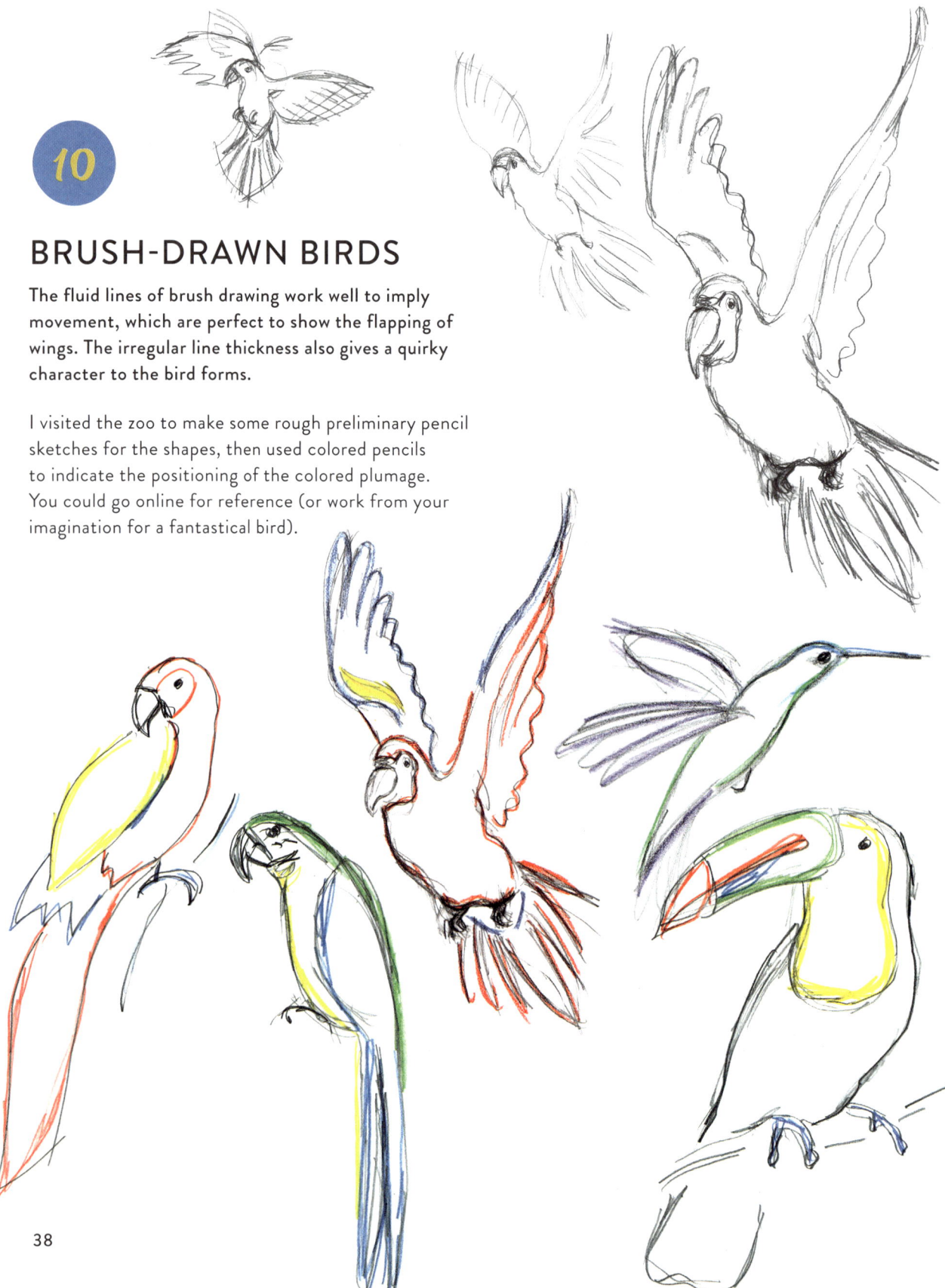

10

BRUSH-DRAWN BIRDS

The fluid lines of brush drawing work well to imply movement, which are perfect to show the flapping of wings. The irregular line thickness also gives a quirky character to the bird forms.

I visited the zoo to make some rough preliminary pencil sketches for the shapes, then used colored pencils to indicate the positioning of the colored plumage. You could go online for reference (or work from your imagination for a fantastical bird).

If you are working digitally on a tablet, you have the opportunity to make corrections, but not if you are drawing with brushes and ink. Try to practice the various forms beforehand because it will make you more relaxed when you draw the whole bird, and you can experiment with various shapes and methods for capturing the character.

For each of the birds on the next page, I did a few test drawings, some parts would work fine while another section would be slightly out of proportion. Don't get disheartened if you don't get it right the first time. I found the color sketches from the zoo helped, a little like a color road map for each of the brush strokes.

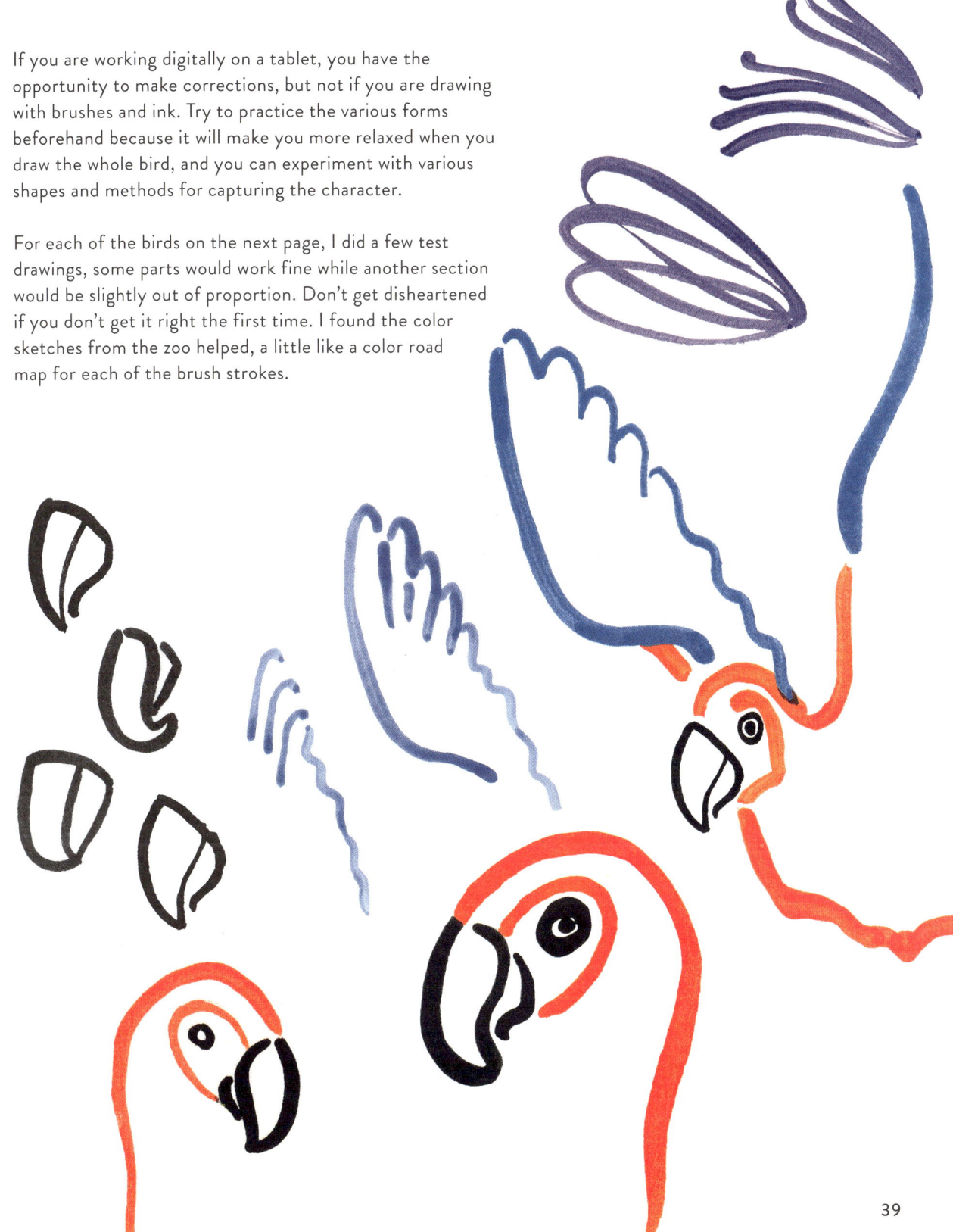

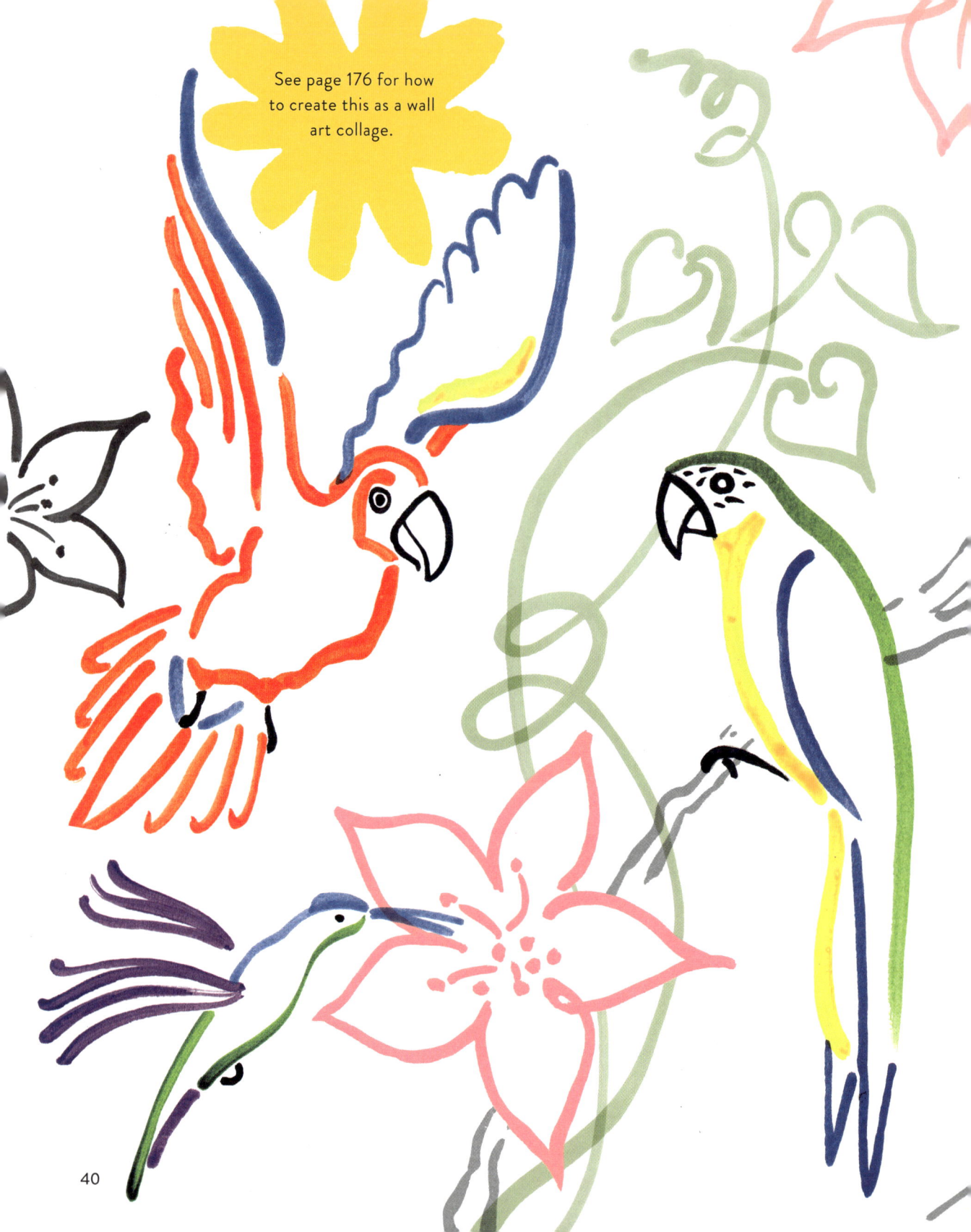

See page 176 for how to create this as a wall art collage.

40

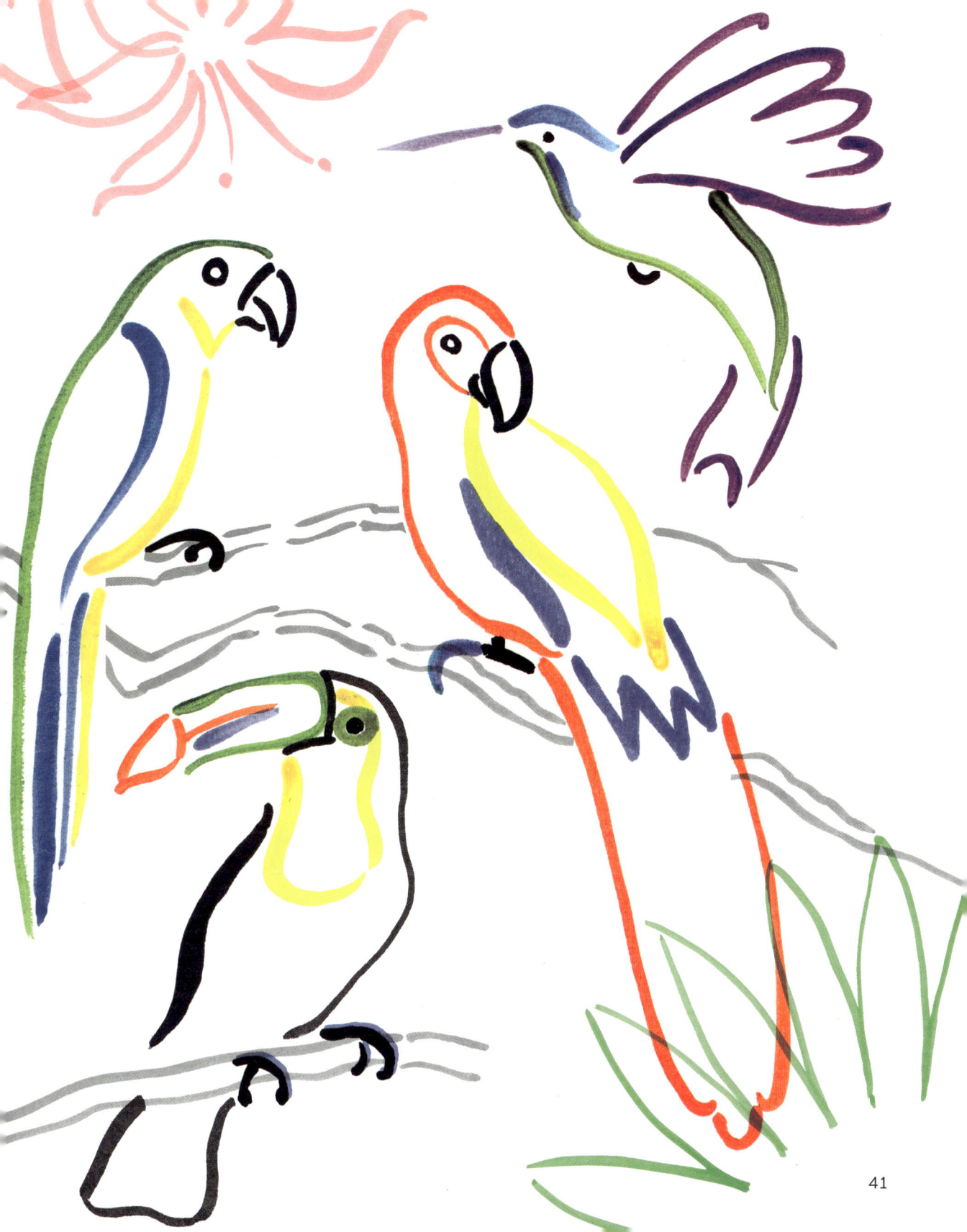

41

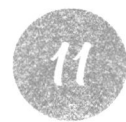

DRAWING WITH TONE

You've used lines, circles, curves, drawn brushstrokes, and even squares. Now try something else. You can use different tones to describe a subject. Part of the fun is analyzing the tones, also called values, in what you see, then translating this into a drawing.

First, look for the light source (sun or artificial light). The areas facing the light will have a paler tone, and the ones farthest away or on a converse side will be darker. Try to also observe any shadows and small reflected highlights.

Light source

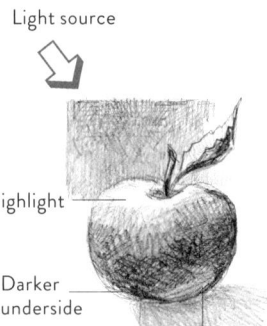

Highlight

Darker underside

Cast shadow

Reflected highlight from white table top

Drawn tone

Pencil marks can be overlaid to create various gray tones depending on the degree of hardness of the graphite, the pressure you use, and the number of layers. Black felt-tip pens and fineliner pens are almost opaque. The gradations of tone are achieved by the density of the marks you make.

Graphite pencil
Swatches from a 2H pencil (scratchier and lighter tones) on the left to a 4B (softer and denser). Draw with a medium pressure and build up layers.

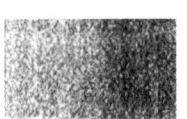

B and 2B
I find a single B or 2B will give a good range of tones depending on the brand and pressure you apply.

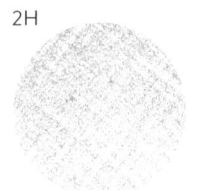
2H

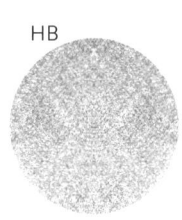
HB

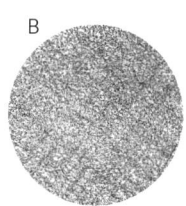
B

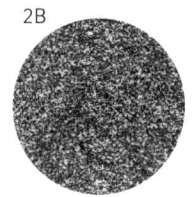
2B

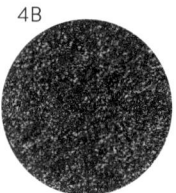
4B

Marker pen or fineliner
To give the impression of tone, you can create more or less space between your lines, or you can overlap, hatch, or cross-hatch them.

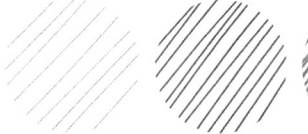
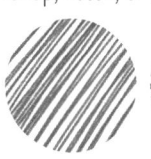
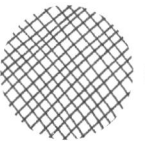
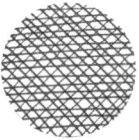
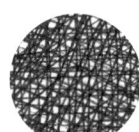
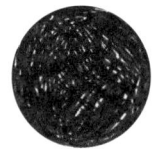

Tonal collages

This is a great way to hone your eye to translate something you see in color into black and white tones for an image. Even if you only want to draw in color, it's useful to be able to see subtleties of tone in the shadows and highlights. This enables you to explain the form or even exaggerate and add emotion to your color palette. Collect papers of approximately four tones of gray, plus black and cream or white. It doesn't matter if the papers have tinges of color, but they should range from dark to light. For the type of glue/adhesive see page 189.

Easy leaf shapes
Tear out leaf and stem shapes in one or two mid-tones. For the planter, tear out a mid-tone circle of paper, adding a dark tone to represent the inside and use pale tones for decorative details and highlights. Going back to the leaves, add dark or light veins to each side, torn or cut.

Cut veins

Backlit cactus
Using mid-tones, tear a round shape for the cactus and planter shape. Tear darker, curved rib shapes for the cactus and dark shadows for the planter. Cut the white spikes (see below) and add some curved highlights to show the light hitting the side of the pot. Add a dark mid-tone background, making the spikes glisten as if backlit.

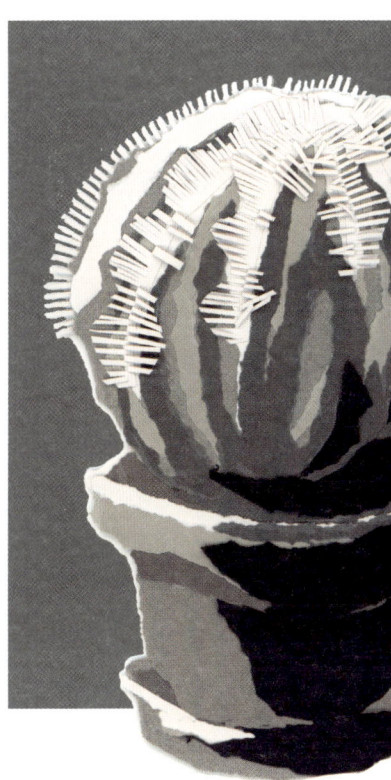

Torn veins

The leaf veins (left) and cactus spikes (above) were cut with scissors, then folded down alternately.

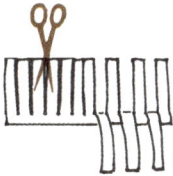

Create your own tonal values

Draw four or five areas of different tones. These are drawn in a small sketch pad, using a 2H pencil for light tones, a B pencil for the mid-tones, and a 4 or 6B for the rich, dark tones. You can make the swatches scribbly, as on the right, or with very soft transitions, as below. The latter is more time consuming but it can be mindful or something to do while watching a movie.

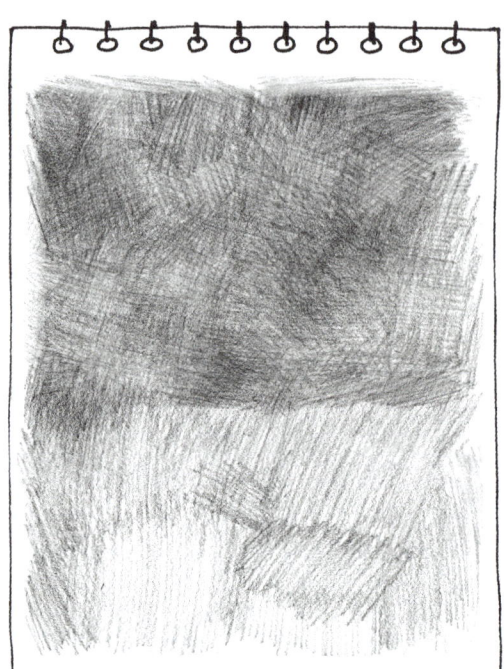

Scribbly gray tones
Work in blocks of different pencil directions to make attractive areas of tonal texture

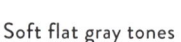

Soft flat gray tones
The pencil can be held at a lower angle than normal, applying light pressure. Gently move your hand with a diagonal action letting the pencil rest on the paper surface. The tip will build up layers of tone, changing the direction of the pencil to hide any faint texture lines.

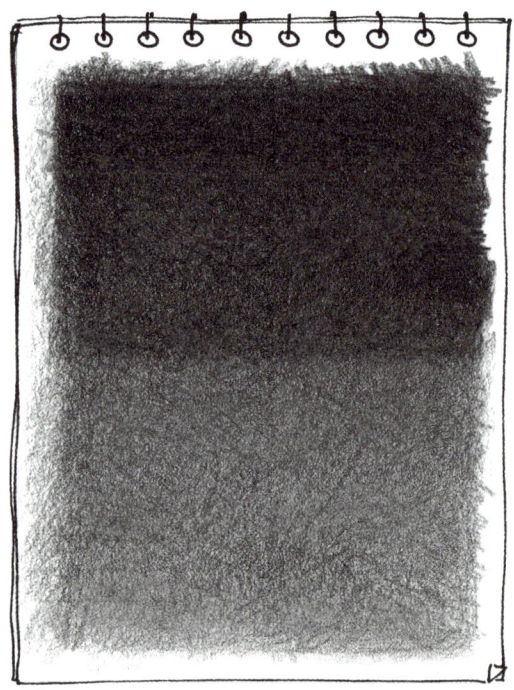

Easy collage portrait

Since your medium is torn paper, you cannot agonize or put pressure on yourself for an absolute likeness because you are not drawing fine details. Study your model to see the different tonal areas. Then create the tonal papers (opposite page) and tear the shapes to build up the features. Even if the torn shape is not quite right it is easy to tear a bit more and stick it over the top. For the type of glue/adhesive see page 189.

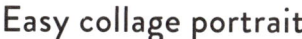

1. Tear out a large oval shape for the face in a light tone, and a bit of shadow under the chin. This will be the base on which you glue all the smaller tonal pieces. Position the eyes and mouth.

2. Keep analyzing the tones. Here highlight is used for the nose shape and darker tones for adding dimension.

3. During the process it might look a bit ghoulish! Here, I didn't position one pupil correctly, and the cheek shading was too low and dark. If the glue hasn't dried, carefully move the papers and adjust, or just add a correct paper tone over the top.

4. Keep adding more tonal details such as shades for the cheeks and highlights for the lips and pupils. Finally, place sections for clothing and some rough scribbly hair textures (use the angle of the scribble to describe the direction of the hair style).

It's useful to tear some curvy shapes before you start, then modify the shapes to the tonal areas as you see them. You can use scissors, or more organically torn edges, or mix them. It helps to have fingernails!

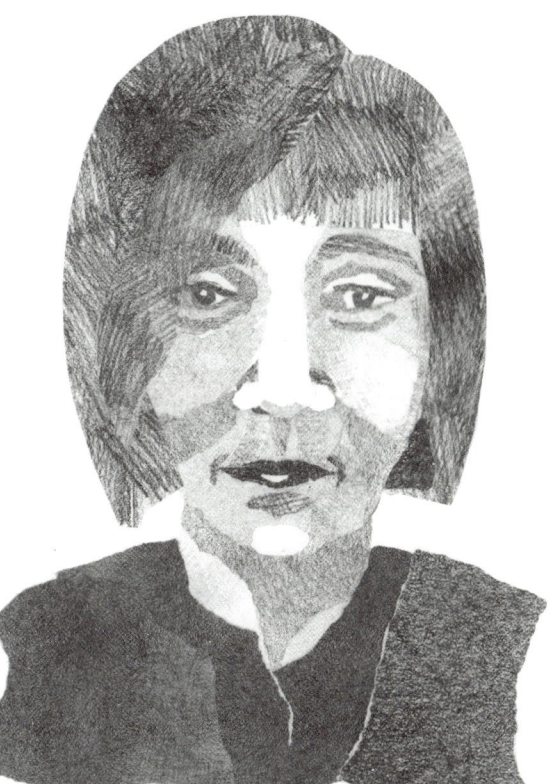

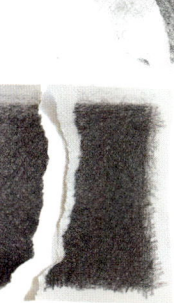

Tearing paper will create an edge with a white margin and a clean tonal edge, experiment tearing toward and away from you. Both are useful and the white margin can be a highlight or just to add textural interest.

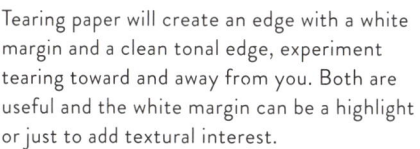

PIXELS TO TONE

Another way to see the tones in a colored subject is to work in monochrome pixels. Choose a limited range of tones, as this will help you to plan and edit down visual information. Always a useful skill!

Start with some patterns

These were all done with HB and 2B pencils in just two tones plus the white paper. They are fun to draw and you get to practice making the right pencil pressure for each tone. Try just moving and repeating one pixel tone to see the visual effect it will have—it becomes a bit addictive . . . The dragon (right) was drawn with four tones plus white.

These three are the same diagonal cross design but with the tones in different squares.

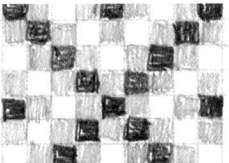

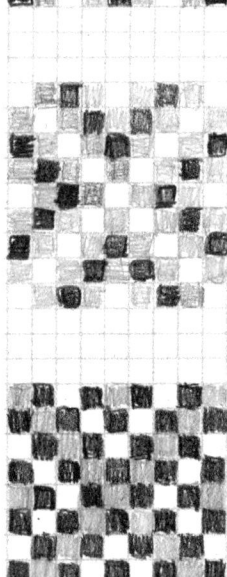

These three are based on an offset, giving different zigzags.

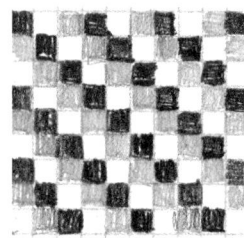

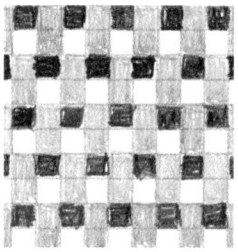

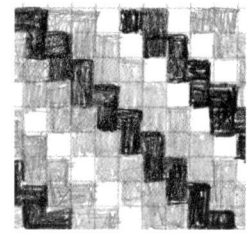

Central flower, with cross, diamond, and square.

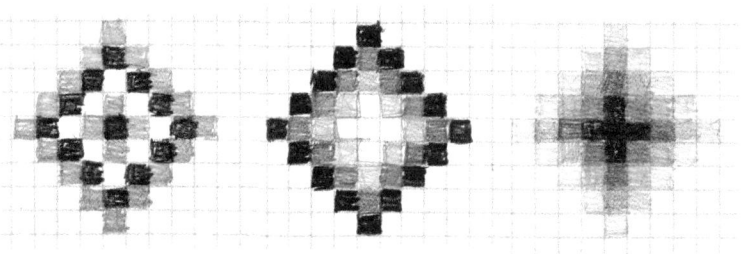

These three are all based on a diamond.

A diamond with corners.

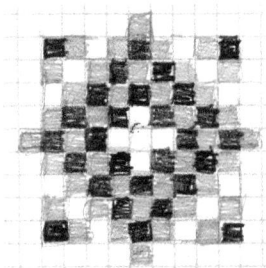

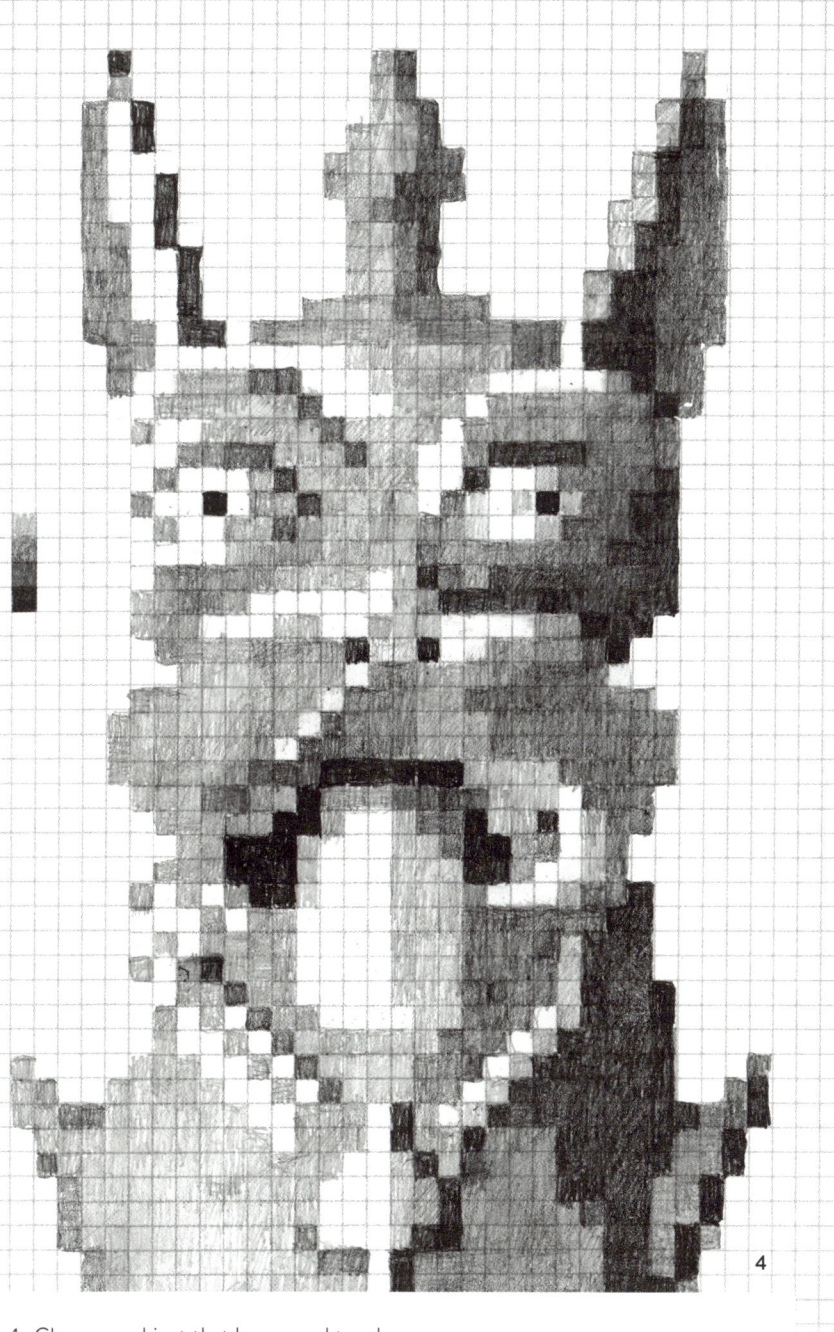

1. Choose a subject that has a good tonal range.
2. Roughly draw the outline proportions on the graph paper, mark small dark points for reference, here the eyes, and nostrils.
3. Working from top to bottom so your hand does not smudge the tones, shade a paler tone, leaving highlight squares white.
4. With the general shape in place it is easier to add mid-, then finally dark tones. It doesn't matter if you get the odd pixel in the wrong place.

47

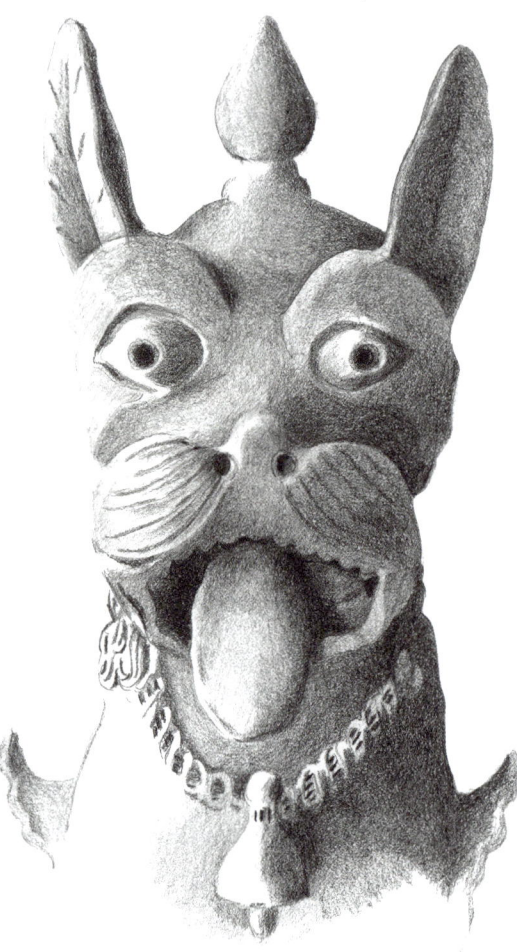

Drawing tones

Having honed your skills of seeing and translating tone into collage and pixels, now try some different drawing media. Keep some white highlights of the paper and draw some very dark tones, to prevent the drawing from looking flat.

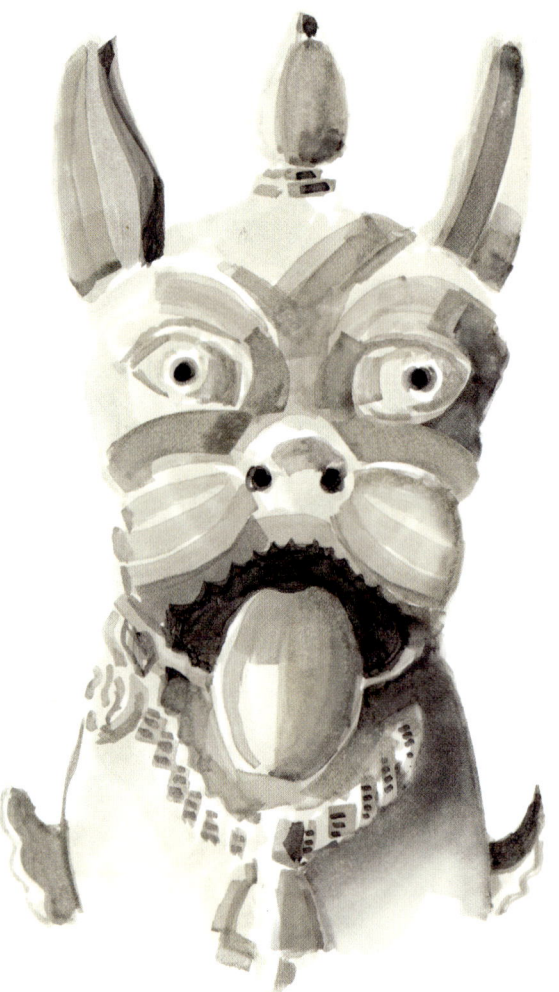

Dramatic Dragons
A good subject for black monochrome drawings. Above, subtle, graded tones were built up with thin layers of graphite using pencil stroke in different directions. Don't press on the pencil, just let the thin veils build up until you reach the tone you want. This method takes more time, but is satisfying to create. You will need a good quality paper for the best result.

The dragon drawing on the left has a loose-textured approach. The pencil strokes are visible using the hatching technique from page 13.

Using a set of five gray tone chisel tips, plus black alcohol markers, tones can be built up from light to dark. You can either make a feature of the marker's linear shape, or use the marker edges to help describe the curves and forms. The edge is best for adding whiskers as in the top section, or blending the tones as in the lower.

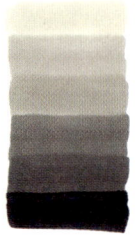

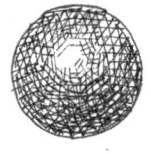

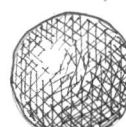

Use a fineline pen or nib pen to build up a variety of tones by hatching in different directions and creating layers. Practice with some globe shapes first.

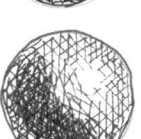

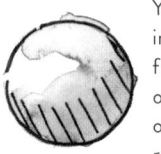

You could add a monochrome indigo wash to a waterproof fiber-tip black line as shown on the bottom globe. Indigo or any dark blue being a cool recessive color works well for tonal shadows.

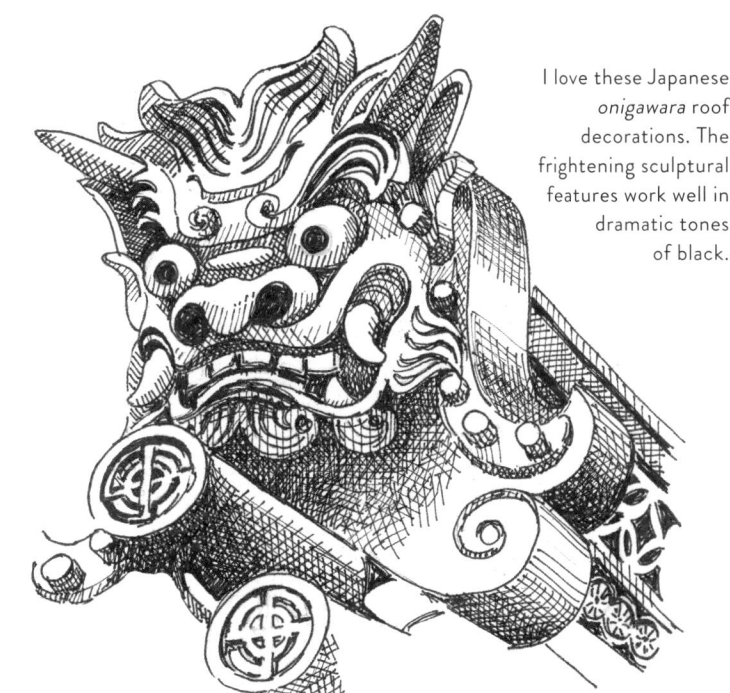

I love these Japanese *onigawara* roof decorations. The frightening sculptural features work well in dramatic tones of black.

The sketch below was drawn with a water-based graphite pencil. It is a quick way of adding tone to your drawing. The line work was drawn first, then water brushed loosely from the pencil lines to create the tone. When dry, add the details of dragon scales and the decorative circle roof tiles using a normal 4B pencil.

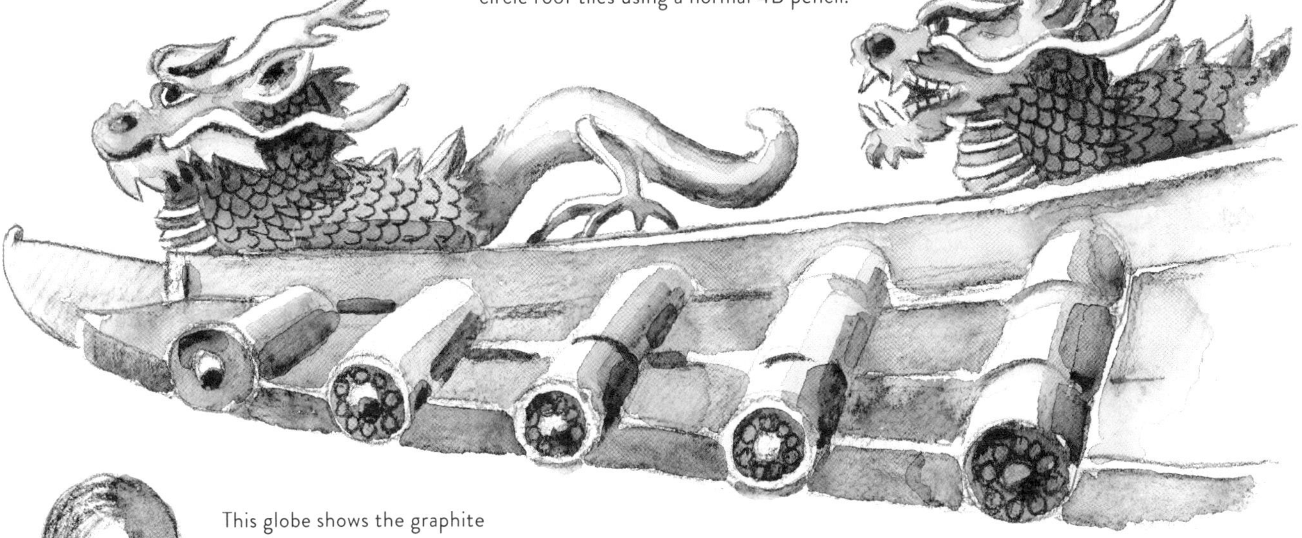

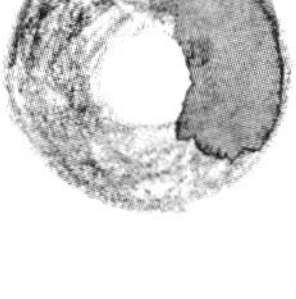

This globe shows the graphite marks from the pencil on the left, then how the water spreads the tone on the right

LAYERS AND TEXTURES

It's fun thinking in layers, and color often offers a mix of surprises (in a good way). Choose a subject, such as a landscape, that has broad color range and layers.

Using alcohol-based chisel-tip markers on mid-weight paper as shown here, or colored pencils on drawing paper, think how to simplify the subject. Normally, the shadow sections are added at the end. For these, try violet or blue, since they generally combine well with previous color layers and are recessive cool colors.

First, block in a base background layer.

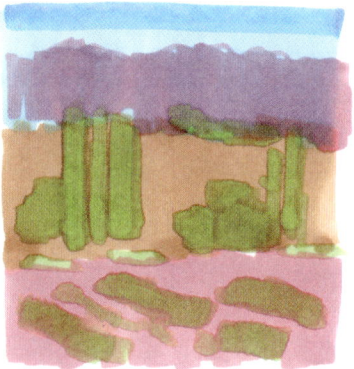

Add a second layer of large shapes.

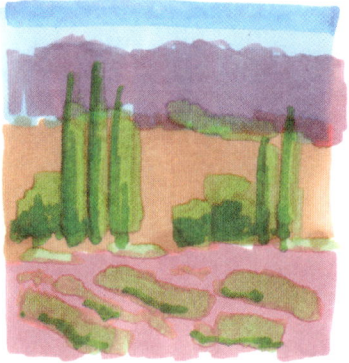

Start drawing shadow areas, adding more as in the final image (right).

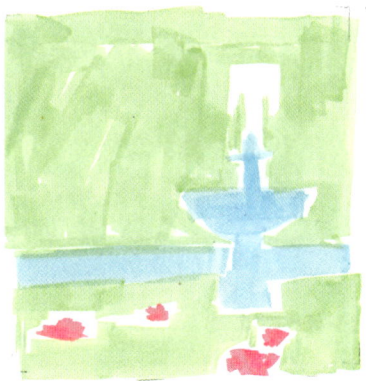

Block in a base background layer.

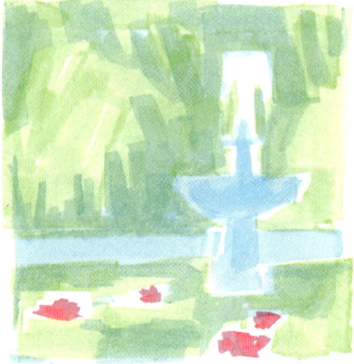

Block in shadow background so the paler leaf shapes are defined.

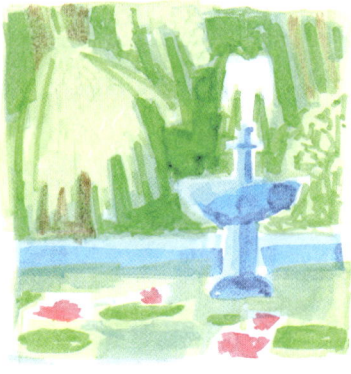

Continue to add green details, and finally shadows as on the opposite page.

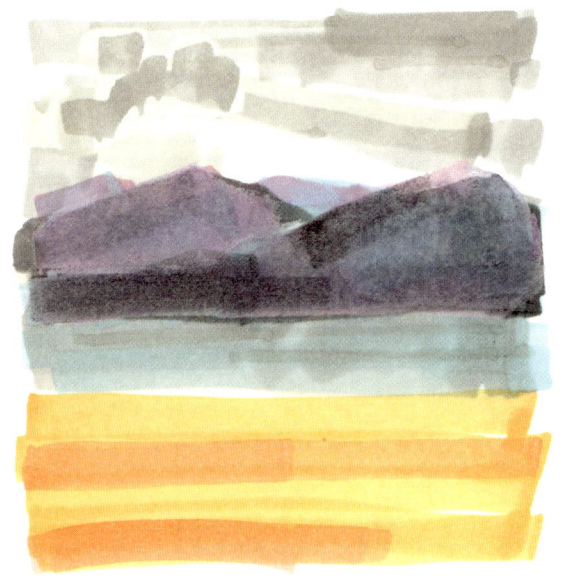

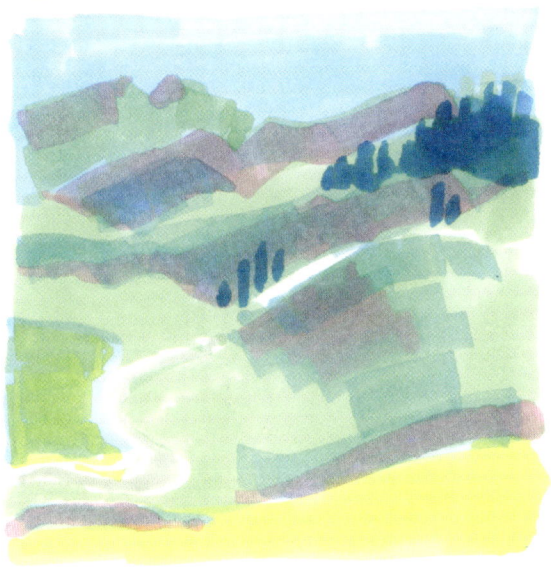

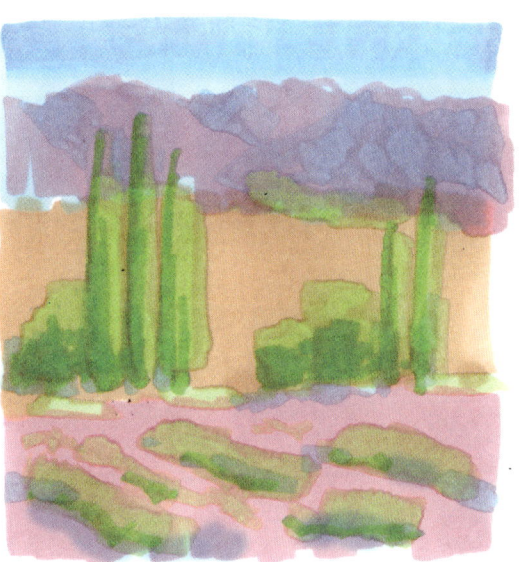

Texture layers

Colored pencil or chalk pencils work well on colored papers, which have a textured surface (see page 186). The resulting color over the top of a bright or rich colored paper can be surprising. I started the Marjorelle garden drawing (opposite page) on a lovely gray paper, but it looked a bit dull, so I tried a rich blue, which makes the greens and yellows glow. Work by creating veils of color layers in a similar way to the markers on the previous page. Don't block in the color, let the texture and glimpses of the paper show through. Unlike with markers, you can add shades of white to blend or modify a color, and for highlights.

This actual size detail (opposite page) shows how slightly textured paper allows the base paper color and subsequently the veils of color to show through in lively textures.

Make little sample swatches of color on different colored papers and the results might be very different to your expectations after working on white paper.

I didn't have a violet pencil for the lavender field, so tried a cool red layer, then a blue. I think it works.

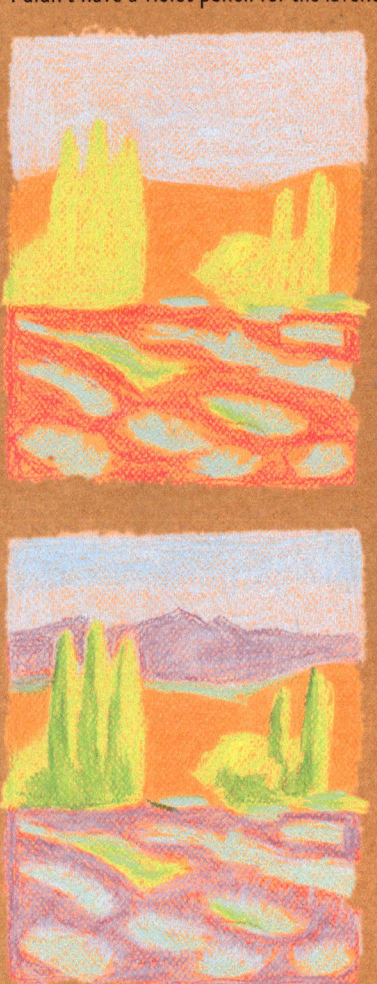

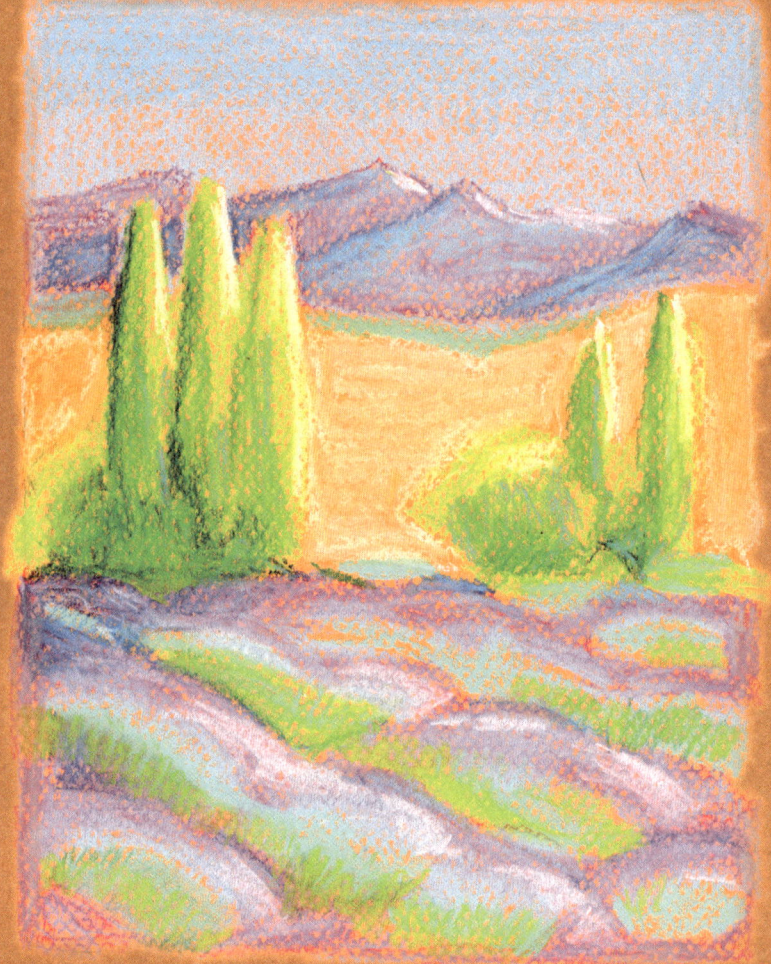

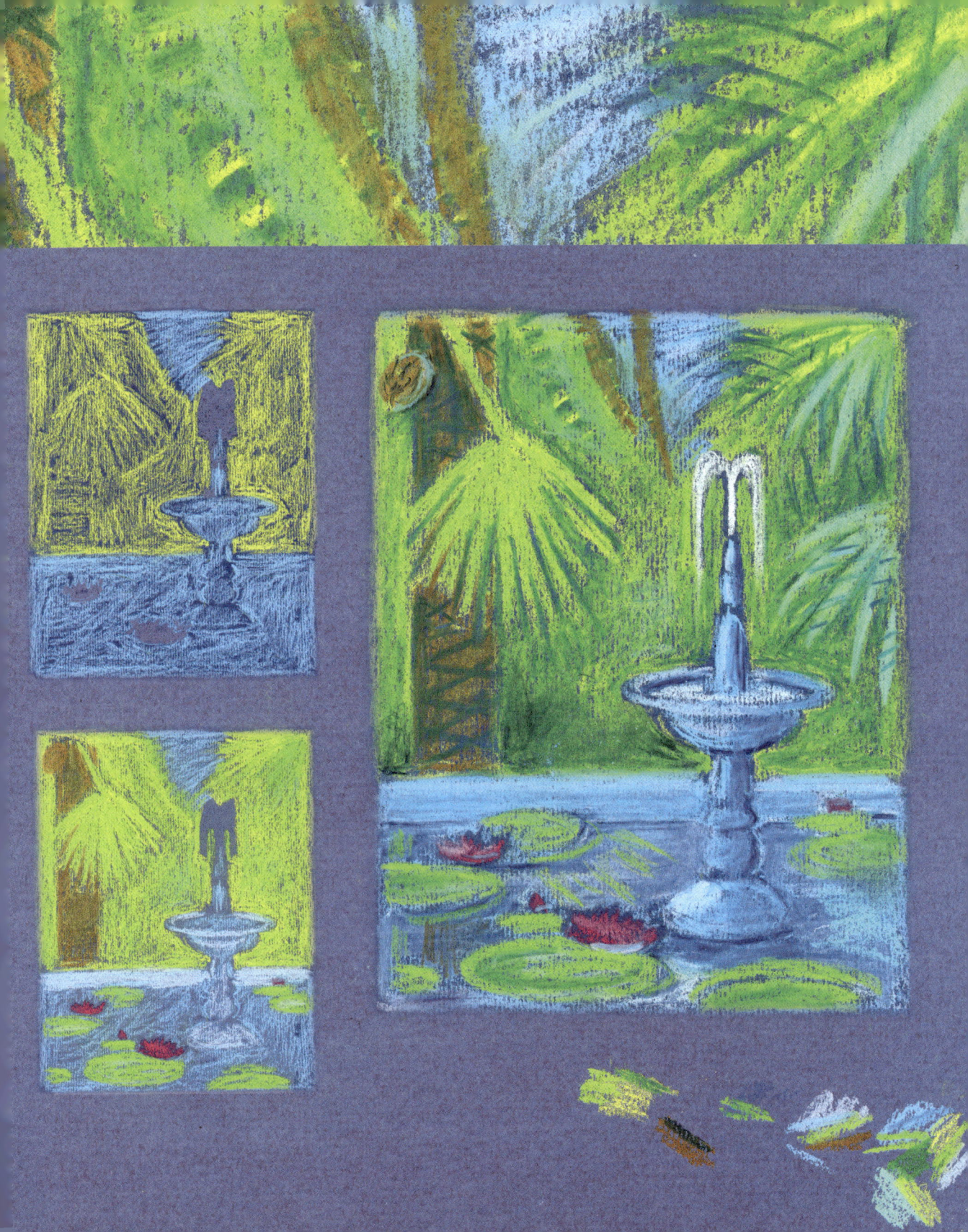

DRAW SOMETHING SMALL, BIG

Changing the scale of an object makes you look at it in a different way. It can be examined in more detail and elevated from something small and inconsequential to a large piece of art that takes on abstract qualities.

You might not have considered the little paint pans that can be bought singly or part of a watercolor box. There is always the excitement when you unwrap a new color and start using it. Magnify them to see how each little pan has its own story or landscape—some with deep recesses, others with cracked, dry paint tops. The overspill around the pans is another element to draw.

Other ideas include the inside of a watch, the center of a flower, a close-up of the iris of an eye, and a butterfly or moth's wing.

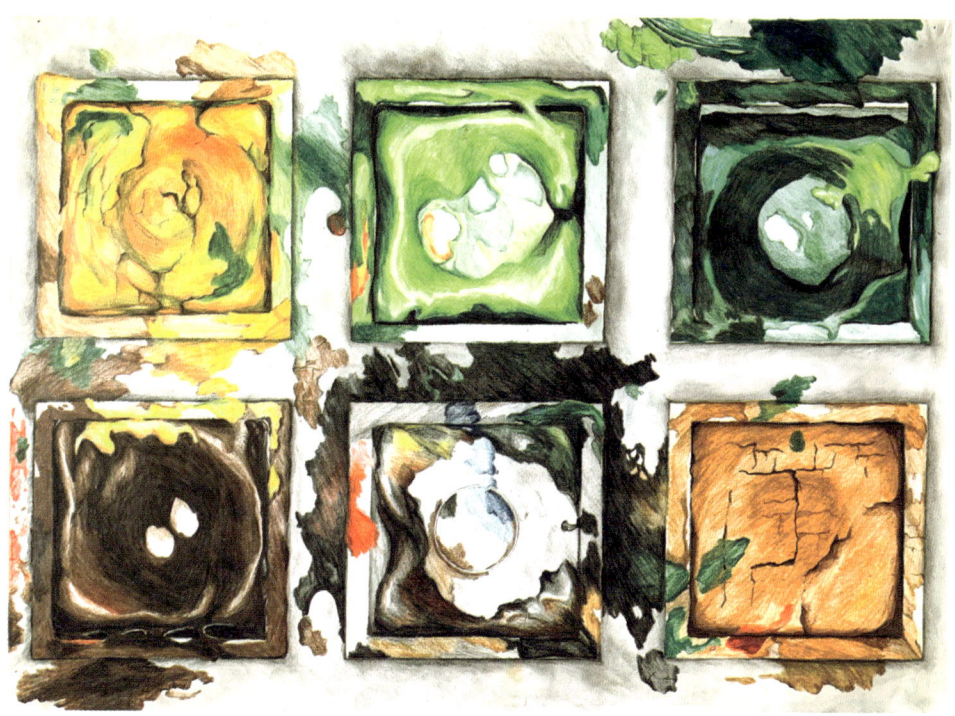

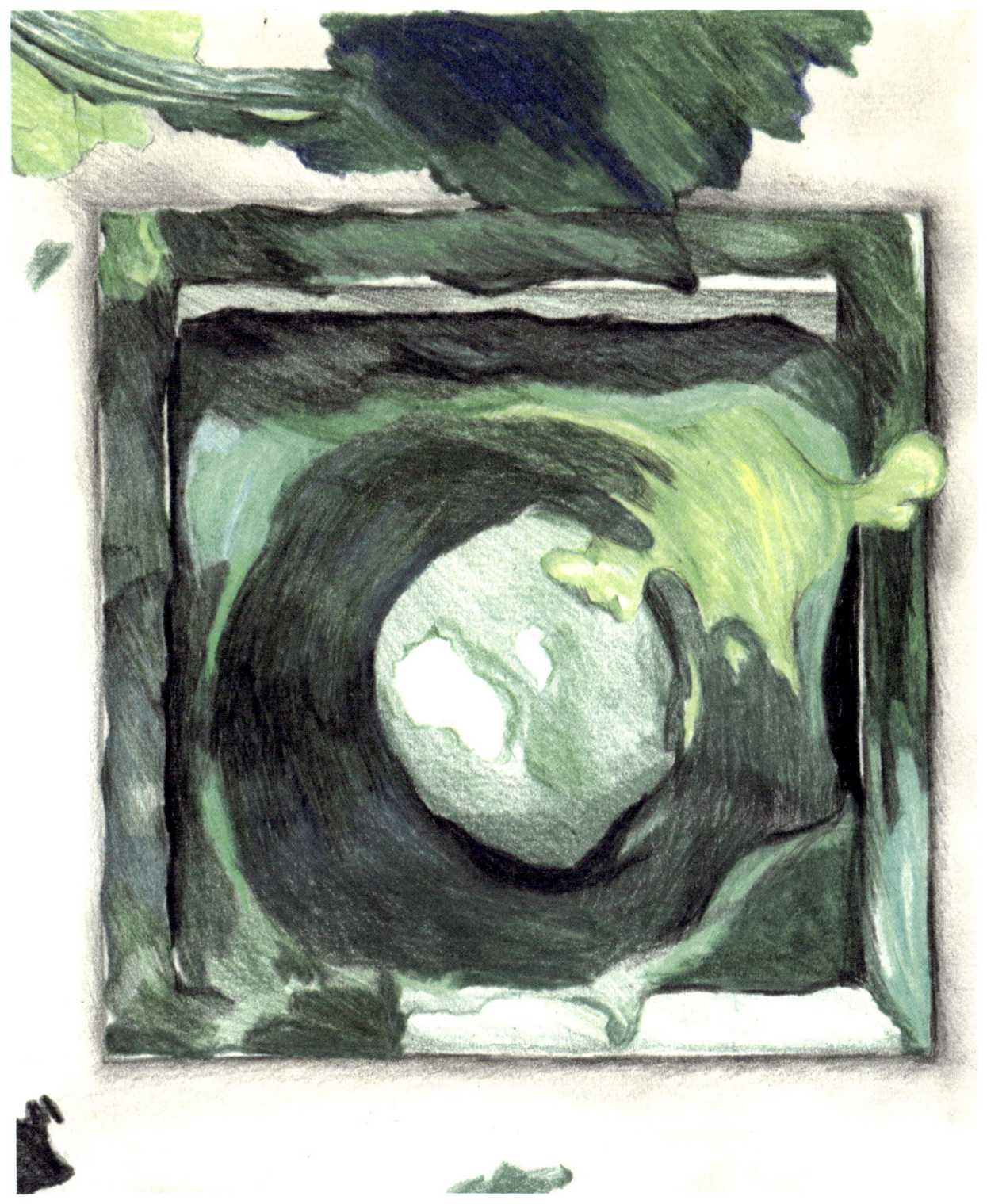

ADD DIMENSION AND DRAMA

Rotate some objects through various degrees, both horizontally and vertically and decide which angle gives you best view to draw. This thought process is something you should go through *every* time you are about to sketch. A flower head looks very different depending on whether you are looking down on it or up from the side.

Take a box . . .

It could be open or closed but drawn from different angles and heights you will see the subtle differences when you move the box around slightly. The open box is useful to understand how to draw interior room or building spaces.

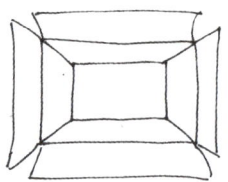

Start from directly overhead and add some color so you have light, mid-, and dark tones. This will help give dimension.

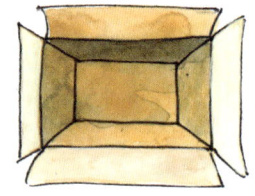

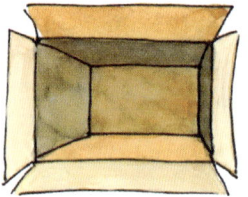
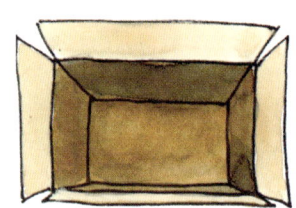
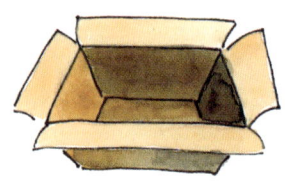

Then move the box (or your viewpoint) so you see more of one internal side and none of the opposite. (The angle could be such that you start to see an external side of the box.)

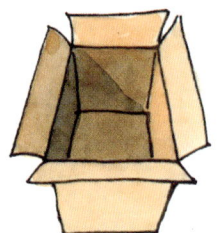
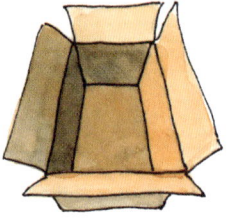

See how the front and back sides of the box vary in height and visibility depending on your viewpoint.

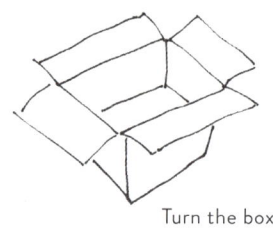
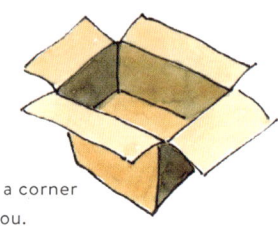

Turn the box so a corner is facing you.

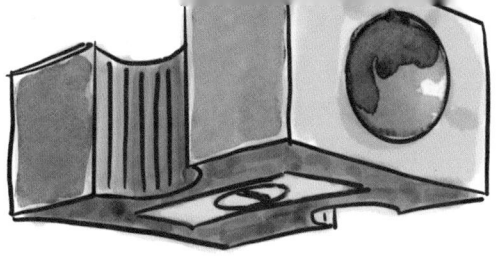
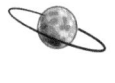
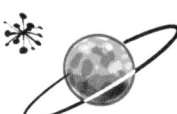
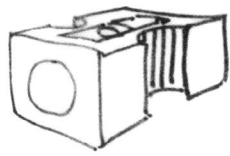

Or a pencil sharpener

Choose another subject (it doesn't have to be a pencil sharpener) and sketch it from a few angles. Think about which best describes its shape. Choose the most dynamic view and draw it big at the top or bottom of the page, transforming its use by adding a figure. Think sci-fi spaceships flying, like in *2001: A Space Odyssey*, or *The Martian*, or the dynamic skyscrapers from *Batman* or *Spider-Man*.

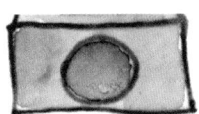

From straight on you wouldn't know what this is.

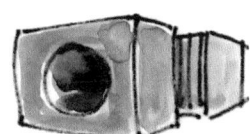

Turn it slightly to the side and you might.

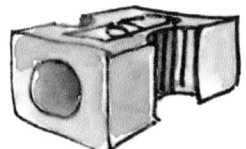

As you move around and above, it becomes clear that it is a sharpener.

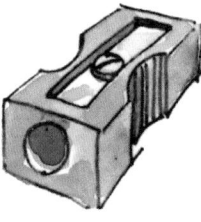

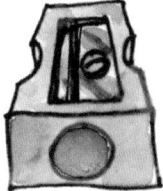

Drawn from above and straight on, you can see that the back end of the sharpener that is farthest away is smaller than the front, giving the impression of distance.

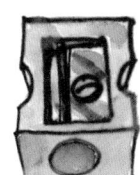

Here, the width of the sharpener is the same at the front as the back (as in reality) but it just doesn't look as three-dimensional.

See how many different angles or viewpoints you can find.

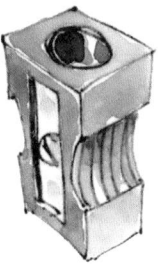

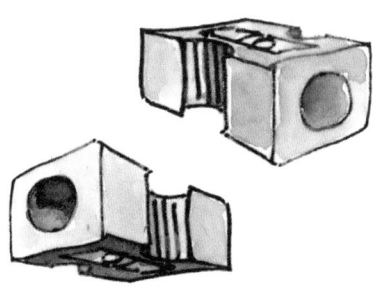

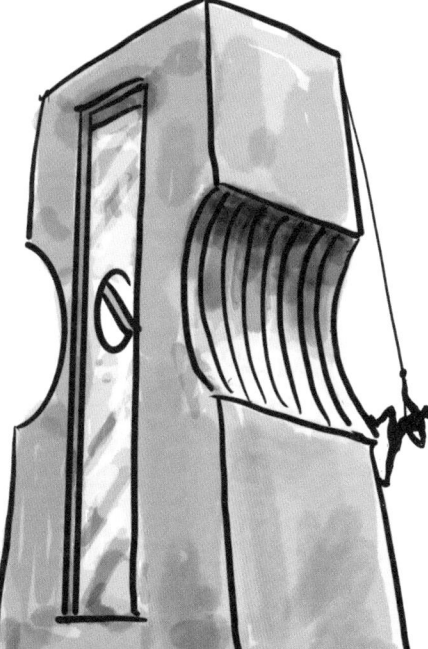

Simple perspective

While sketching the box or sharpener, you have been using perspective. With perspective, drawings look more dynamic and three-dimensional. It's useful to understand a few basic concepts and then use them or not, as you see fit. (Rules are made to be broken.) Many artists in the early twentieth century abandoned the perspective system altogether.

It is a method used to imply three dimensions on a flat paper surface. Your brain will interpret distance when an object is smaller—such as the road or telephone poles (right). This system will help you draw the objects to look as if they are receding. There are three basic types: one-, two-, and three-point perspective.

How to do it

Draw a horizontal line that will represent the horizon line or your eye level. Then, use an "air pencil" to see the convergent lines. Hover and angle your pencil in the air and align it with the angles formed by the receding edges, such as the lines of the disappearing road, then roughly sketch or transcribe that angle on your paper.

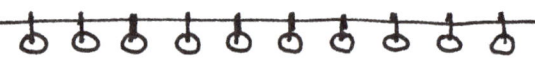

Jargon buster

There are many different terms and abbreviations for elements used in perspective drawing. These are the ones used in the book.

H (red) Horizon line. Where the sky meets the land, it may be hidden behind mountains or buildings.

EL (also red) Eye level. Generally similar to the horizon line.

CL (blue) Convergence line. The line that you visualize and will help plot how various elements recede into the distance.

CP Convergence point. The point at which the convergence lines and the horizon intersect.

VP Viewpoint. The angle that you are looking at the subject. You might be looking up at something, or down, from the right or left side or just straight on.

One-point perspective

The convergence lines (CL) all meet at one point, the convergence point (CP), where they cross your eye level (EL). Here your eye level is central on the height of the box. You can see how finding the CP will help you draw the receding internal edges of the box.

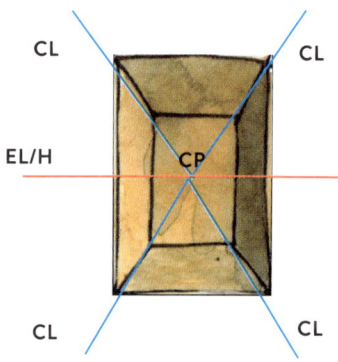

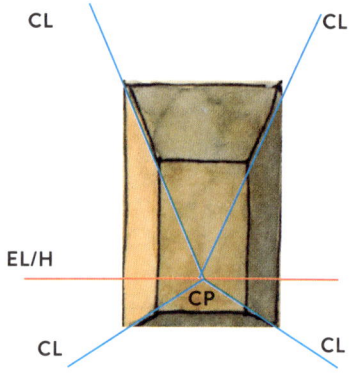

For compositional reasons, you may want the EL to be higher or lower. In the box above, and the Gothic hallway (right), the eye level is lower. You can see the CLs recede downward to the lower CP.

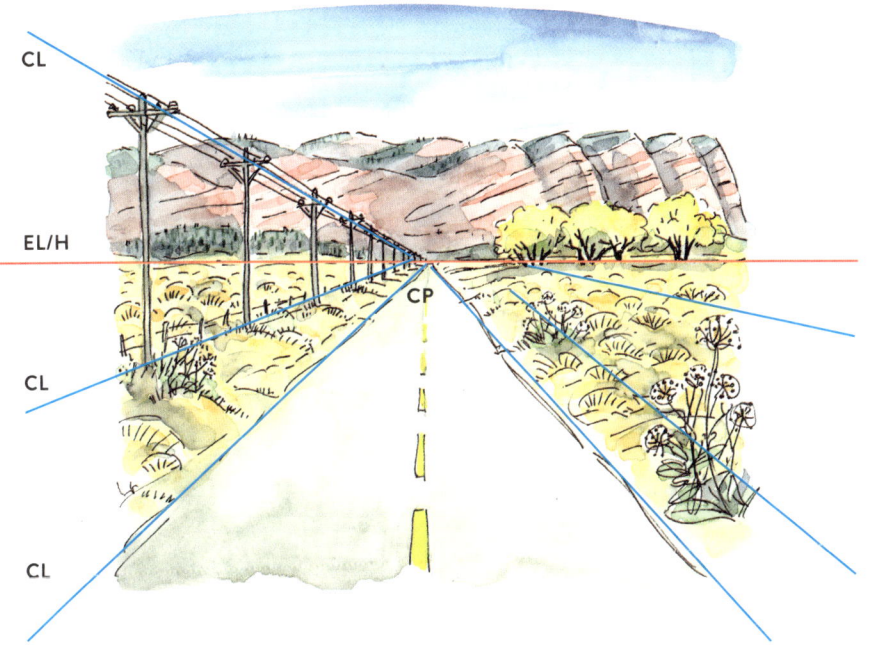

CL

EL/H

CL

CP

CL

The road to nowhere

You have probably seen this sort of image before, since it explains one-point perspective well. Your eye level is at the same position as the horizon line indicated by the red line. You can see the CLs drawn along the top and bottom of the telephone poles and the curbside, which all meet at the central CP. Seeing these lines will help you draw elements as they recede into the distance at one convergence point in the center. Even the diminishing size of the plants can be plotted using this.

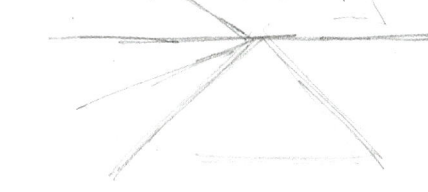

Air pencil sketch

This shows the plotting of the horizon line and convergence lines. It is the first stage of the drawing above.

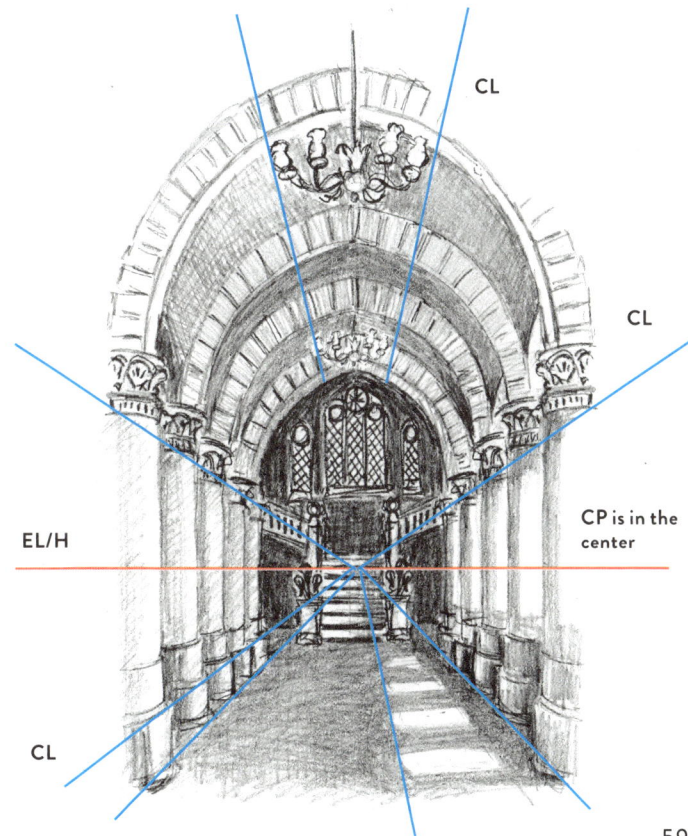

CL

CL

CP is in the center

EL/H

CL

Gothic hallway

Here, the eye level is positioned in the middle of the stairs. All the tops and bases of the columns, even the sunlight cast on the floor, follow the convergence lines to the center. You can scale items using the convergence line, such as the chandeliers.

Try a corner angle

This seating pavilion (below) was drawn using classic two-point perspective. Get used to analyzing where your horizon/eye level line lies and how the convergence lines recede to a CP on either side. I bet when you do this you will realize that many of the drawings you have done are already in this category.

Two-point perspective objects or buildings
Your VP is looking at the corner projecting toward you so you can see both sides recede, each to its own CP. The upright sides remain vertical.

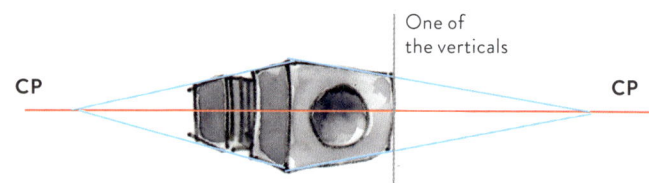

CP   One of the verticals   CP

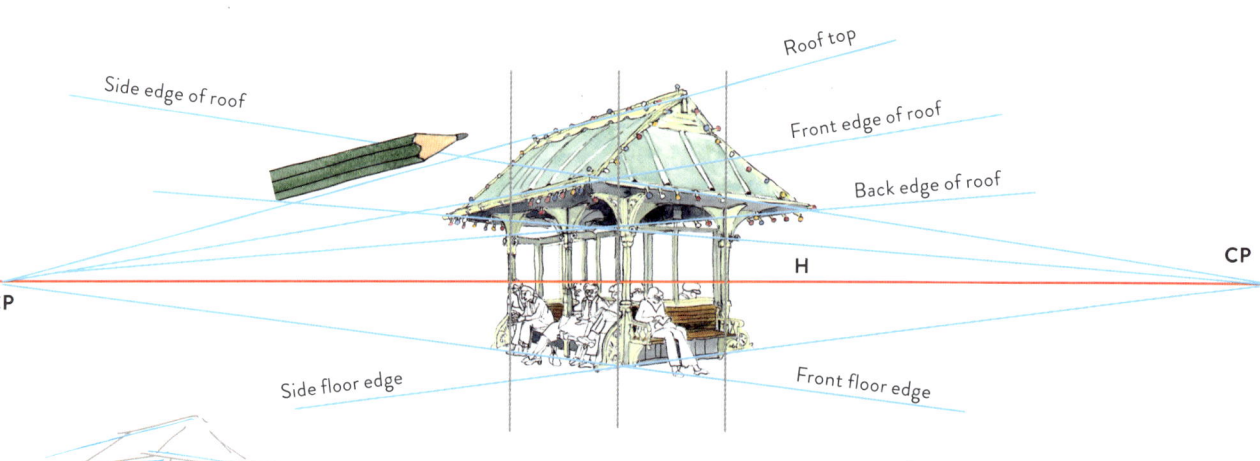

Side edge of roof

Roof top

Front edge of roof

Back edge of roof

H

CP

CP

Side floor edge

Front floor edge

See the angles
Hold an "air pencil" while looking with one eye to the edge of the object. Then quickly mimic the same angle with a drawn line on the paper. Repeat with roughly positioned lines for the sides of the structure. Then draw the vertical lines to roughly indicate the shape of the object or building. The inside roof edge at the back can be drafted using the same method.

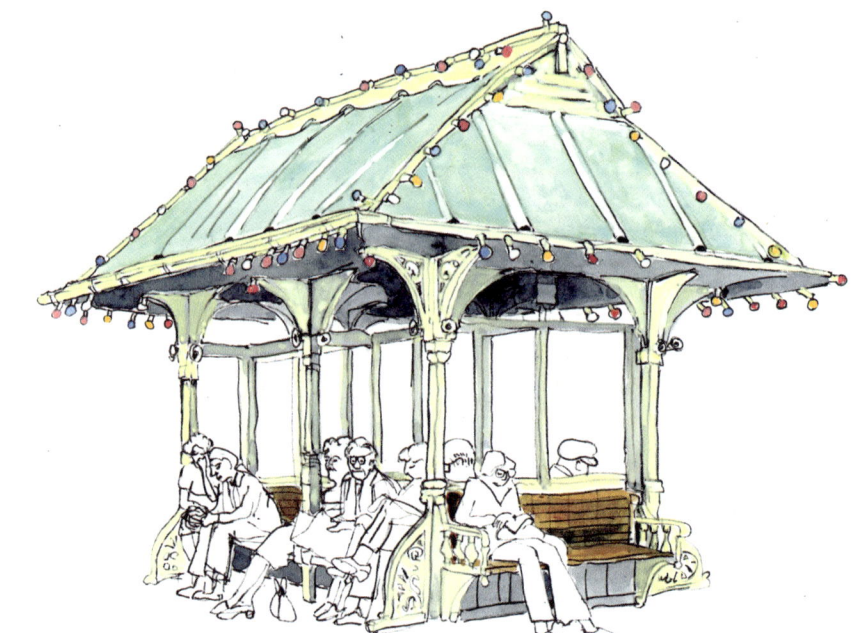

Two-point perspective interiors
Using the box concept, you can see the CPs help to plan the interior side edges of a room.

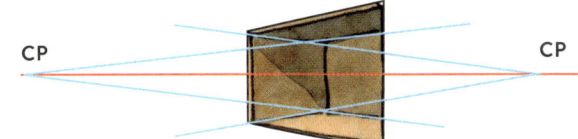

CP   CP

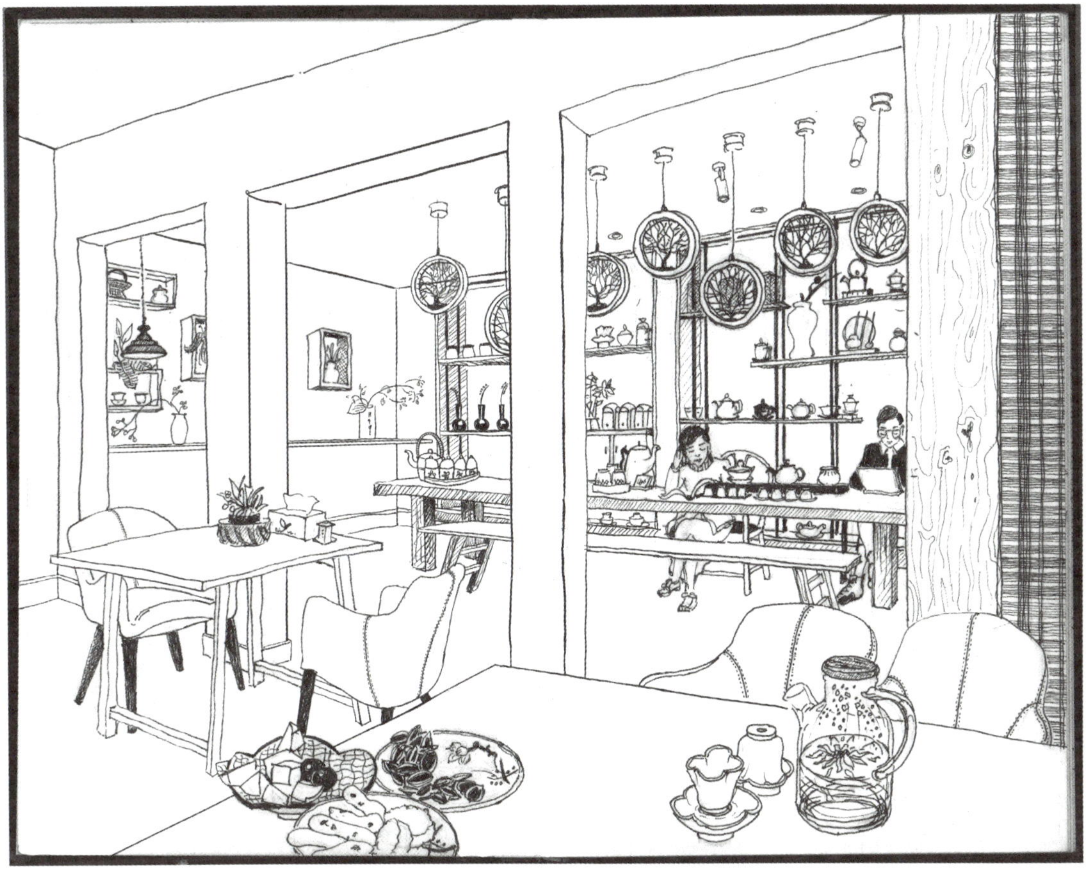

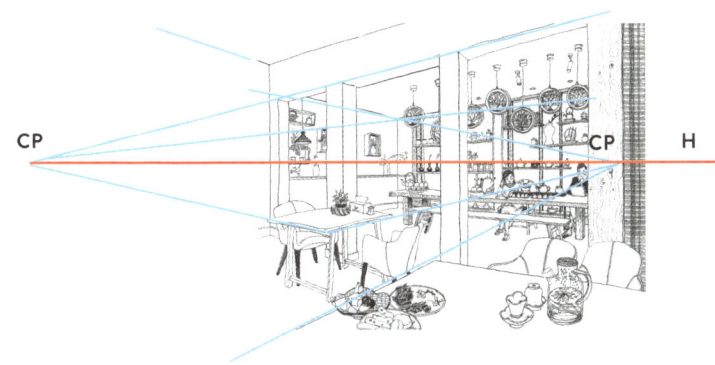

Hidden points
Sometimes the CPs will not be where you expect them. Sitting at the table with my sketchbook, I found the horizontal for my eye level, then angled my pencil to find the convergence lines. I discovered one CP was outside my sketchbook whereas the other was behind the wall within the sketch. However you can see the main wall structures work to the convergence points and indeed the tables, chairs, shelving, and even picture frames.

CP   CP   H

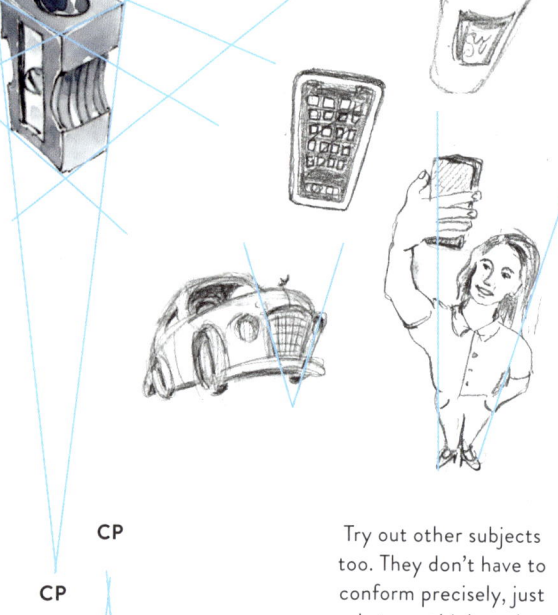

From above or below?

Three-point perspective is used to create a sense of looking up or down. By adding in a third CP and playing with the angles of the convergence lines, you can create a subtle or exaggerated spatial effect.

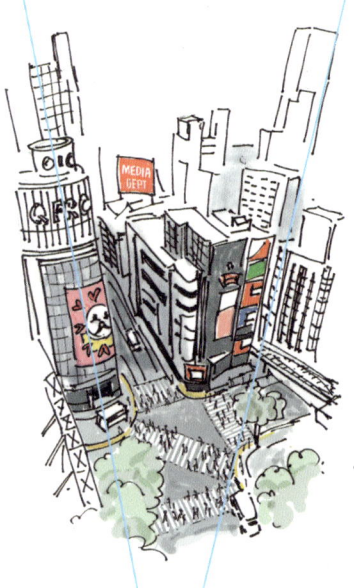

Three-point perspective
Your eye level or horizon line will either be in the sky or at/near ground level. The CPs will probably be way off the sides of your sketchbook or paper. To calculate the line angles, do it by eye or hover a ruler at the angle over the top of your paper surface. Of course you may decide to exaggerate the angle for extra visual drama.

The side walls will follow to the normal two-point perspective convergence points at the sides, but unlike one- and two-point perspective, the vertical will **not** remain vertical. Instead it will zoom up or down to the third CP.

Try out other subjects too. They don't have to conform precisely, just what you think works.

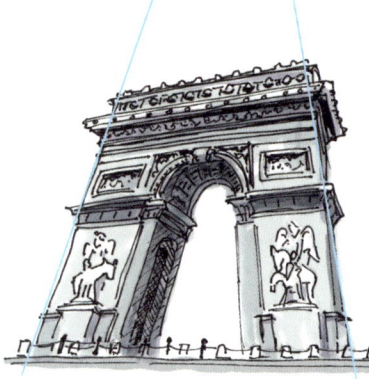

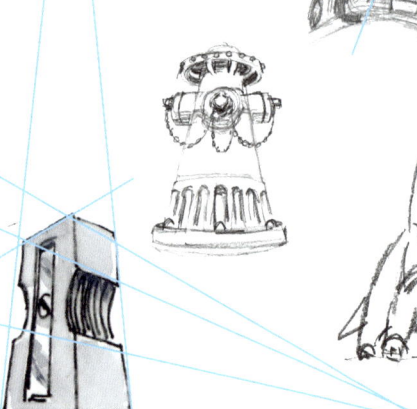

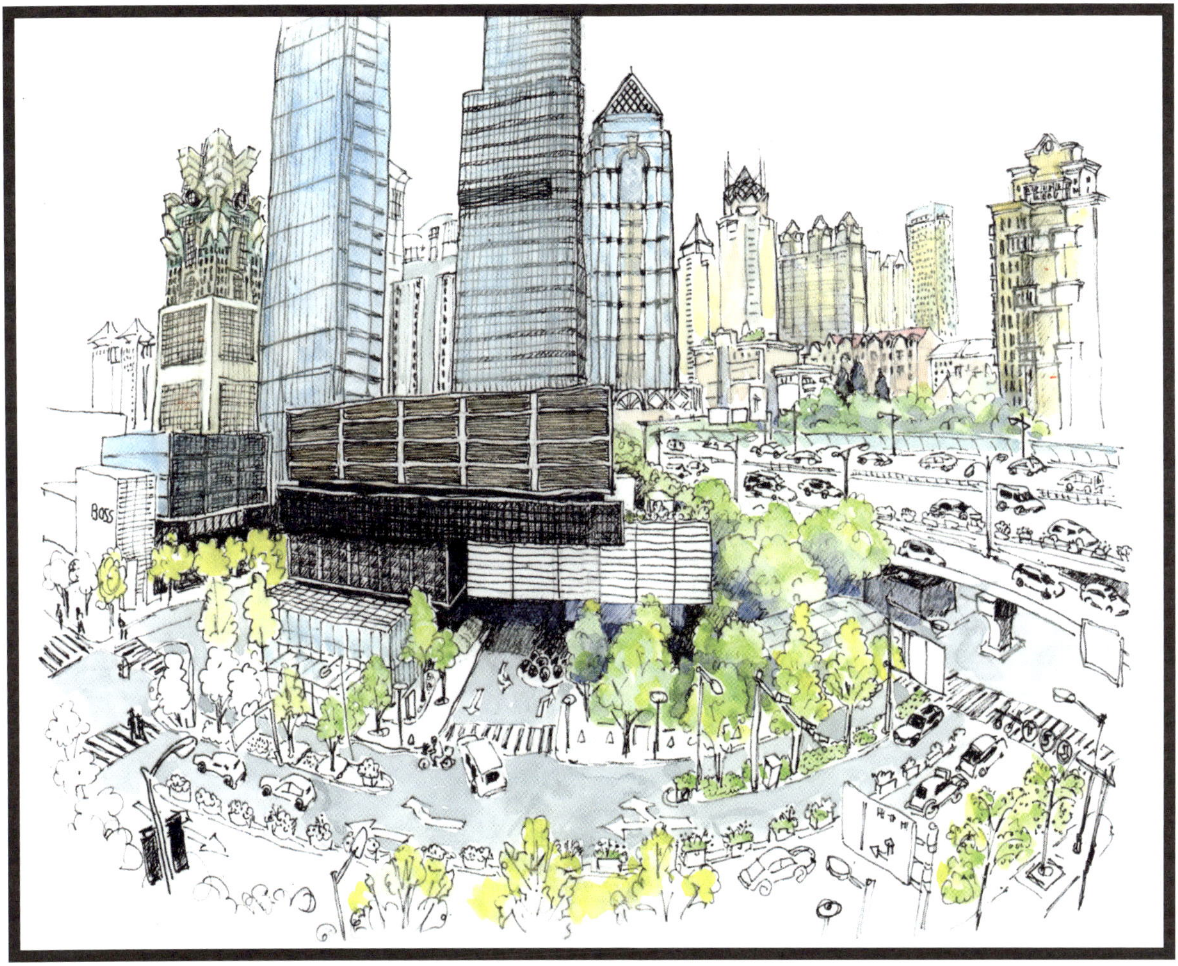

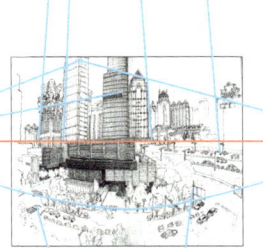

Mash up and bend it

The sketch above shows manipulated perspective.
(it's only a concept after all). The sketch combines
two types of three-point perspective, giving a warped
effect. The sketchbook wasn't wide enough, so the
lower part of the sketch is curved to include more
of the foreground below and create an interesting
composition. Objects such as the lamppost work to
the downward CP. Look online at fish-eye perspective
drawings—there are some great examples.

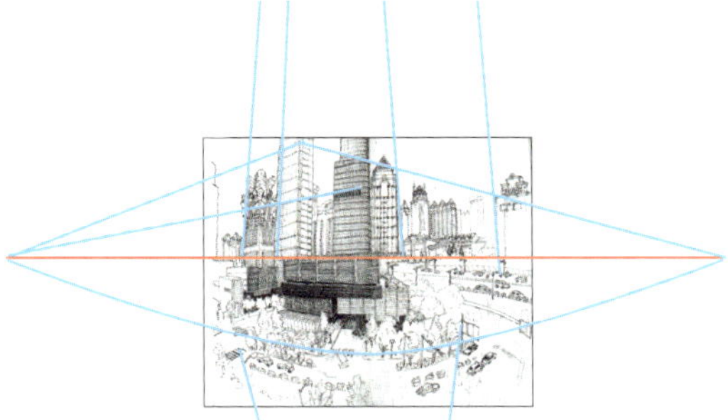

All the convergence points
are well off the page so just
guess at them!

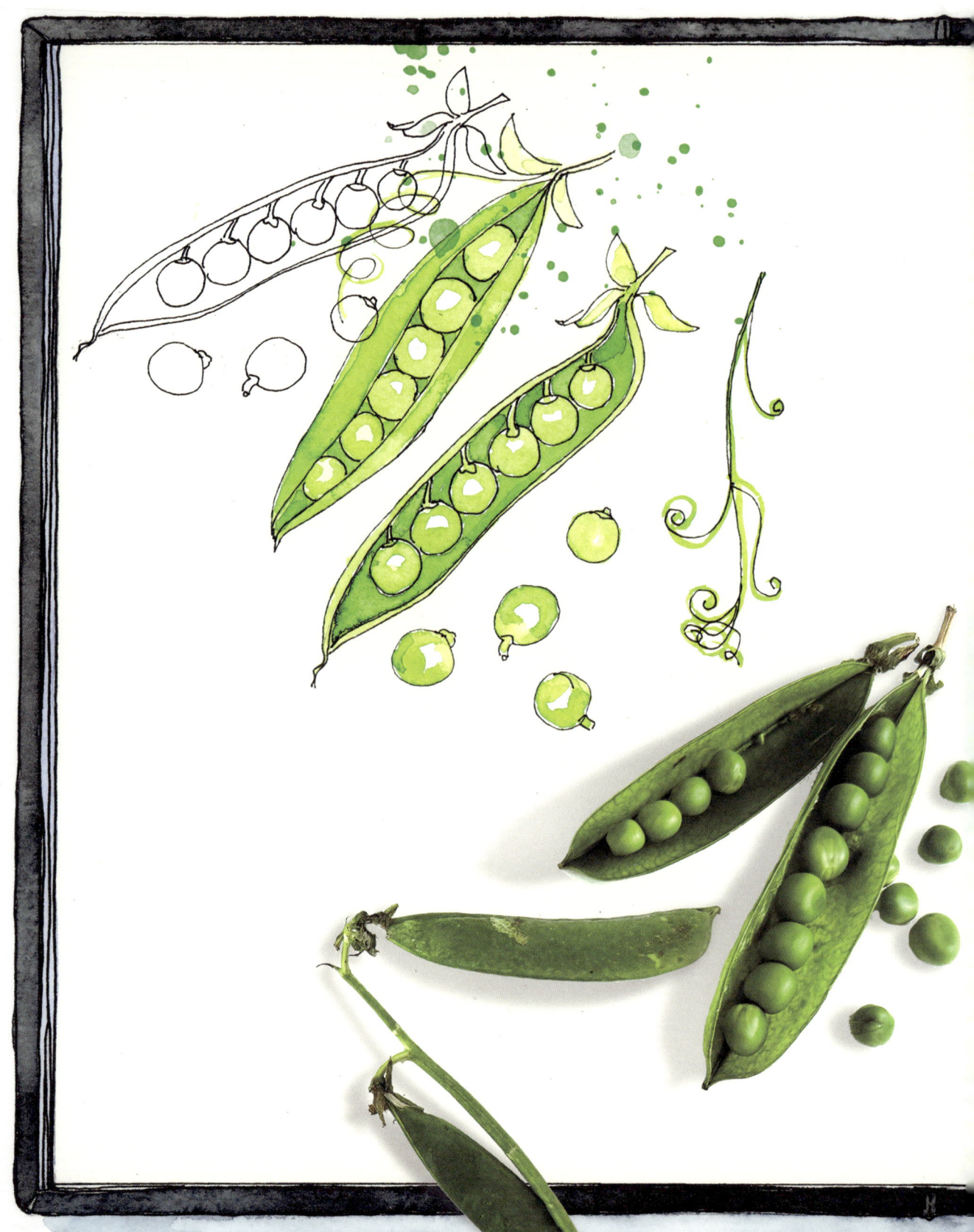

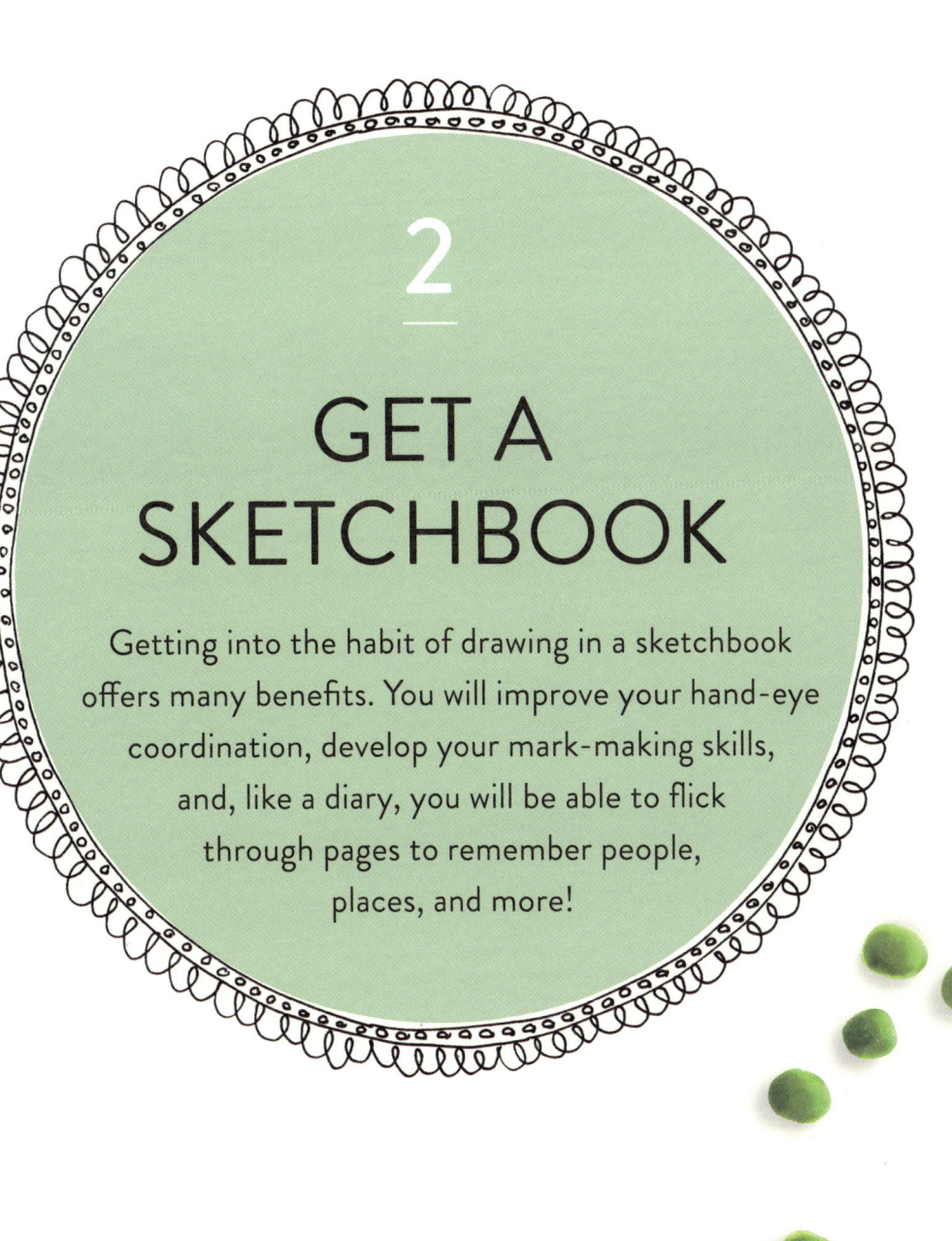

2

GET A SKETCHBOOK

Getting into the habit of drawing in a sketchbook offers many benefits. You will improve your hand-eye coordination, develop your mark-making skills, and, like a diary, you will be able to flick through pages to remember people, places, and more!

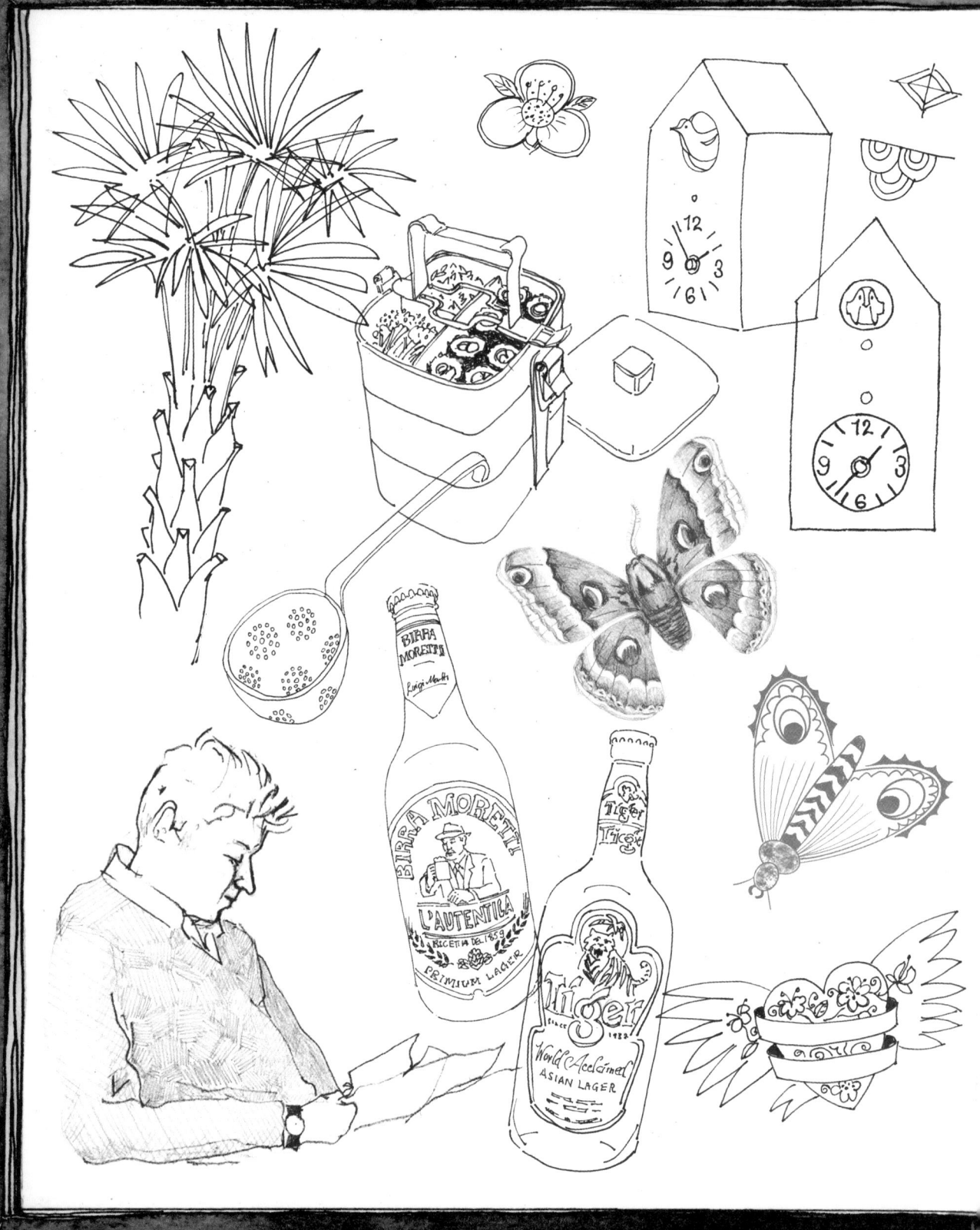

START A SKETCHBOOK

If you want to make drawing a habit, purchase a sketchbook. It's a place to experiment and make mistakes without worrying—you just learn from them! The sketchbook is a place to enjoy yourself. You might have one or two books on the go at any time. One can be a "thinking" sketchbook, for scribbles and thoughts (a lot of the ideas in this book started off like this). The other is a visual journal of drawings you want to keep. When you build up a few books you will surprise yourself looking back through them to remember moments with friends, family, vacations, and more.

Which book or pad?

There are a vast array of books on the market. If you know you are going to work in dry media—pencils, fineliner, felt tips, or colored pencils—then medium-weight paper is the choice. For your visual journal try to get a good quality book; over time the sketch discolors and disappears on poorer quality paper. It may not seem important at the time of drawing but a few years later it might.

If you think you will want to add some color to your sketches with water-based or wet media such as inks, then you need to have a heavier weight paper so that it doesn't buckle, as the color dries [110–140 lb paper (250–300 gsm)] is a good weight). A sketchbook with a surface that is not too textured allows you to draw across the surface smoothly, while still having some interesting texture for the color washes. To use alcohol-based markers you will need a special marker pad.

There are a variety of formats you can use—portrait, landscape, spiral bound, or soft- and hardback books. Initially, I would suggest spiral bound, because you can tear the odd page out without spoiling the binding.

Mash up
I have some pages in my sketchbooks where I just draw random objects, usually when I know I am not going to have much time to finish or there is space to fill on the page.

What to draw with?

Generally, sketches are drawn using a single pencil or pen for speed, and can be easily transported when working away from home. If you want to add color, take a limited range of colored pencils or paints to capture what you see; you can always add more color when you get back home. Let's look at some common sketching materials. Refer to page 182 for more specific details.

Graphite pencils

Available in many grades—from very hard (2H to 6H) that give a pale mark to very soft (2B and higher), that give a rich, dark black. Pencil grades often vary between manufacturers, so don't assume they will be the same.

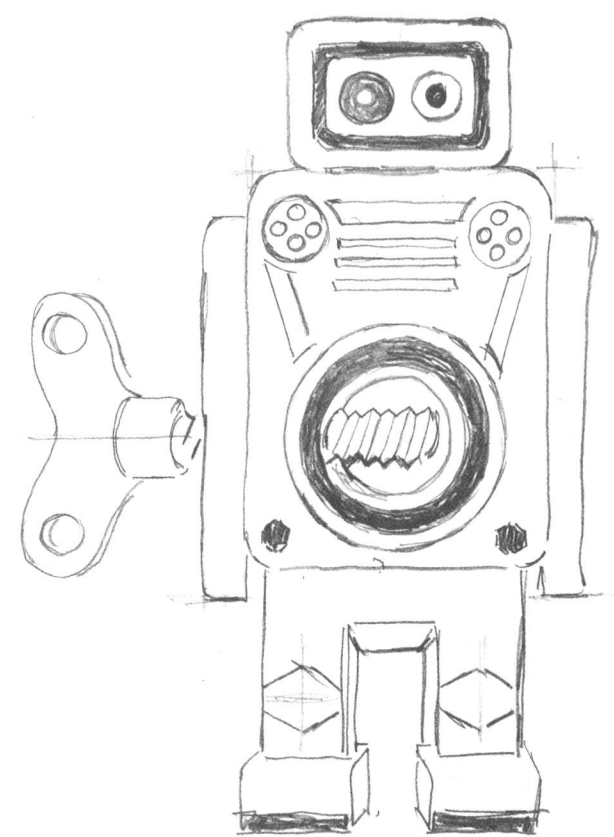

This 2B pencil line, has a nice strength of tone for vibrant sketches, but can smudge slightly (as can any grade above 2B). A typical No. 2 pencil (HB) or B are good options but the former can look slightly underwhelming throughout a whole sketchbook. You can, of course, mix grades of pencil in the drawing, to give a nice variety of tone.

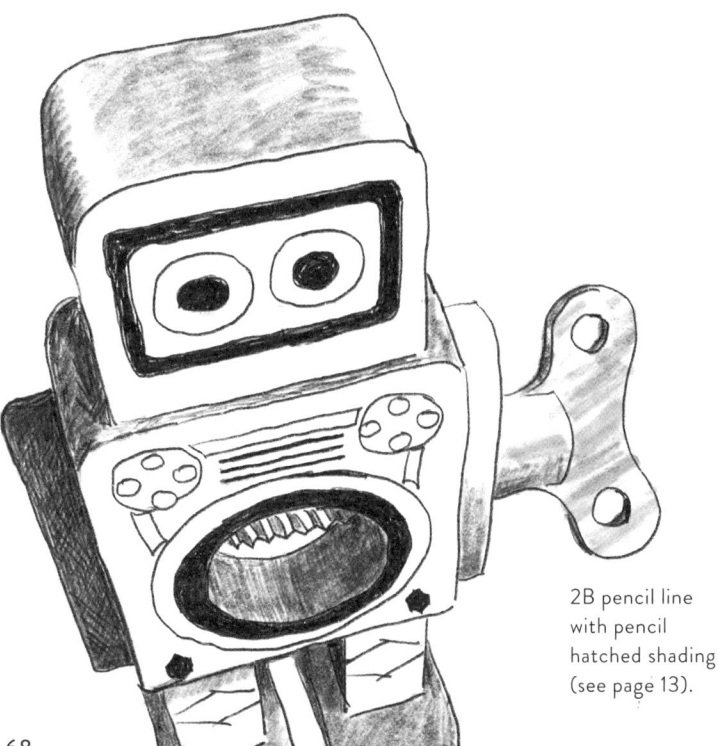

2B pencil line with pencil hatched shading (see page 13).

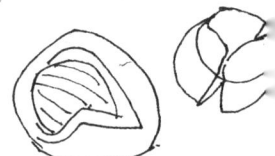

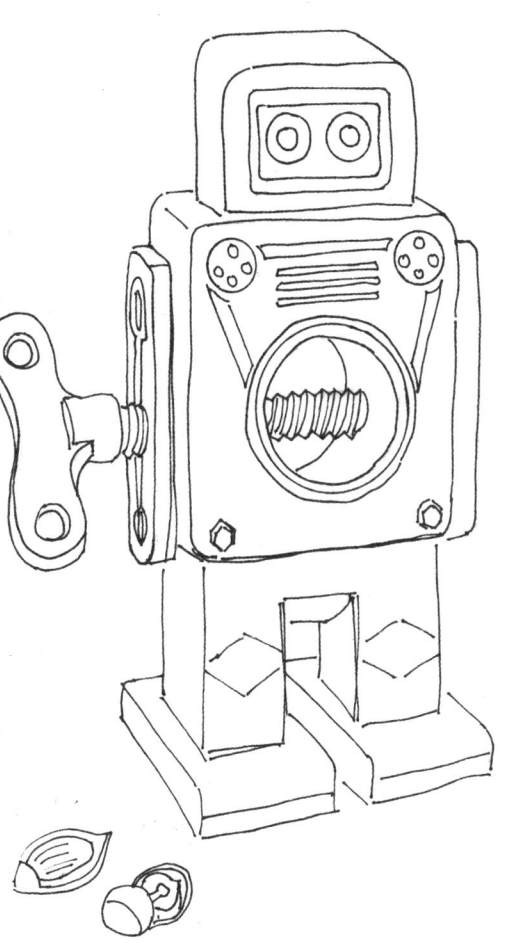

Fineliner and felt-tip pens

These come in many thicknesses of point and in different colors. They can be bought individually or as bargain packs so you can experiment. They are more dynamic than pencil, but obviously not erasable so you might want to do a very rough pencil grid or guidelines before committing your sketch to ink.

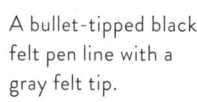

A bullet-tipped black felt pen line with a gray felt tip.

Fineliners make simple ink lines (right) with hatching and cross-hatched shading (see page 13). You can also try a nibbed art pen, like a fountain pen. These come with ink cartridges and result in a quirkier line since they are less smooth to use.

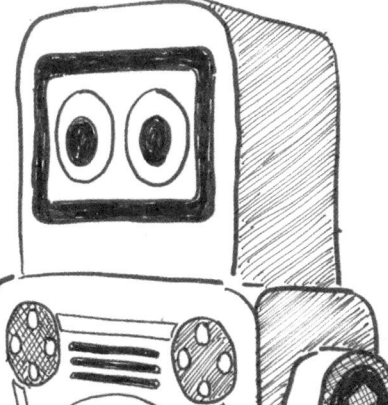

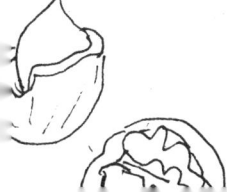

Color

There are many different ways to add color. Watercolor pencils, or watercolor markers are a good starting point. Either leave the drawing as a colored line or blend color with water and a brush. Or try a water brush (see page 189). You can get a small pack with a good range of colors that is easy to transport—good for sketching on the move.

Colored pencils can be used to build up layers of color, (right). Press lightly and build up pale layers of the color to create an even tone. This is time-consuming so not for a quick sketch, but is relaxing and mindful. A quicker technique can be seen below.

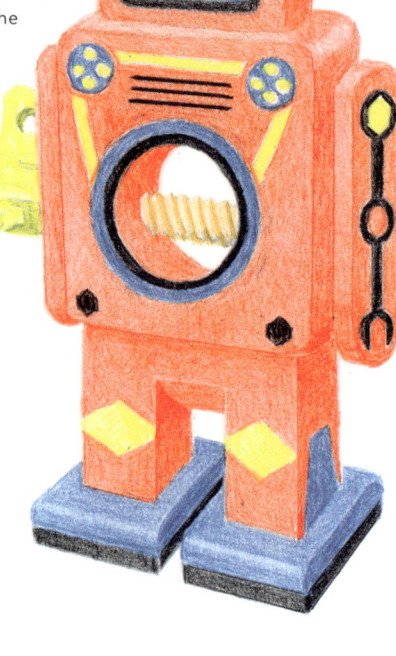

Use the pencil point to create a lively textured surface.

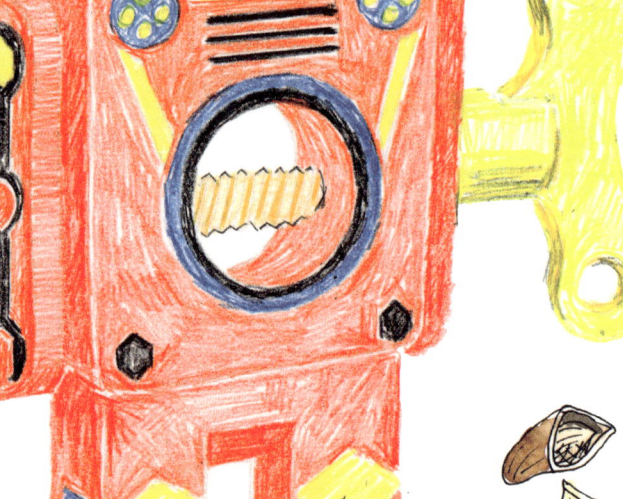

Watercolor pencils (above) or watercolor markers are a quick way to add color. Draw outlines of all the shapes and some solid areas, then brush the lines with water to release the pigment. Allow each color to dry before applying the next.

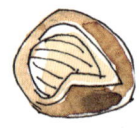

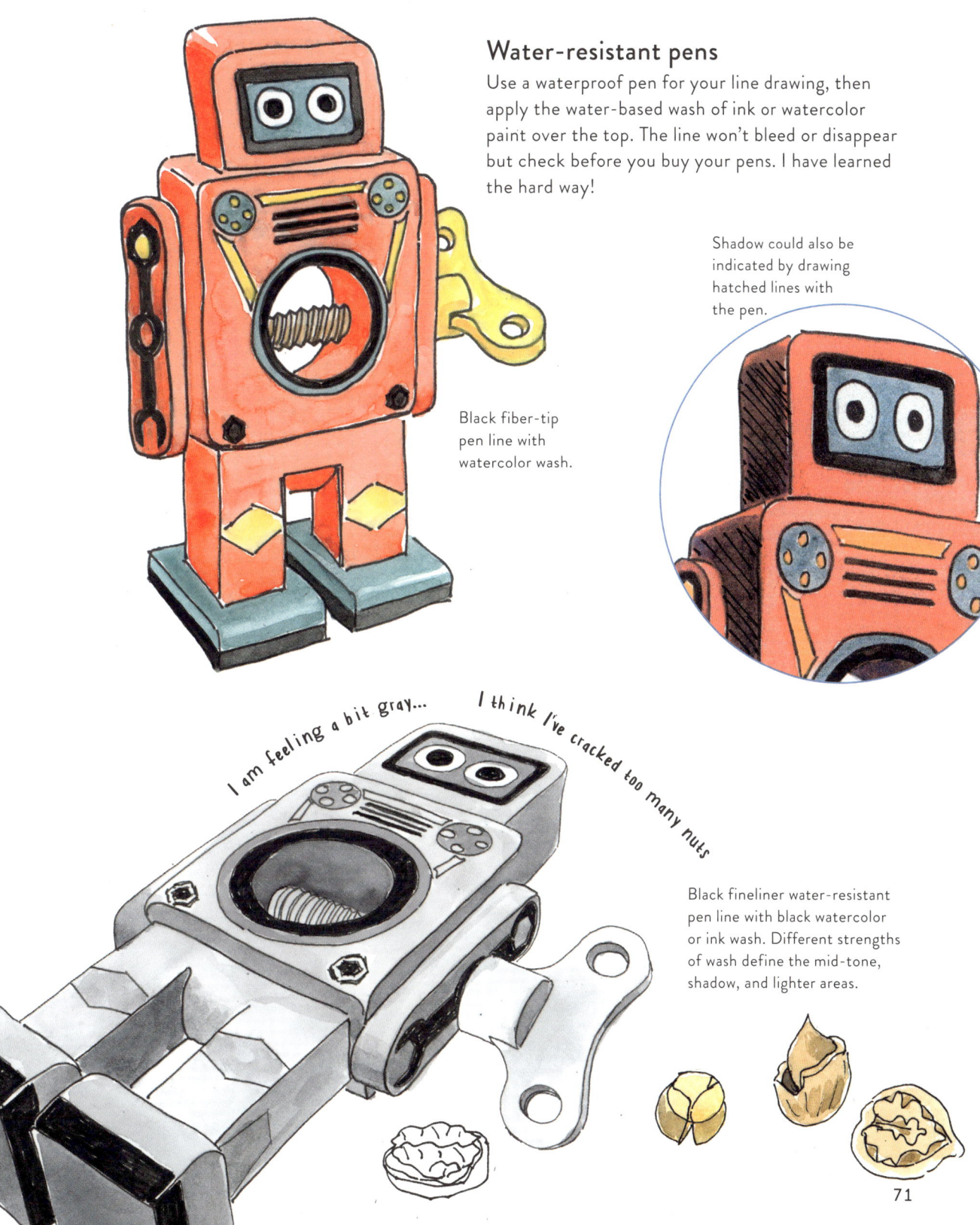

Water-resistant pens

Use a waterproof pen for your line drawing, then apply the water-based wash of ink or watercolor paint over the top. The line won't bleed or disappear but check before you buy your pens. I have learned the hard way!

Shadow could also be indicated by drawing hatched lines with the pen.

Black fiber-tip pen line with watercolor wash.

I am feeling a bit gray...

I think I've cracked too many nuts

Black fineliner water-resistant pen line with black watercolor or ink wash. Different strengths of wash define the mid-tone, shadow, and lighter areas.

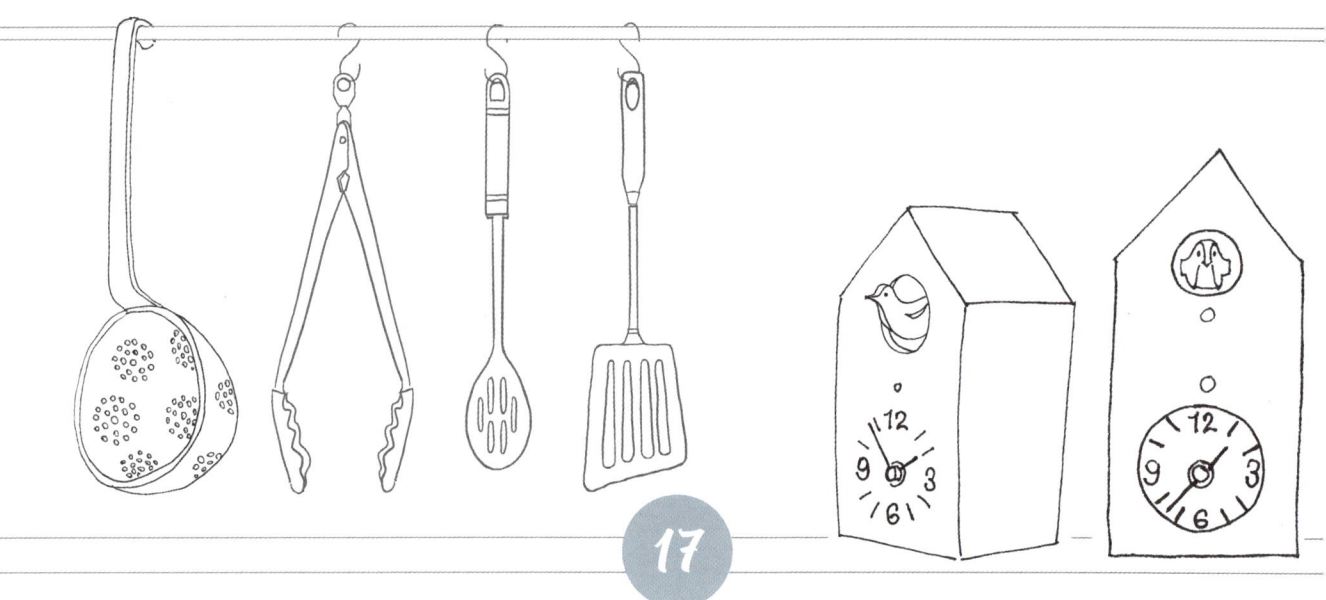

17

SKETCH THINGS AROUND YOU

Find some easily available objects you like or that have good shapes to draw. These could be from the kitchen, the shed, or even contents of your work bag. The drawings above are done in a sharp, 2B pencil to make a crisp drawing. Try sketching the objects from different angles (see page 56).

Thinking about how the object fits in a square or rectangle will help you see its shape and proportions. Sometimes you can just draw straight away, but for more tricky subjects follow the method below.

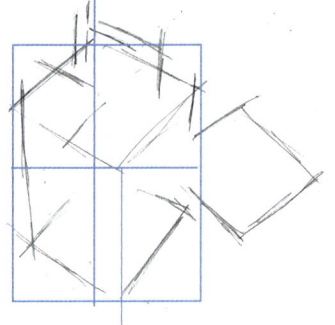

1. Draw a pale rectangle in pencil (here drawn in blue so you can see how the corners of the bento box, especially the front and back ones, fit). Draw in some extra horizontal and vertical lines to help you.

2. Once you have your basic shape you can sketch in the sushi and the metalwork handle.

3. Then you can erase the guidelines and firm up your final lines. Add some darker tones around the sushi rolls.

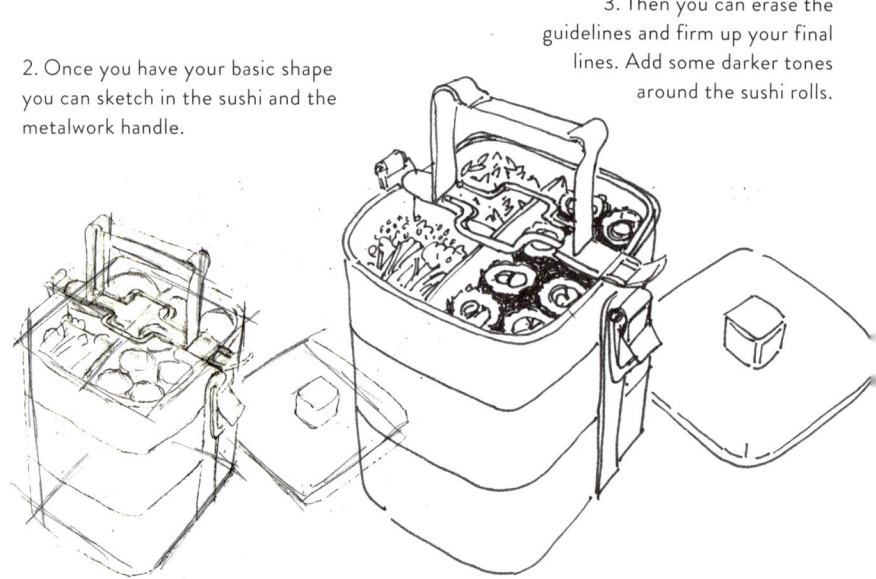

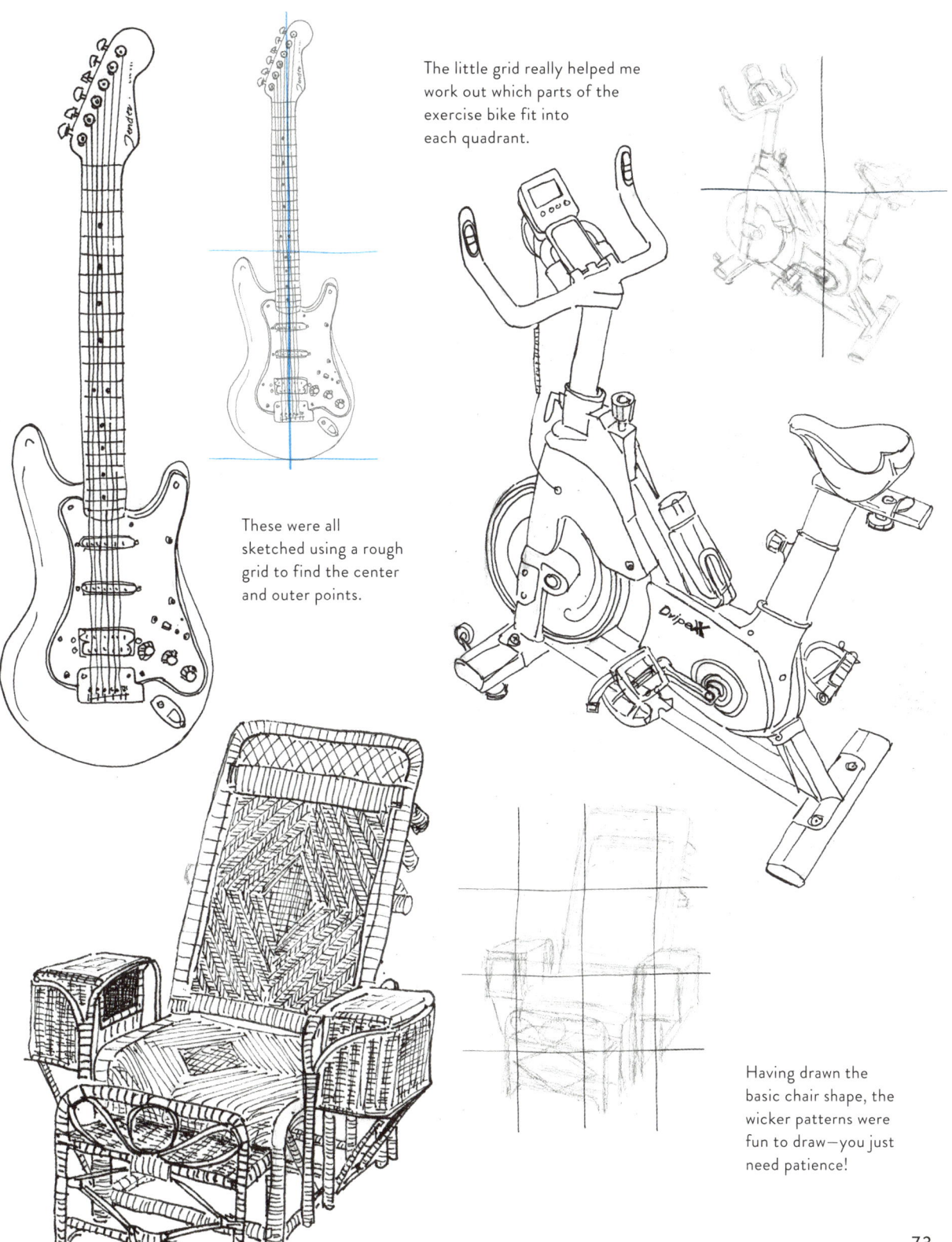

The little grid really helped me work out which parts of the exercise bike fit into each quadrant.

These were all sketched using a rough grid to find the center and outer points.

Having drawn the basic chair shape, the wicker patterns were fun to draw—you just need patience!

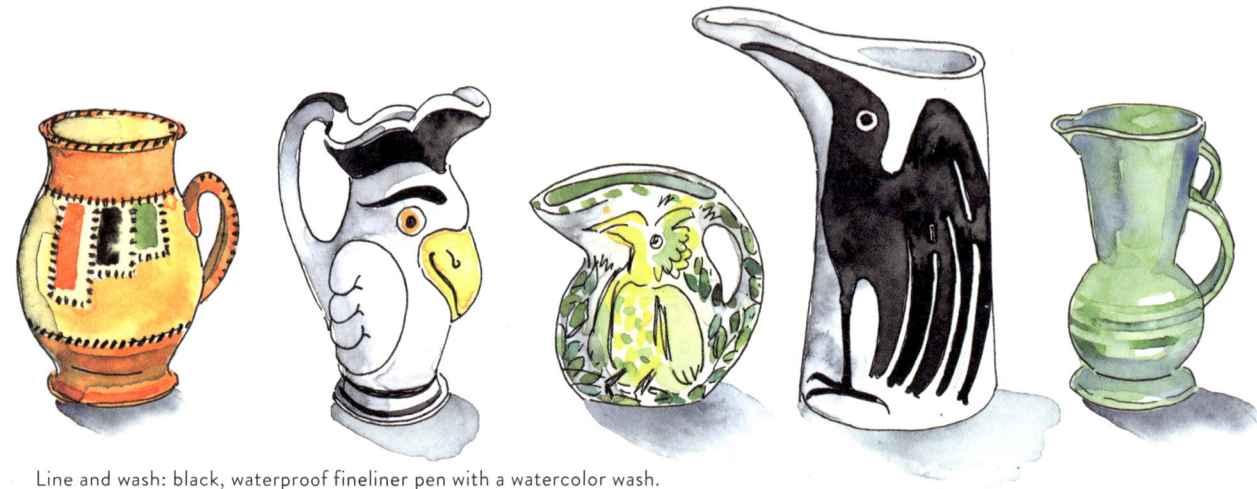

Line and wash: black, waterproof fineliner pen with a watercolor wash.

Make a collection drawing

Drawing a collection is a great way to explore how to capture the various shapes and surface textures of similar objects. It helps if you like a particular subject. You may have some objects at home, such as a collection of art deco and bird jugs, as above, or beetles from your yard. If you can't find anything, visit a natural history museum for inspiration. Think how you want to arrange your drawn collection, formally or more randomly.

Watercolor marker: your drawing can look as if it was painted.

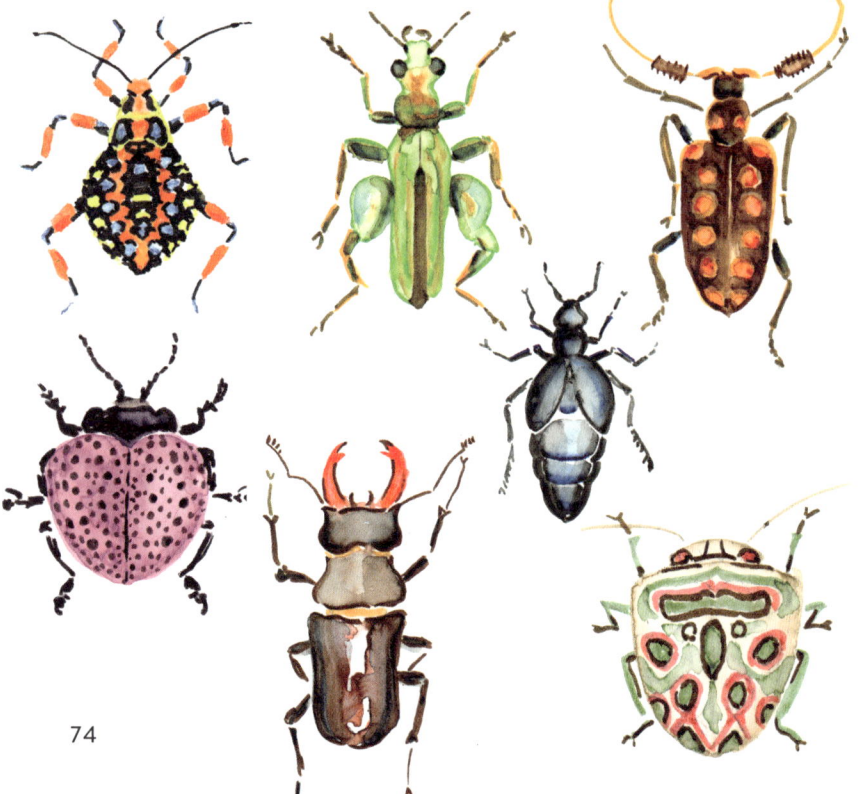

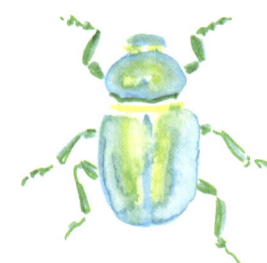

1. Draw colored lines.

2. Brush lines with water to release color, dry, then repeat the process with more colors.

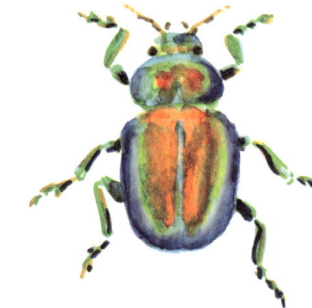

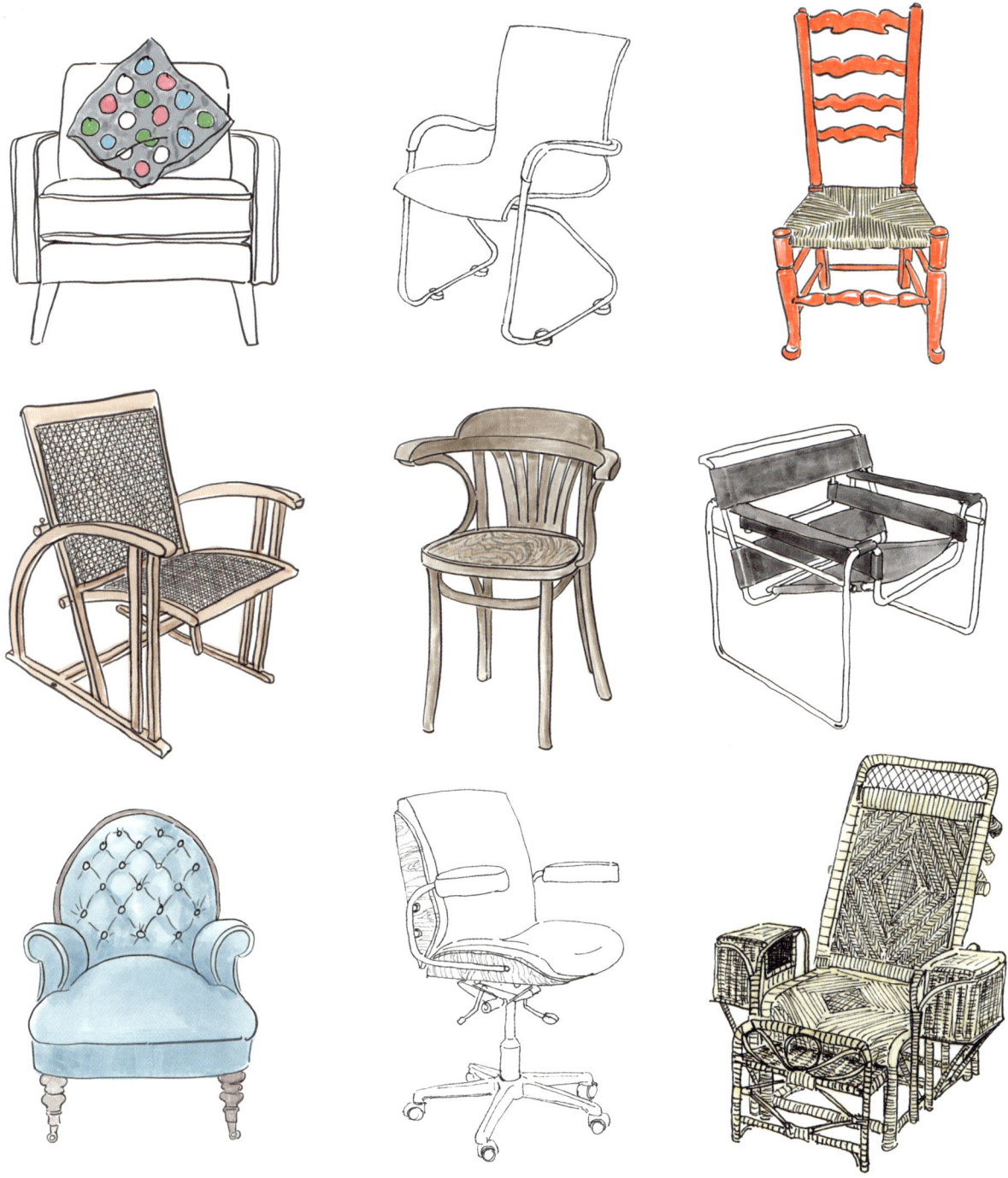

Work from different angles to explore the various shapes and styles. Some of the subjects could be from your own home or "collected" when visiting friends. Starting from a viewpoint that is straight on is easier at first, since you don't have to think about the perspective of all the legs.

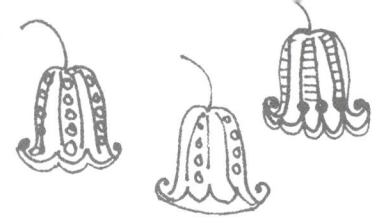

18

DECORATIVE FLOWERS

Some common
flower forms
Symmetrical or
  asymmetrical,
Star,
Ray or pompom,
Trumpet,
Bell,
Bearded or lipped,
Bowl or cupped,
Cruciform,
Coronate.

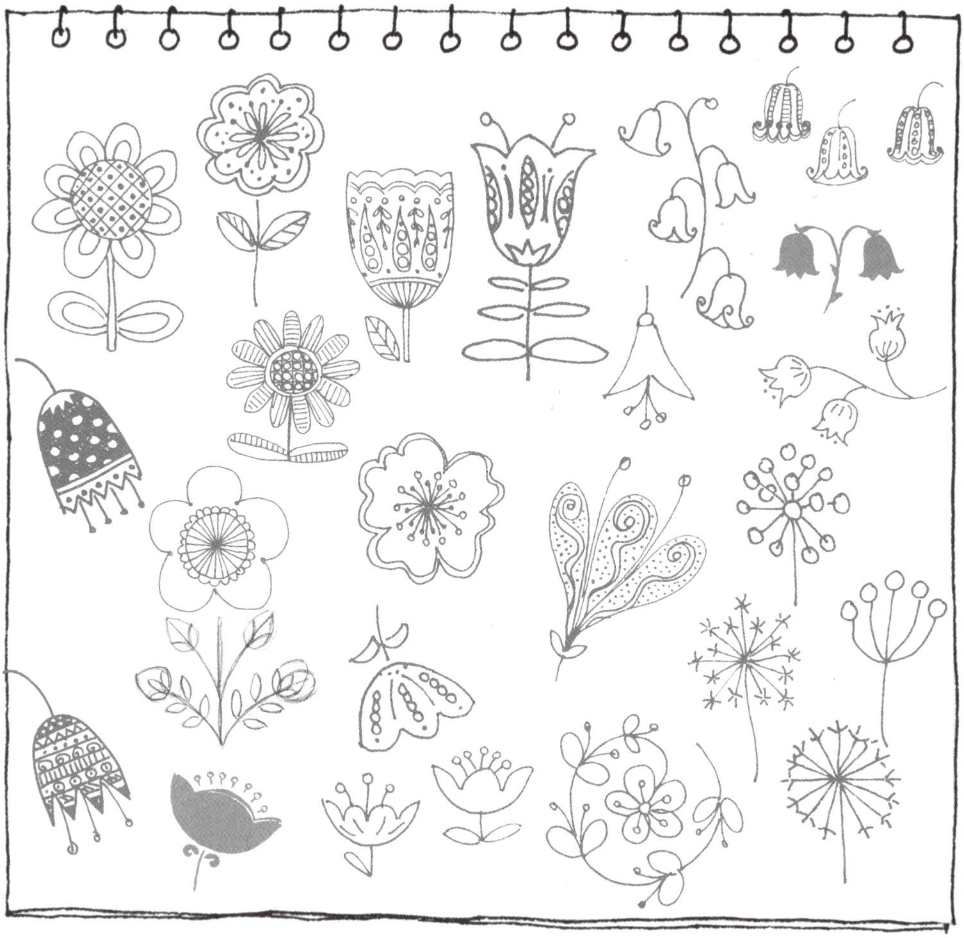

You can sketch realistic-looking flowers or you might prefer a more decorative approach. Use your sketchbook to develop stylized shapes and decorations.

There are many flower shapes to choose from (see the list on the left). Think about how to simplify or stylize the shape, add decorations to the petals, and don't forget the leaves. Another starting point could be the folk art tradition of flower painting. Take a look online at *rosemaling* (rose-painting) or Scandinavian folk art for inspiration.

I have this Mexican folk art gourd painted with decorative flower patterns. I used it as a starting point for some of the sketches.

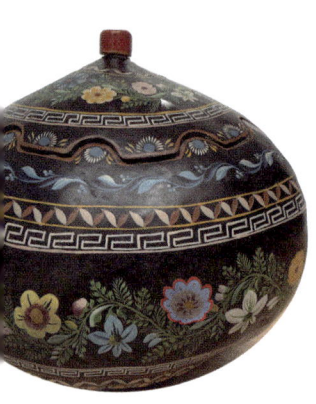

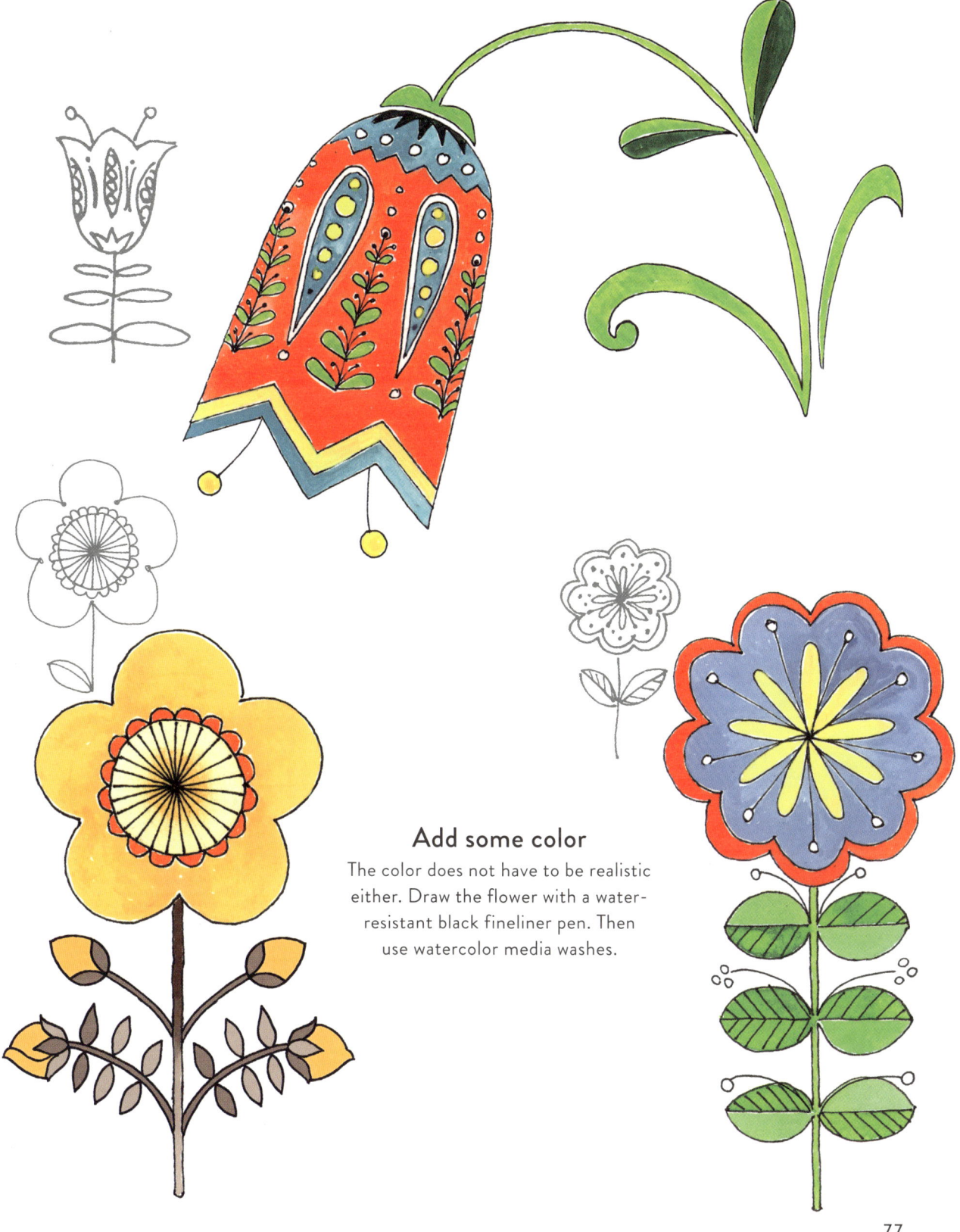

Add some color

The color does not have to be realistic either. Draw the flower with a water-resistant black fineliner pen. Then use watercolor media washes.

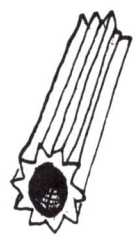
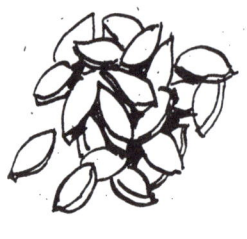

19

PERFECT PASTA

Little pasta shapes are great to draw because they represent so many of the forms you will find yourself sketching—shells, spirals, cylinders, even aspects of architecture. They are pinched and twisted, making their shapes intriguing to draw. The pasta on the following page was drawn with a waterproof ink pen so that color could be added later.

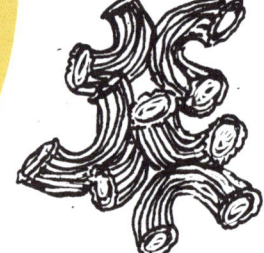
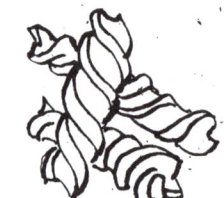
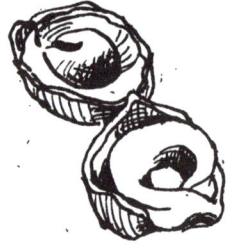
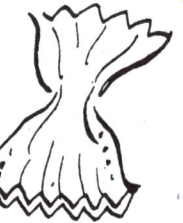
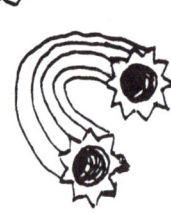
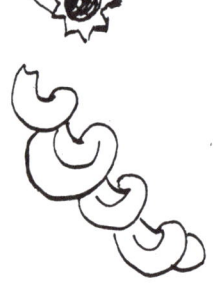

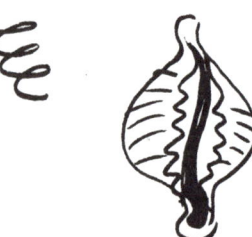

Art pen
These were drawn with a fountain pen and an old-fashioned nibbed calligraphy pen, which have a quirkier line than a fineliner or felt marker.

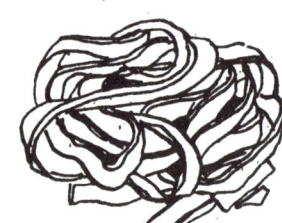

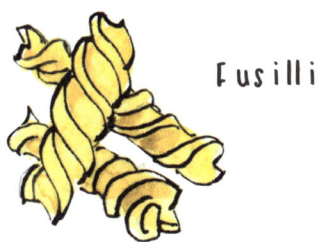

Fusilli

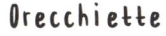

Orecchiette

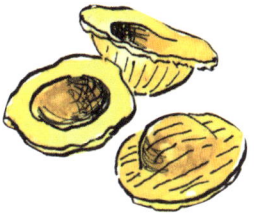

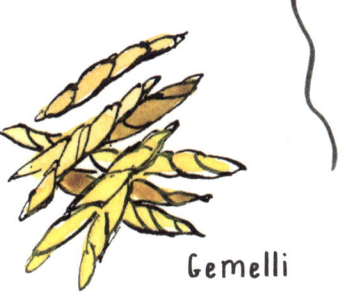

Gemelli

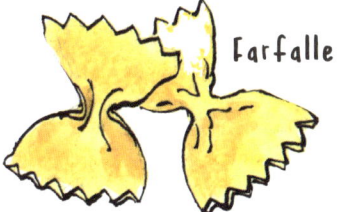

Farfalle

Fettuccine

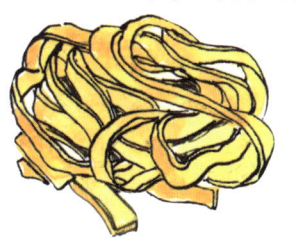

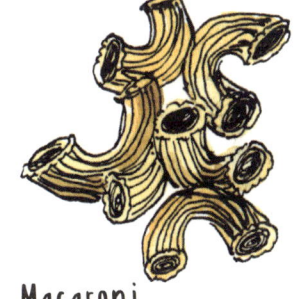

Macaroni

Ravioli

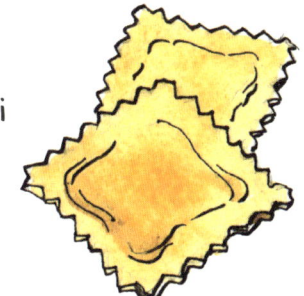

Orzo

Add some color

When you have drawn the pasta shapes, add some color. To keep the line work visible you will need to use something transparent such as watercolor or ink—these will let the line show through the color.

Penne

Spaghetti

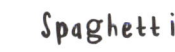

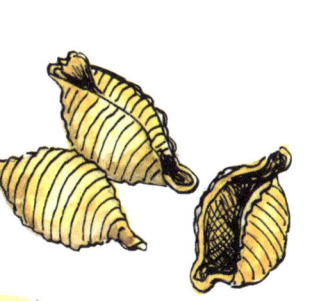

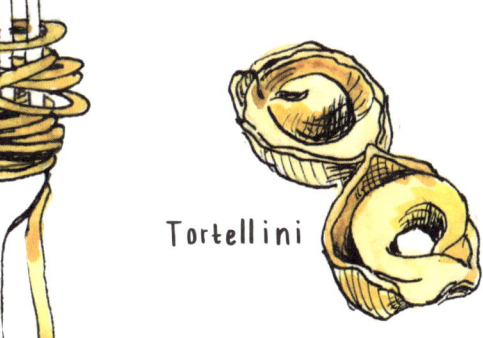

Tortellini

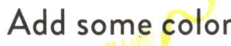

Conchiglie

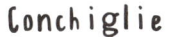

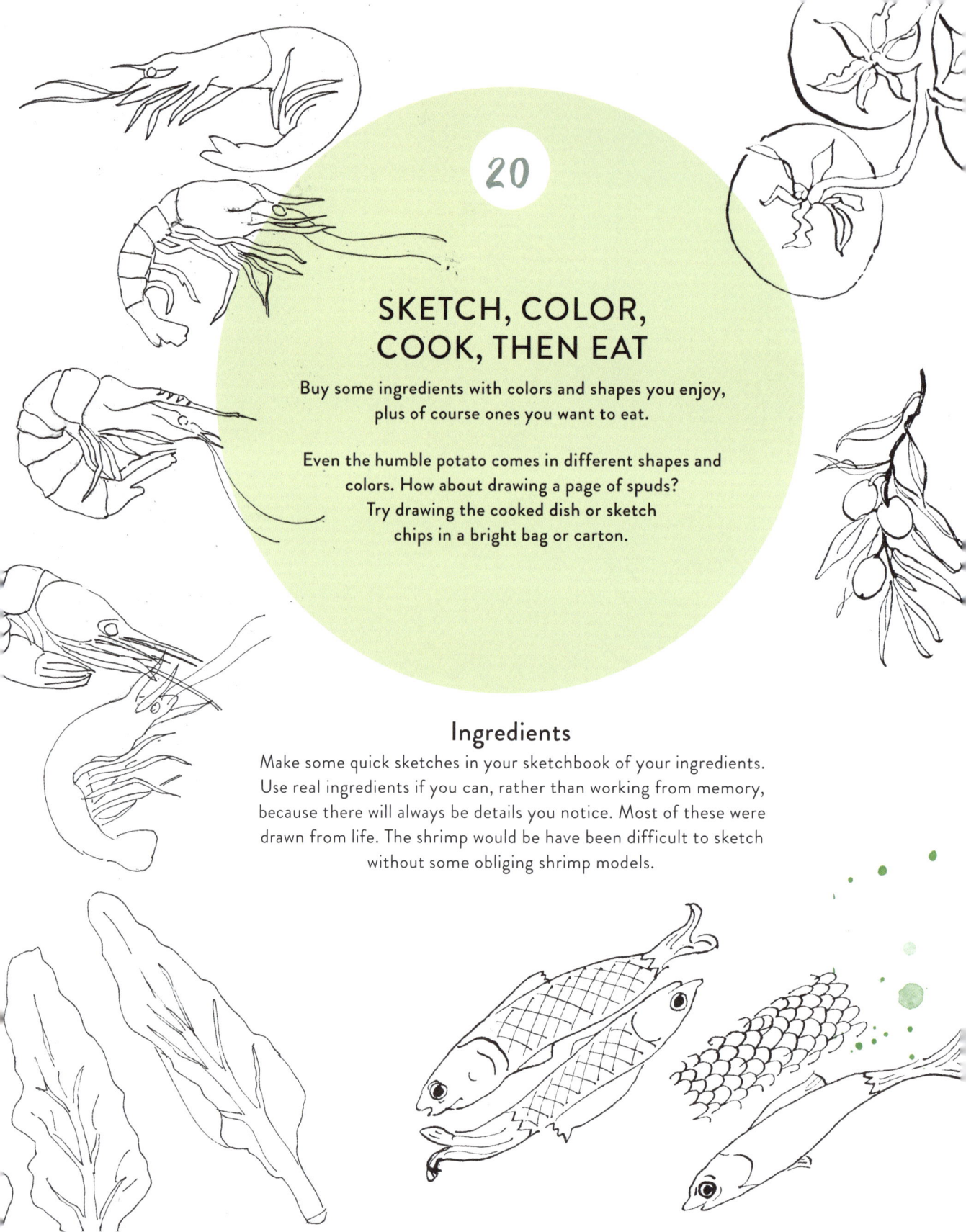

20

SKETCH, COLOR, COOK, THEN EAT

Buy some ingredients with colors and shapes you enjoy,
plus of course ones you want to eat.

Even the humble potato comes in different shapes and
colors. How about drawing a page of spuds?
Try drawing the cooked dish or sketch
chips in a bright bag or carton.

Ingredients

Make some quick sketches in your sketchbook of your ingredients.
Use real ingredients if you can, rather than working from memory,
because there will always be details you notice. Most of these were
drawn from life. The shrimp would be have been difficult to sketch
without some obliging shrimp models.

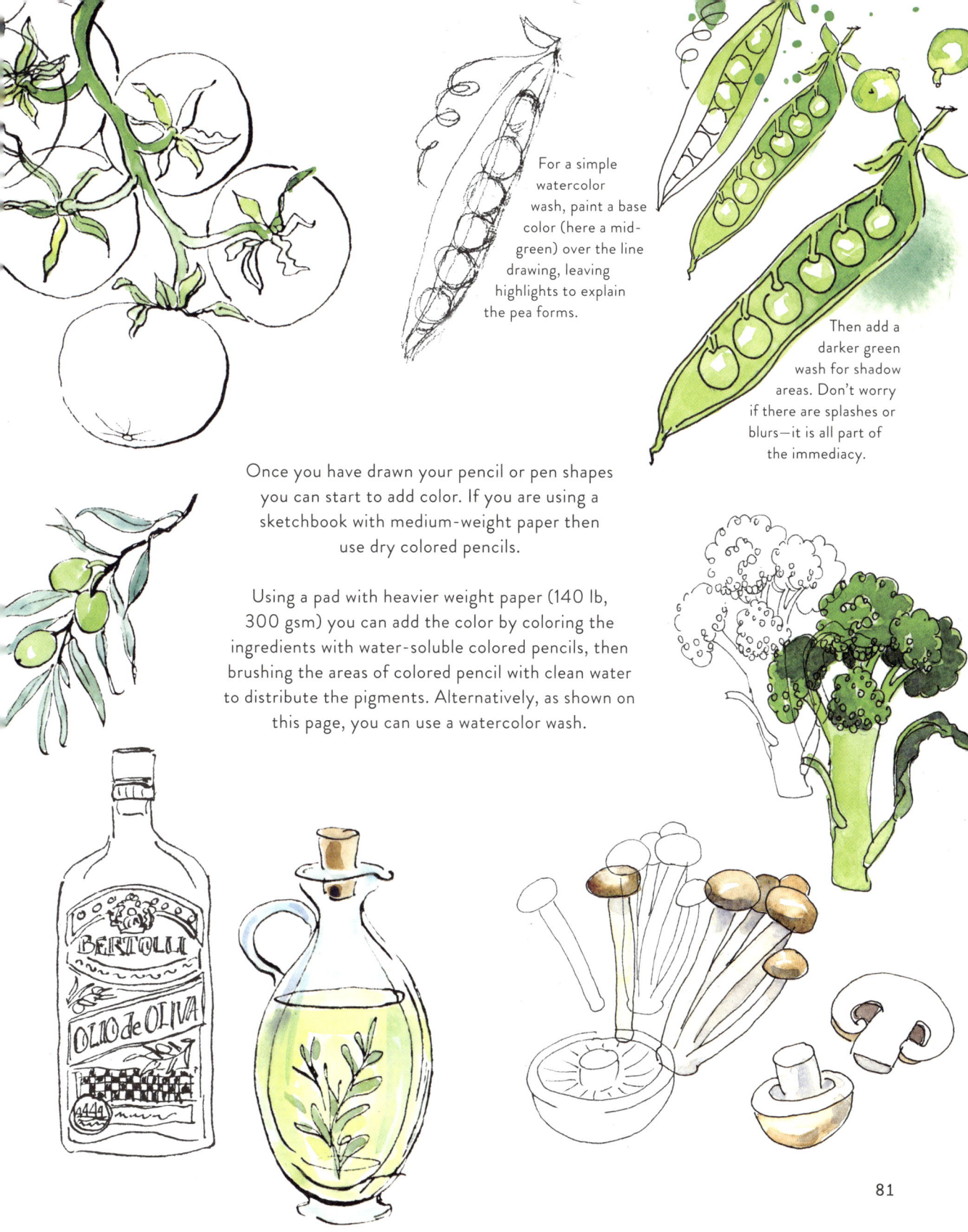

For a simple watercolor wash, paint a base color (here a mid-green) over the line drawing, leaving highlights to explain the pea forms.

Then add a darker green wash for shadow areas. Don't worry if there are splashes or blurs—it is all part of the immediacy.

Once you have drawn your pencil or pen shapes you can start to add color. If you are using a sketchbook with medium-weight paper then use dry colored pencils.

Using a pad with heavier weight paper (140 lb, 300 gsm) you can add the color by coloring the ingredients with water-soluble colored pencils, then brushing the areas of colored pencil with clean water to distribute the pigments. Alternatively, as shown on this page, you can use a watercolor wash.

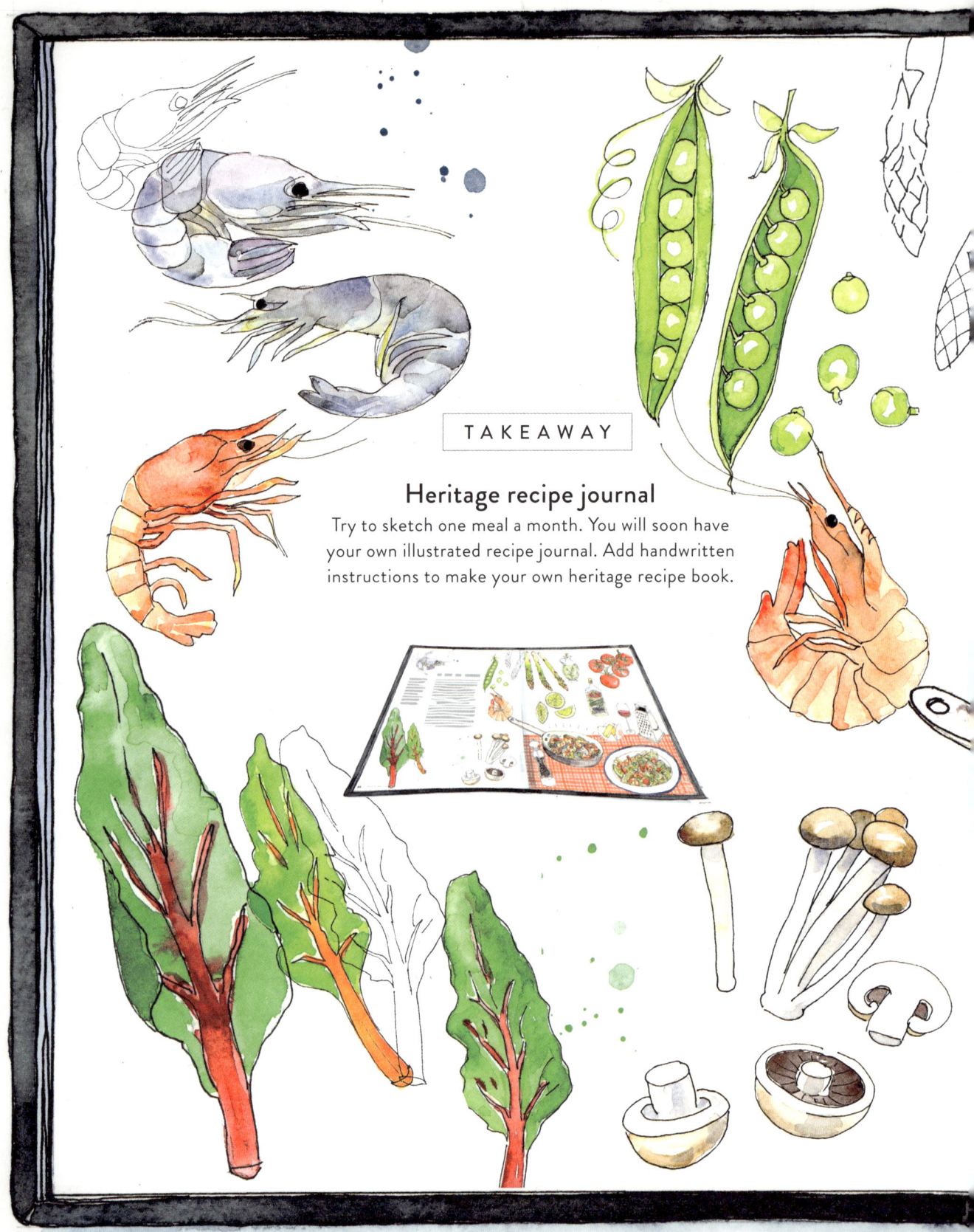

Heritage recipe journal

Try to sketch one meal a month. You will soon have your own illustrated recipe journal. Add handwritten instructions to make your own heritage recipe book.

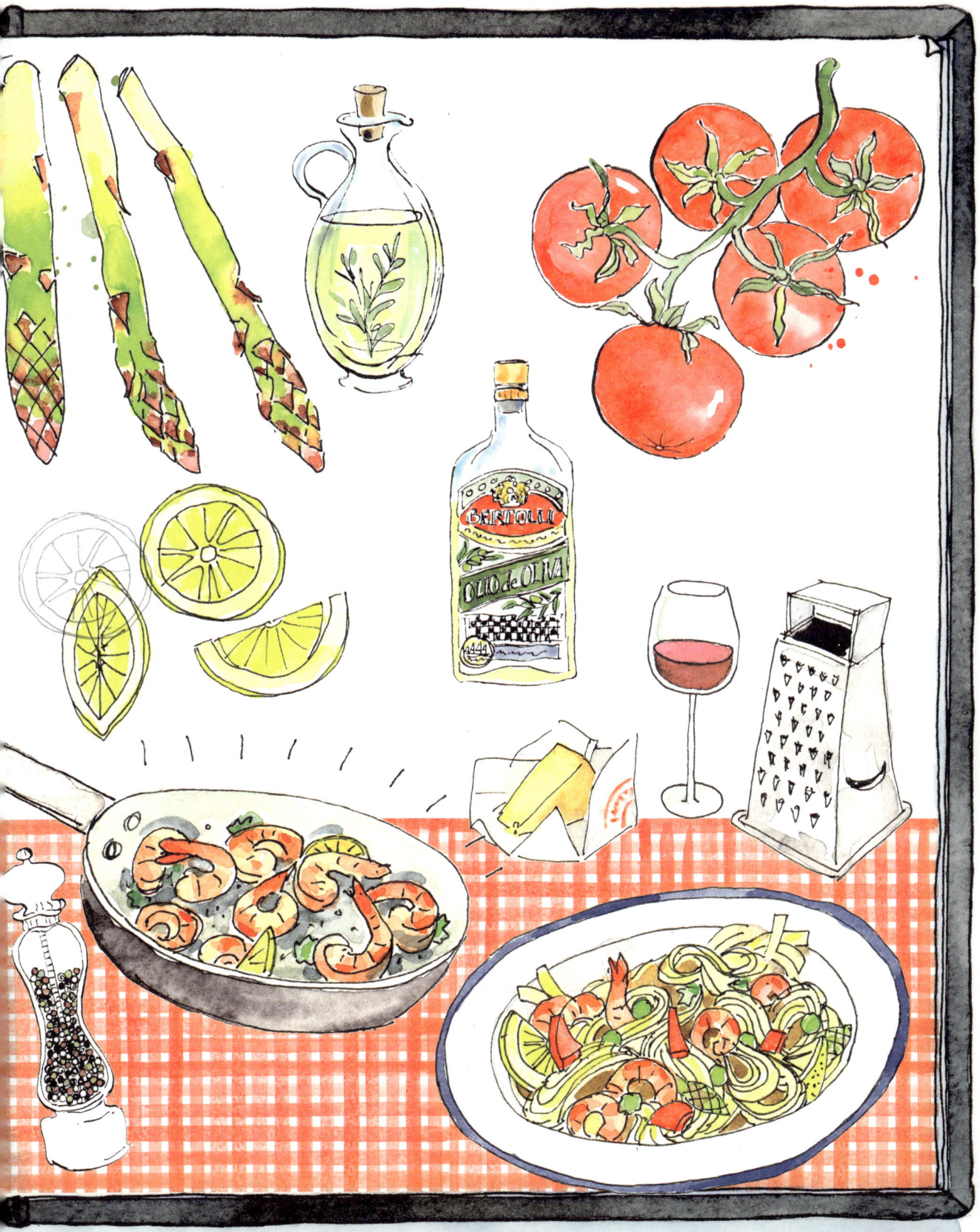

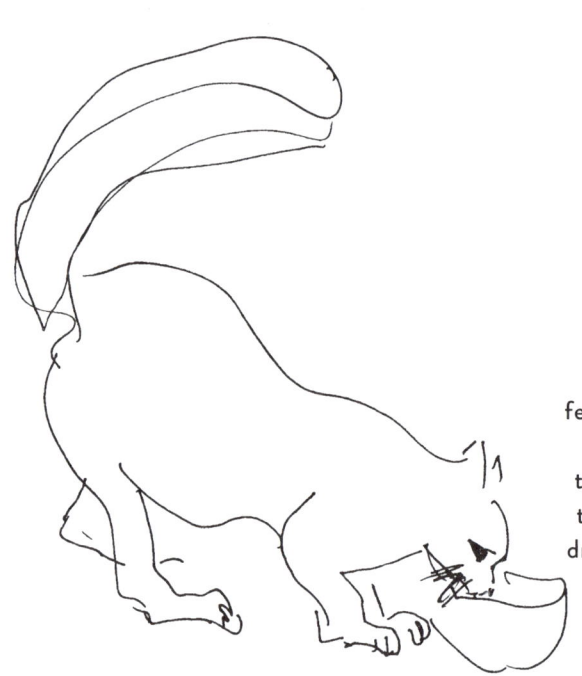

21

CAPTURE THE CAT

It's fun making quick sketches to capture feline characters and their movements. Eating at a bowl provides a moment or two where the model will be in the same pose, although the tail may keep waving! Work quickly, and draw the cat a few times. Some will work well, others not!

Add a color wash

Adding a gray-blue wash to your line work gives the cat shapes more volume. You can use colored pencil to shade in some areas close to your line work, then add water and with a brush move the color pigment around. Keep the paint wash loose to add to the sense of fluidity and movement.

You can try something different with clear water. Wet the cat shapes, then drop the color inside the wet shapes. The blue-gray wash will magically fill the shape.

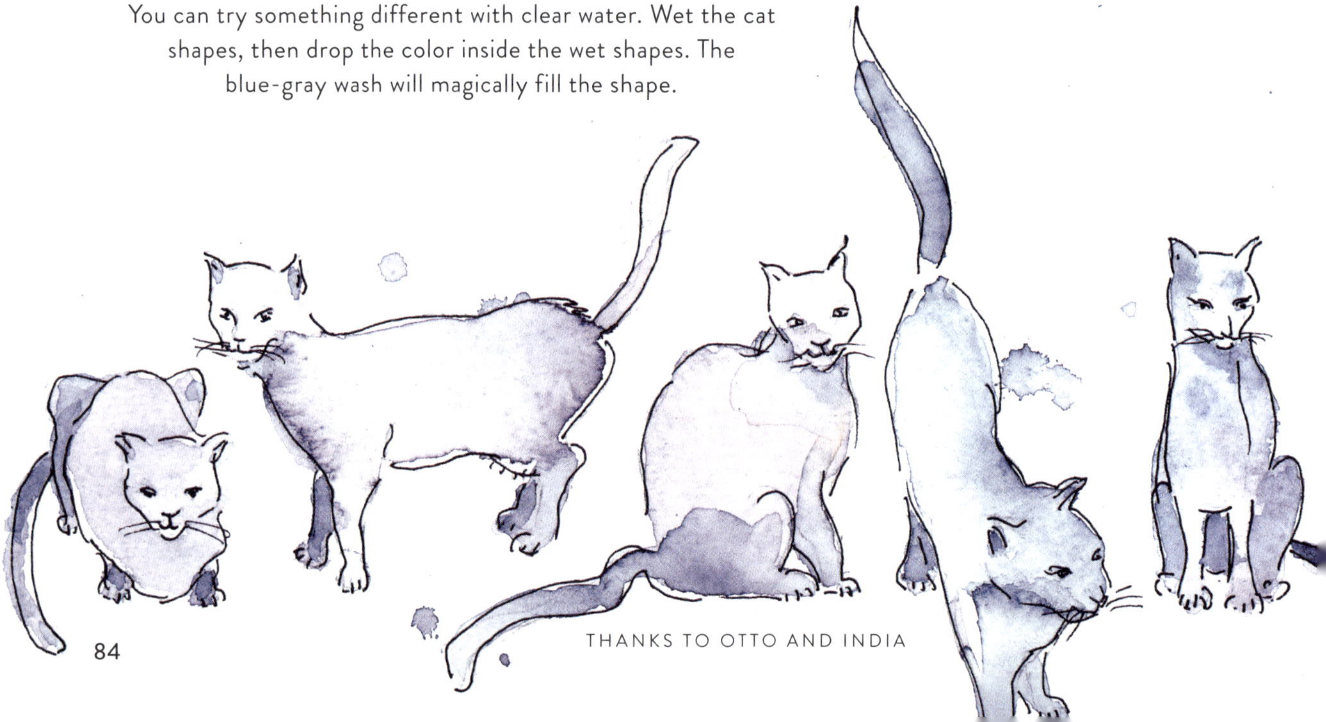

THANKS TO OTTO AND INDIA

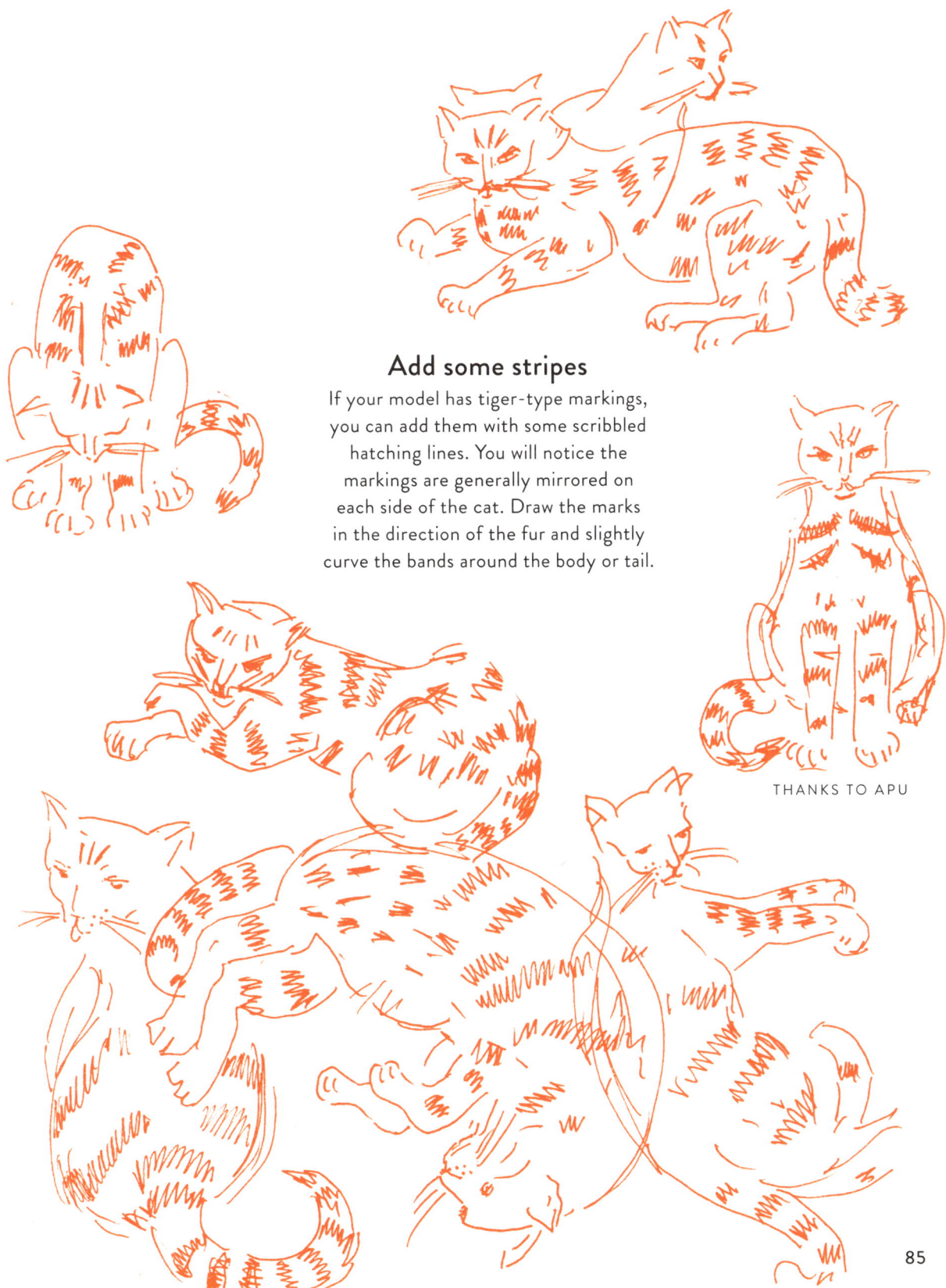

Add some stripes

If your model has tiger-type markings, you can add them with some scribbled hatching lines. You will notice the markings are generally mirrored on each side of the cat. Draw the marks in the direction of the fur and slightly curve the bands around the body or tail.

THANKS TO APU

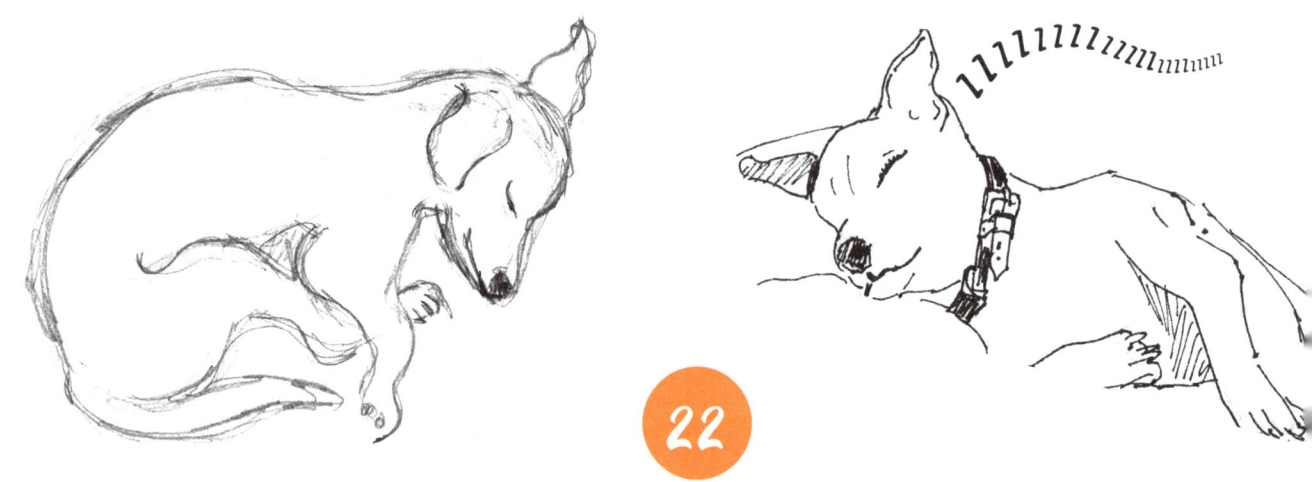

22

MAKE IT A DOG DAY

Man's best friend generally makes a better model than humans, since they can't talk back, and, unlike cats, they may obey commands to "sit" or "stay." Better still, catch them curled up on a sofa or snoozing on their owner's lap.

You may own a dog, or, if you have friends with a dog, make a mental note to take your sketchbook with you when you next visit so you can draw the pet. They make great images for birthday cards for the owners . . . or their pet.

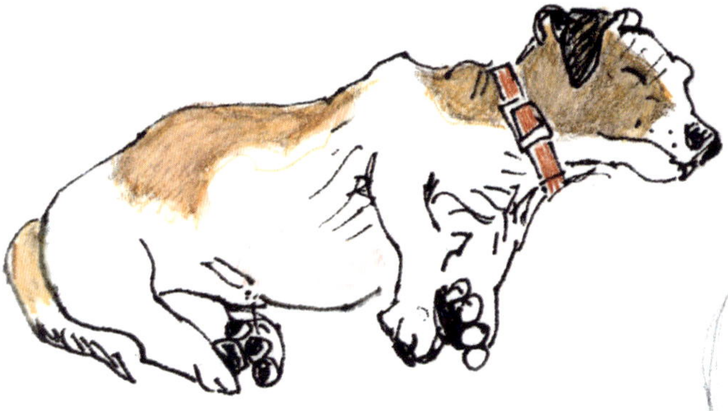

Let sleeping dogs lie.

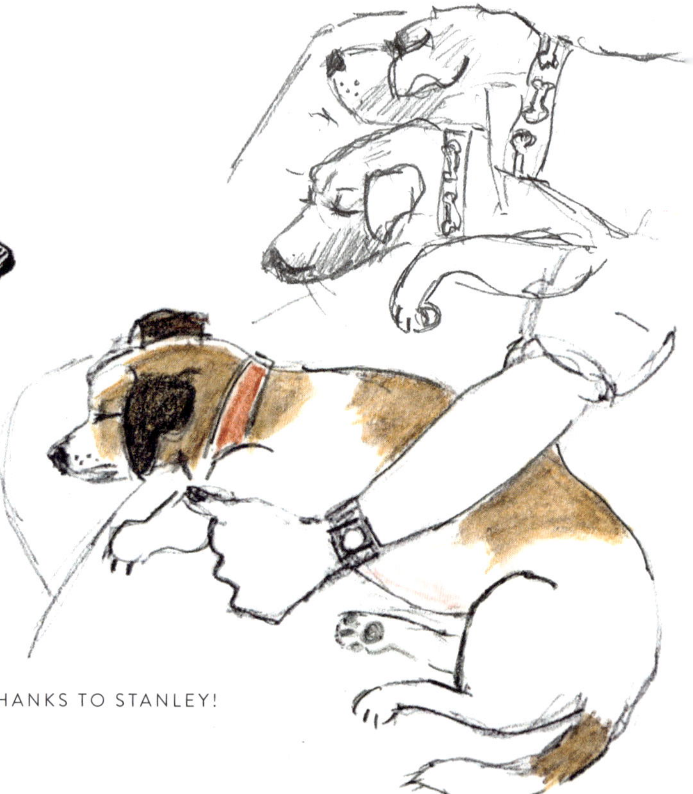

THANKS TO STANLEY!

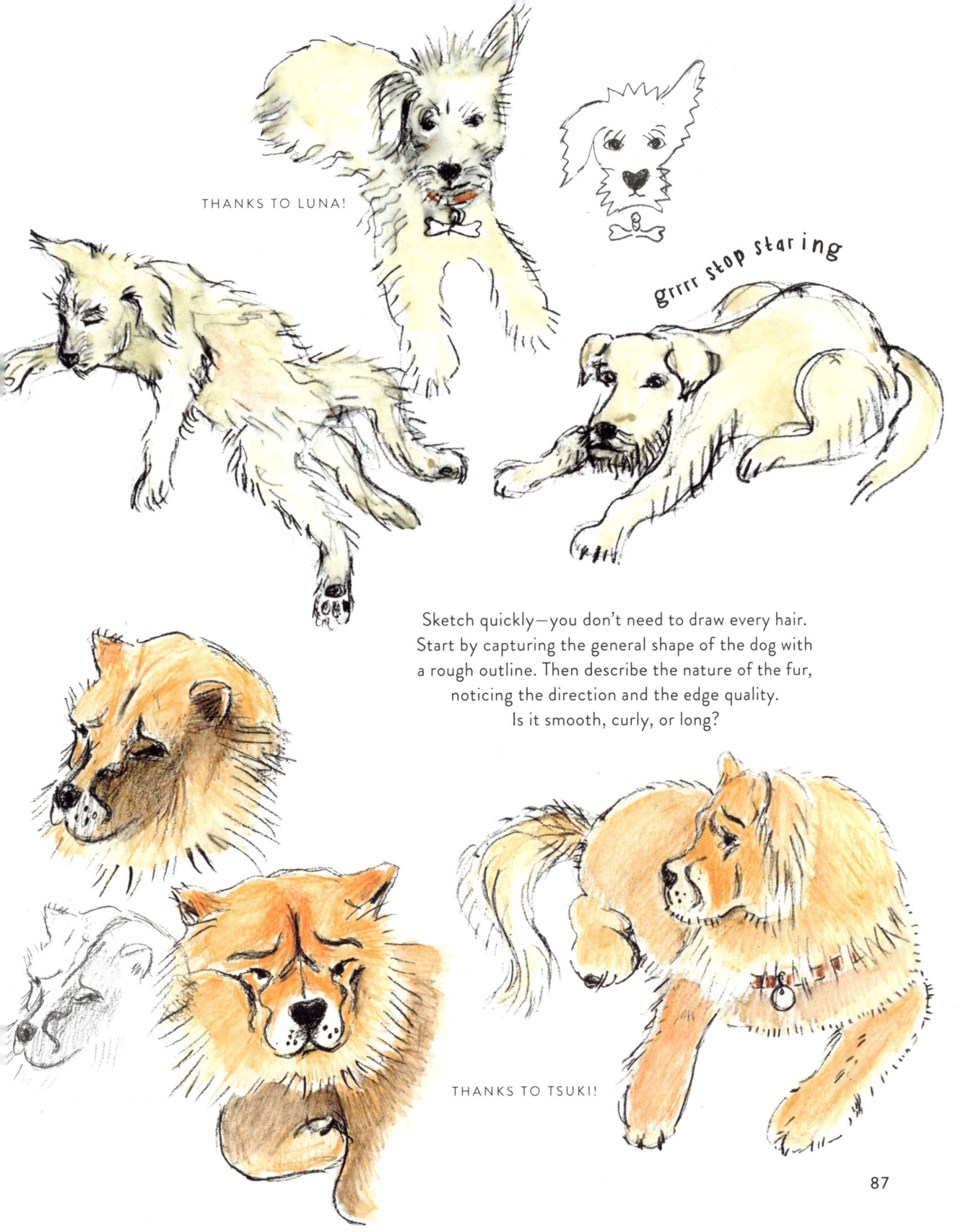

THANKS TO LUNA!

grrrr stop staring

Sketch quickly—you don't need to draw every hair.
Start by capturing the general shape of the dog with
a rough outline. Then describe the nature of the fur,
noticing the direction and the edge quality.
Is it smooth, curly, or long?

THANKS TO TSUKI!

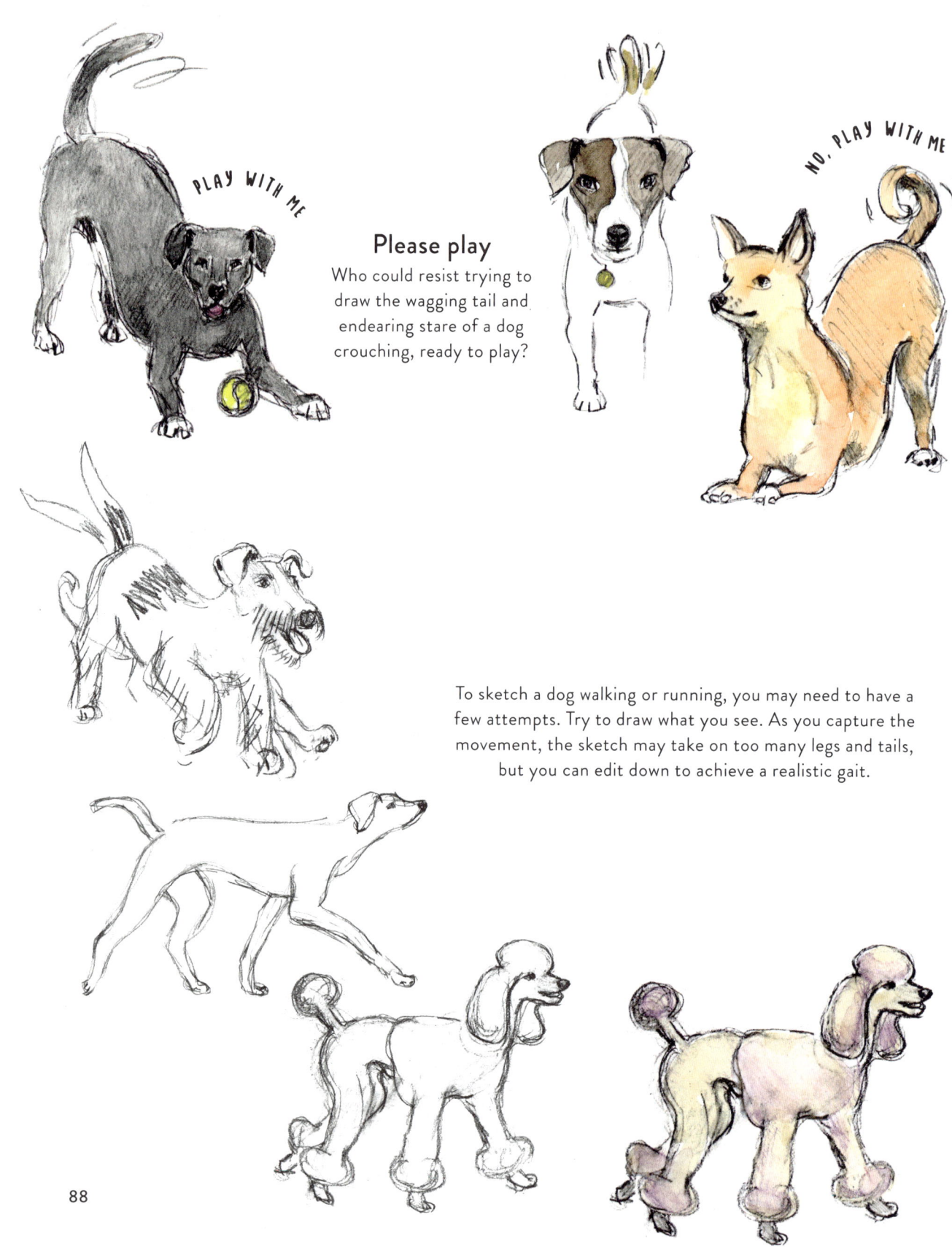

PLAY WITH ME

NO, PLAY WITH ME

Please play

Who could resist trying to draw the wagging tail and endearing stare of a dog crouching, ready to play?

To sketch a dog walking or running, you may need to have a few attempts. Try to draw what you see. As you capture the movement, the sketch may take on too many legs and tails, but you can edit down to achieve a realistic gait.

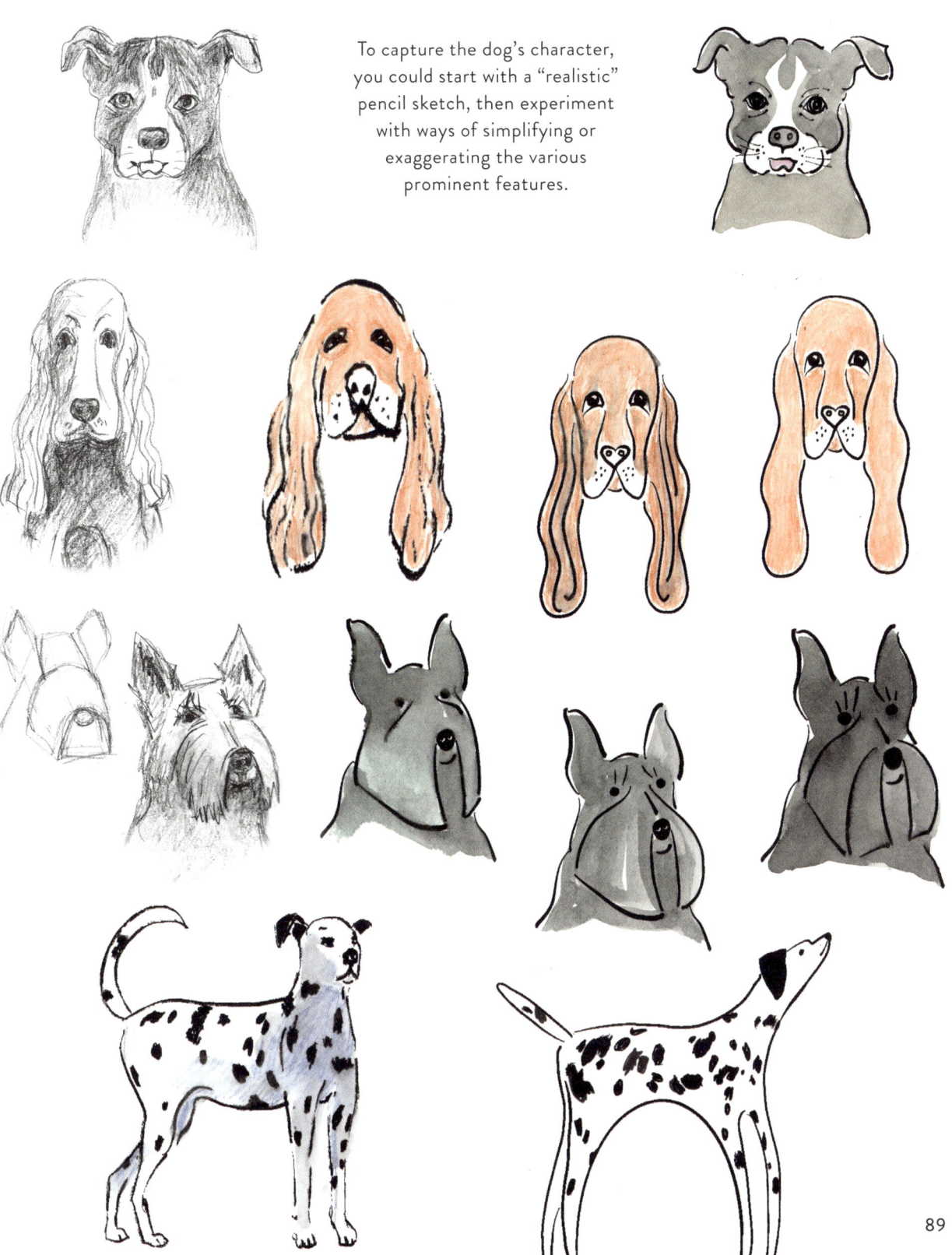

To capture the dog's character, you could start with a "realistic" pencil sketch, then experiment with ways of simplifying or exaggerating the various prominent features.

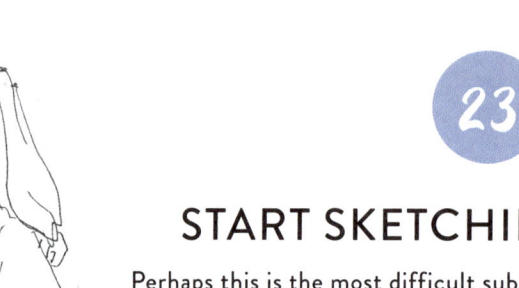

23

START SKETCHING PEOPLE

Perhaps this is the most difficult subject, because you might feel under pressure to achieve a certain likeness. Don't worry if you don't, just keep practicing. Sometimes the quickest off-the-cuff sketch or caricature can capture someone better than any labored drawing.

I used to have a long, boring journey home on the bus, so I started drawing people. I would draw discreetly in my sketchbook behind my backpack on my lap. The sketches never captured a likeness, partly due to the movement of the bus and because I wasn't very good at it. But they were lively, and it gave me a love of sketching people in all sorts of situations.

A word of caution: Obviously be discreet if you are sketching strangers. They might ask why you are staring at them, and they may ask you to stop.

Make it easy on yourself

Sketching profiles or three-quarter views are a good place to start. You still observe the shapes and proportions of the face, but you don't have to worry about mirroring the facial details, (see page 94).

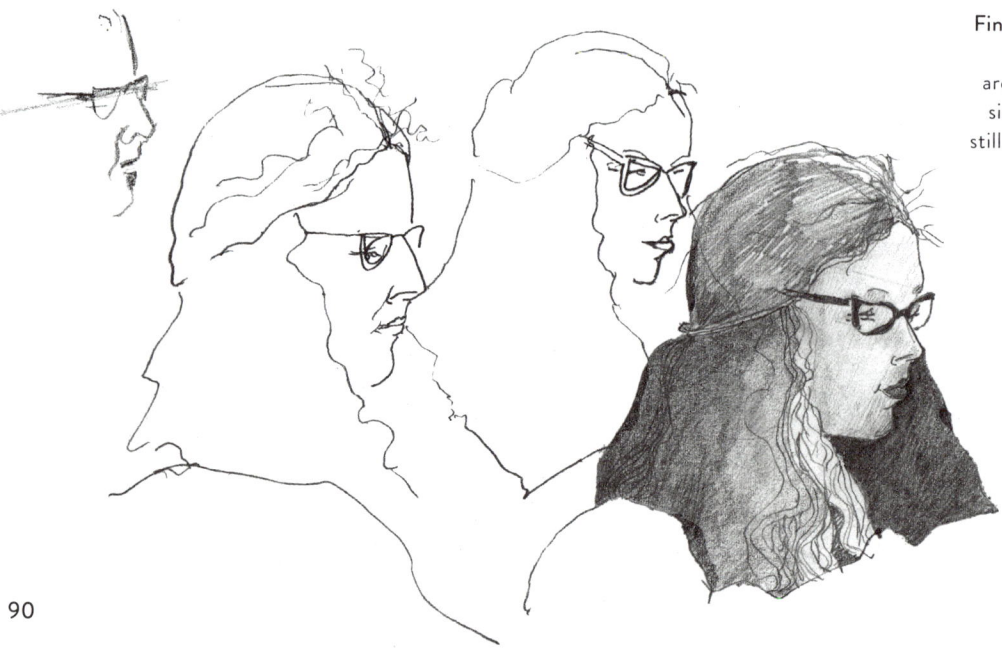

Find the perfect model
Reading or sleeping are two obvious poses, since they will remain still. Or you might have a willing friend who will sit for you.

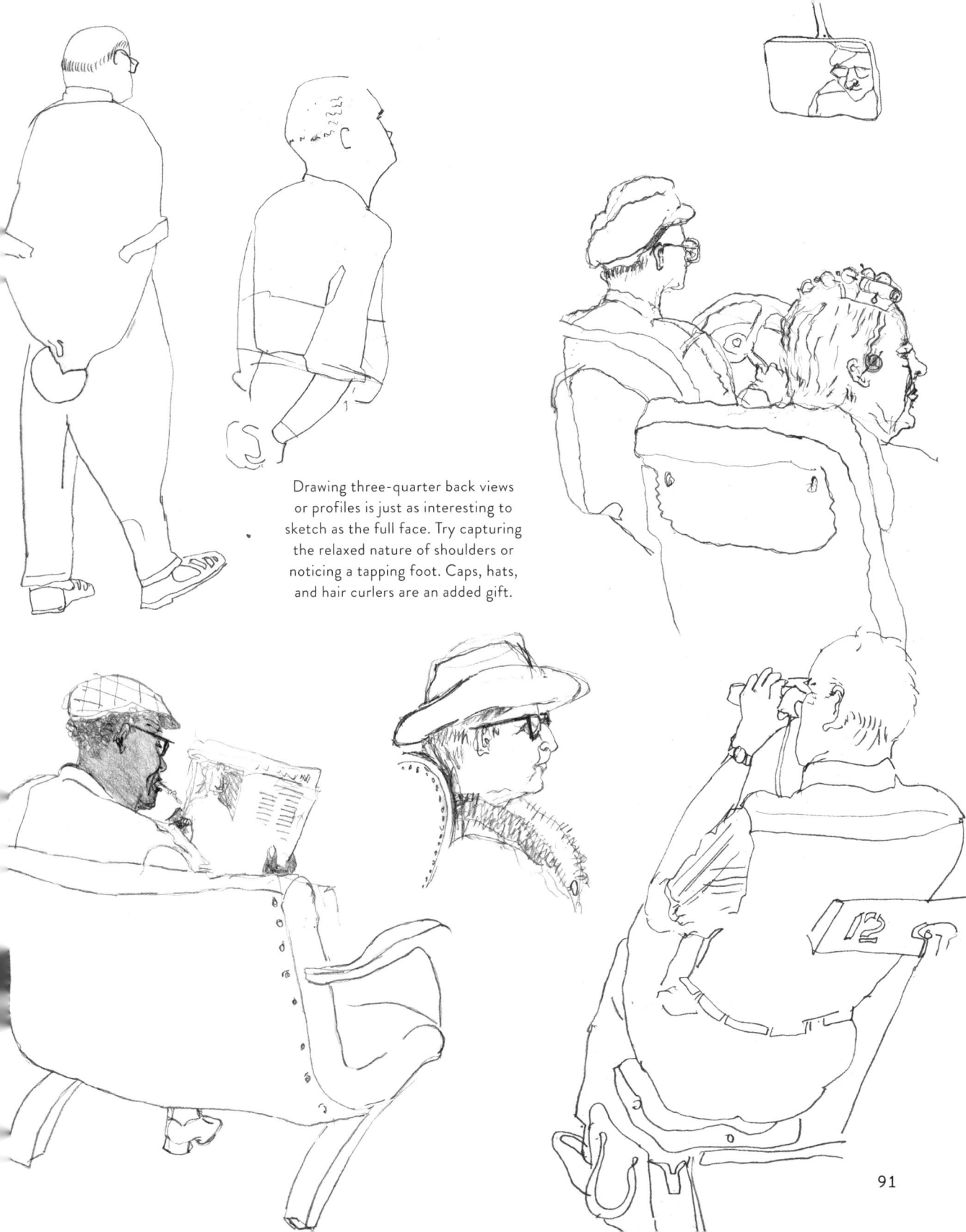

Drawing three-quarter back views or profiles is just as interesting to sketch as the full face. Try capturing the relaxed nature of shoulders or noticing a tapping foot. Caps, hats, and hair curlers are an added gift.

Collect eyes, noses, and mouths

Sketching the individual elements will encourage you to see, draw, and enjoy the differences between the various shapes. It will create a great drawn collage in your sketchbook.

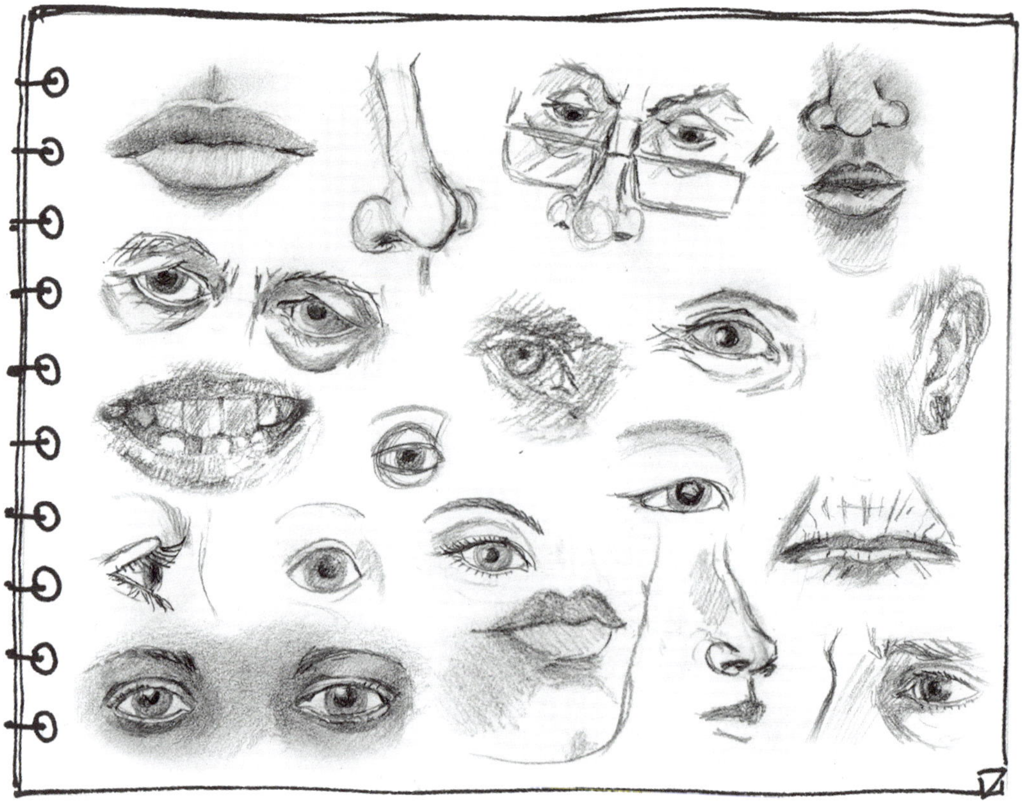

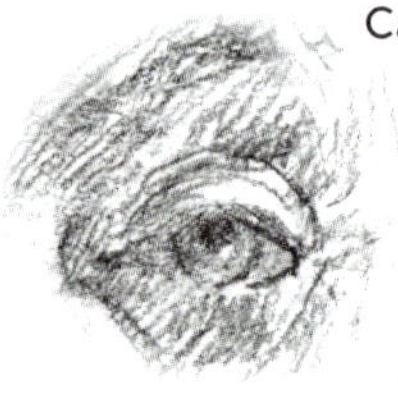

Capturing character

The structure of a young person's eye is very different to the wrinkles or glasses of an older person. It is good to practice the features of different ages and ethnicities. You will also have a great reference if ever you want to create an imaginary character. You can sketch with areas of shading or just a simple line.

Symbolic eye

The eye has be an important motif in many cultures. Three are shown below, or look online for more examples. In your sketchbook, draw and collect your own interpretation of the symbols.

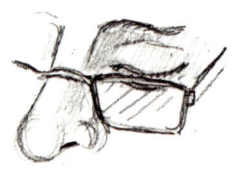

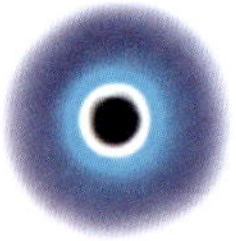

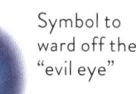
Symbol to ward off the "evil eye"

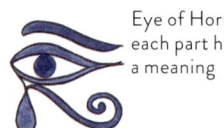
Eye of Horus: each part has a meaning

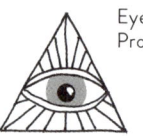
Eye of Providence

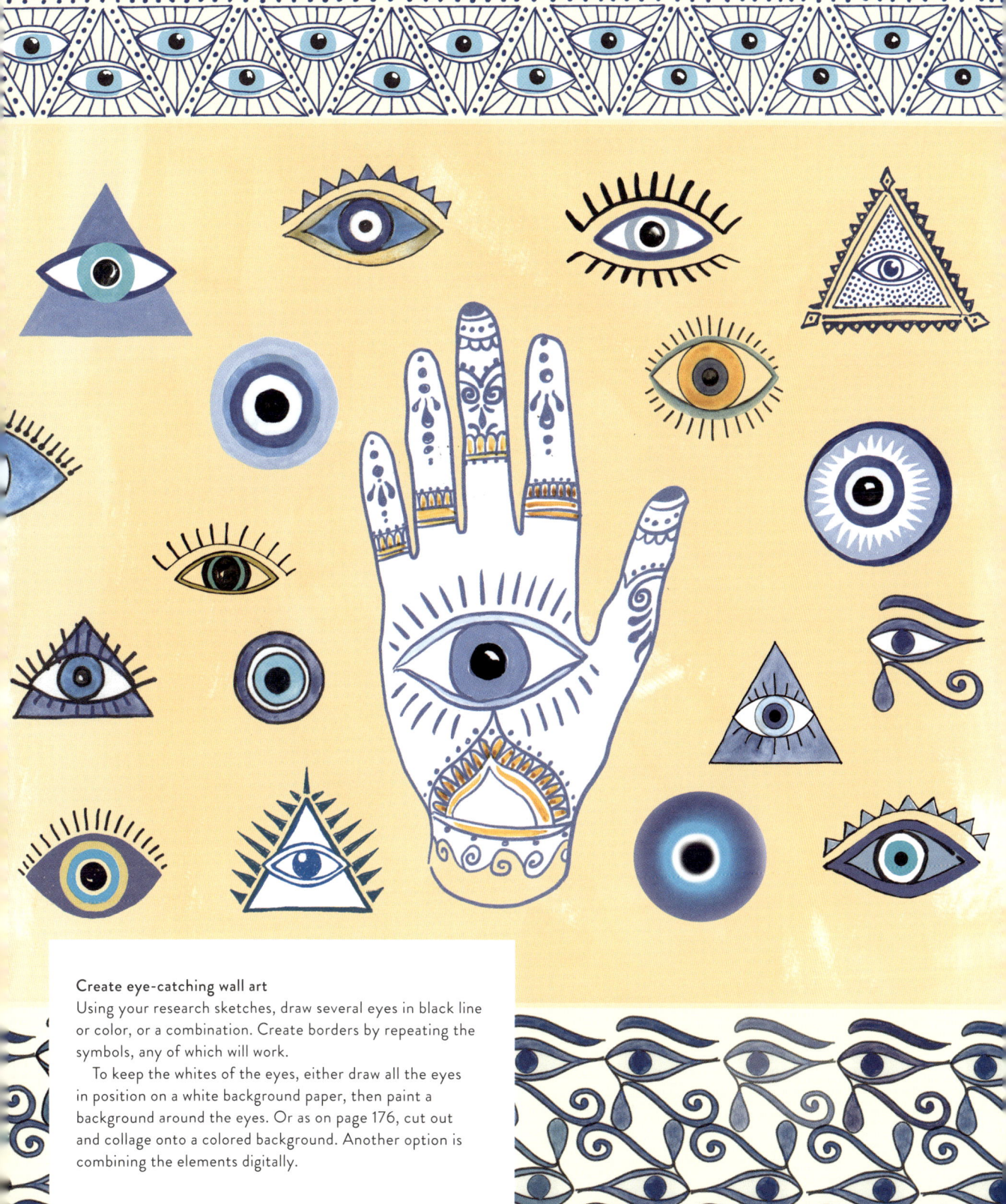

Create eye-catching wall art

Using your research sketches, draw several eyes in black line or color, or a combination. Create borders by repeating the symbols, any of which will work.

To keep the whites of the eyes, either draw all the eyes in position on a white background paper, then paint a background around the eyes. Or as on page 176, cut out and collage onto a colored background. Another option is combining the elements digitally.

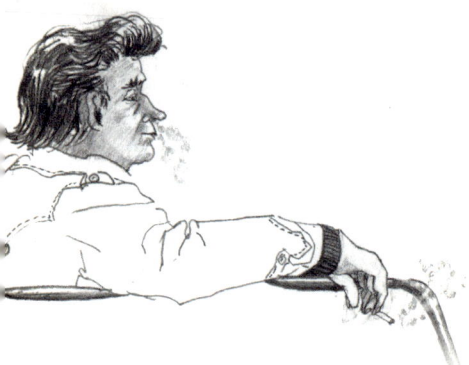

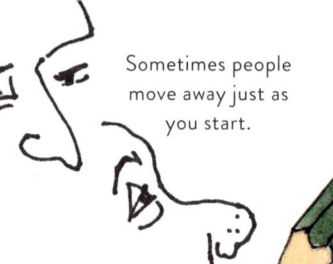

Sometimes people move away just as you start.

24

PEOPLE WATCHING

Take the opportunity to sketch people in everyday life when you can predict they will be in the same position for a while. Good locations are cafés, airport lounges, or waiting rooms, especially if people are reading. Obviously be discreet and don't invade anyone's personal space. Initially you might find it daunting, however the more you do it the more fun it will become.

Facial proportions

There are lots of online websites with complex information for facial proportions. Take a look and see which one you think works for you. Features vary greatly depending on age, ethnicity, and genetics—some people have button noses and others long aquiline noses. Since sketches are quick observations, here are some guidelines that I find useful to keep in mind.

Simple guidelines

Draw the face as an egg or oval shape, then add a vertical line for the center of the face. Position the eyes about halfway down the face, then the end of the nose about midway between the eye and the chin. (Or you can draw a circle from the top of the egg. The end of the nose is at the bottom of the circle.) The mouth position is halfway between the bottom of the nose and the chin.
See how the same guidelines can help when the face is looking up or down.

Vertical center line curves if face is at an angle

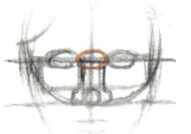

The distance between the eyes is always greater than you think. A useful quick guide is to imagine a third eye in the middle. Of course, this is only useful if the face is viewed straight on.

The red lines show the basic shapes of some of the sketches on the following page. Notice that to get the body posture right you need to set the shoulders at the right angle and make sure the neck sits properly within them.

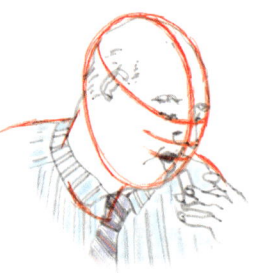

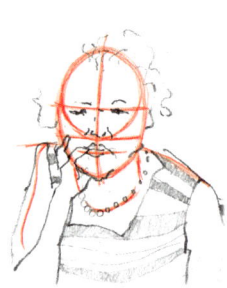

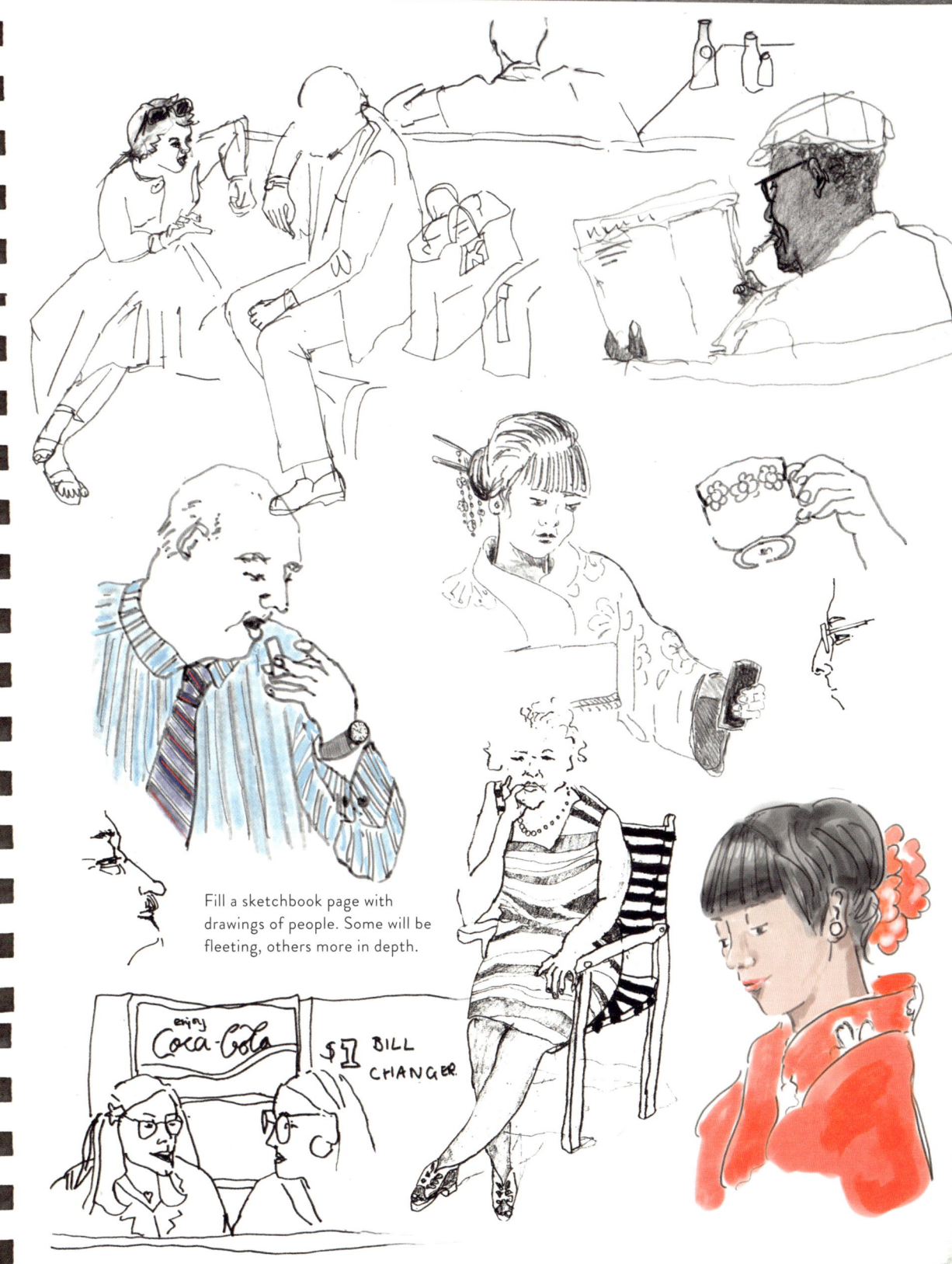

Fill a sketchbook page with drawings of people. Some will be fleeting, others more in depth.

Sketching on the move

Friends will normally be good humored when being drawn as a passenger or driver. Drawing or sketching in a car, or any form of transport might seem strange, but it is a great way of loosening up, especially if you are trying to draw figures for the first time. Your friends can't really expect the sketch to look like them with the turns and bumps, and the wobbly lines will just add to the character of the drawing. I tend to draw the car interior and clothing when the car is on the move, then when stopped at traffic lights I can draw the facial features, often returning to them several times.

Try it—the journey will go much quicker, and a few years later your friends will enjoy seeing the sketches as memories of the journey.

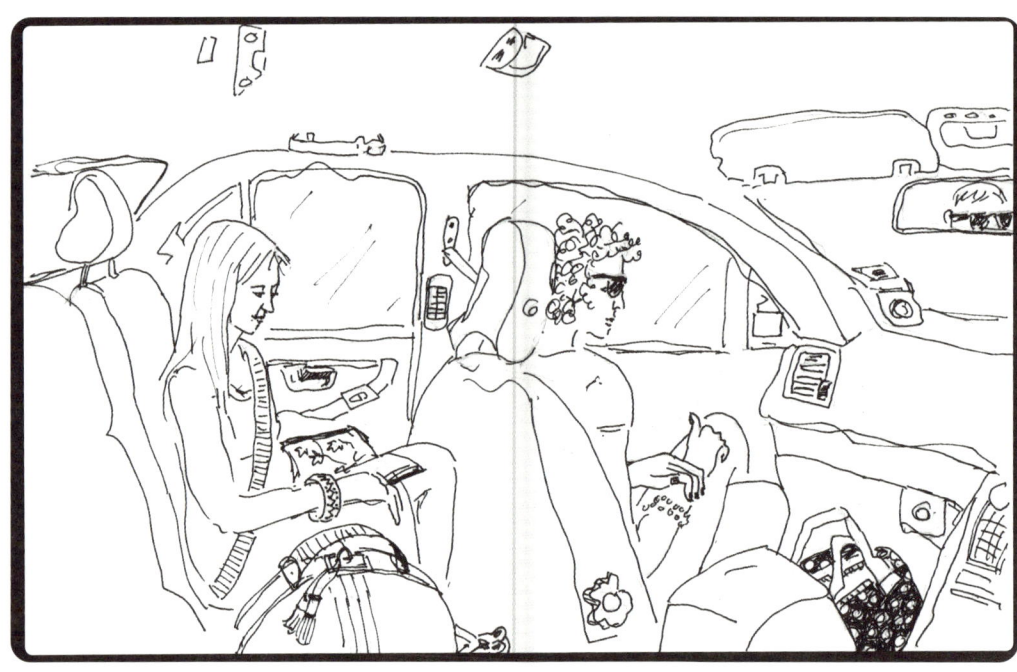

This interior uses a quirky one-point perspective (page 58). Slightly curving the lines gives a panoramic effect.

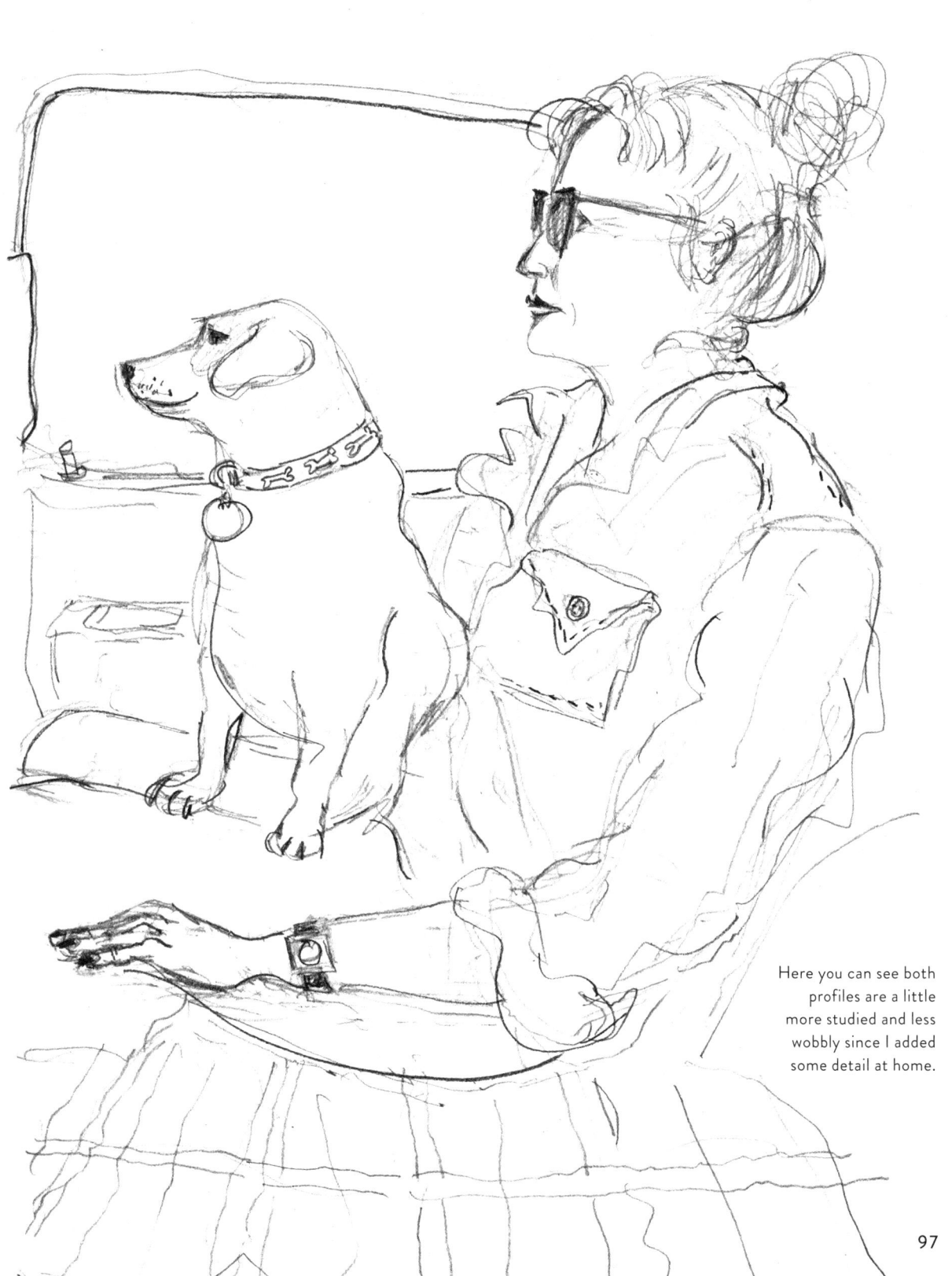

Here you can see both profiles are a little more studied and less wobbly since I added some detail at home.

CELEBRATE YOUR FRIENDS AND FAMILY

Sketching friends and family is a great way to enjoy and remember special occasions.

Drawing while people are eating is tricky, since they move quickly and are talking, and normally you are eating too. I find the best way is to wait until everyone has finished the main course—they are more relaxed than when they have just arrived. Between courses, cell phones come out and people look at them or at the menu, and will often hold that position for a few minutes so that you can capture them. You can draw the stationary elements of the table and all the paraphernalia at any time.

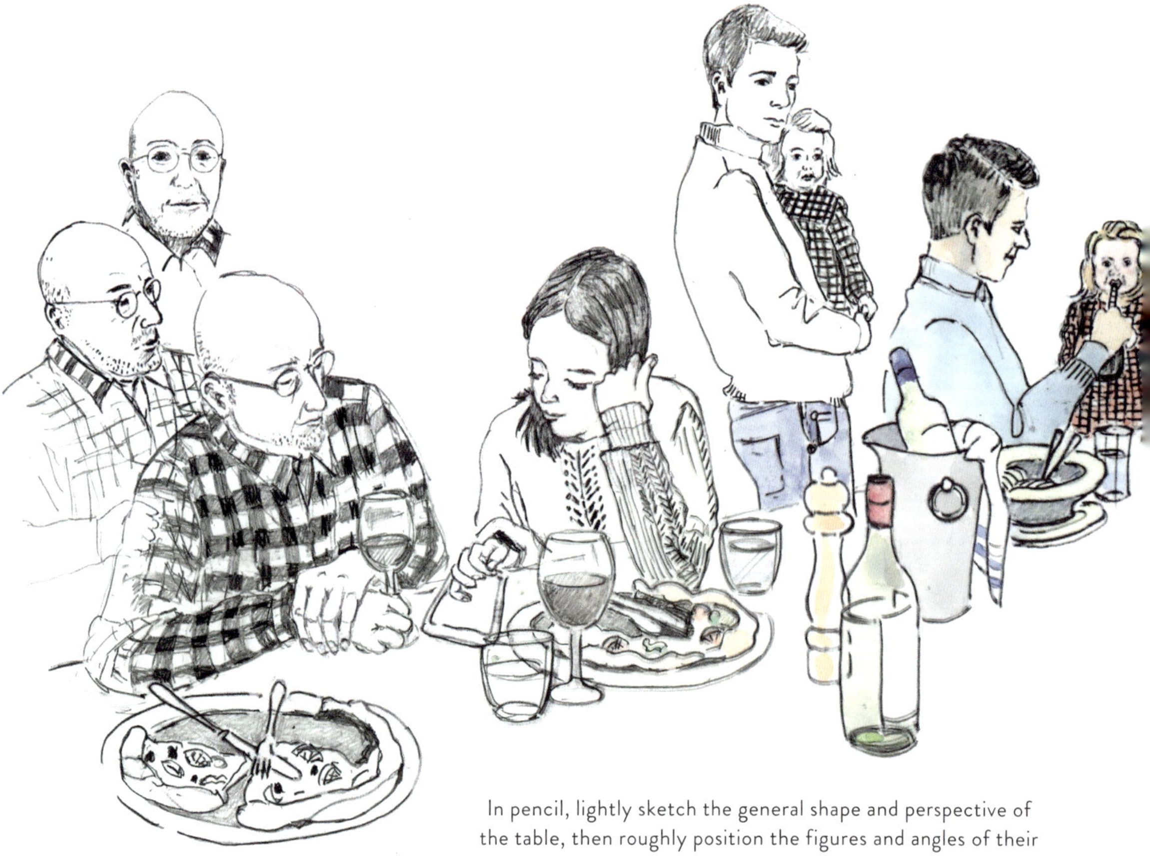

In pencil, lightly sketch the general shape and perspective of the table, then roughly position the figures and angles of their heads (see opposite page, top right). Once you have the general proportions sketched out, you can add more detail. I often do several versions of each head. . . Generally, one will capture a likeness! You can always add color another day.

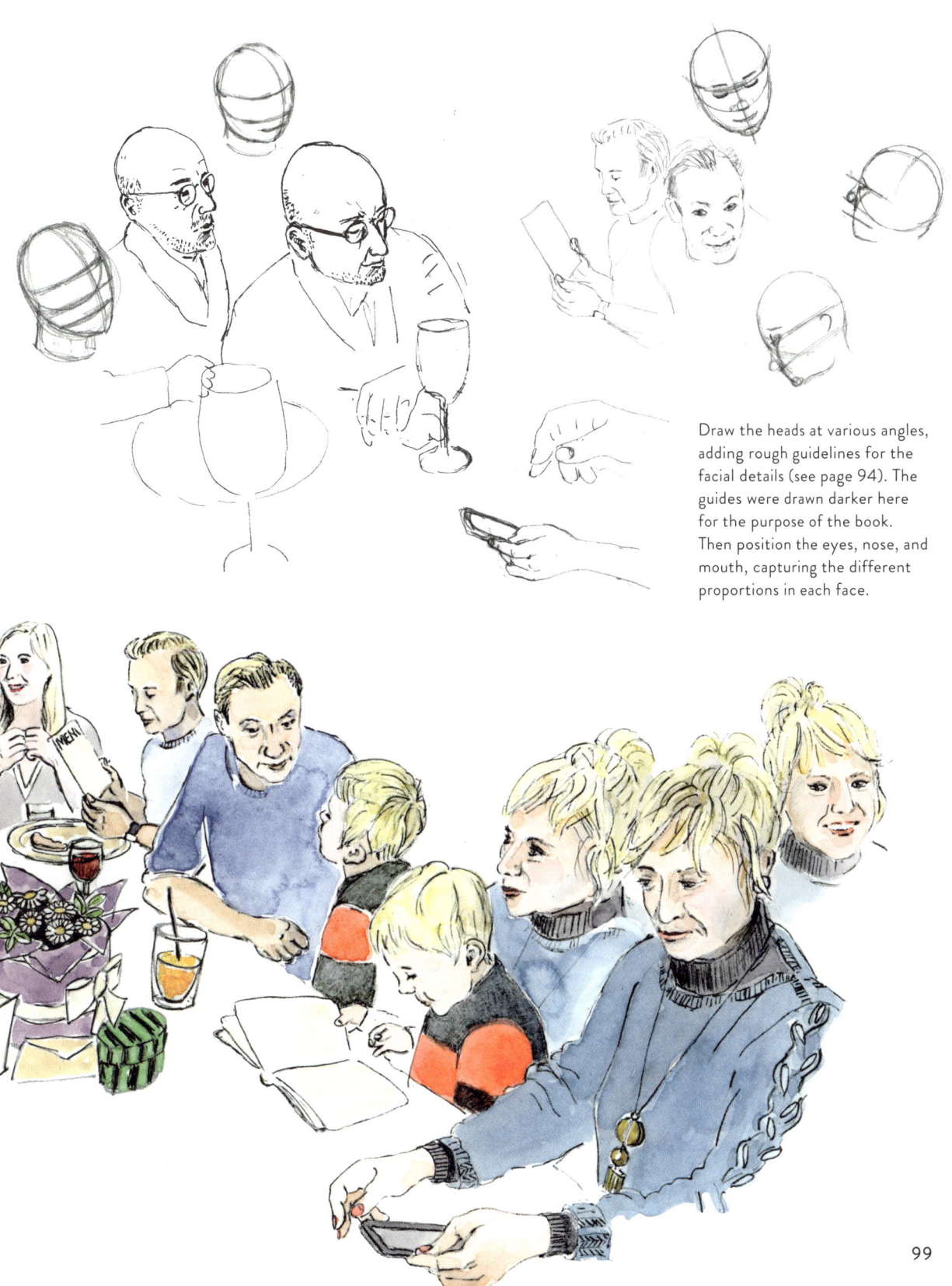

Draw the heads at various angles, adding rough guidelines for the facial details (see page 94). The guides were drawn darker here for the purpose of the book. Then position the eyes, nose, and mouth, capturing the different proportions in each face.

URBAN SKETCHING

Drawing from your surroundings will provide inspiration and ideas every day. A great website is urbansketchers.org where you can discover the international urban sketching community and see the range of subject matter shared from around the world.

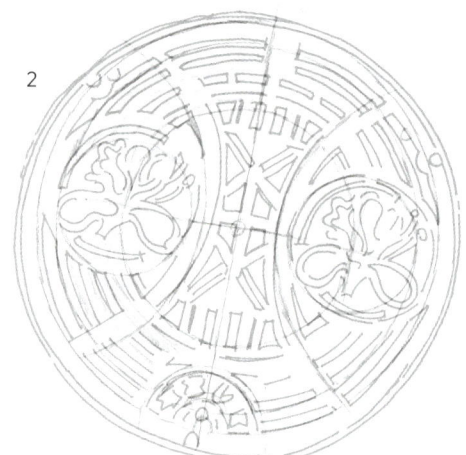

1

2

Street furniture

Take note of what might be regarded as a mundane or atypical subject for drawing. Mailboxes, telephone poles, fire hydrants, and vending machines all make great subjects.

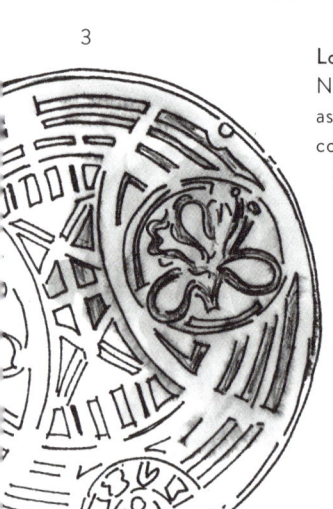

3

Looking down

Not all manhole covers are as charming as these in Japan, but simple geometric covers also have a simple beauty. To help you see the proportions, most can be divided into three or four segments. (1) Sketch the basic divisions in pencil (2) then plot the metal design. (3) Finally, ink the line with a permanent pen and add a monochrome or colorwash.

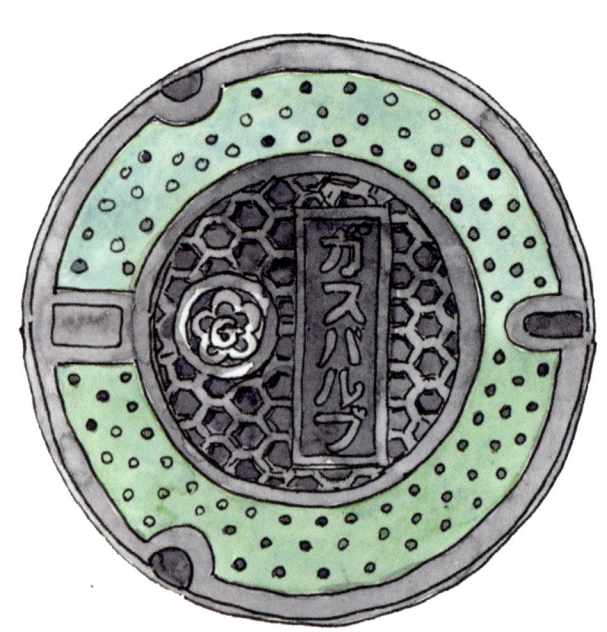

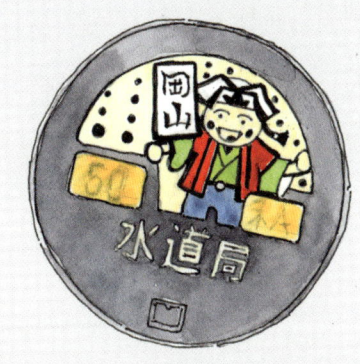

Urban sketching group vision and values

1. We draw on location, indoors or out, capturing what we see from direct observation.
2. Our drawings tell the story of our surroundings, the places we live, and where we travel.
3. Our drawings are a record of time and place.
4. We are truthful to the scenes we witness.
5. We use any kind of media and cherish our individual styles.
6. We support each other and draw together.
7. We share our drawings online.
8. We show the world, one drawing at a time.

www.urbansketchers.org

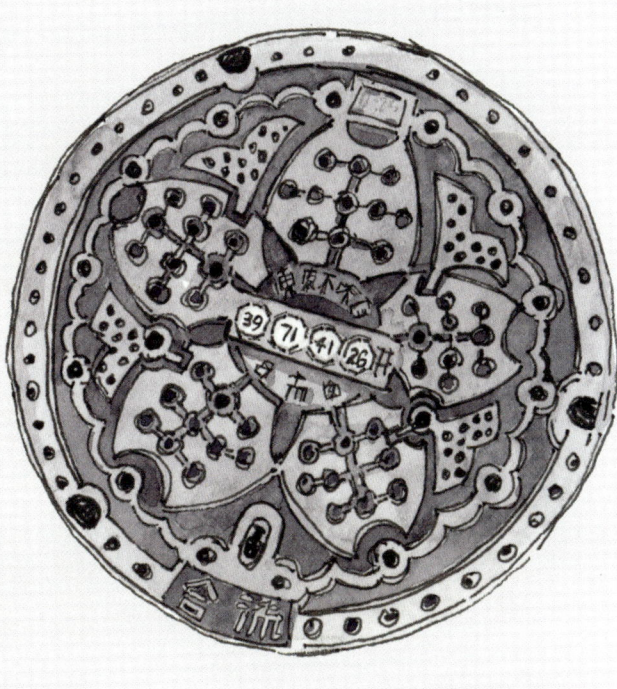

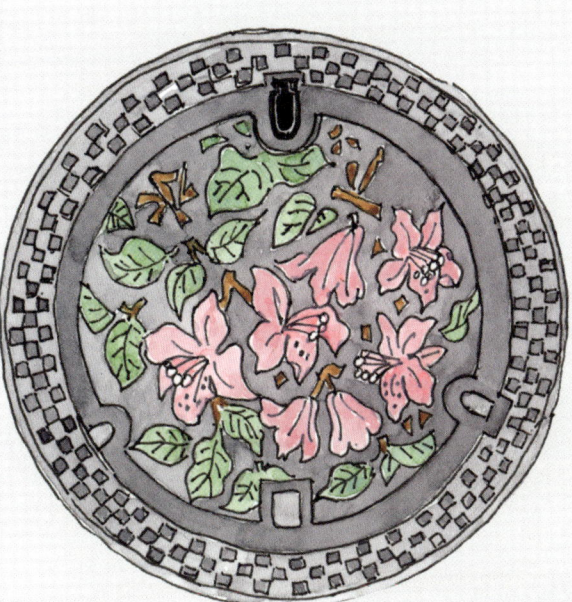

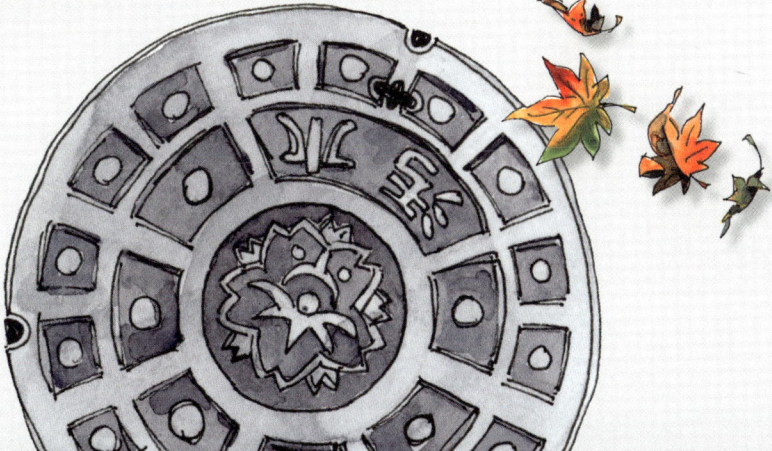

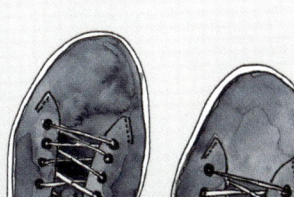

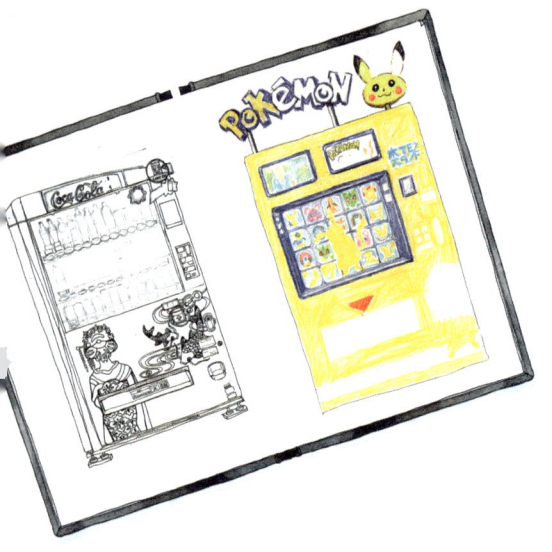

Vending art

These amazing vending machines are part of the Japanese graphics street culture. They seemed so bizarre they had to be drawn. Not only are the graphics great, but you can add all the buttons, coin return slots, and the little dinky feet.

The geisha and koi carp machine just was outside my hotel, so I was able to make a pencil sketch and start the waterproof black line work before adding the color at home. Although fiddly, the bottles and cans are repeating shapes, so you soon get into a rhythm while drawing them.

The Pokémon machine was in the airport waiting area, and working with colored pencil was a quick way to get most of the color started.

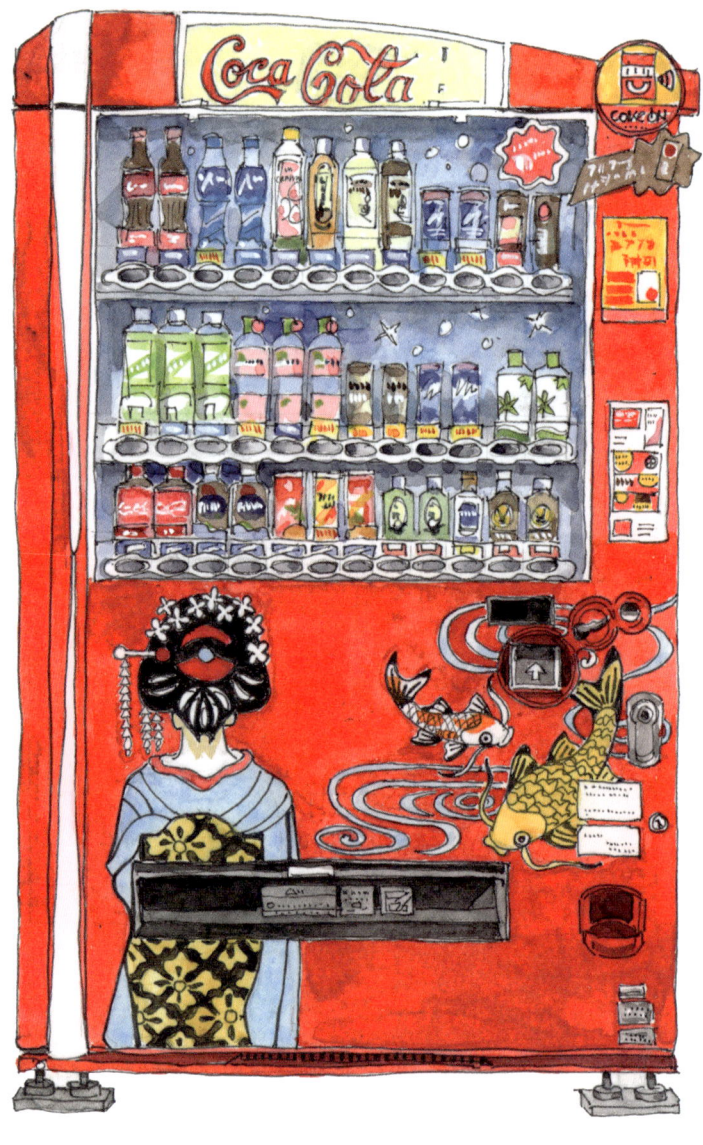

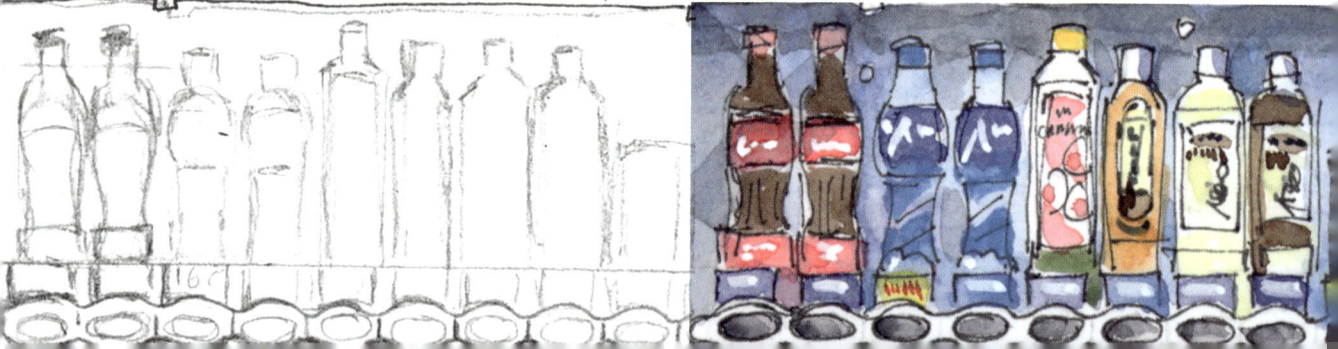

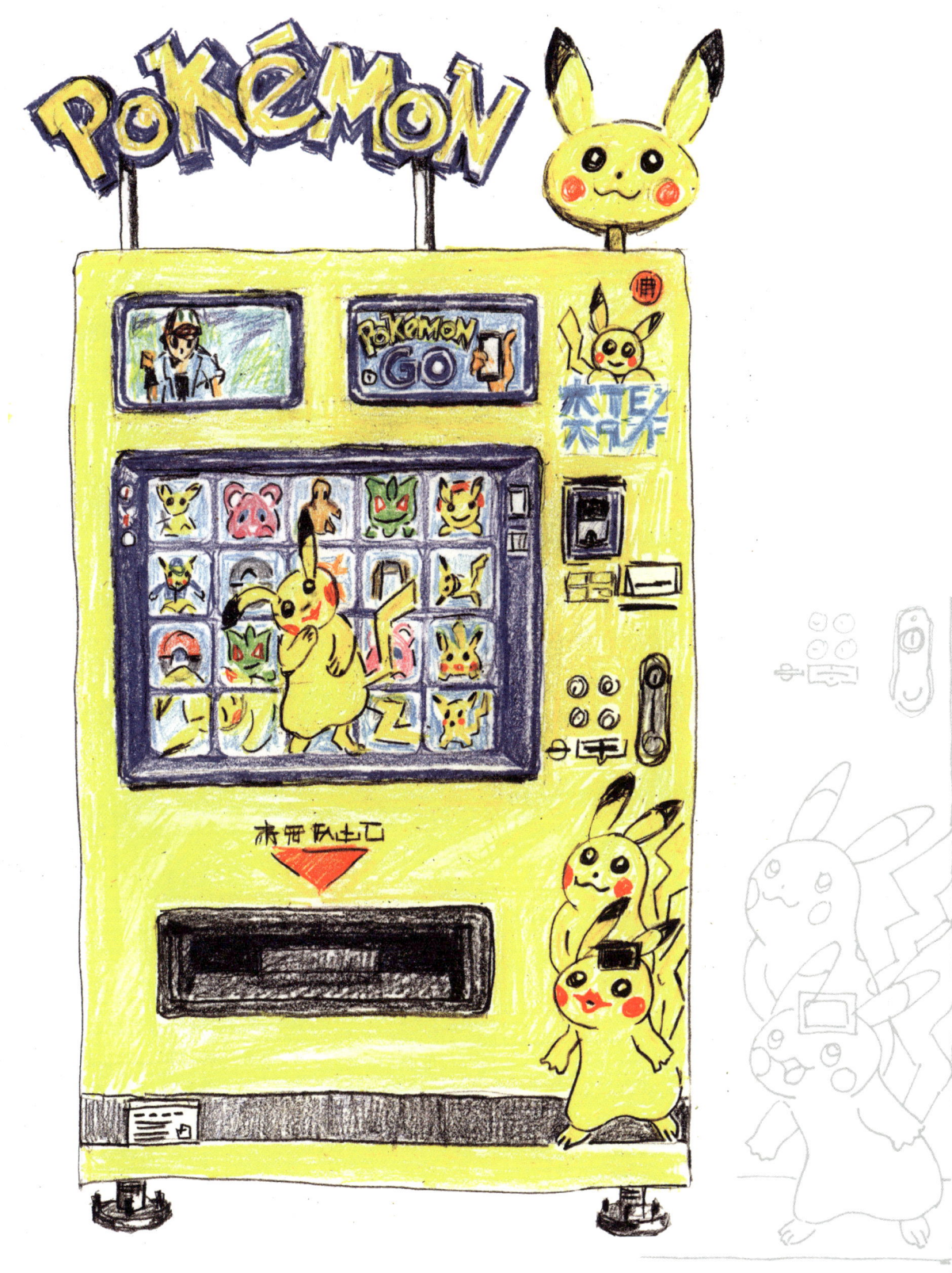

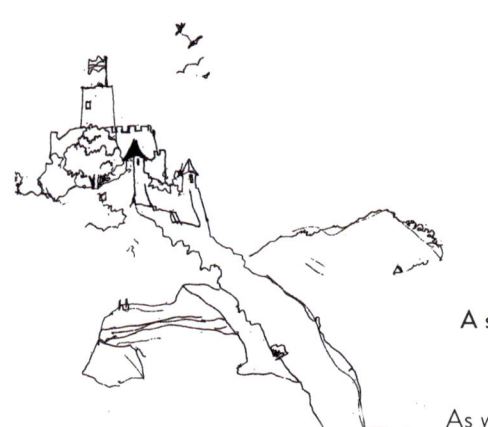

TRAVELING

A sketchbook while traveling is essential for any aspiring artist.

As well as sketching friends and family by the pool, in the ocean, or just having a good time, sketching is the best way to capture the culture, food, people, and landscape of the country you are visiting. Much more personal than photos on your phone!

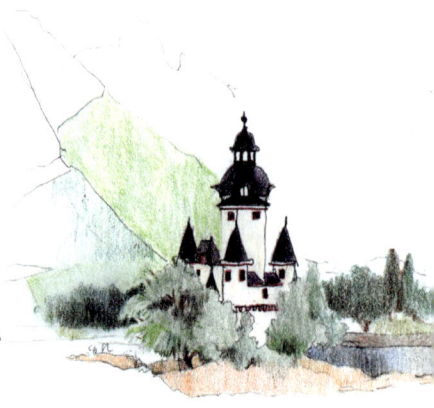

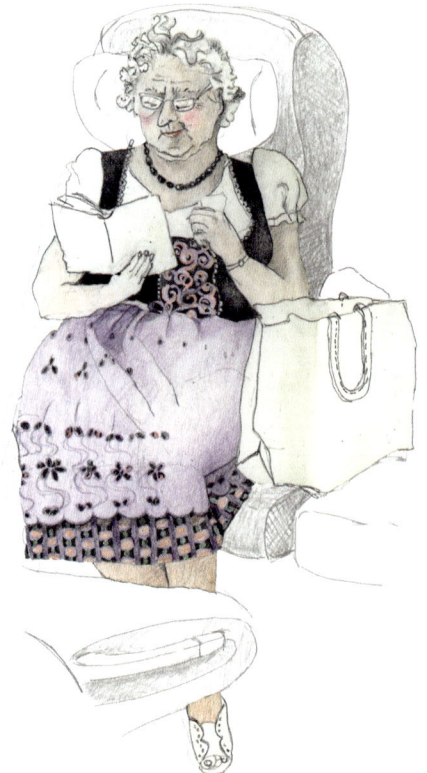

Who could resist this lady in her traditional outfit on a train in Germany? I wonder where she was going.

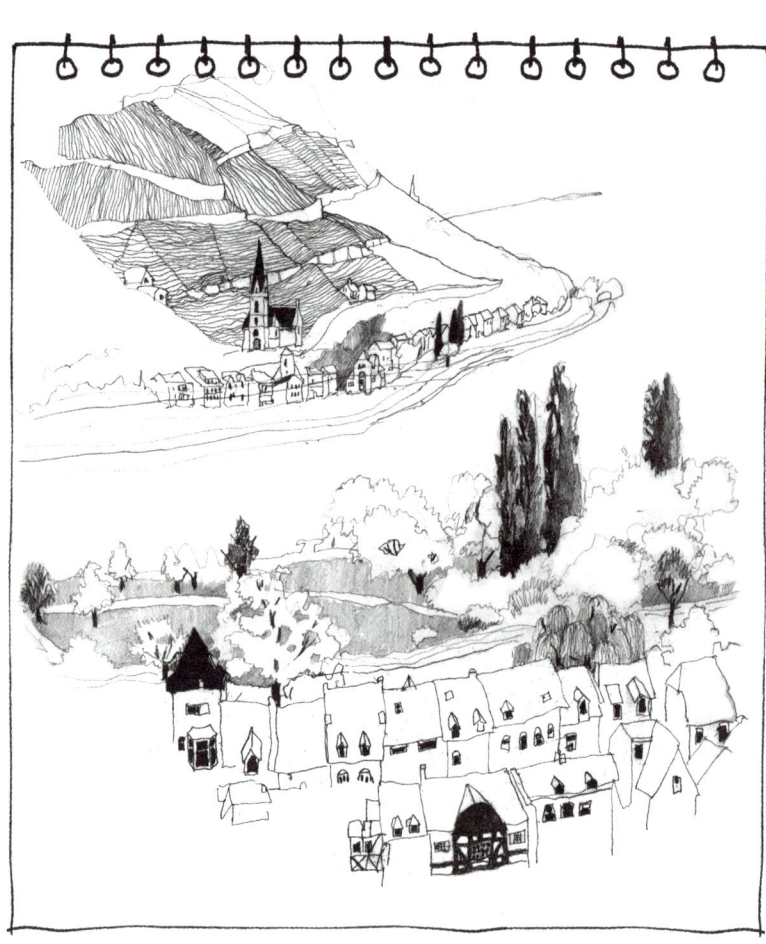

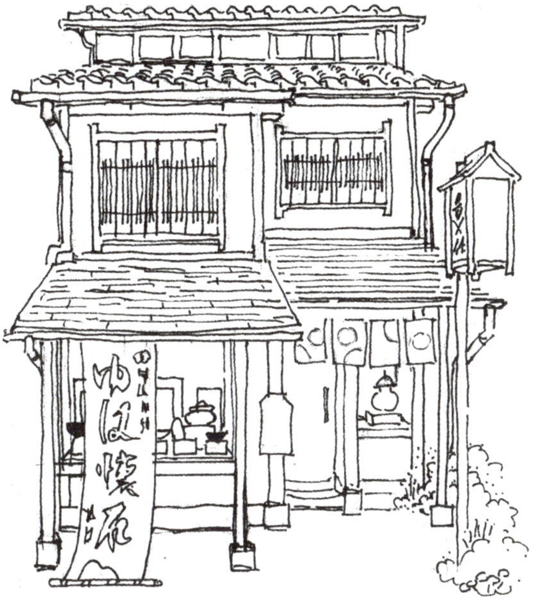

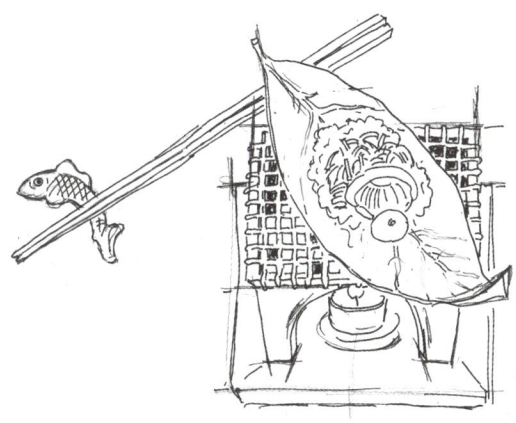

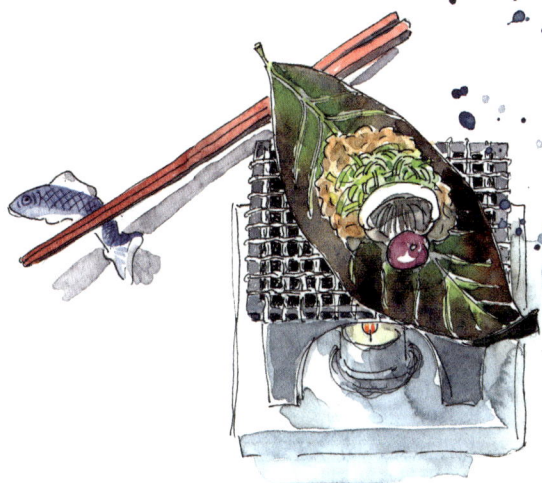

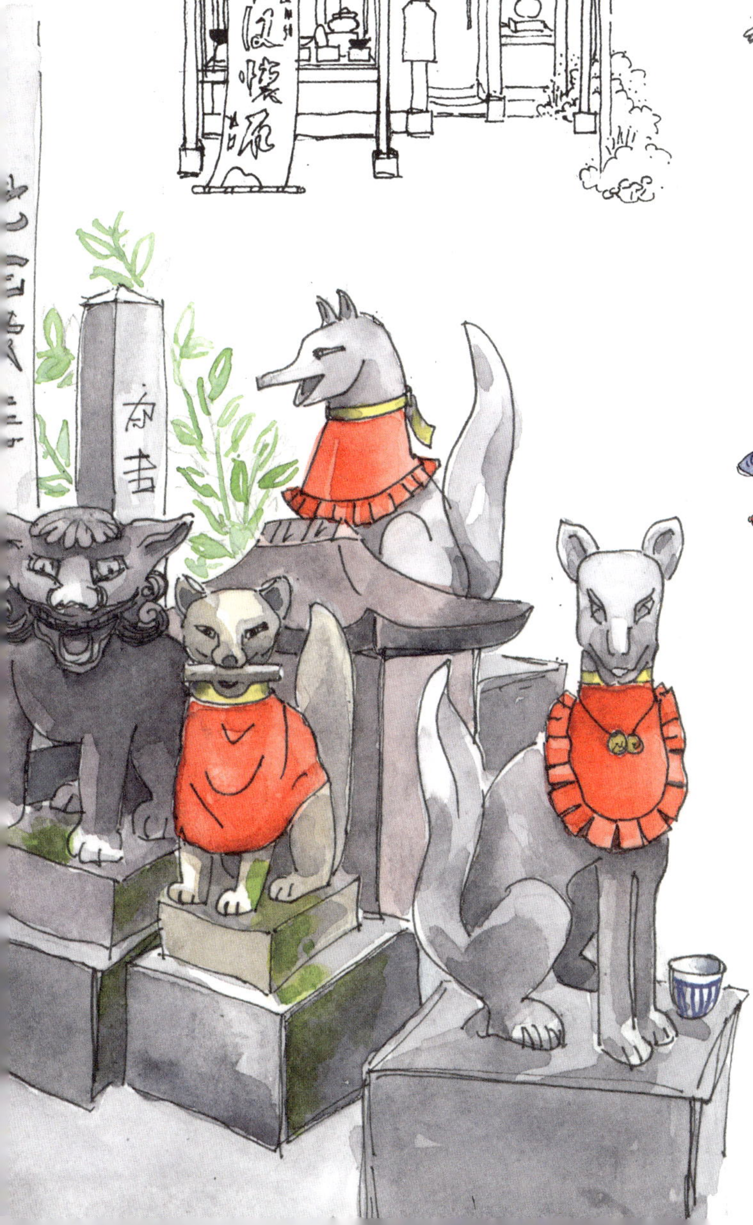

Map out a faint pencil sketch, then work with a black, waterproof pen for the line work before adding wet media washes over the top. Some sketches can have color added on the spot while you can add to others when you arrive back home. What a great way to relive the vacation!

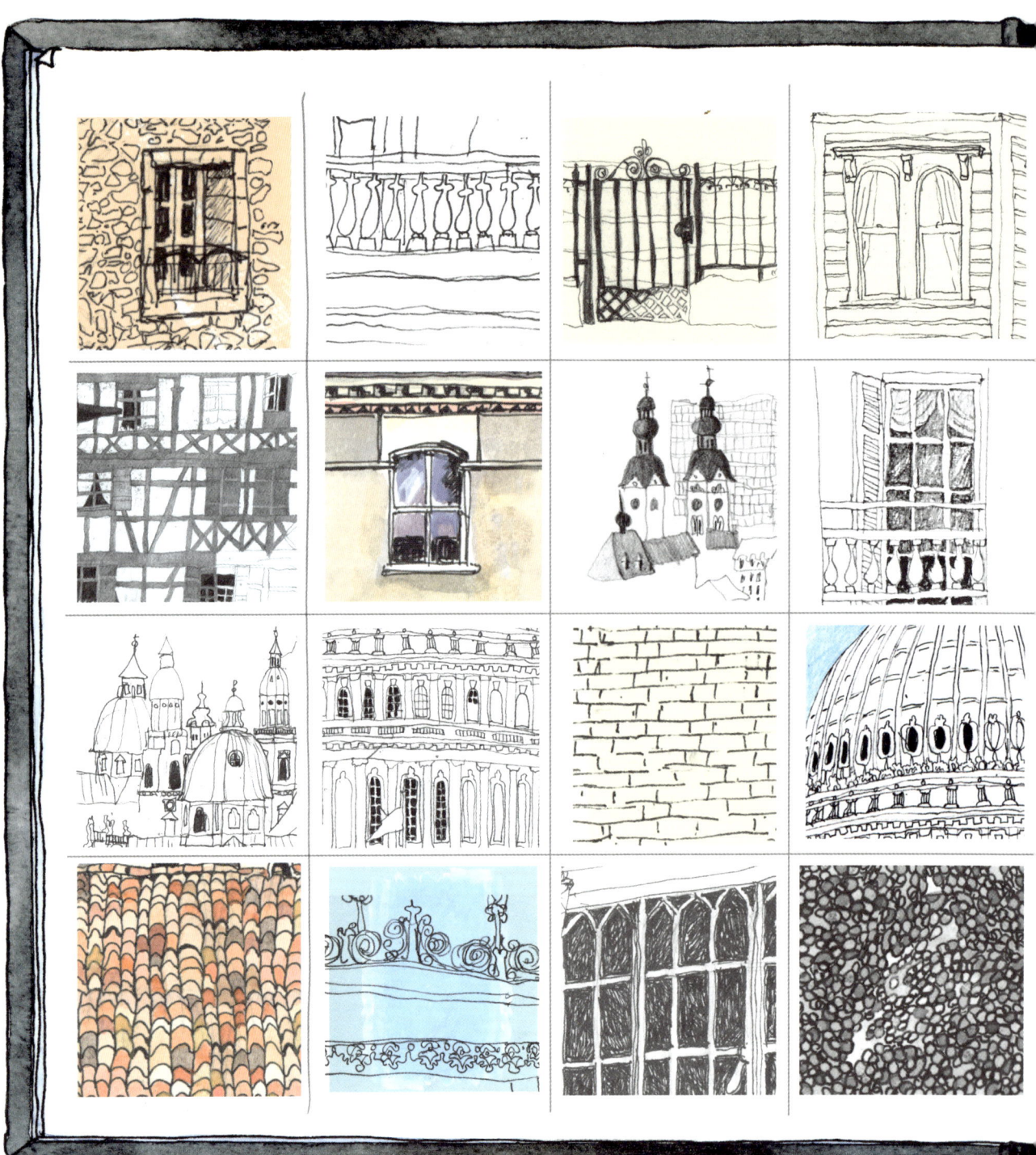

106

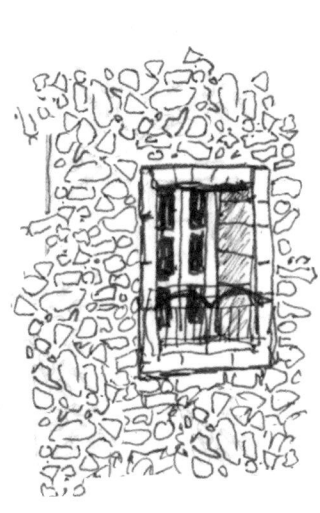
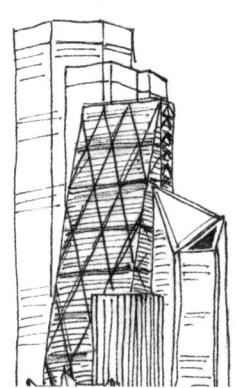
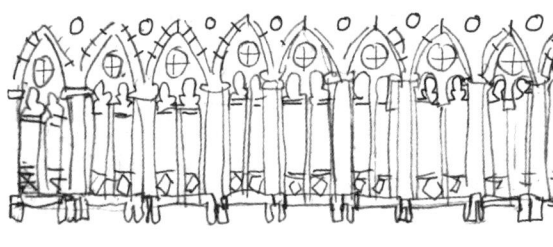
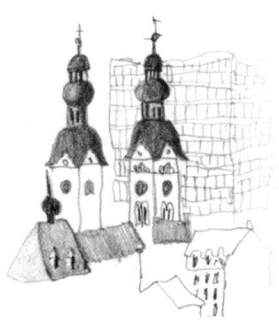

Old travel sketches

Most of these are scraps from sketches that remain unfinished but are kept, since they are a reminder of times and places. Each one was an observation of different windows, stone work, roof tiles, or wall treatments. You can either create your own collage from cut-up scraps, or draw a grid in the back of your sketchbook and fill in a square whenever you see a new architectural detail. This sort of gathered reference is great for drawing fantasy or imaginary illustrations.

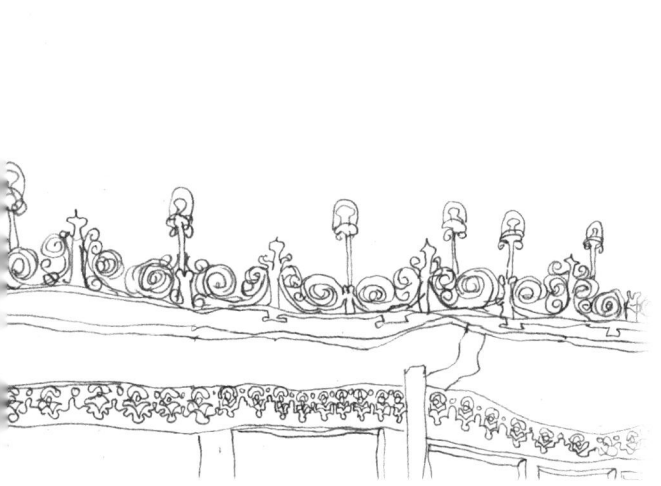
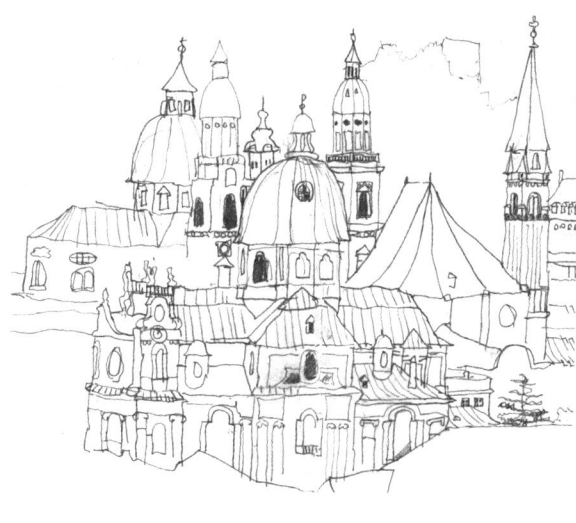

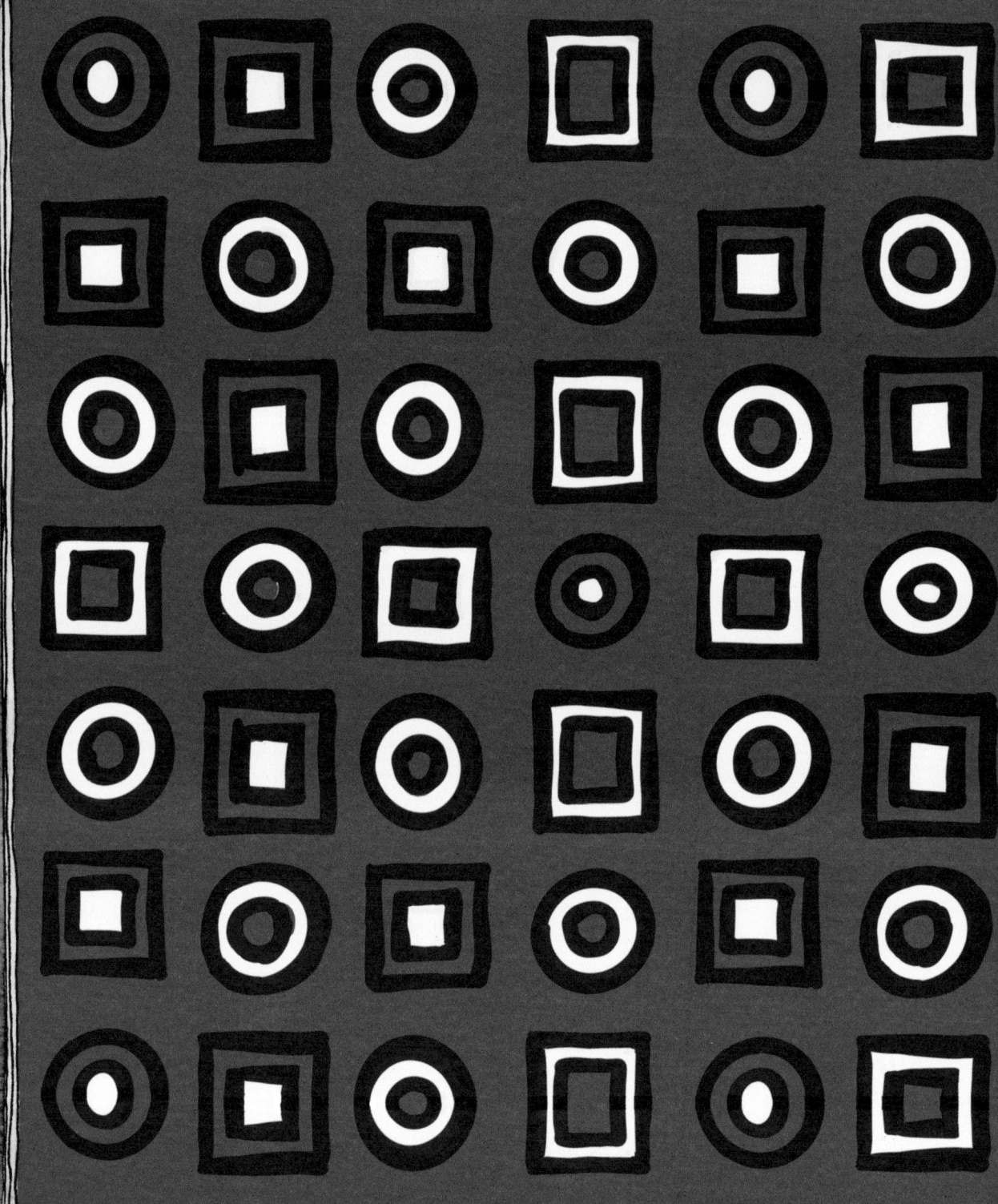

3

PRACTICE MAKES PERFECT

It doesn't matter if it's not perfect, but practice does make progress. Patterns are satisfying to create and the eye responds well to repetition, enjoying the different rhythms. Drawing the same thing several times will help refine your drawing skills, and is fun and relaxing to do.

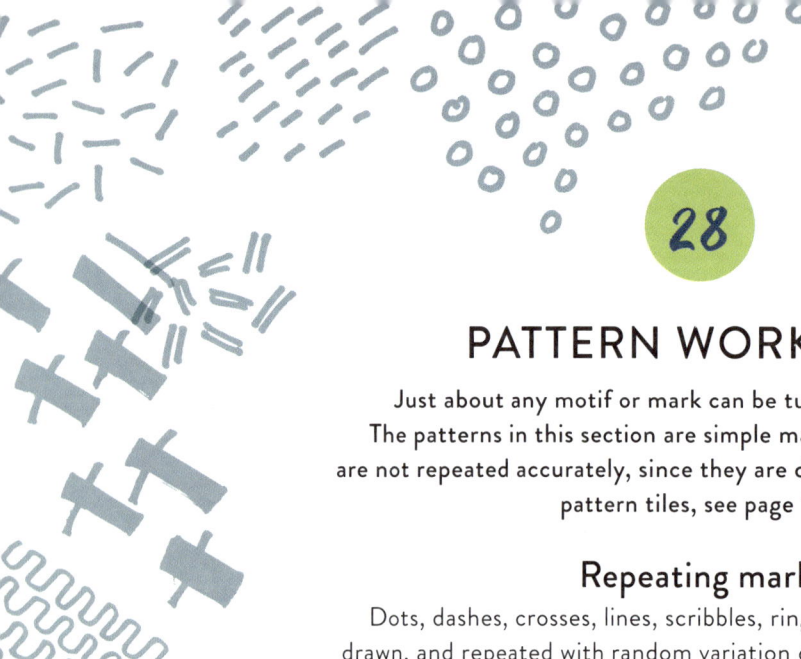

28

PATTERN WORKSHOP

Just about any motif or mark can be turned into a pattern. The patterns in this section are simple marks, and the elements are not repeated accurately, since they are drawn by hand. For repeat pattern tiles, see page 170.

Repeating marks

Dots, dashes, crosses, lines, scribbles, rings, and more can all be drawn, and repeated with random variation of spacing, size, and color to create very different results. Alternatively, the little motifs can be arranged more formally, putting them together roughly in equally spaced or staggered rows. Try drawing blocks of these patterns and see how many variations you can create.

Circle collage

Choose twelve of the patterns. Paint your own or buy some colored paper. The paper should be heavy (about 140 lb, 300 gsm) and pale toned, since some of media listed below can be transparent, which will mute the pattern color. Draw the patterns on the colored paper in blocks of about four inches square (or whatever size you are comfortable with), then cut them out using a craft circle cutter or drawing around a circular object and cutting with scissors. (For ease, you could work with diamond shapes.) Finally, arrange and glue circles to a white or colored background.

For drawing the patterns you could use:
- Acrylic markers
- Colored pencils
- Watercolor markers
- Standard felt-tip pens

The white patterns were drawn with a white acrylic-based marker. The concentric circles (bottom left) were brush drawn with gouache.

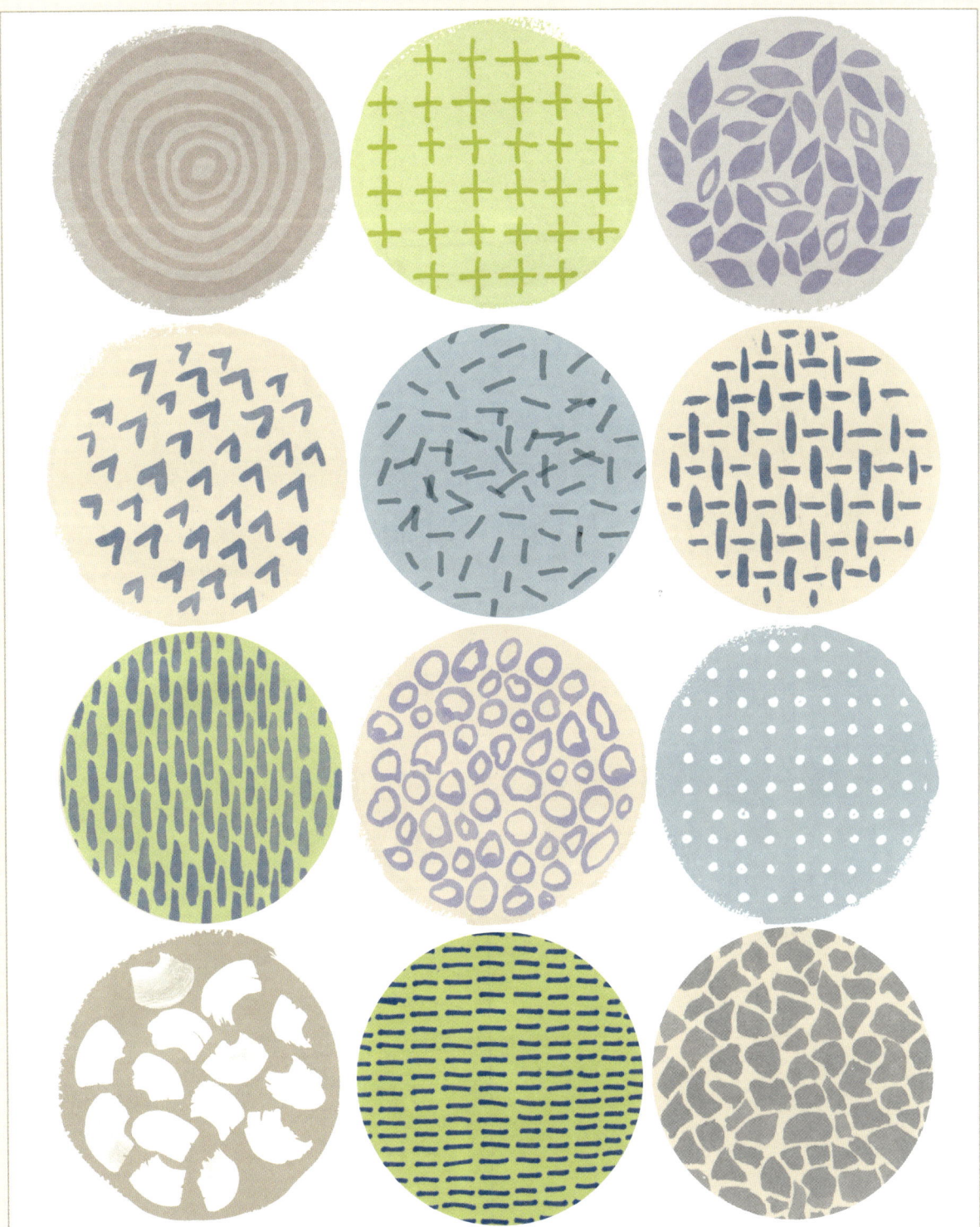

Patterned tawny owl

Patterns can be used to fill in shapes within a drawing, since the different marks and directions of the patterns will define various areas. This drawing was planned as 8.5 x 11 inches, and at this size, any normal paper would buckle with the background water washes; the paper used here is a 160 lb (350 gsm) watercolor paper. Ideally, stretch the paper (see page 177), or the paper might be slightly uneven.

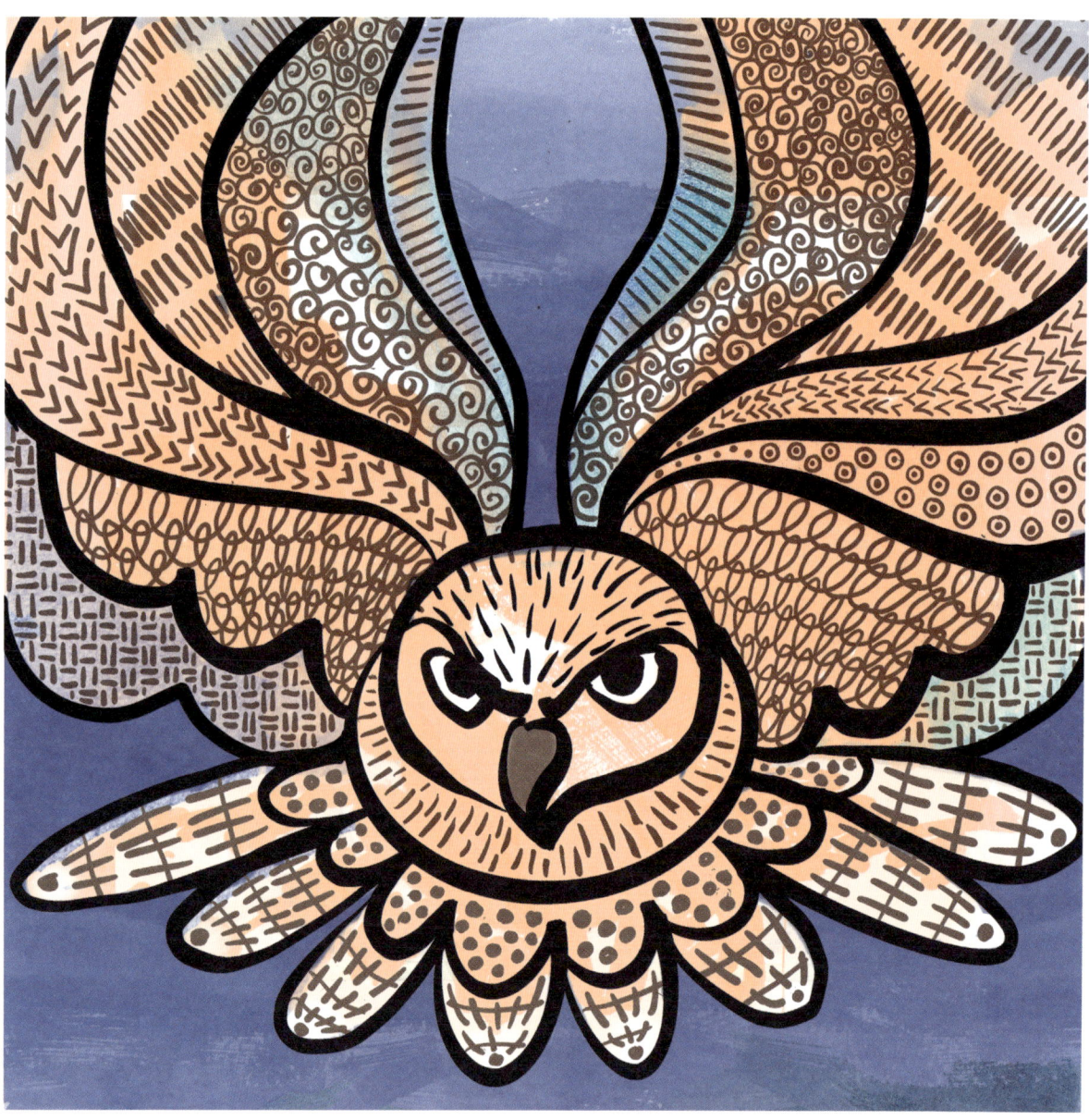

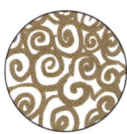 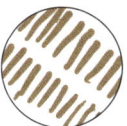 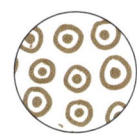 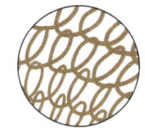 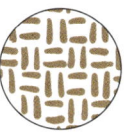 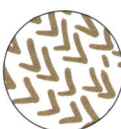 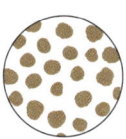 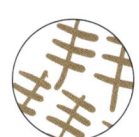

Here are the drawn patterns. It's a good idea to create a small block of each before you fill in the main drawing to get a feel of the size and spacing.

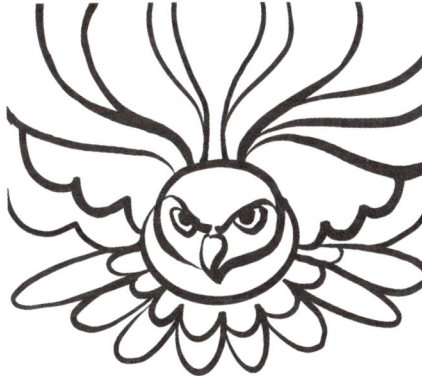

Draw a faint pencil line of the owl, then, using a waterproof black brush-tip pen, draw the bird outline. Applying different pressures will give nice variety to the line. You can erase any pencil lines. (Practice a few times on some scraps of paper, until you gradually get the strokes all to work).

I saw this fantastic coffee shop window—what a great idea for random patterns! Imagine trying it on an interior wall using brush drawing (see page 32). Use a decorating brush and decorating paint in pale neutral or bright primary colors.

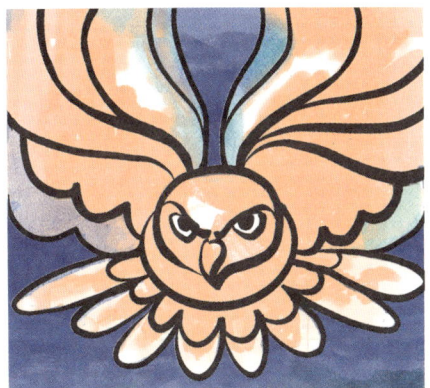

For drawing the patterns you could use:
• acrylic markers
• colored pencils
• watercolor markers
• standard felt-tip pens

Apply a color wash (watercolor markers or watercolor paint). Blues for the sky and pale brown for the bird. Leave some areas almost white, then add some green to vary the blue. Allow to dry. Finally, draw patterns in the wing shapes. Use a dark color so that it will be opaque over the background washes.

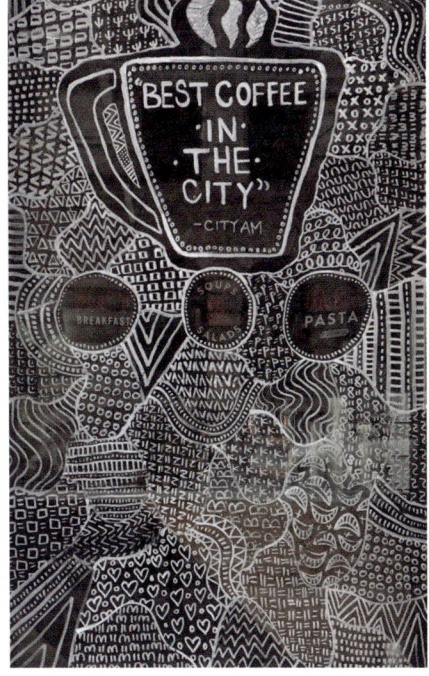

REPETITION AND SYMMETRY

You can repeat the marks at random, make them into a line, or create a radial effect. While this can be done by hand (using a grid to arrange the pattern in your desired order), digital tools and apps will make the process much faster and more accurate.

A friend introduced me to the symmetry function on my tablet, and it is both a fun and useful way to replicate marks. Simply draw one set or segment of a shape and *voila*, it magically duplicates it.

Try practicing your symbols and marks, and then you can make fun patterns, choosing between a simple mirror image or multiple repeats.

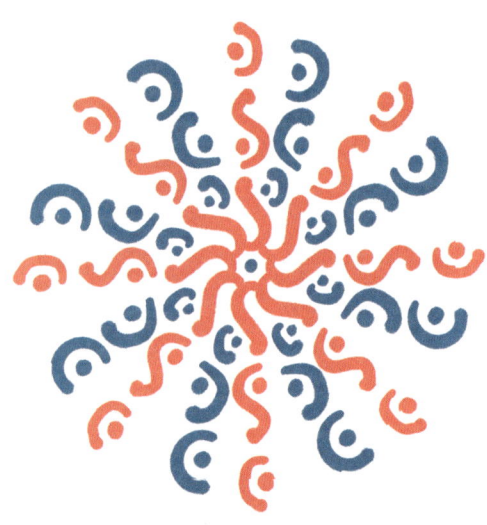

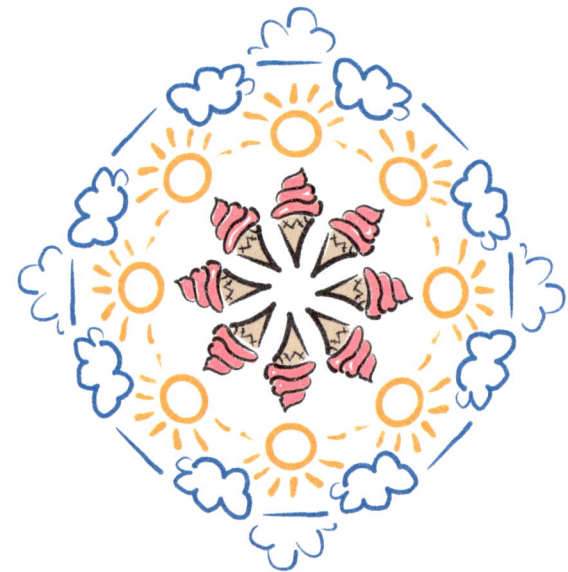

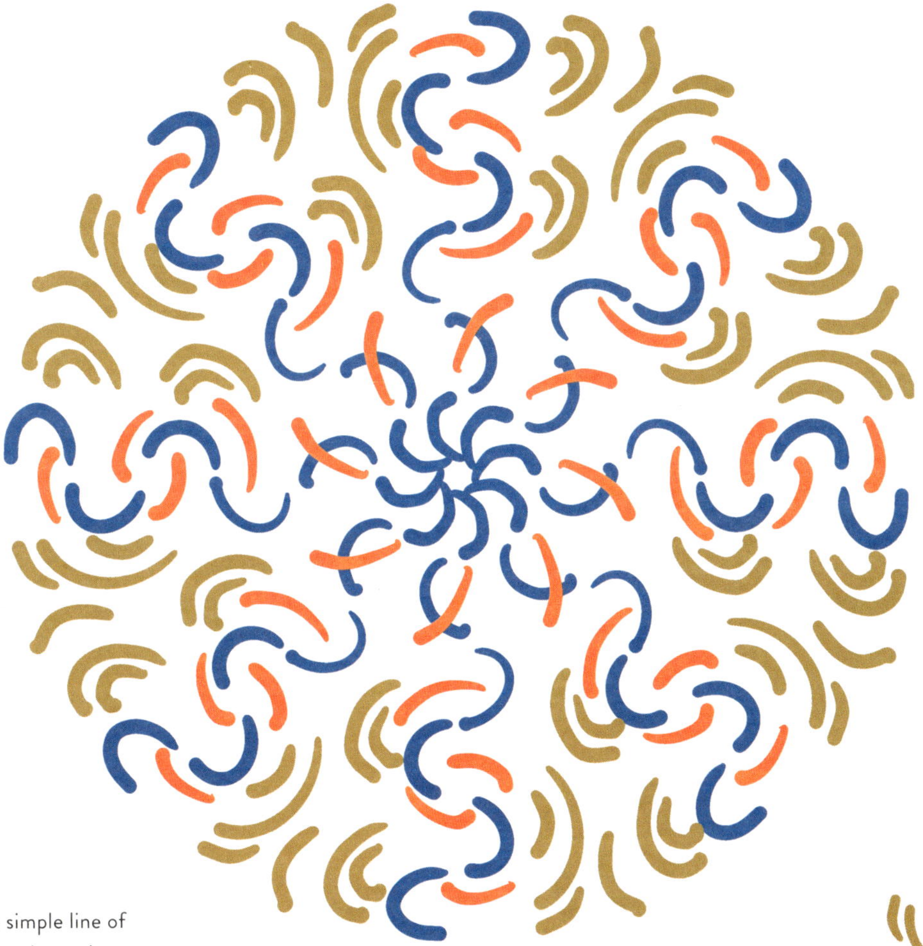

Duplicate a simple line of
curves, to create a set
in three stages.

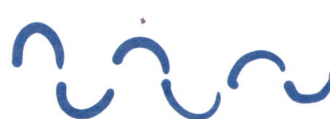

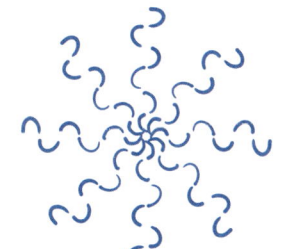

Draw more curves around the first set.

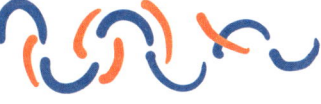

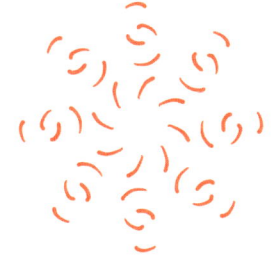

Add another set to
fill in the space.

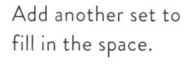

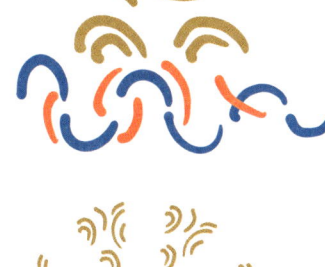

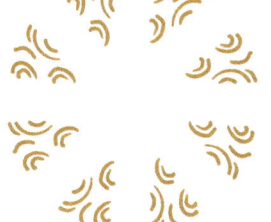

GEOMETRIC PATTERNS

The mathematical shapes of triangles, circles, and squares are ideal for repeat patternmaking. Experiment with spacing, twisting, and resizing to see surprising results, or combine with other elements such as lines and dots for added detail.

Try some triangles

A simple triangle can be repositioned to make different patterns. Here are just a few examples that can be done quickly during a spare moment (although you will always be tempted to add just another row or try another combination).

Doodle in a note pad
The little pages (right) show pattern play with triangles. Try adding lines and outlines, zigzags, different sizes, or joining the triangles together. Copy one, then create your own.

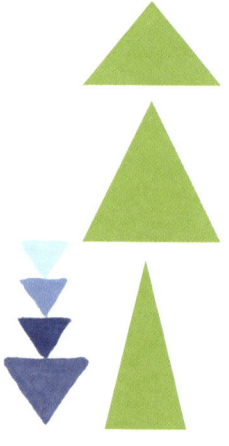

You can try different shape and size triangles.

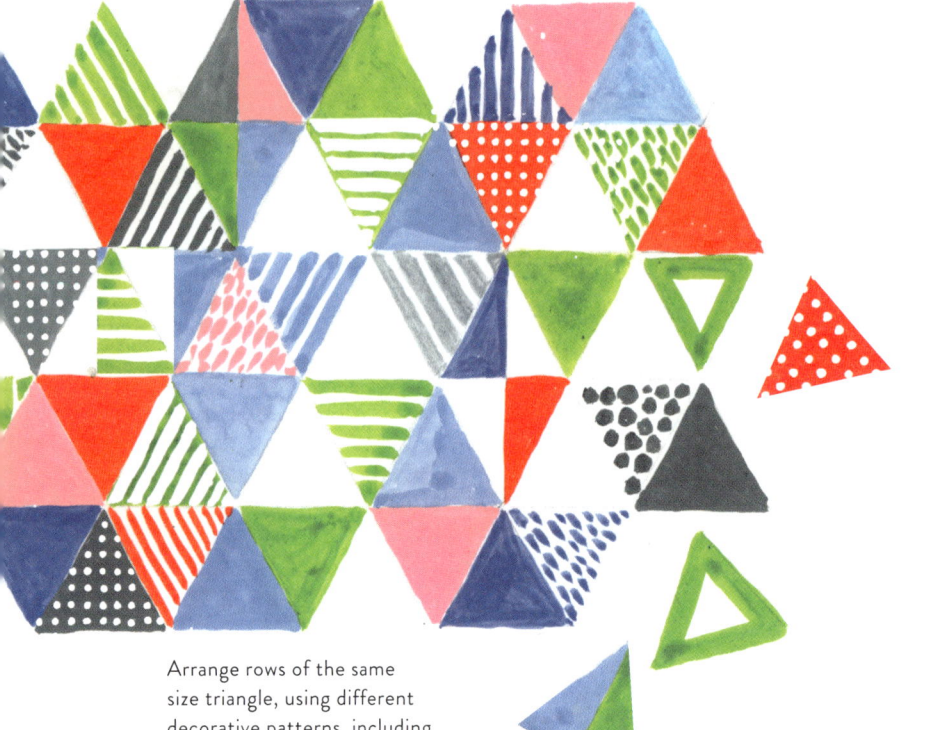

Arrange rows of the same size triangle, using different decorative patterns, including coloring a triangle into two halves.

Draw a basic background pattern of colored triangle shapes with wide gaps in between, then add a staggered pattern of stippled and lined triangles over the top.

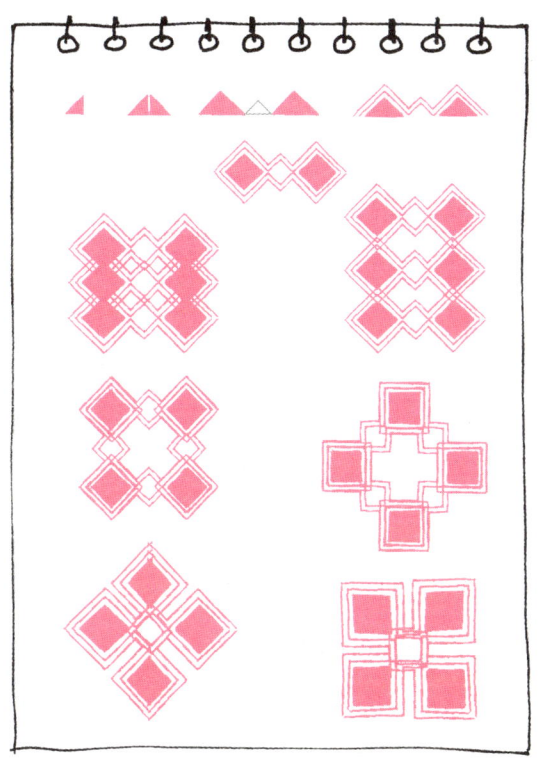

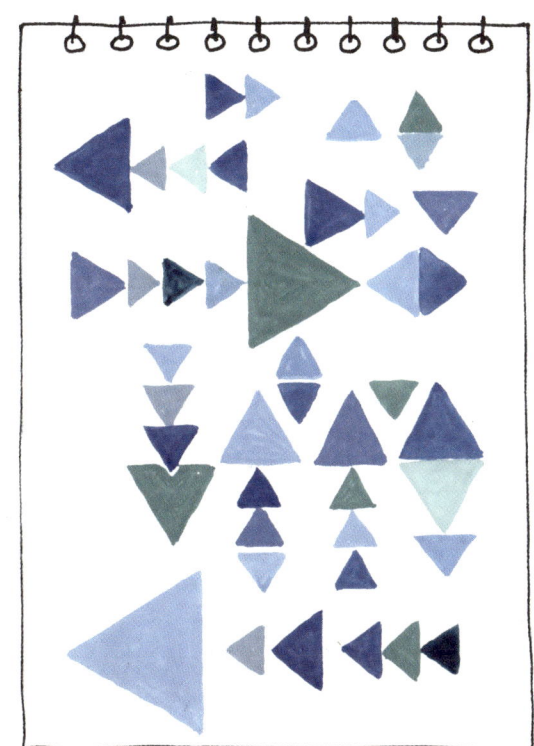

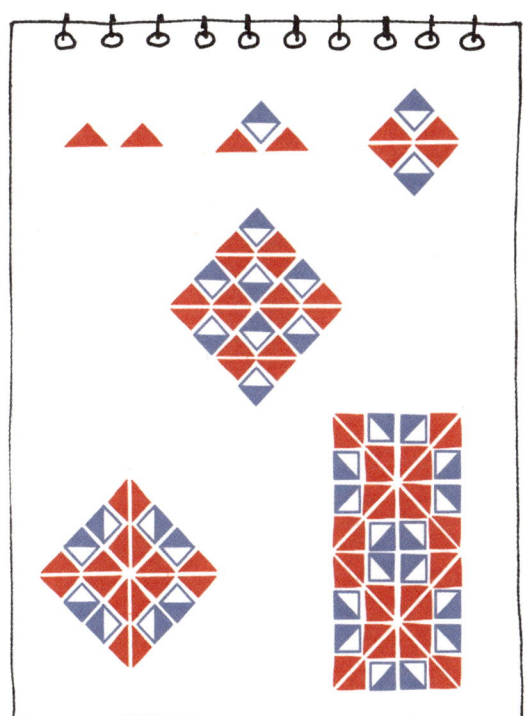

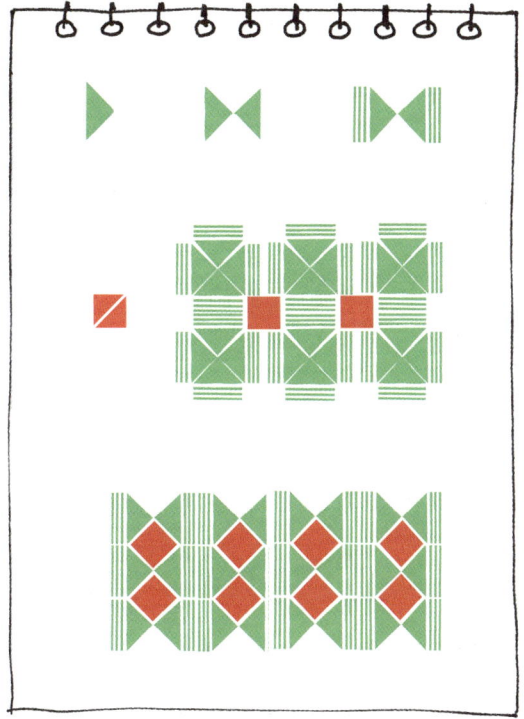

BOOK COVERS

Design your own note pad cover with these simple geometric shapes. Draw a pencil grid so they are roughly evenly spaced.

Circles and squares

You can use geometric shapes for patternmaking on their own, or you can mix the shapes, either by drawing them next to each other or by overlapping in various repeats.

If you are drawing them as outline shapes you can overlap them in various trellislike patterns (as in the middle book cover below), or having sections of circles fitting into squares (as in the collage on the opposite page).

Acrylic marker on colored paper.

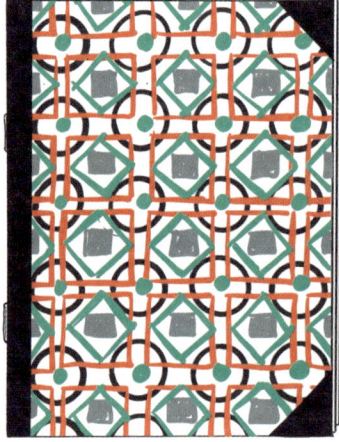

Felt tips on white paper.

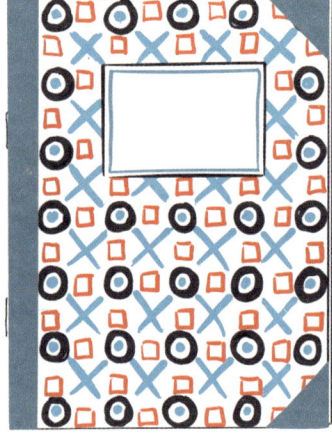

Felt tips on white paper.

Little booklet covers
These are about 3.5 x 5 inches. You can enlarge them to wrap around whatever size softcover notebook you have. You could even make your own blank book using sheets of paper to fold, trim, and staple.

The spine and corners can either be drawn and colored as part of your design, or you could glue on extra colored paper to protect the edges of the cover. Make sure the paper you add is not too thick and can fold neatly.

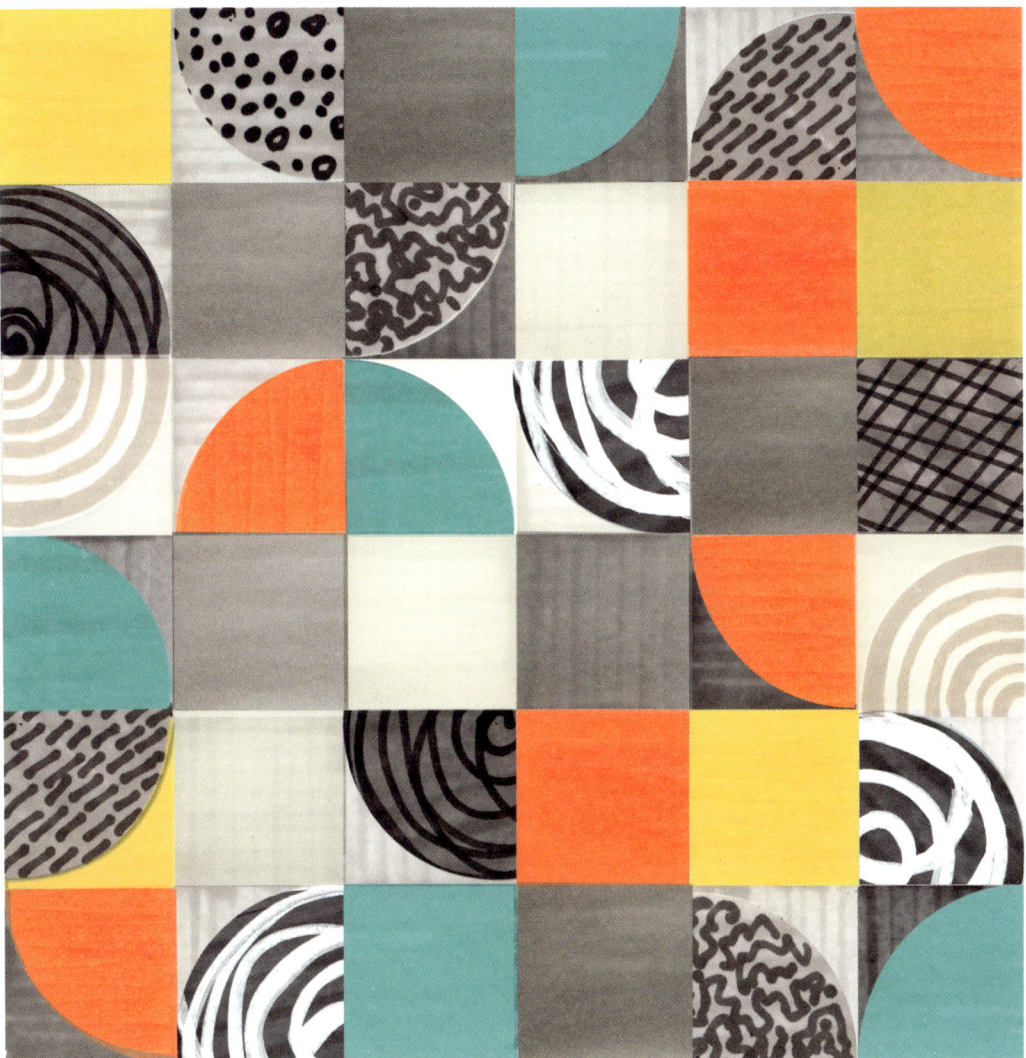

This collage could be for a larger book cover or for a small piece of wall art. The size of each square depends on how comfortable you are at creating areas of color with professional alcohol-based marker pens. Use special bleedproof marker paper to help the flat areas look smoother.

Draw areas of color and decorate some with patterns. Then cut out squares and circles to the same width/radius. I used a craft circle cutter but you could draw circles and cut with scissors. Assemble and glue (see page 189) to a backing sheet of paper.

Note: If you don't have alcohol-based marker pens, you can use anything else.

Marker paper

Non marker paper

For the white circles, use an acrylic marker pen

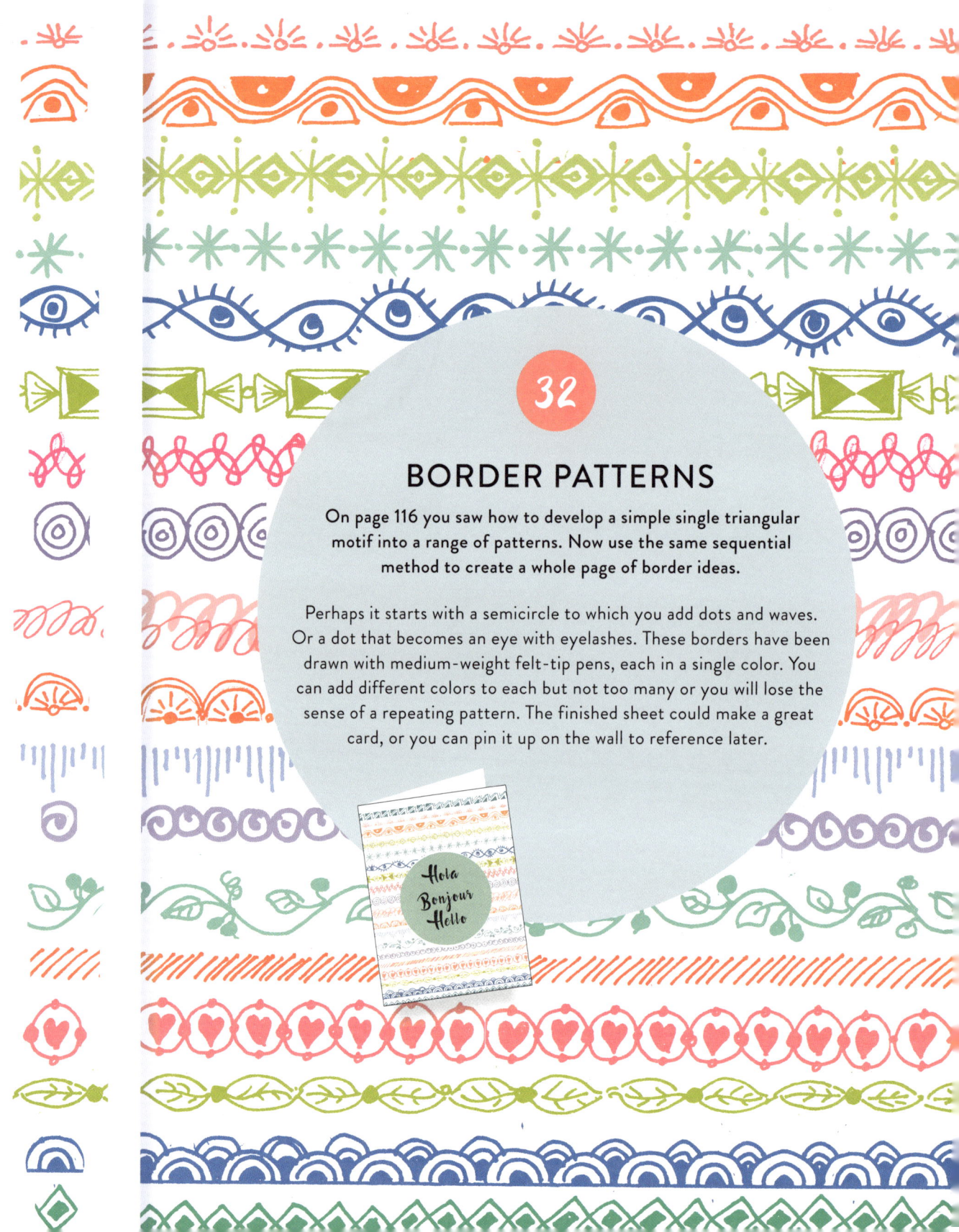

BORDER PATTERNS

32

On page 116 you saw how to develop a simple single triangular motif into a range of patterns. Now use the same sequential method to create a whole page of border ideas.

Perhaps it starts with a semicircle to which you add dots and waves. Or a dot that becomes an eye with eyelashes. These borders have been drawn with medium-weight felt-tip pens, each in a single color. You can add different colors to each but not too many or you will lose the sense of a repeating pattern. The finished sheet could make a great card, or you can pin it up on the wall to reference later.

Hola Bonjour Hello

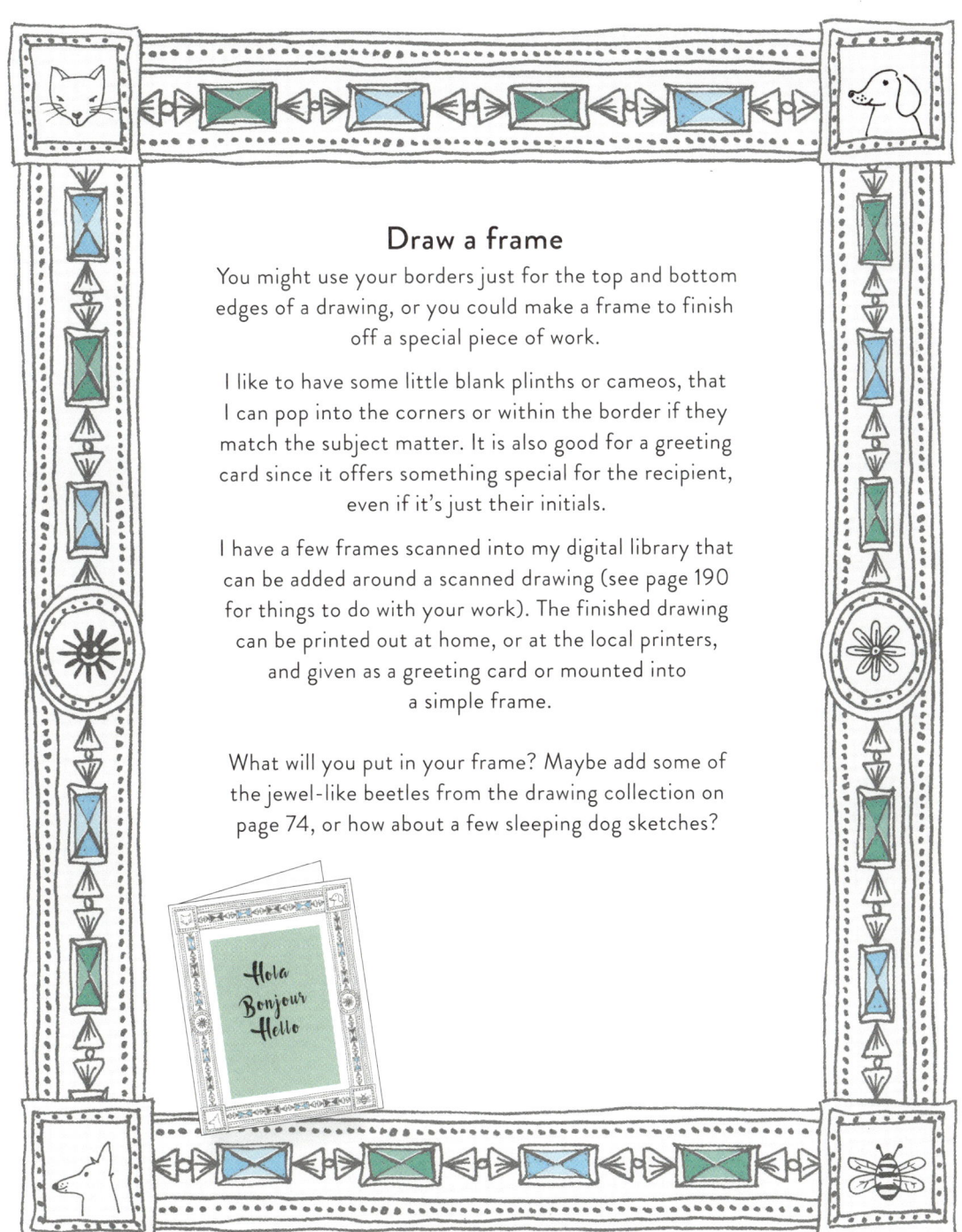

Draw a frame

You might use your borders just for the top and bottom edges of a drawing, or you could make a frame to finish off a special piece of work.

I like to have some little blank plinths or cameos, that I can pop into the corners or within the border if they match the subject matter. It is also good for a greeting card since it offers something special for the recipient, even if it's just their initials.

I have a few frames scanned into my digital library that can be added around a scanned drawing (see page 190 for things to do with your work). The finished drawing can be printed out at home, or at the local printers, and given as a greeting card or mounted into a simple frame.

What will you put in your frame? Maybe add some of the jewel-like beetles from the drawing collection on page 74, or how about a few sleeping dog sketches?

Hola
Bonjour
Hello

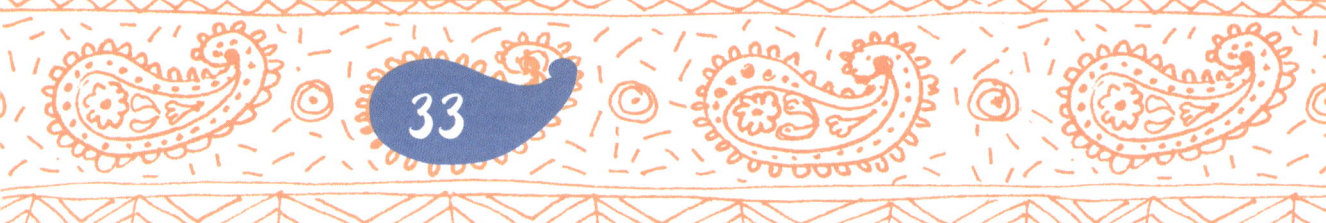

33

PAISLEY PATTERN SHAPES

There is something very satisfying about the organic teardrop shape of the paisley motif. It has a history going back to 200CE and was used in textiles and ceramics in Persia (Iran). The teardrop paisley will hone your skills in drawing curved lines. Look online to select your favorite shapes and decorations to embellish your paisley (or decorate with contemporary patterns).

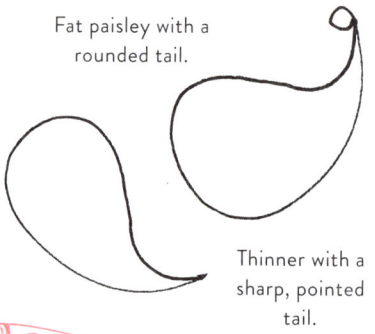

Fat paisley with a rounded tail.

Thinner with a sharp, pointed tail.

Smooth curves

Draw a few paisley outlines with a pencil to start. Then try with a medium-size fine-tip pen. Notice how the two edges have different diameter curves, giving the paisley its teardrop shape. To achieve a smooth edge, try "ghost drawing" above the paper to get a rough idea of the hand movement. Then position your hand so it is comfortable on the paper surface and start at the point, drawing around the whole shape before joining back at the point.

As most paisley patterns have a border, you will need to draw a second outline inside the first, keeping it as equidistant as you can!

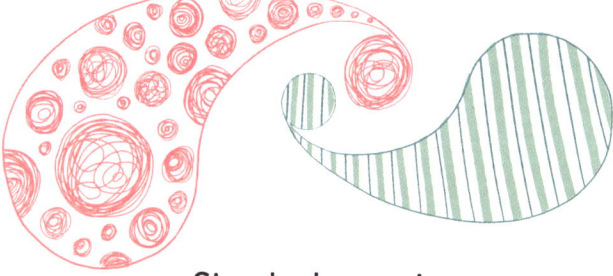

Simple decoration

Add some simple decorations. Here they are all drawn in one color. You could draw each motif in different colors, or you could color in the blank areas inside each of the little shapes.

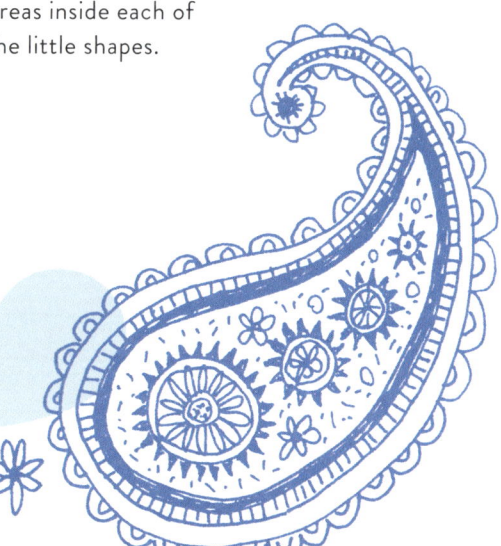

Just five motifs make up the blue paisley.

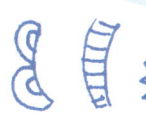

122

Pattern border

These paisley teardops have a border pattern (right). It works well with little dots or flecks in the background. For alternative ways of repeating or orienting the pattern see page 170.

see page 170.

The motifs are mostly petal or tear drop shapes.

Traditional paisley

For inspiration, look at how traditional craftspeople drew border patterns and created irregular shapes on the interior space of the paisley. The floral decorations can have a fully open flower in the wider top section, then smaller buds and leaves in the narrower part. Since the motifs all repeat, it is not complicated to construct—you can see all the individual parts of the motifs shown for the paisley lily (above, right). Once drawn you can add color.

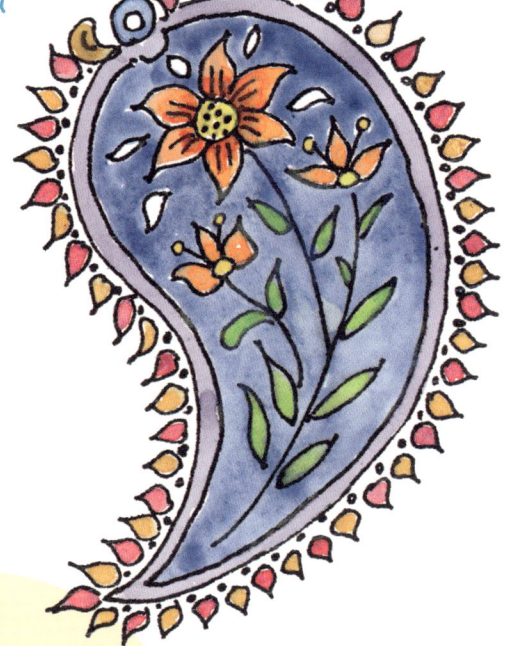

You could place the motifs off-center and even break out of the edge of the teardrop, giving a more contemporary or retro design.

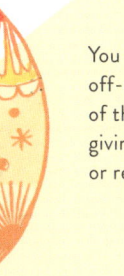

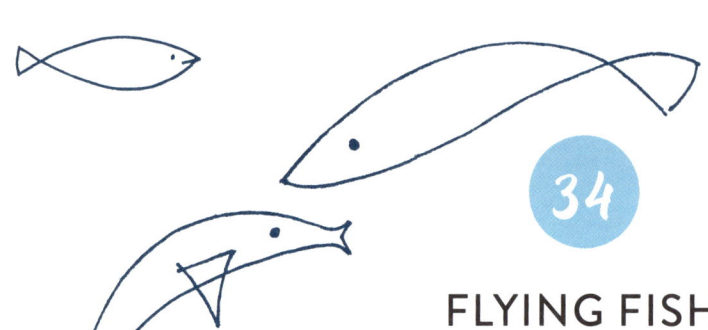

34

FLYING FISH

Draw some simple fish shapes. The sketches above started as horizontal fish, then gradually morphed into a curve, giving me the idea of waves and jumping fish.

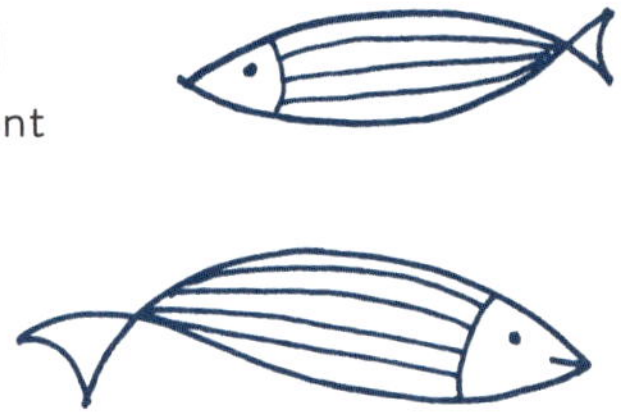

The sketchbook pages on the right show some of the initial drawings (there were a couple more pages). Don't be impatient and think you will draw the motifs correctly on your initial attempts. Sometimes, the first quick, unconscious sketch could be the best; other times you need to keep experimenting and refining your drawing. Try out different patterns inside the fish shape. Most of the examples reference fish scales or follow the contour of the fish's circumference.

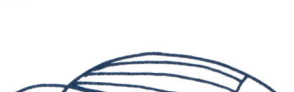

You can also arrange the fish in various pattern repeats (see page 170). Here, the pattern is just alternating rows of the fish flying in opposite directions, but you could draw a random pattern as in the goldfish bowl on page 127.

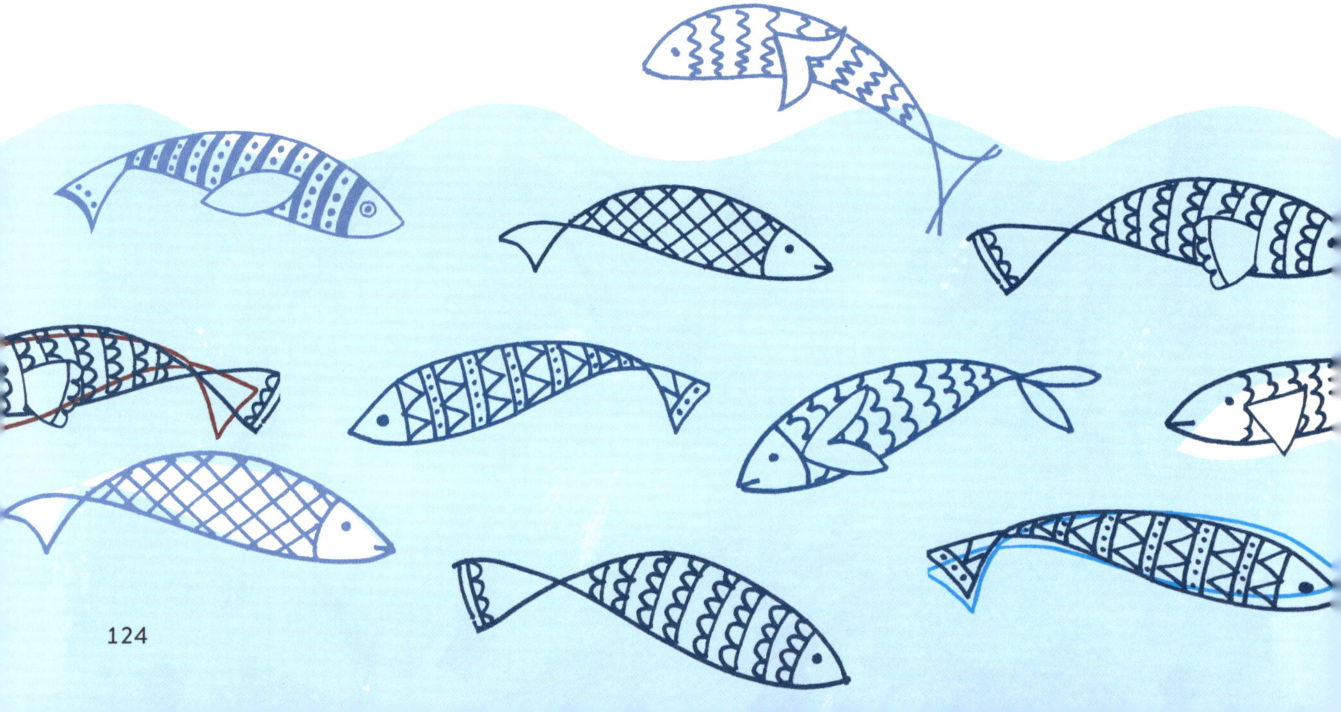

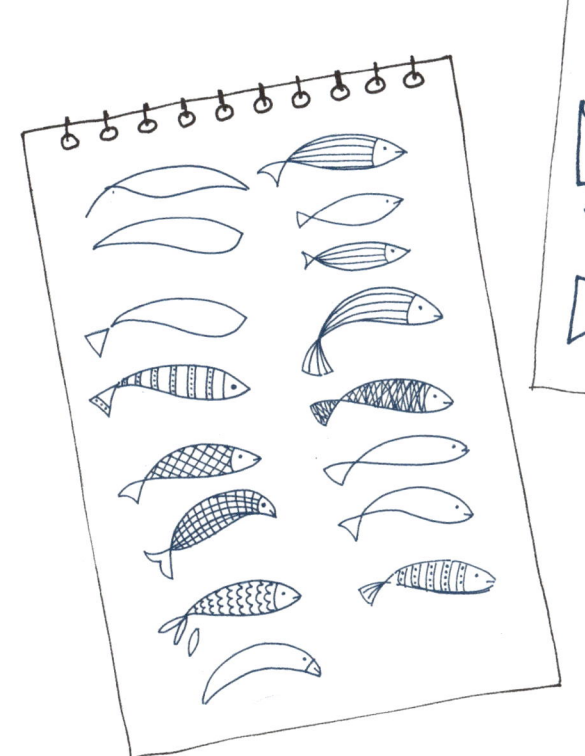

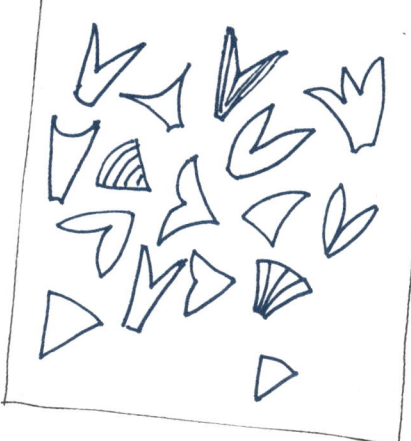

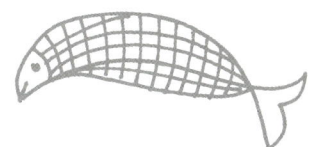

Doodle fish
The sketchbook pages show lots of initial sketches for shapes, patterns, tails, and fins. Work quickly so the body curves are drawn with one or two strokes, like the continuous line drawings on page 146. Tails can be included in the initial lines or drawn at the end with the fin.

As you can see, looking at the banana fish above, the sketches don't always work!

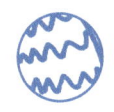 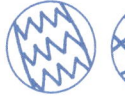 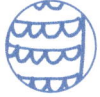

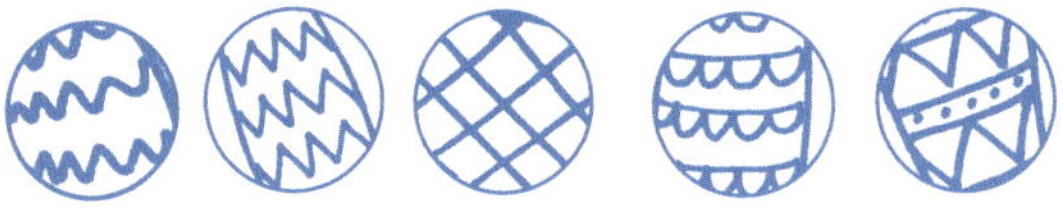

Zigzags, crisscrosses, or looped rows are a good starting point for decorating your fish.

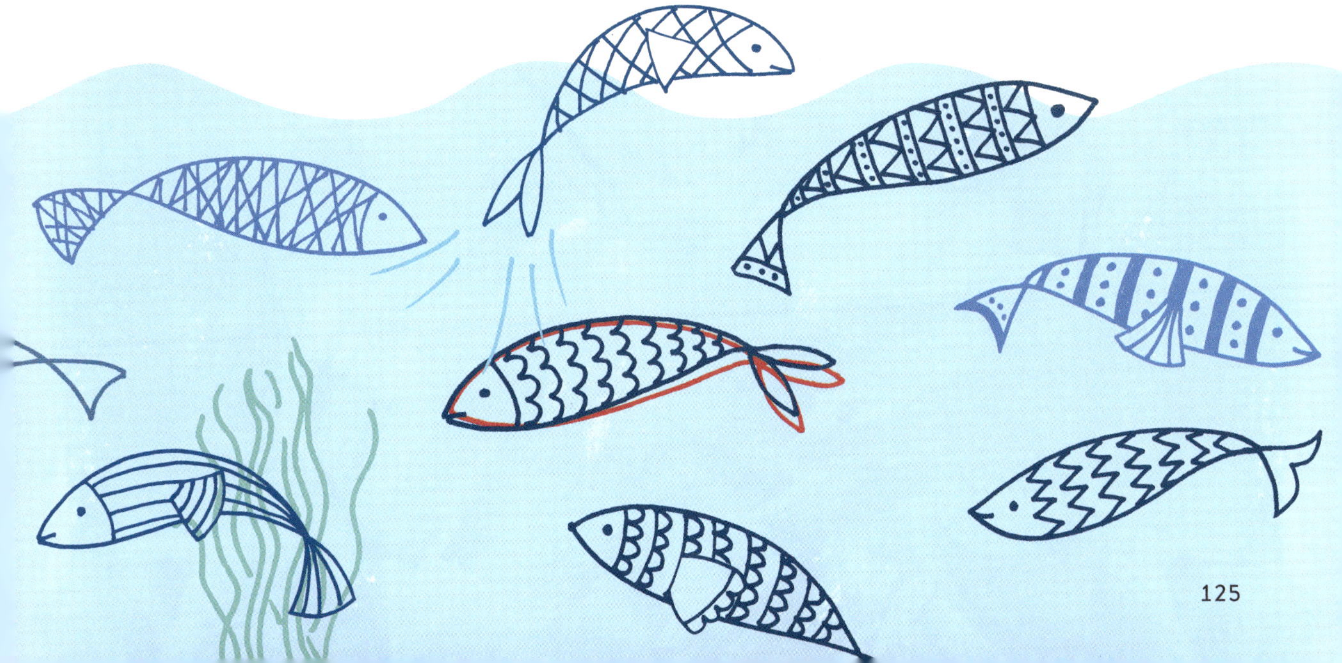

Fins and fishy tails

The shape, size, position, and decoration all give you extra options to play with.

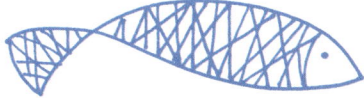

The tail might simply extend the decoration from the body of the fish . . .

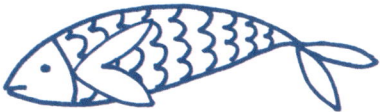

Or the fin and tail could coordinate and be the same shape . . .

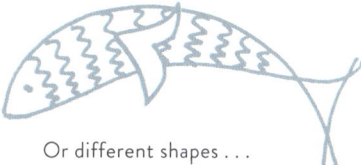

Or different shapes . . .

Or just have a matching decorative edge pattern.

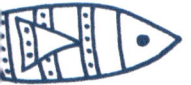

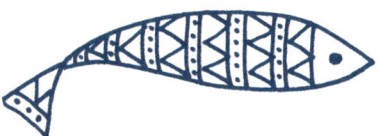

How many fins? This fish looks sleek with no fins.

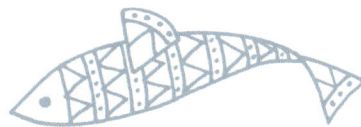

Adding one gives more options on shape and decoration.

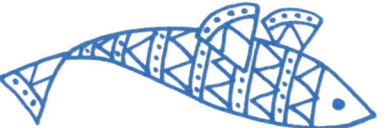

Adding two gives extra dimension so the fish is less like a profile.

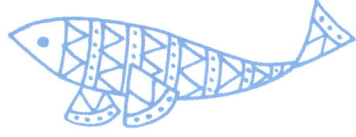

The fins could go above or below.

More color?

You could keep the colors a simple range of blues, or spice it up with orange for goldfish, like in the bowl on the right.

The decorative elements give many opportunities for adding more jewel colors.

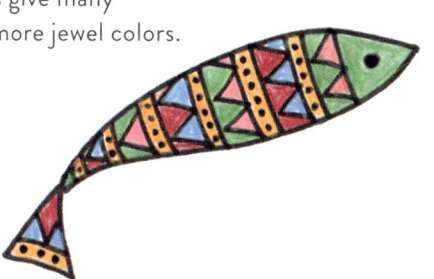

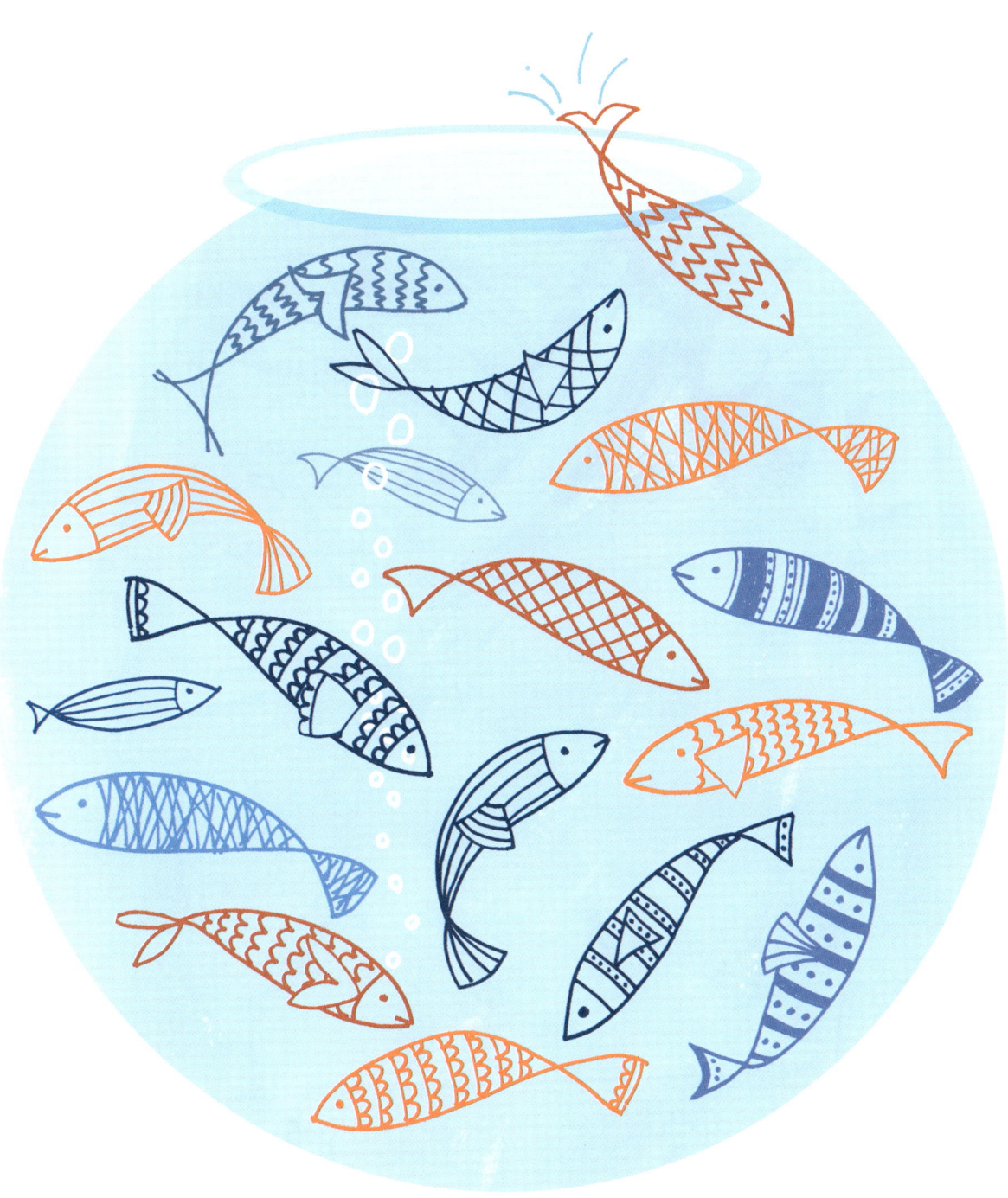

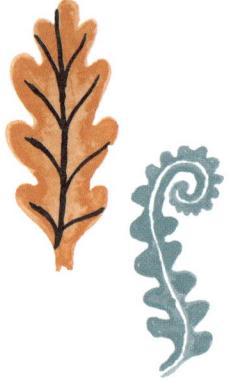
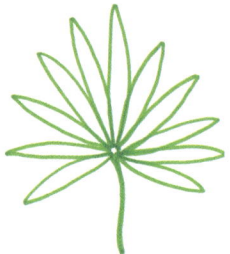

35

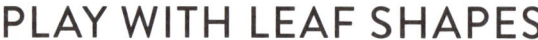

PLAY WITH LEAF SHAPES

I love the organic nature of leaves—and they don't have to be drawn perfectly! Even in nature leaves have irregularities. Draw a few to see which ones you like best. I enjoyed the simplicity of the long, lozenge-shape willow leaf below, and the wavy-edged oak leaf on the right.

These were all drawn with watercolor pencils or watercolor markers. Draw a strong outline shape, then either leave it as a simple outline or, using a brush, add some water and blend the color away from the line. (Make sure to use a paper that can take water washes—see page 187).

This process of investigating and playing with a shape can be done with many natural objects, a shell, fruit, insects, or even something mechanical such as cogs and wheels.

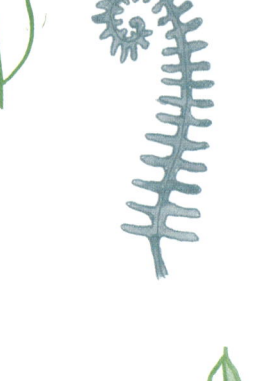
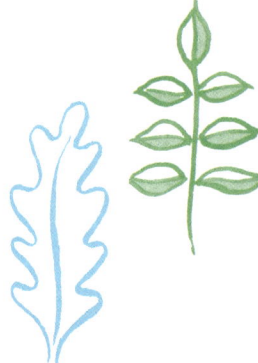

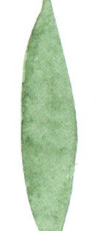

Willow leaf

You might think the simple lozenge shape of the willow would be a bit dull for making patterns but you'd be wrong . . . here are just a few. You could try a different range of colors, they don't have to be green!

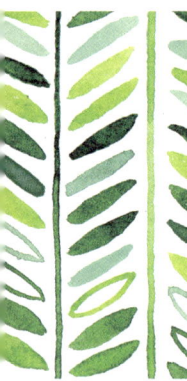
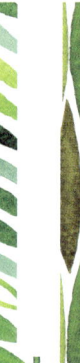
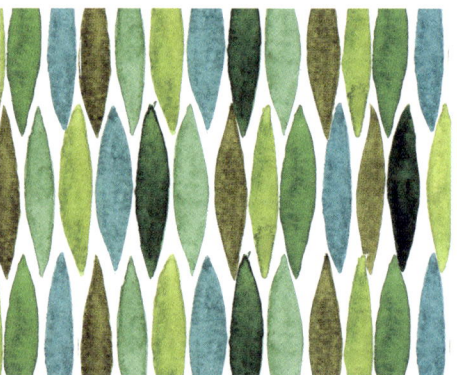
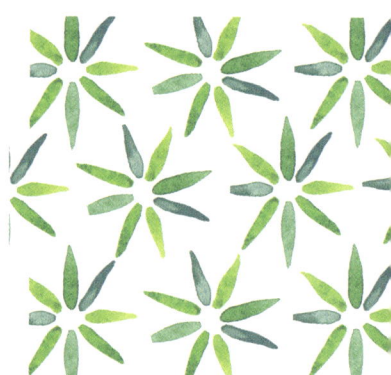

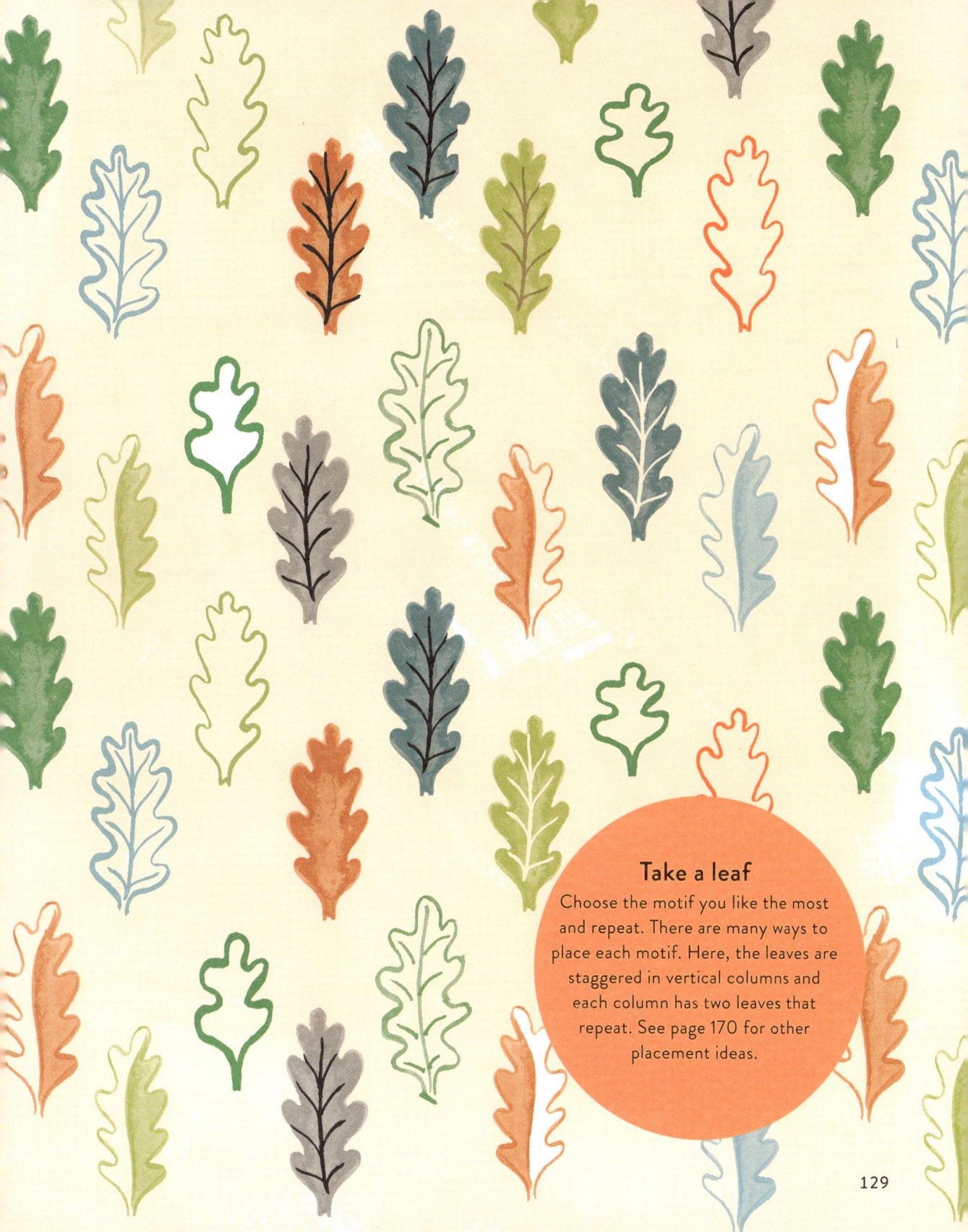

Take a leaf

Choose the motif you like the most and repeat. There are many ways to place each motif. Here, the leaves are staggered in vertical columns and each column has two leaves that repeat. See page 170 for other placement ideas.

PLAY WITH FLORALS

Flower images are the most popular motifs for creating patterns. Find inspiration on textiles, wallpapers, ceramics, and stationery and start planning by making rough sketches or doodles. The patterns here are made from various flower motifs and randomly arranged. (If you want to create a repeat pattern, see page 170).

Consider viewpoint
Do you want to draw the flower heads so they look like stars (above) or in profile (right and below). Consider the spacing between each, and whether you want the sizes to be the same or to vary. Small ones can be useful to fill gaps.

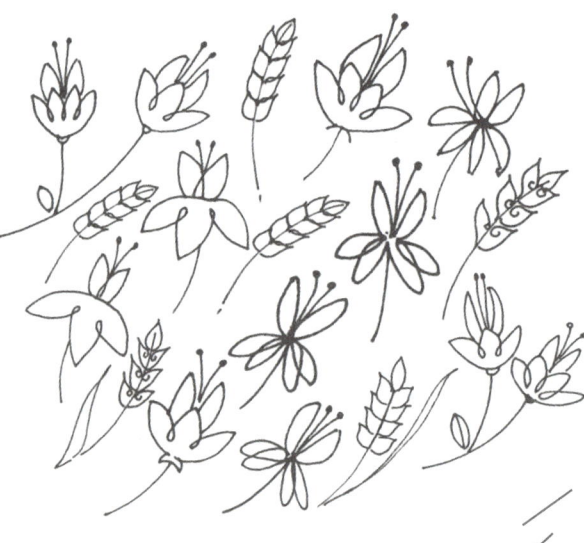

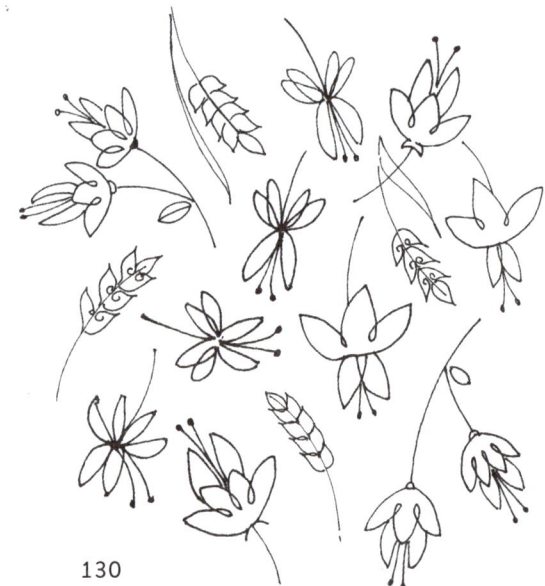

Although it is more difficult to organize than an overhead design, the stalks above create a sense of movement within the pattern. The motifs could be placed in the same direction as above, or scattered so the pattern looks the same when viewed from any direction (as left).

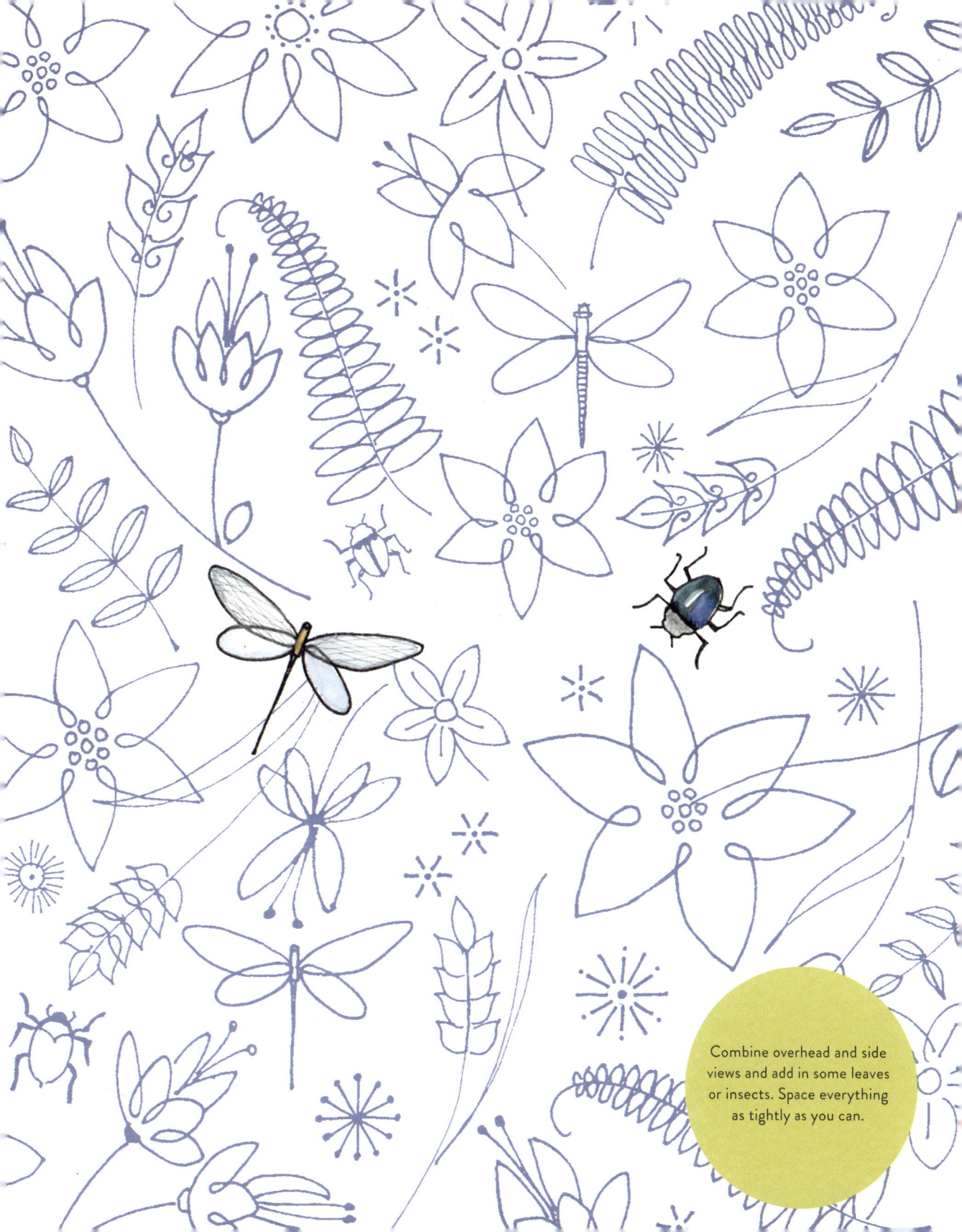

Combine overhead and side
views and add in some leaves
or insects. Space everything
as tightly as you can.

Try different colorways

When you buy a fabric, generally there is a
choice of different colors for one pattern.
This is called a colorway.

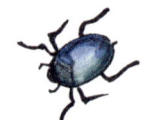

Choosing your colors is an enjoyable challenge
because the options can be endless. You might decide
to keep the colors realistic; if not, look at groups of
colors on fabrics that you like. Make little squares
of colors to help you make a choice. If it's a simple
pattern, try creating a few different colorways.

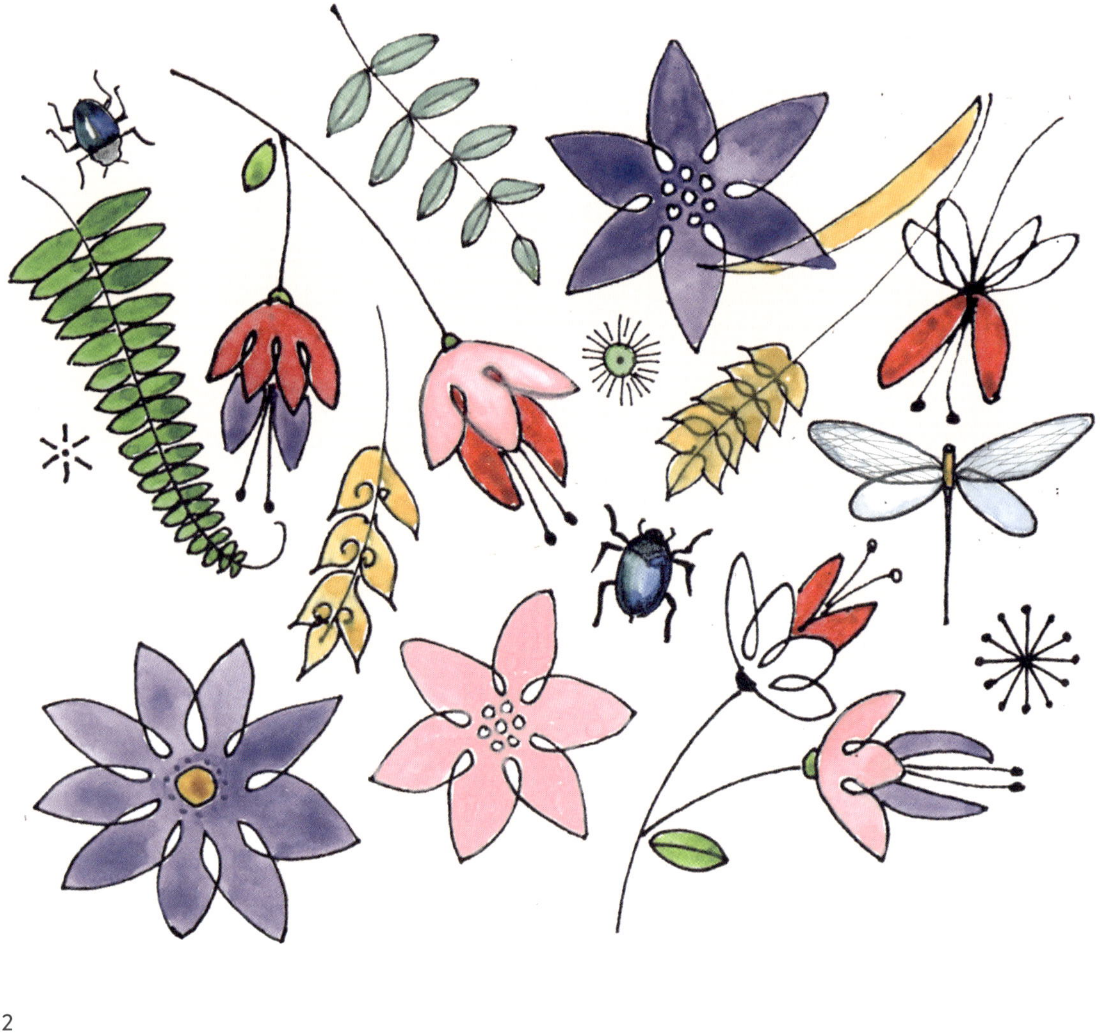

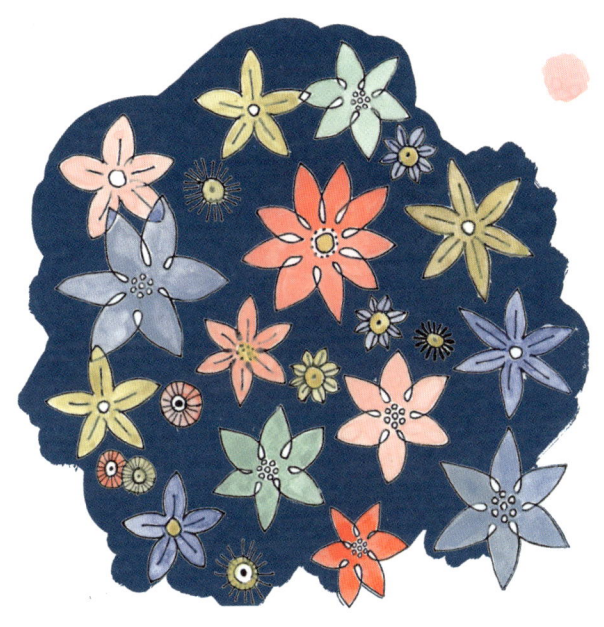

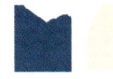

Dark or light background?

You can leave the background white, or you might choose a neutral cream or gray. You could also pick a color from the pattern and use a very pale version of it, or something more dramatic such as dark navy or black.

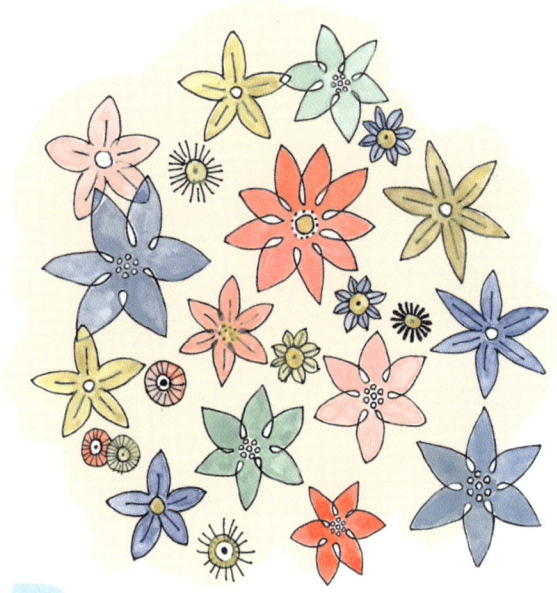

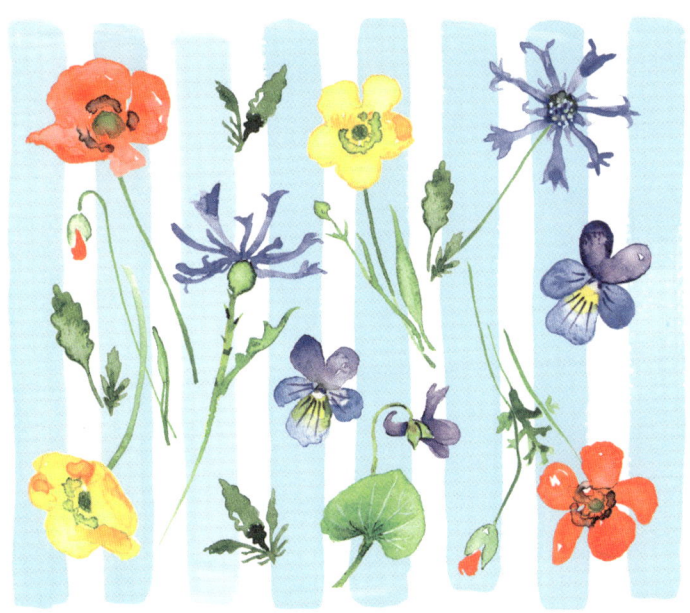

Pattern backgrounds

Look at fabrics to see what is possible, including stripes, spots, abstract organic shapes or even large geometrics. Experiment and see what works for you.

37 LIKE DRAWING PATTERNS?

As well as making your own patterns, you can include observed patterns in your drawings. I love drawing patterns on location—when I see some stripes or unusual patterns I want to open my sketchbook. You can add the found patterns on your drawings of clothing or furnishings, or you could add in the odd imagined stripe to a blazer or a floral print to a dress. Patterns can even be seen in the repeating architectural details on a building, or in agricultural landscapes with the visual rhythms of a vineyard or field of sunflowers.

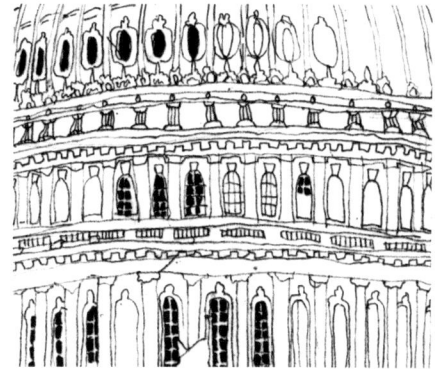

Pattern for shape

A shape is normally defined by an outline, or made by a tonal or color difference between the shape and its surrounding background. Pattern can be used to the same effect. In the sketch below, the cat was drawn with a fineliner, then the patterns on the tartan blanket and embroidered cushion were added. The patterns behind describe the shape of the sleeping cat.

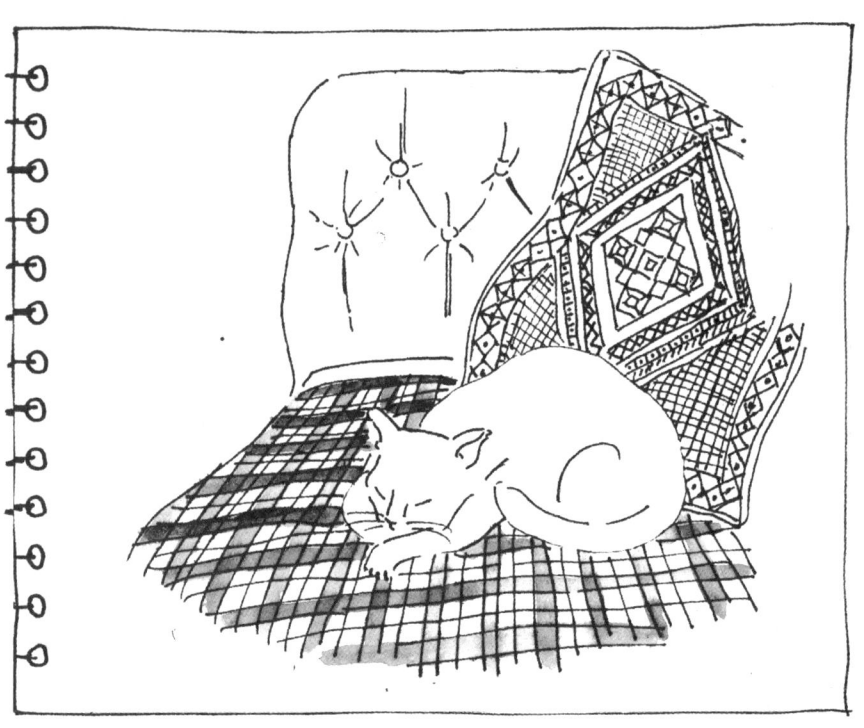

Flat or angled patterns?
The checks of the tartan blanket are drawn in perspective (see page 58). The checked pattern angles away to the end of the sofa, giving the drawing dimension. If you wanted a more abstract composition, you could draw both the rug and the cushion with flat patterns.

Enjoy a fold

Fabrics will fold or join at seams, cushions will overlap, and pockets will bulge. This gives you the opportunity to stagger the pattern. This offset can help explain the curve of an arm or the shape of a pocket.

For the knitting stitch pattern see page 136.

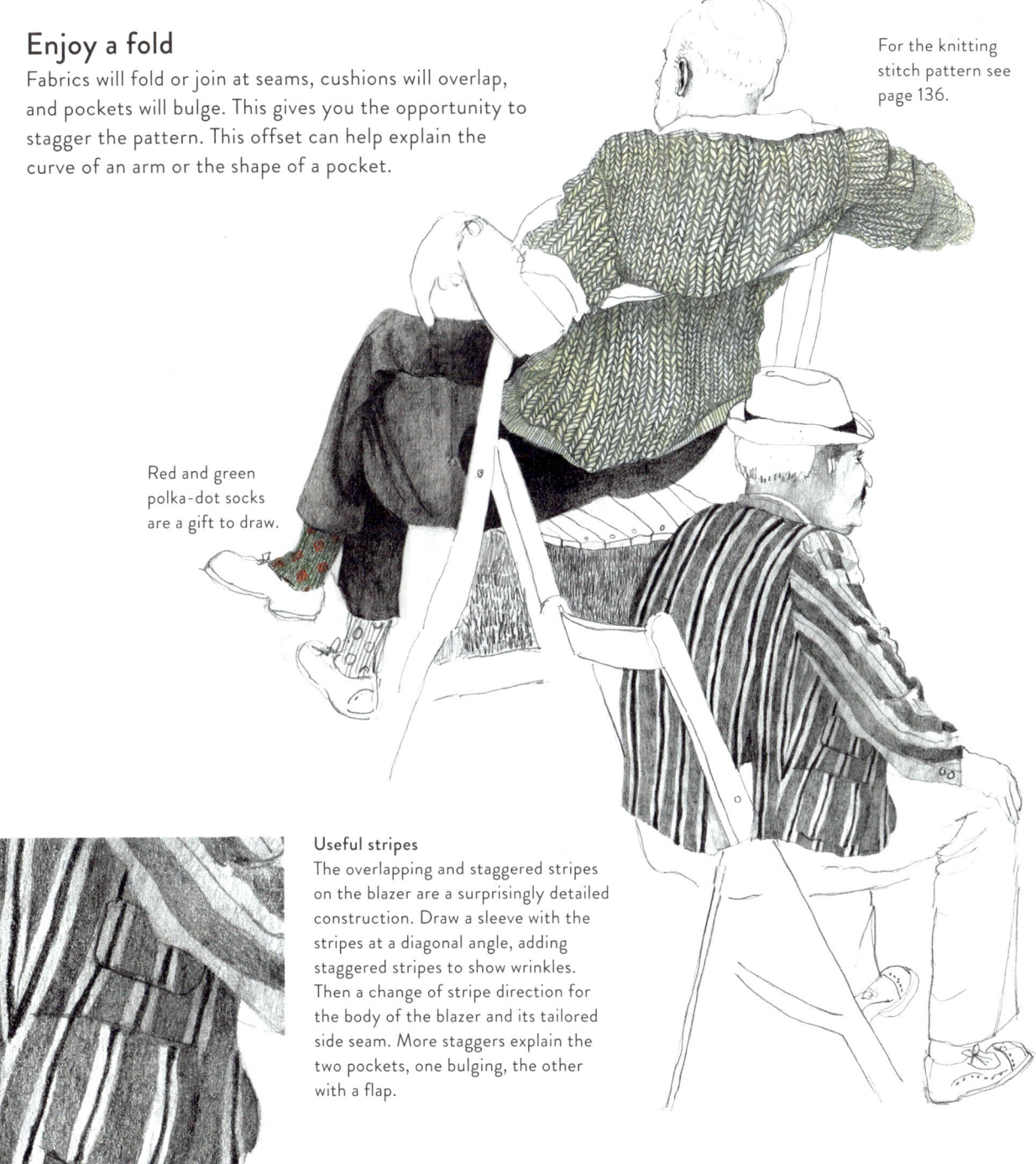

Red and green polka-dot socks are a gift to draw.

Useful stripes

The overlapping and staggered stripes on the blazer are a surprisingly detailed construction. Draw a sleeve with the stripes at a diagonal angle, adding staggered stripes to show wrinkles. Then a change of stripe direction for the body of the blazer and its tailored side seam. More staggers explain the two pockets, one bulging, the other with a flap.

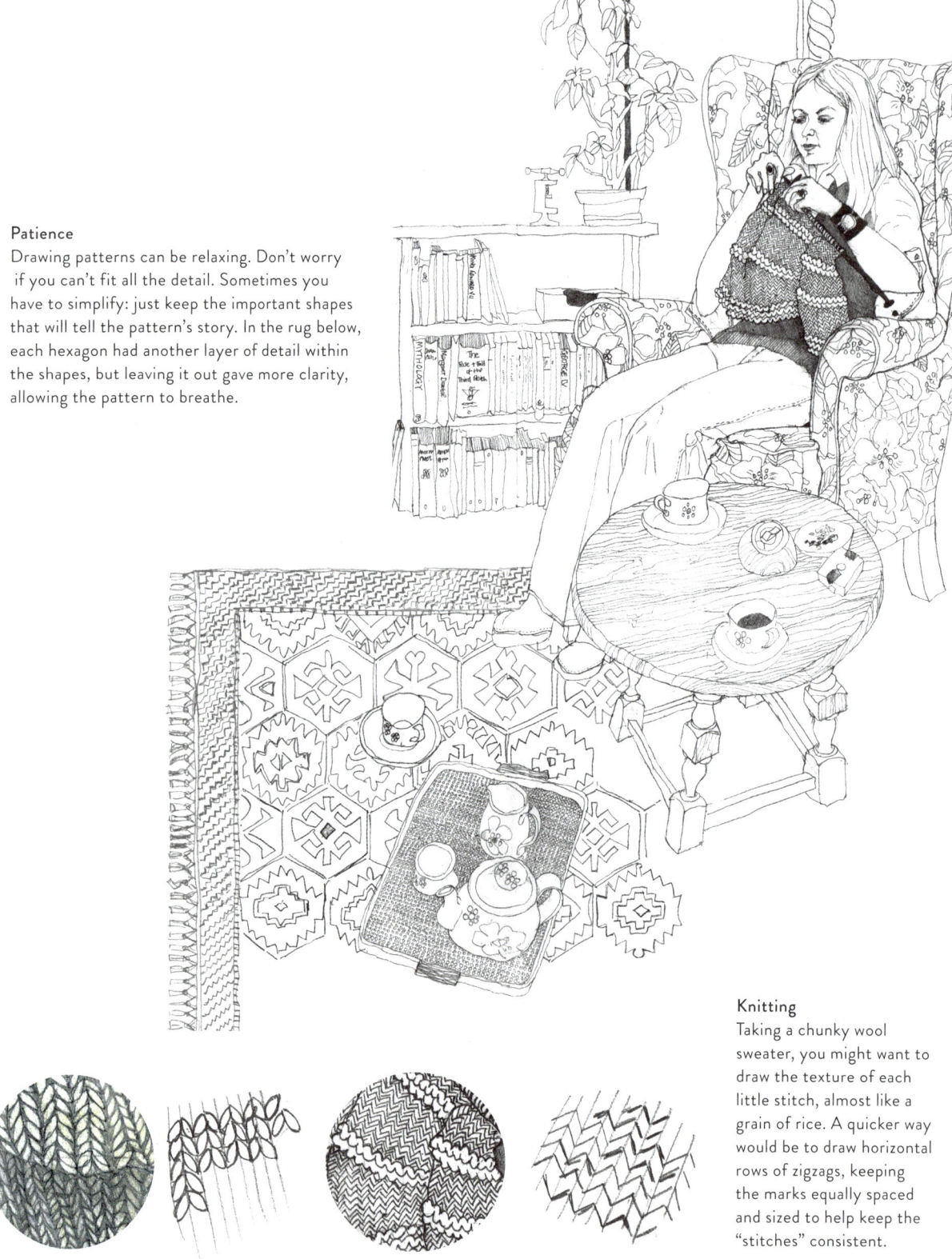

Patience

Drawing patterns can be relaxing. Don't worry if you can't fit all the detail. Sometimes you have to simplify: just keep the important shapes that will tell the pattern's story. In the rug below, each hexagon had another layer of detail within the shapes, but leaving it out gave more clarity, allowing the pattern to breathe.

Knitting

Taking a chunky wool sweater, you might want to draw the texture of each little stitch, almost like a grain of rice. A quicker way would be to draw horizontal rows of zigzags, keeping the marks equally spaced and sized to help keep the "stitches" consistent.

Pattern perspective

Areas of pattern can be drawn in perspective if required. The motifs in the pattern become squashed as they recede, and in the distance will become indistinct. Or you can sketch the pattern flat from overhead. This can be easier and gives the drawing a more abstract quality, as in the drawing with the rug on the left.

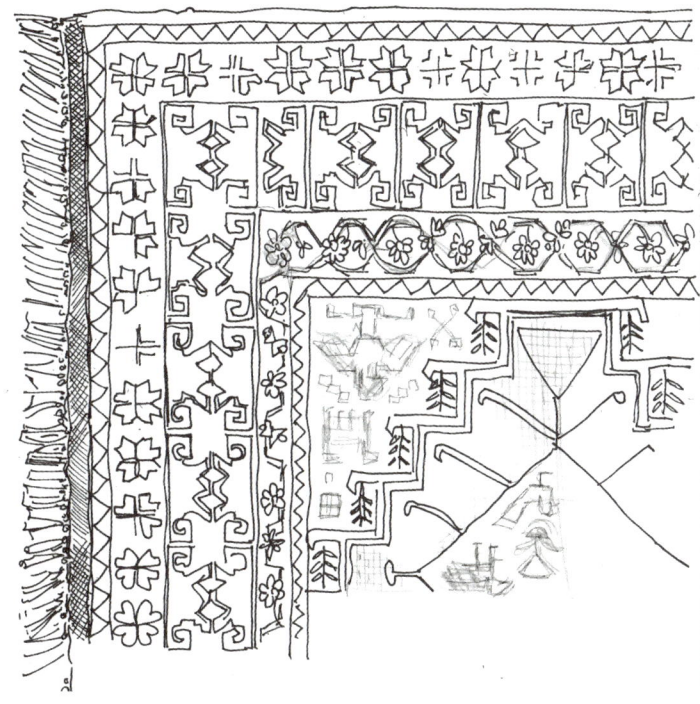

The border on this rug looks complex, but is made up from just four repeating elements.

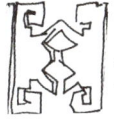 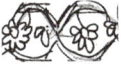 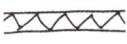

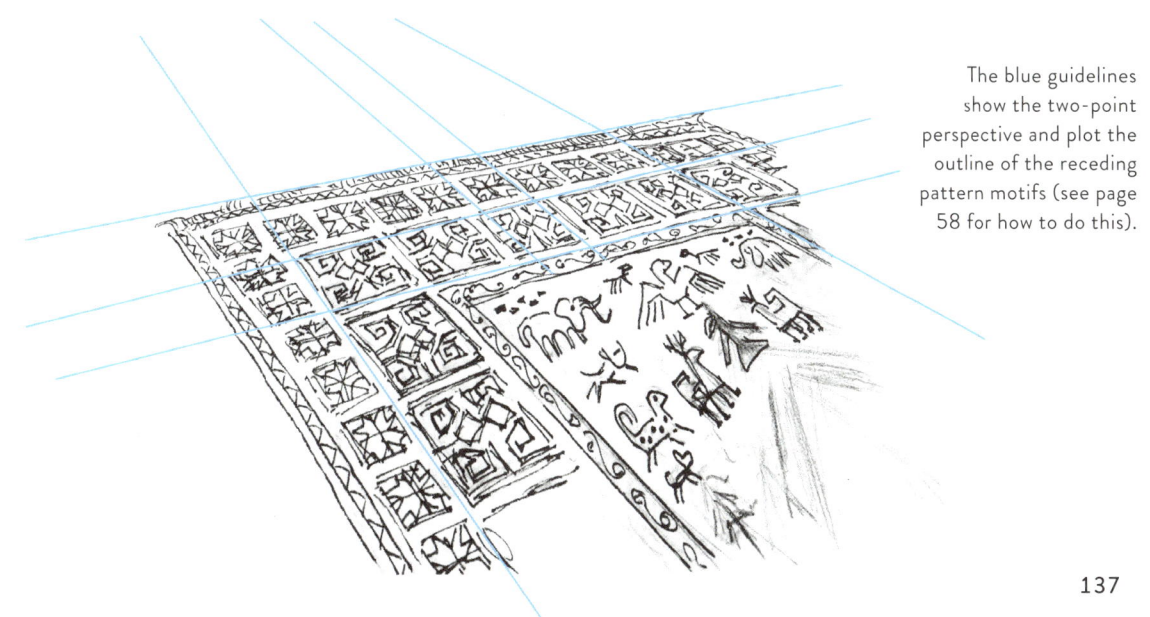

The blue guidelines show the two-point perspective and plot the outline of the receding pattern motifs (see page 58 for how to do this).

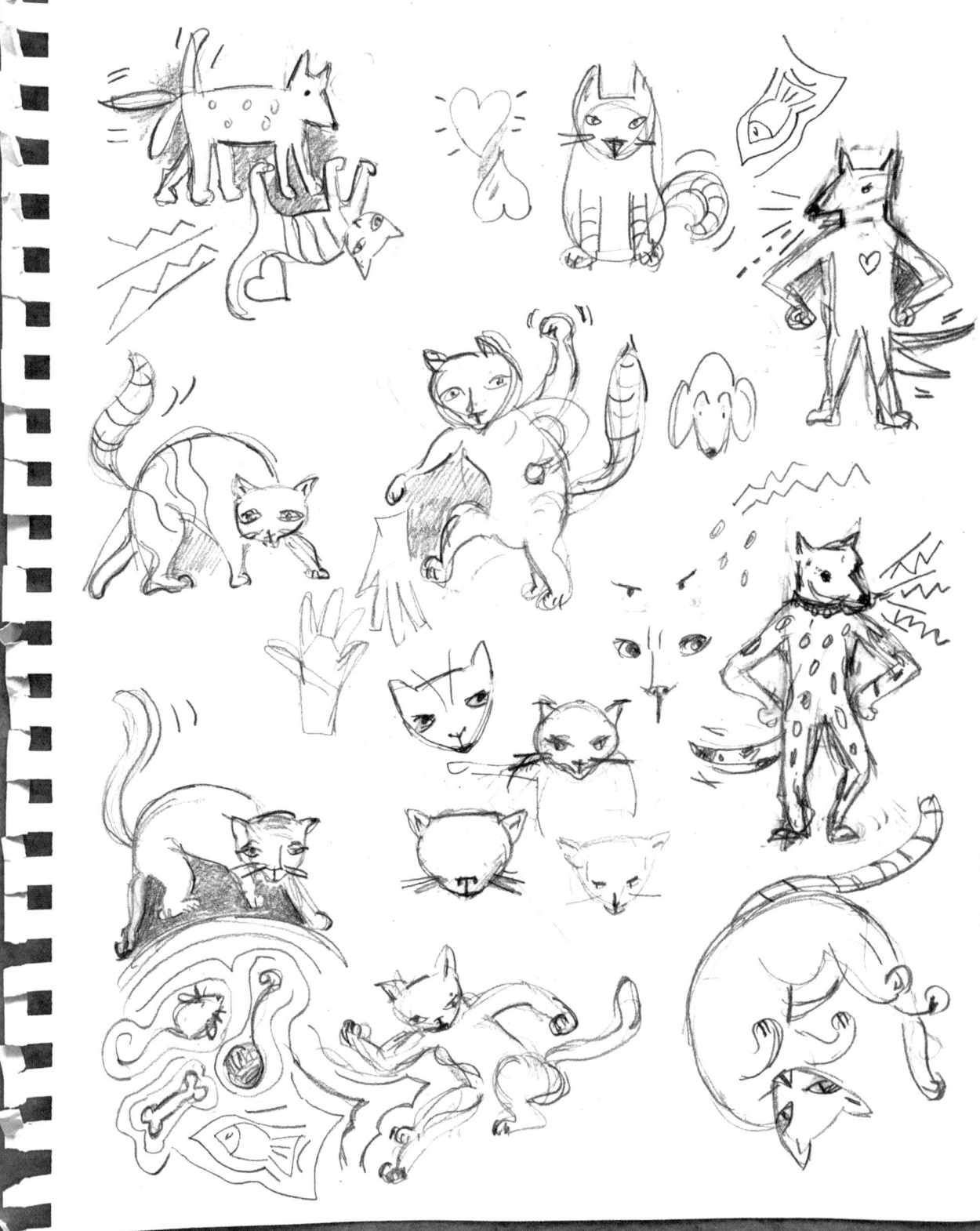

DOODLE SHAPES

Sometimes what starts off as some random doodling while watching a friend's
cat and dog at play can take on a life of its own.

The two simple sketches on the top left were the starting point. The pets were acting
in such an anthropomorphic way, it was a short step to picture each one standing on two
legs with attitude. A bit more doodling of fish and mice bottom left, and the idea for an
interlocking drawing with the motifs and repeating outlines emerged. You could use
different motifs, choosing something with an interesting outline shape. Remember you
are just as interested in the shapes in between the motifs as the motifs themselves.

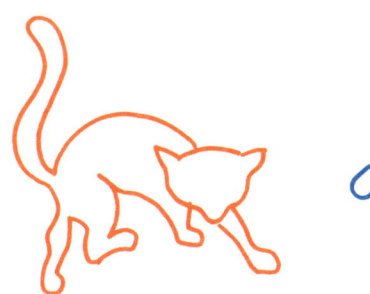
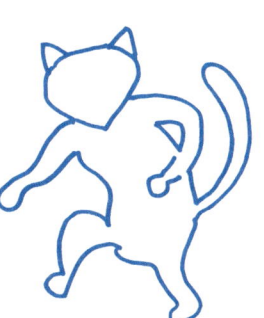
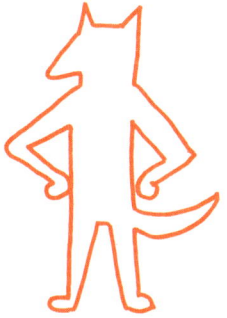
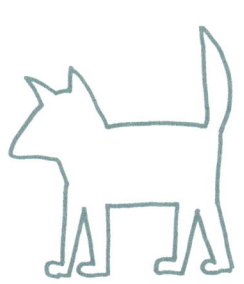

Make your positive shapes
In your sketchbook, make lots of drawings of the main characters you want
to include. Remember, you are concerned with the outline shapes, so think
ahead how you might fit the shapes together. A bit like a jigsaw.

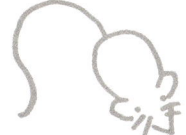
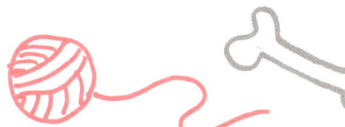
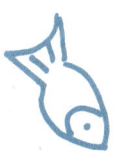
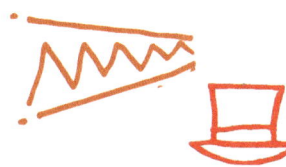

Create some mini motifs
You will need some smaller, interlocking motifs or patterns to fill
in the negative spaces.

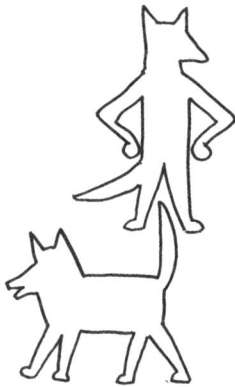

Experiment with interlocking the shapes
Look at various shapes and think how to put the tails, legs, and heads together. It is easier to work in smaller units with just two motifs, and then put the units together.

Draw or collage
To work out how to fit the elements together, you can draw a couple of each motif, cut them out close to the line, and experiment. Or just try sketching it all in position.

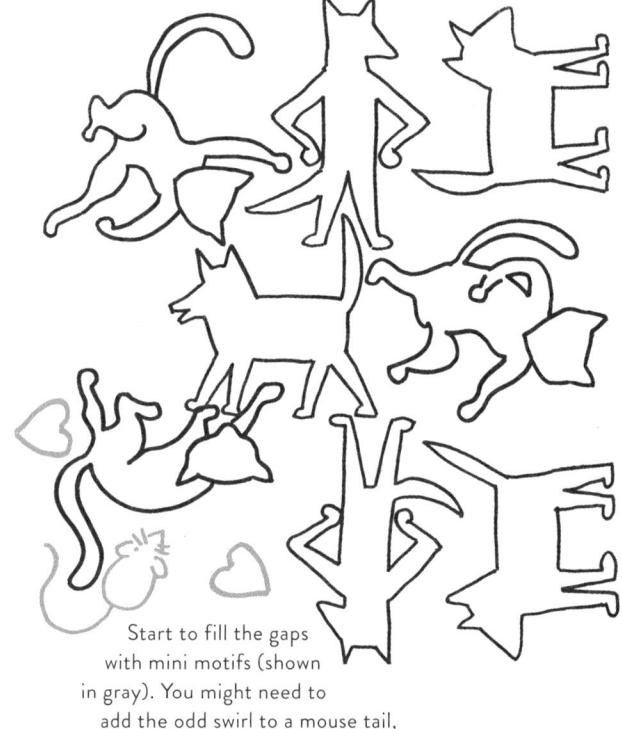

Start to fill the gaps with mini motifs (shown in gray). You might need to add the odd swirl to a mouse tail, like on the finished drawing (right).

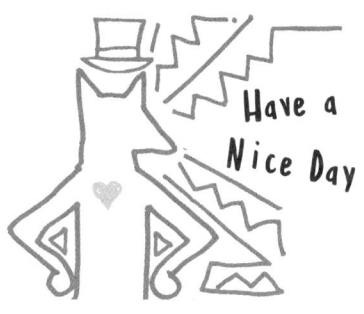

Finish by adding lines, diamonds, zigzags, or even some words.

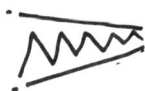

With some of the spaces, draw the negative shape and roughly outline it a couple of times.

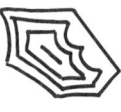

Add some color
Here, just three colors were used to keep it simple. All the cats are in orange, the dogs in brown, and the infill shapes and lines are red. The hearts were filled in with shades of pink.

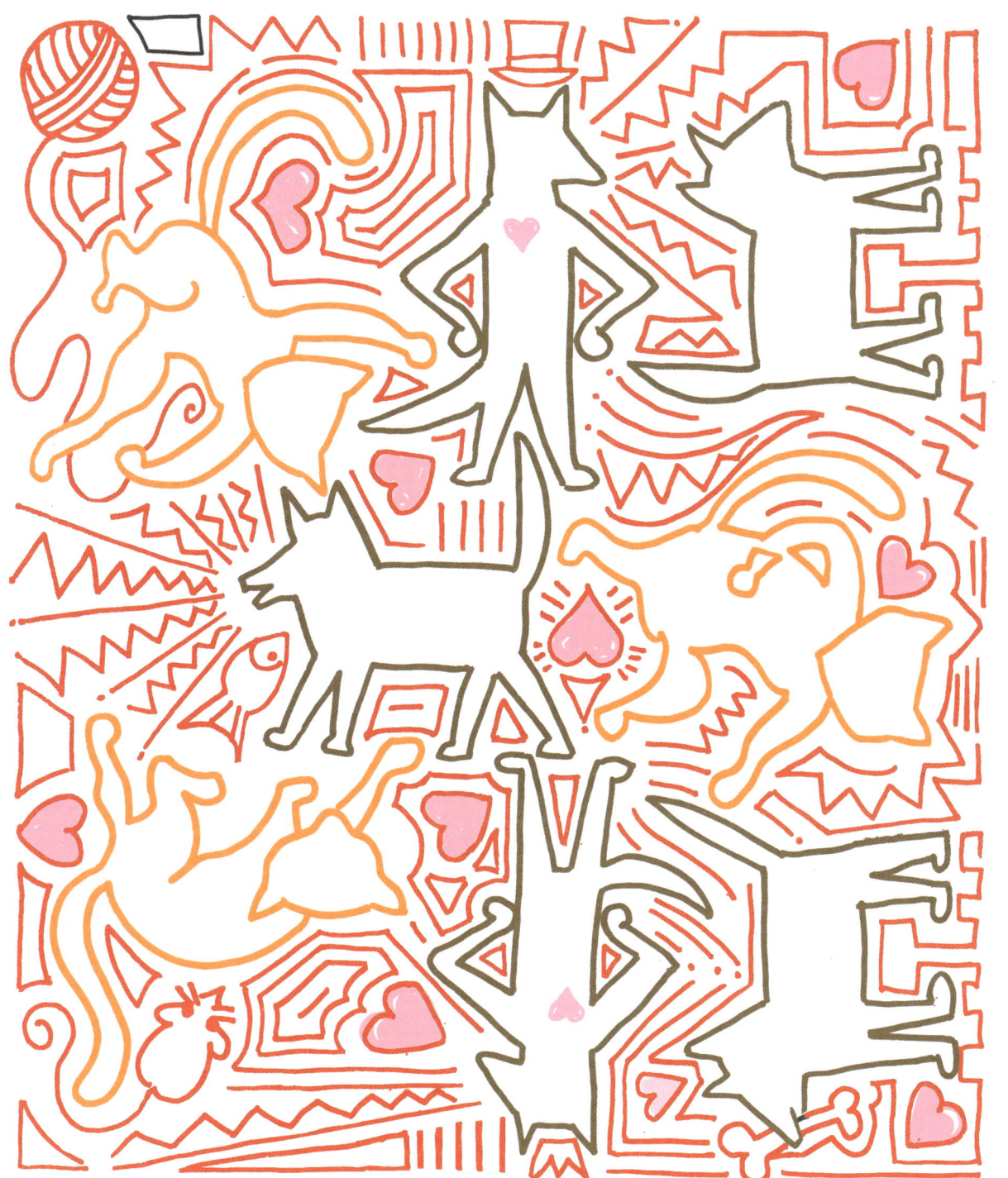

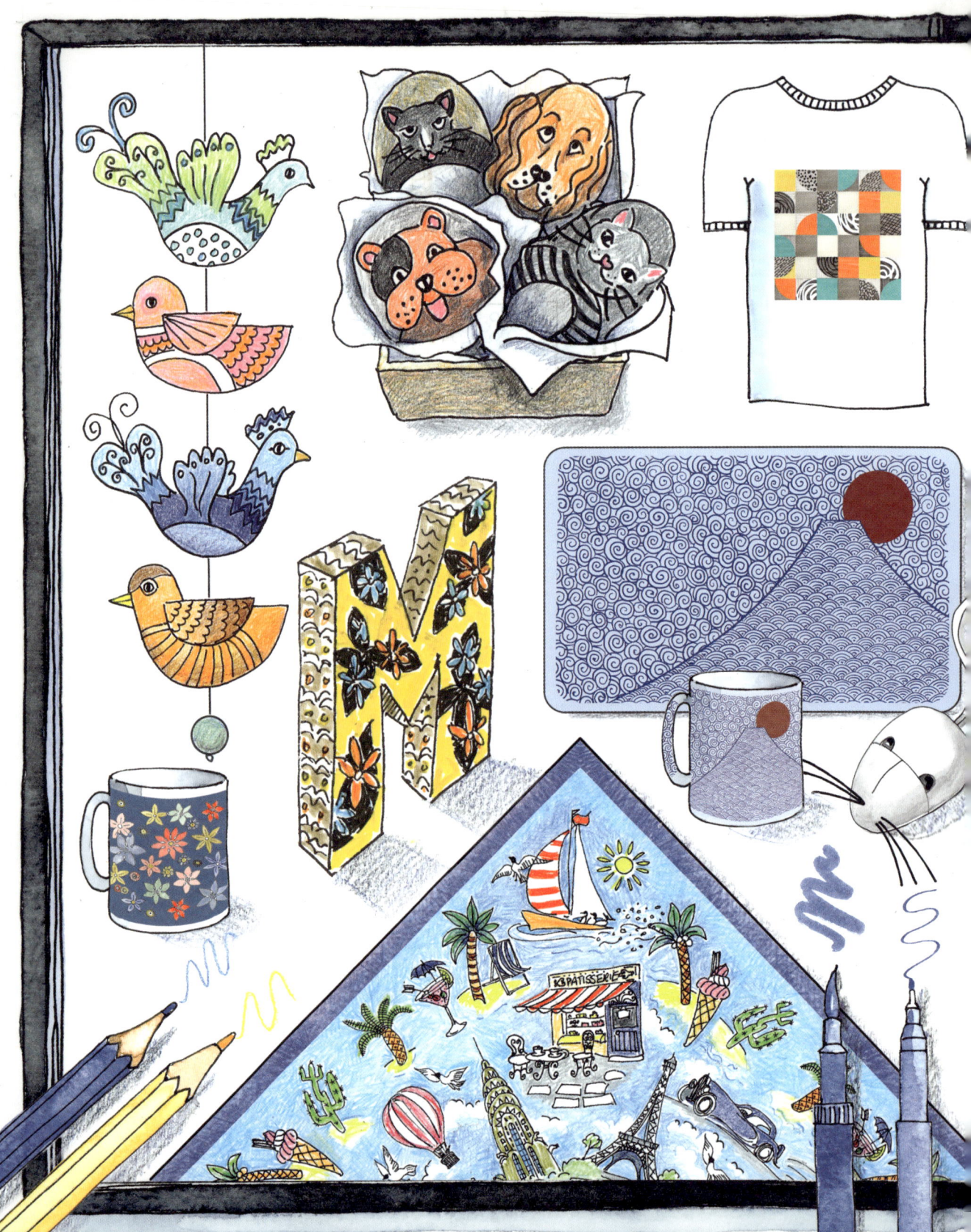

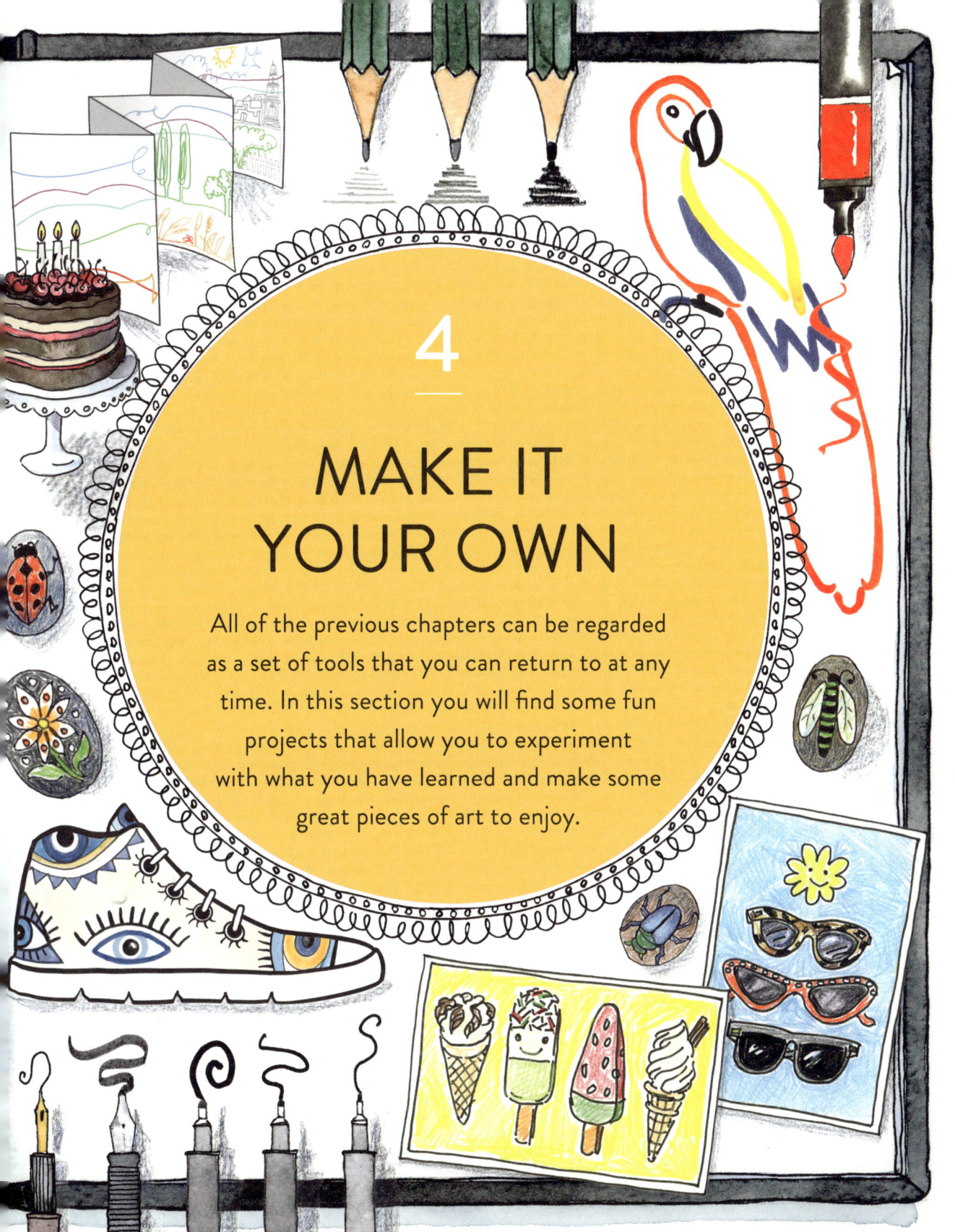

4

MAKE IT YOUR OWN

All of the previous chapters can be regarded as a set of tools that you can return to at any time. In this section you will find some fun projects that allow you to experiment with what you have learned and make some great pieces of art to enjoy.

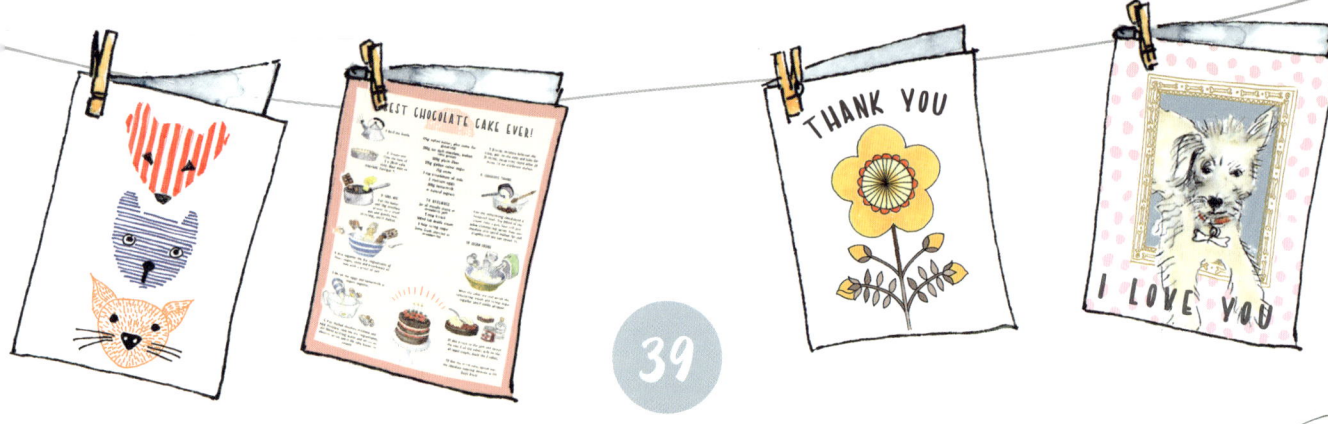

WHAT TO DO WITH YOUR ART

You've created all these great drawings, now the question is what to do with them? Put them in a drawer and look at them once every few years when you are having a clean-up session or moving . . . NO!

There are several takeaway ideas dotted throughout the book but in this final section you can see how to turn your drawings into larger, and different objects. Try creating unique decor for your home, or create something special for a handmade gift.

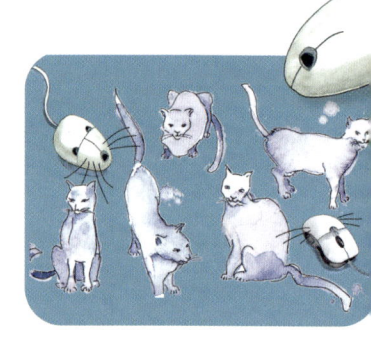

(Cat and) mouse pad. Or draw cover designs for tablets and phones, and then send them off to be printed.

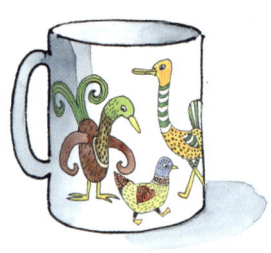

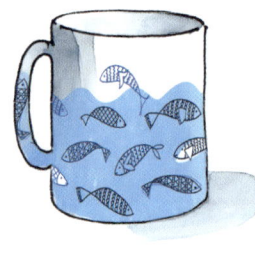

Mugs and T-shirts. Check with your local printing store for the size of the print area.

Pixel sneakers. Drawn with acrylic marker pens.

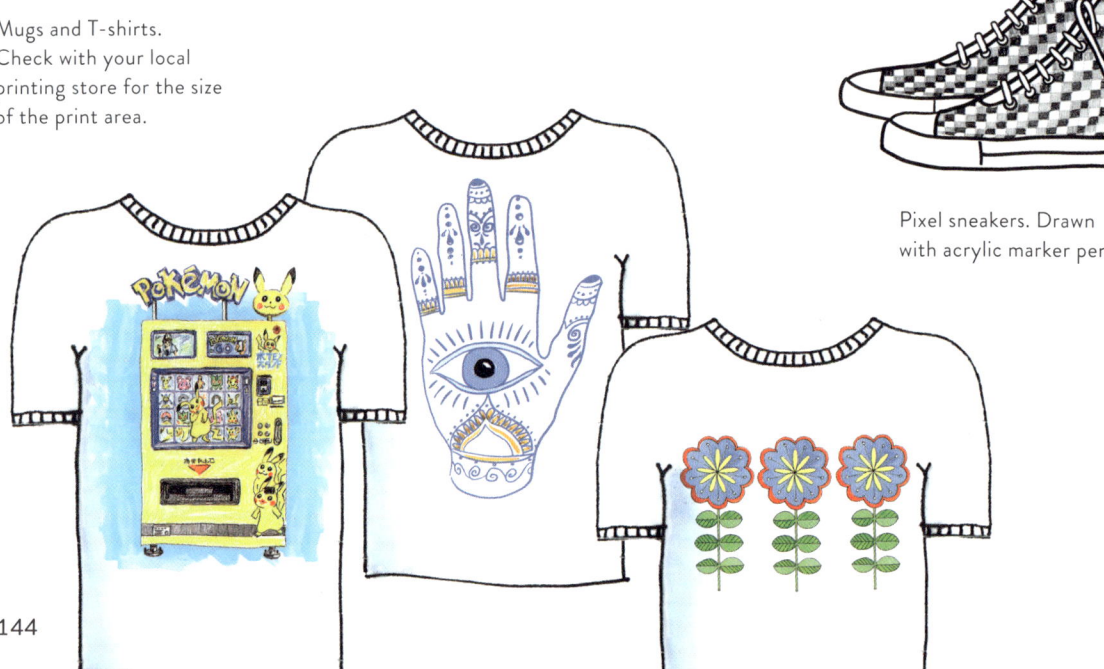

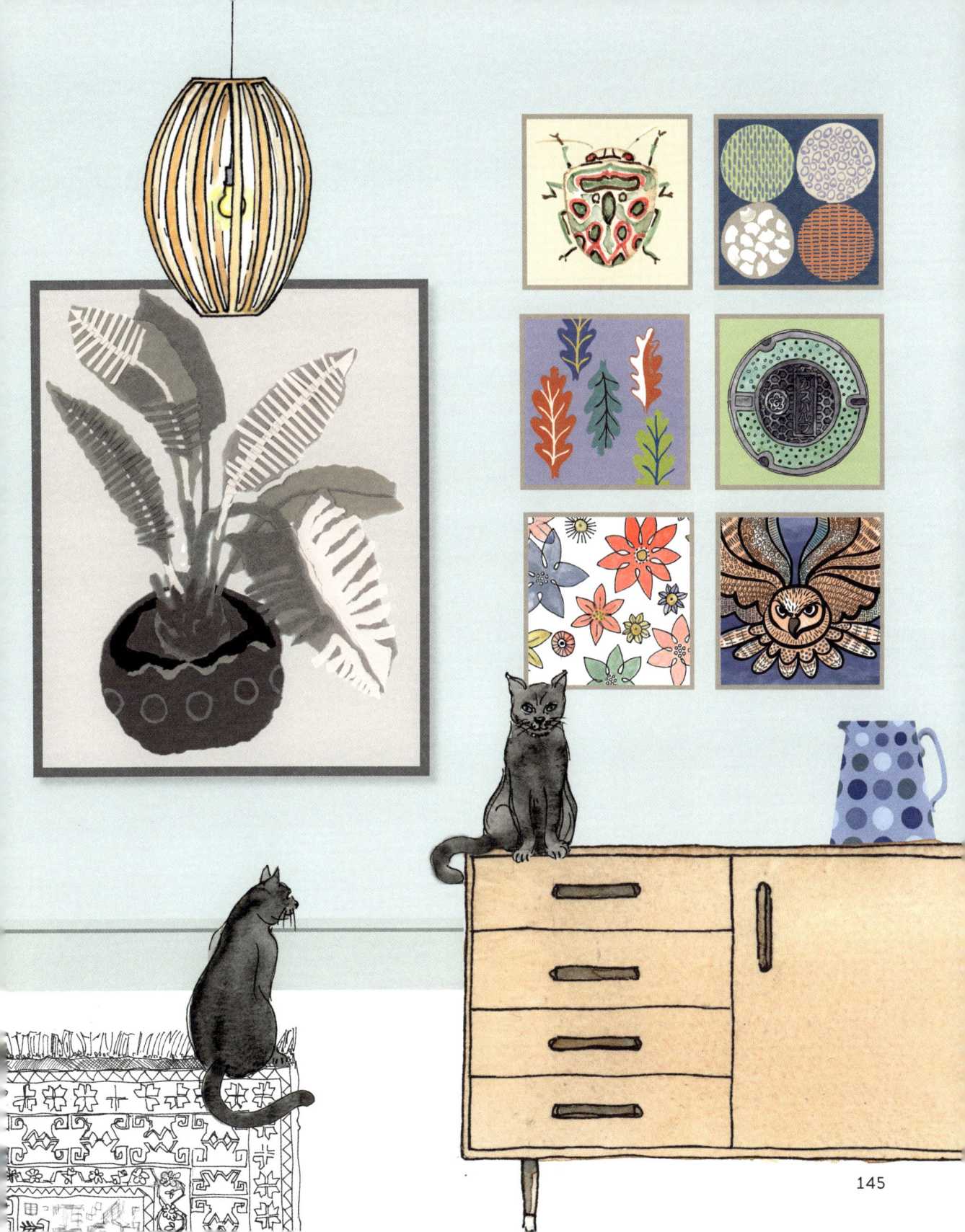

ONE CONTINUOUS LINE

Using a fineliner pen, you can create simple but effective drawings with just one continuous line.

First, sketch out the form and order of direction for the single line so that you have a rough route map to follow. Like calligraphy, don't expect to get it right the first time! You may have to do several sketches to fine tune the proportions.

Look at the drawings and track the start and finish points. Start with a simple form such as the blue bird or the green apple, then you can work out how to add more detail.

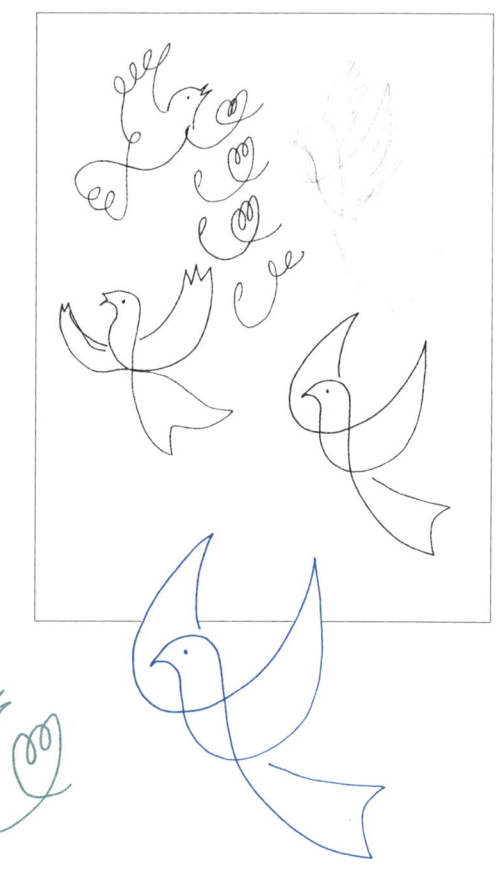

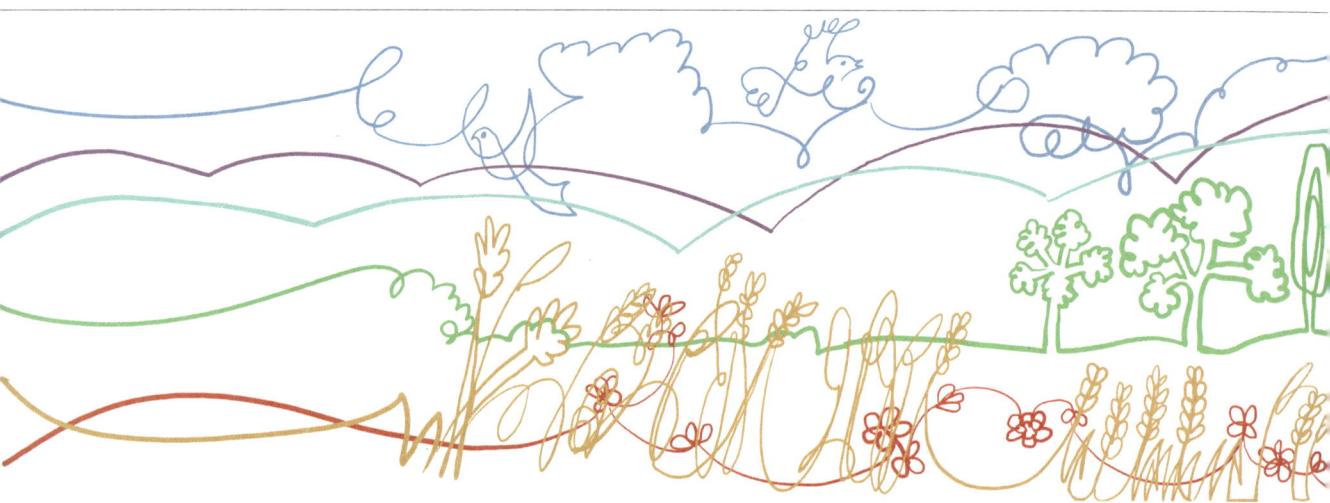

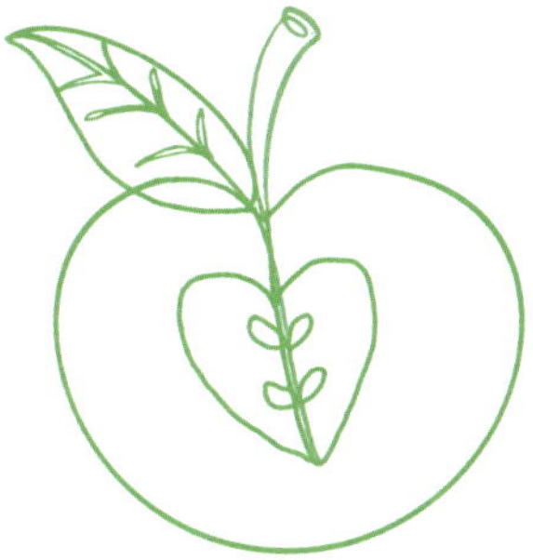

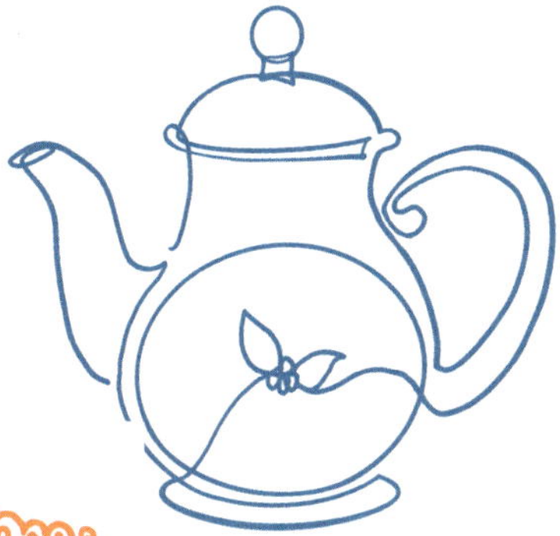

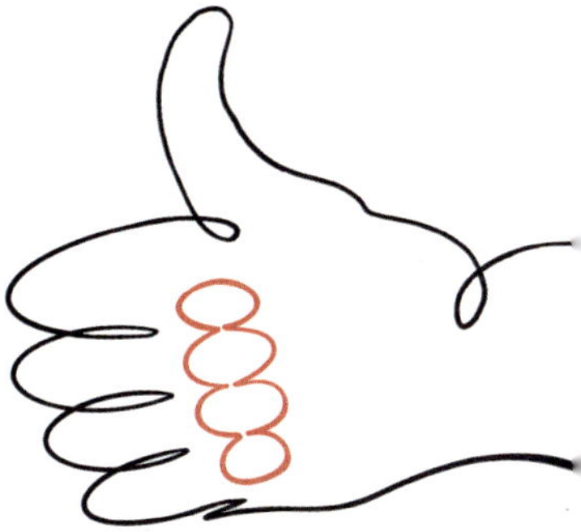

Try two colors to
define certain shapes.

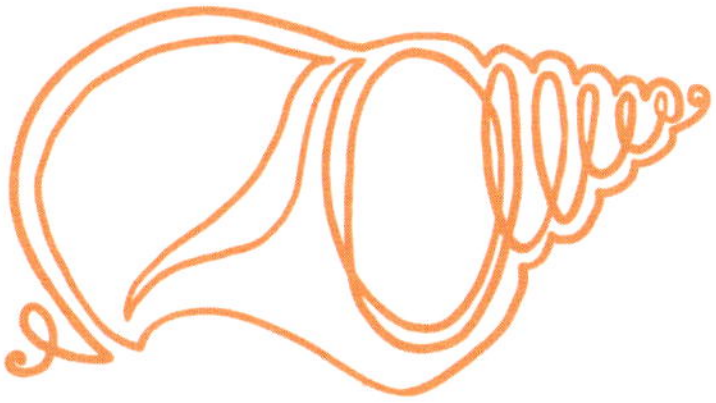

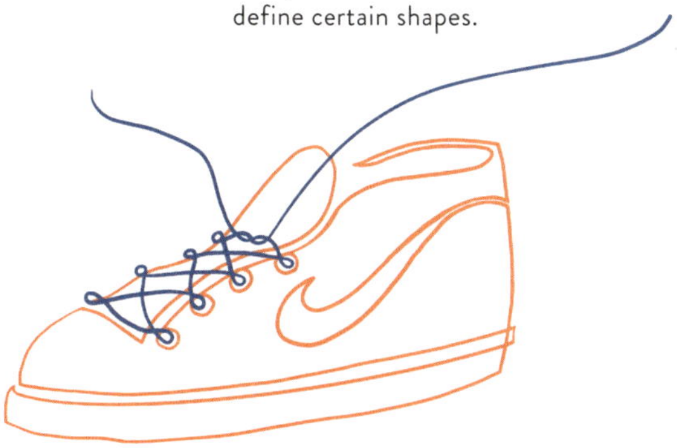

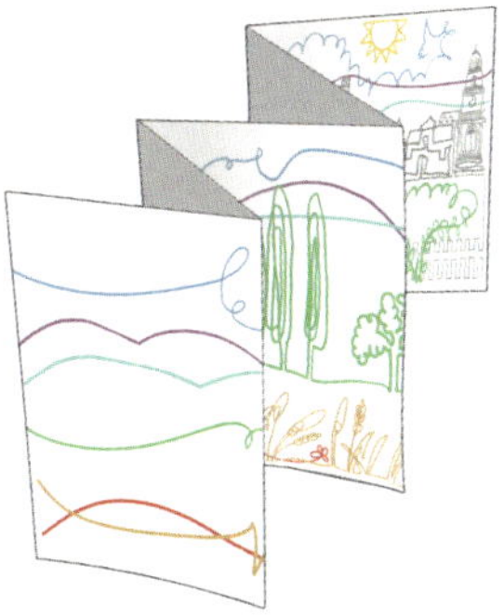

T A K E A W A Y

Draw an accordion book

Take a line for a walk through a landscape. I used a strip from
a sheet of poster paper. The horizontal nature of a landscape
works well for drawing the flow of elements from left to
right. Use a different color for each layer or subject matter
(foreground, grasses, trees, buildings, hills, and sky). Then,
when finished, fold the paper into an accordion. You can see
I had designed one panel of simple lines to be the cover.

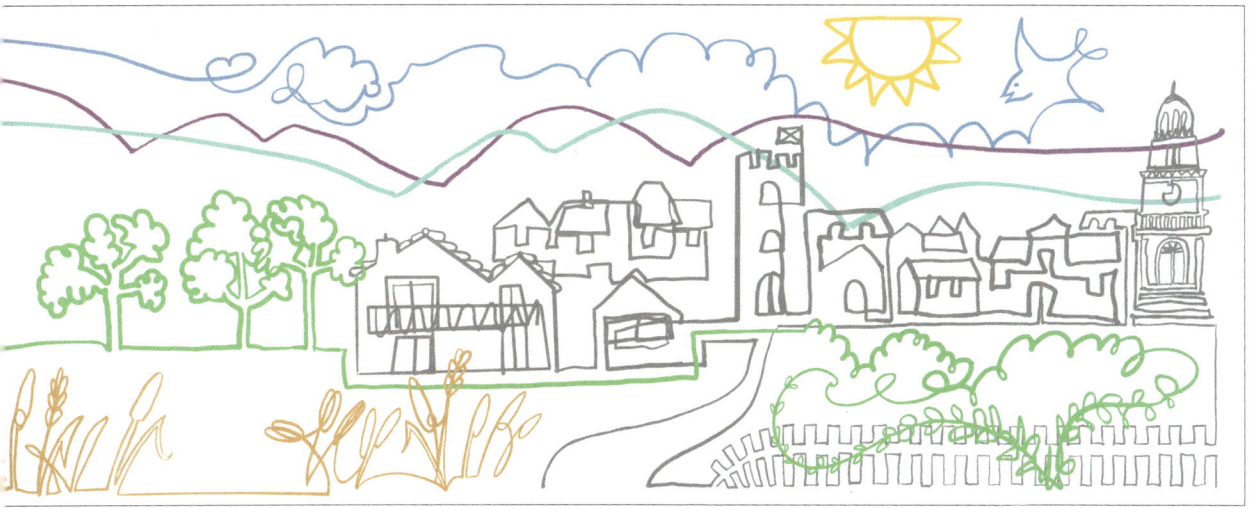

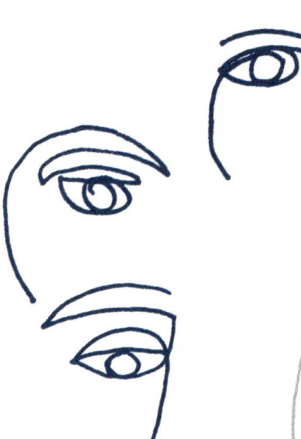

Experiment with the start points and line direction for the individual features. You can see the eyes, nose, and lips shown here are all different. Gradually you will get the best proportions of the details, such as the size of nostril to the whole nose.

Face liner

Continuing the one-line drawings from the previous page, try drawing some faces. It's a good exercise for simplifying and editing down what you see. You also need to plan the "order" of the line.

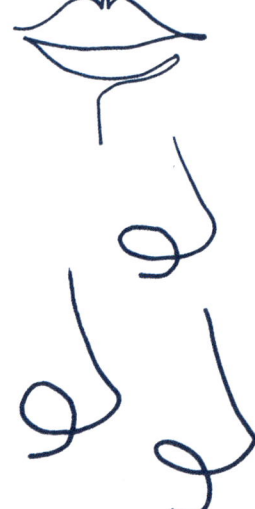

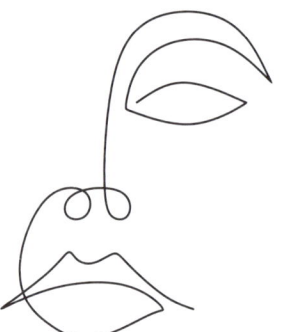

Join the features together
Some faces will be more successful than others. It is difficult to achieve a mirror image of the left and right side of the face when you are just using one line! Try with only one eye; it looks quite effective. You can work from life (possibly a self portrait), or use your imagination or a photograph for reference. Older faces have more continuous lines that help you move around the face!

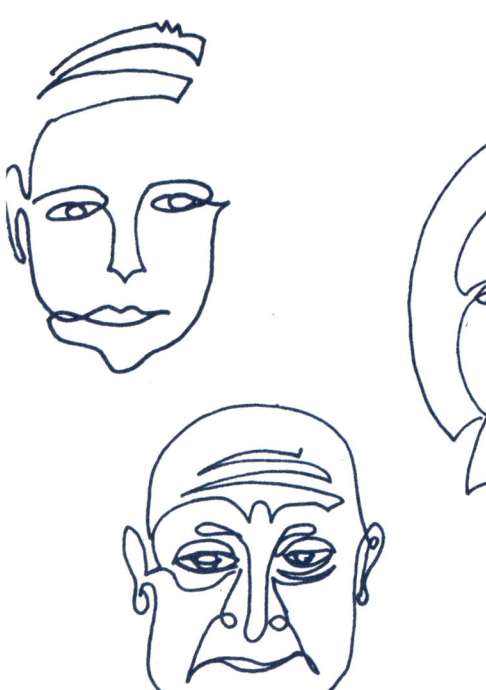

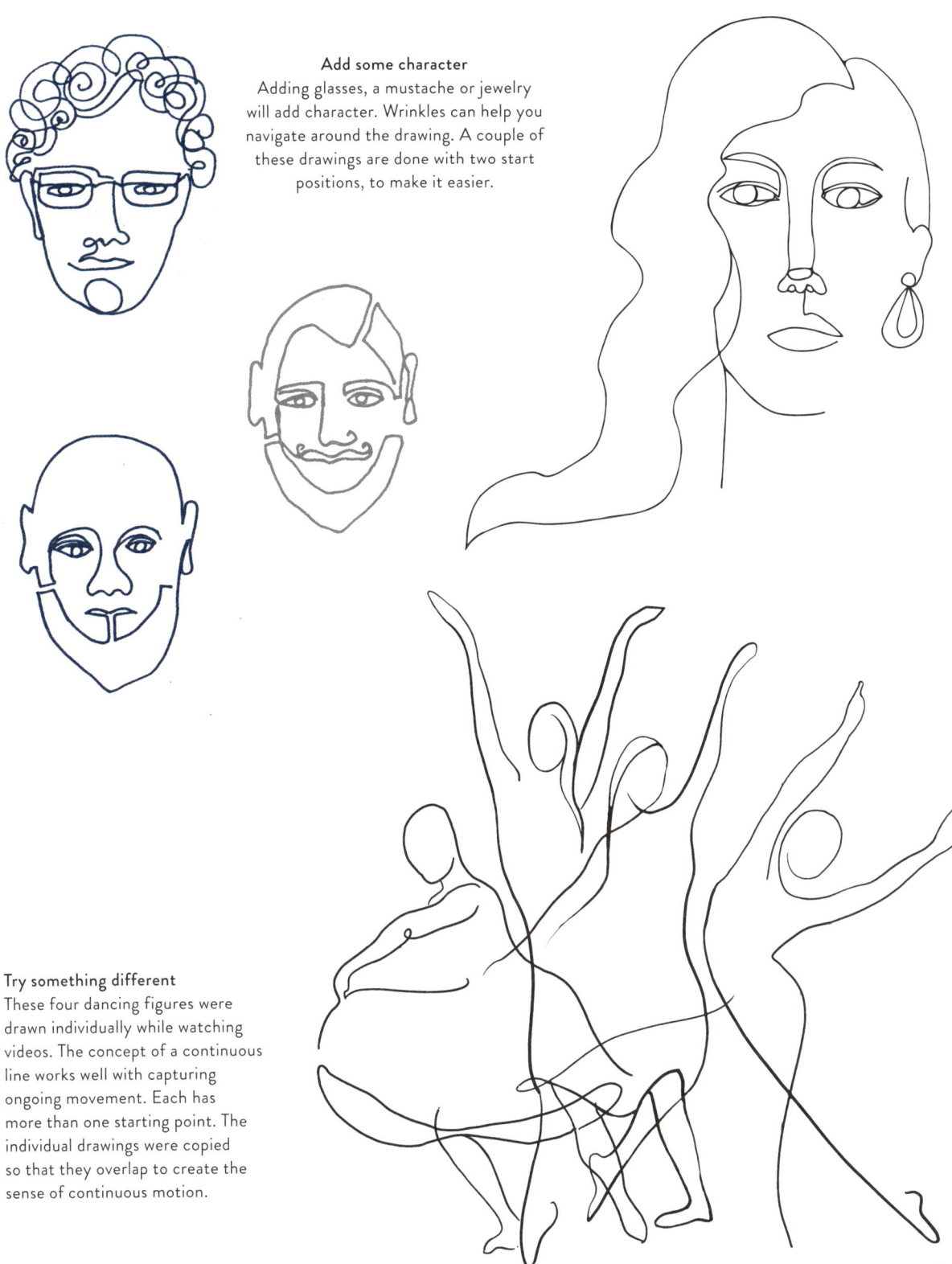

Add some character
Adding glasses, a mustache or jewelry will add character. Wrinkles can help you navigate around the drawing. A couple of these drawings are done with two start positions, to make it easier.

Try something different
These four dancing figures were drawn individually while watching videos. The concept of a continuous line works well with capturing ongoing movement. Each has more than one starting point. The individual drawings were copied so that they overlap to create the sense of continuous motion.

DRAW JAPANESE PATTERNS

Japanese patterns are called *seigaiha*, meaning "blue ocean waves."
The term covers a number of designs and the original is shown in the first
circle below. This motif has also been used for centuries in Egypt, Korea,
Persia (Iran), and around the world.

Practice *seigaiha* patterns

Fill some circles with Japanese patterns using just waves and spirals. There
are many more options using different offset positions and sizes. These were
done with a 1.2 mm fineliner pen. The irregularities of line, repeat spaces,
and the little gaps give the patterns a hand-drawn quality, a bit like the
Japanese idea of *wabi-sabi* (the appreciation of non-perfection).

Draw a *seigaiha* mouse pad

You can design and draw a mouse pad, and then get it printed by a company
online. Find out what size pads they produce to understand the dimensions
and how they want the drawing supplied (see page 189).

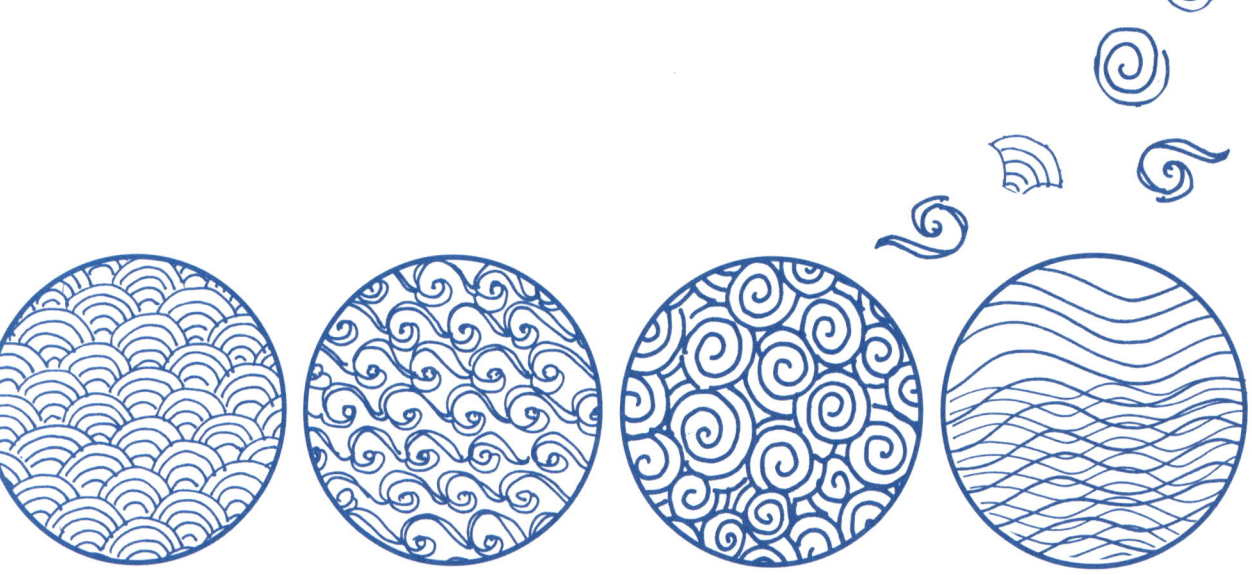

Mt. Fuji Mouse Pad

Using a pale blue paper, draw the basic shape of Mt. Fuji using a blue felt-tip or fineliner pen. Choose two seigaiha patterns and fill in the sky and mountain, putting one in each. Then cut out a circle of red paper for the sun and stick in position.

Circles Mouse Pad

You can either draw the circles in position in a block, or draw them individually, cutting them out to stick together on a background sheet.
1. Draw enough circles to fill the mouse pad (you can overlap them to make them fit).
2. Fill the circles with pale background colors using a felt-tip pen, watercolor washes, or using different colored paper.
3. Where the circles overlap, fill with blue and add more patterns.

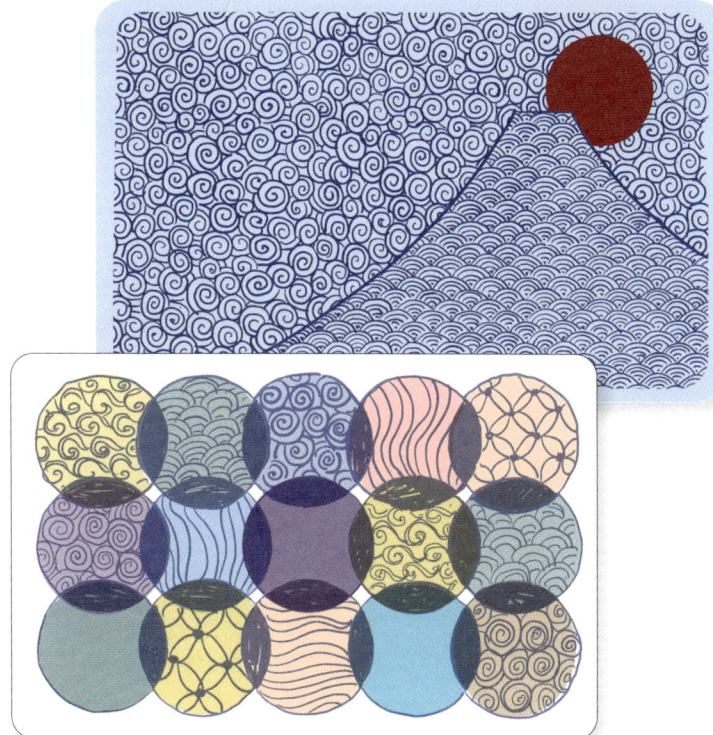

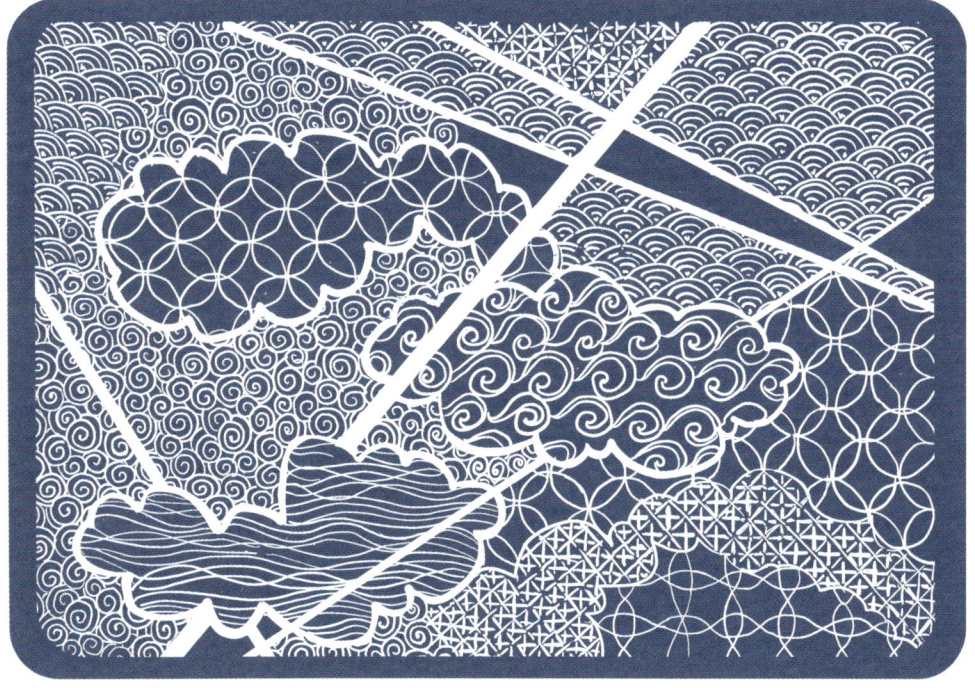

Kumo pad

Draw random cloud shapes, then the angled lines (as lightning or chopsticks). Fill in the areas with patterns.

This was drawn in black line, scanned, then digitally turned into a negative. So the background could be dark blue and the line white. Or you could use a white acrylic pen on a dark background.

Sketch some very simple bird shapes.

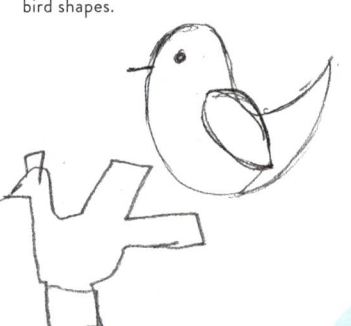
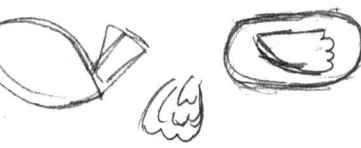
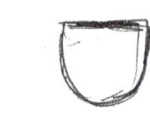
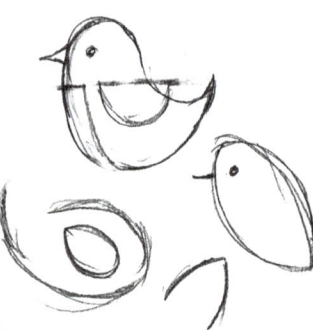

42

DECORATIVE BIRDS

Decoration, like patternmaking, is creative and relaxing. Birds give a fantastic opportunity for adding decoration—their natural markings and feather shapes are a good starting point.

There are many other subjects that can be embellished with decoration, such as butterflies, houses (think of a gingerbread house), figurines (Russian dolls), or even vintage cars. In fact, most things can be decorated if you have the inclination.

Bird shapes

Start by drawing some basic shapes of heads, bodies, wings, and tails. Generally, bird shapes work better from the side, because they have a more interesting form and the wings give a good opportunity for surface decoration.

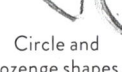

Circle and lozenge shapes

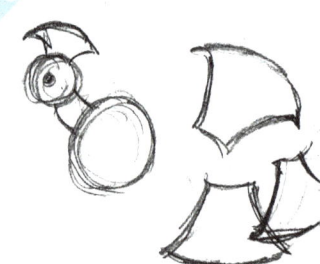

Circle and fan shapes

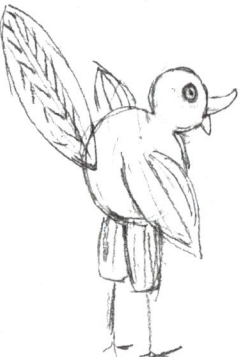

Use geometry

Look at the overall shapes that the wings, tails, and feathers make. Then simplify them into geometric forms. Use circles, ovals, triangles, or simple bird forms, then add some cute feet, a beak, a hairdo and some attitude.

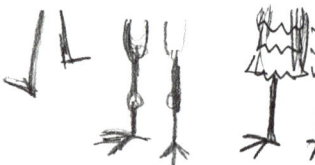
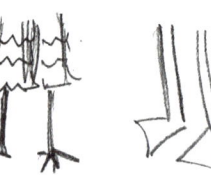

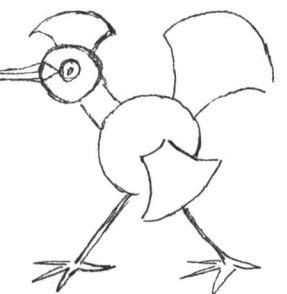

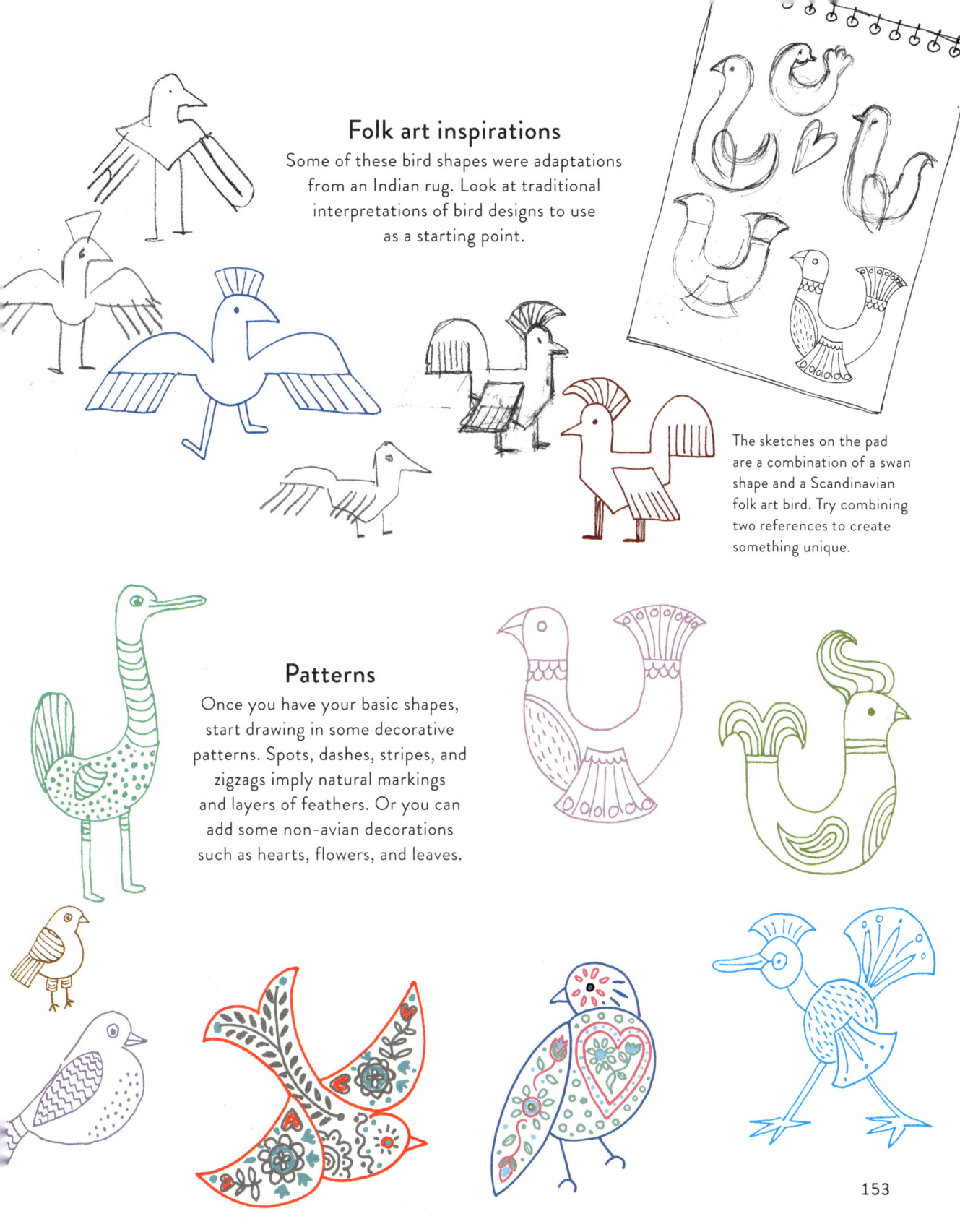

Folk art inspirations

Some of these bird shapes were adaptations from an Indian rug. Look at traditional interpretations of bird designs to use as a starting point.

The sketches on the pad are a combination of a swan shape and a Scandinavian folk art bird. Try combining two references to create something unique.

Patterns

Once you have your basic shapes, start drawing in some decorative patterns. Spots, dashes, stripes, and zigzags imply natural markings and layers of feathers. Or you can add some non-avian decorations such as hearts, flowers, and leaves.

153

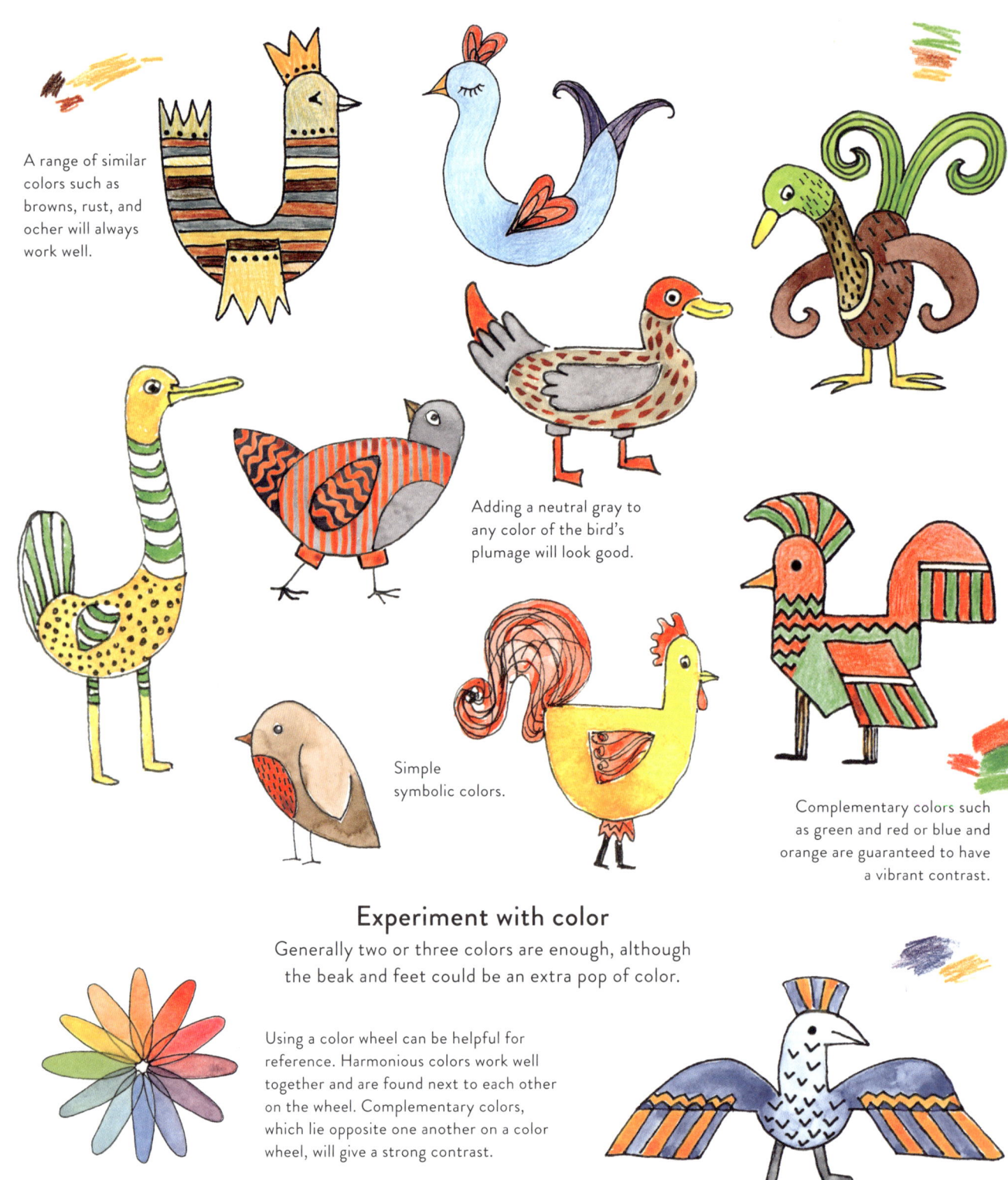

A range of similar colors such as browns, rust, and ocher will always work well.

Adding a neutral gray to any color of the bird's plumage will look good.

Simple symbolic colors.

Complementary colors such as green and red or blue and orange are guaranteed to have a vibrant contrast.

Experiment with color

Generally two or three colors are enough, although the beak and feet could be an extra pop of color.

Using a color wheel can be helpful for reference. Harmonious colors work well together and are found next to each other on the wheel. Complementary colors, which lie opposite one another on a color wheel, will give a strong contrast.

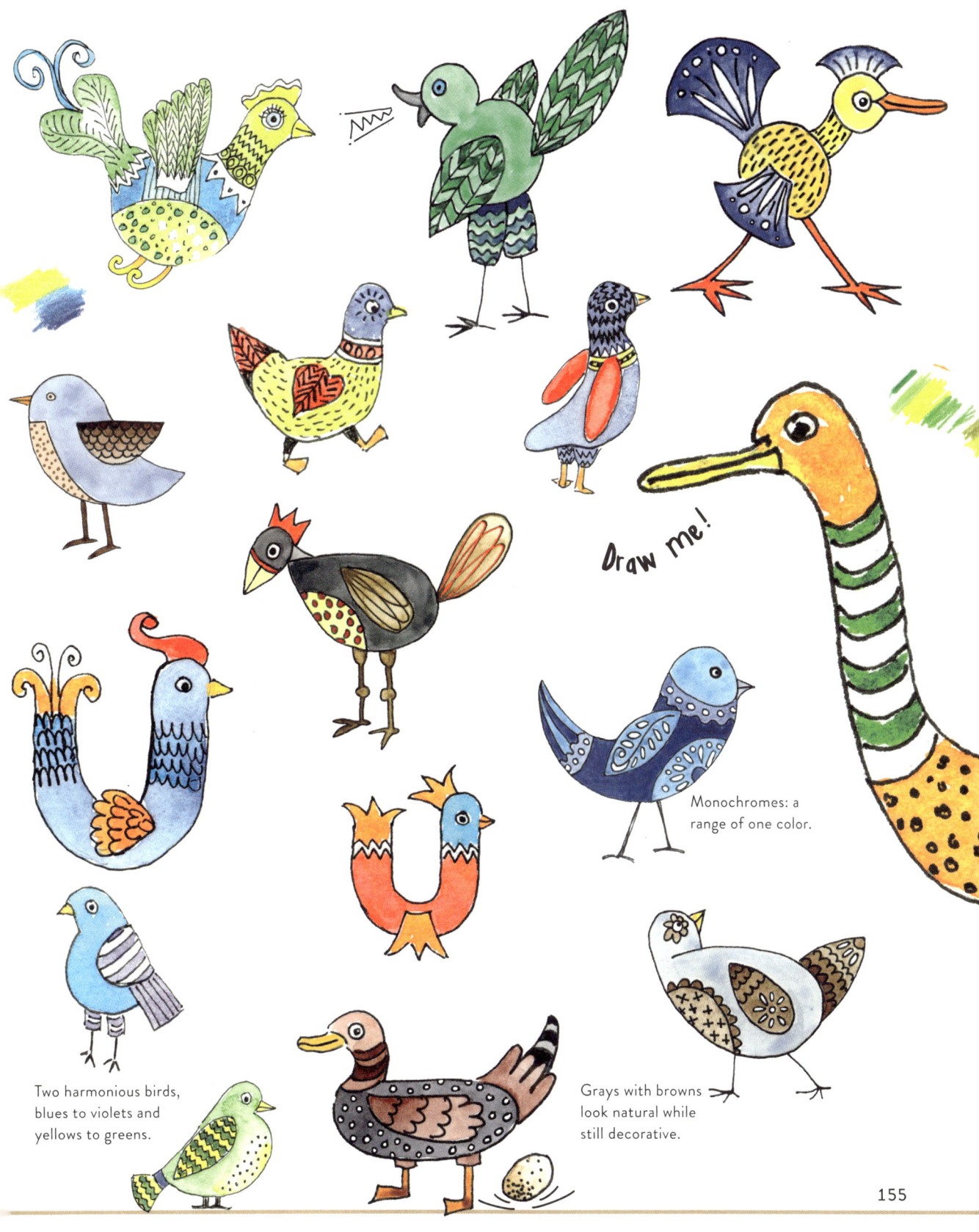

Draw me!

Monochromes: a
range of one color.

Two harmonious birds,
blues to violets and
yellows to greens.

Grays with browns
look natural while
still decorative.

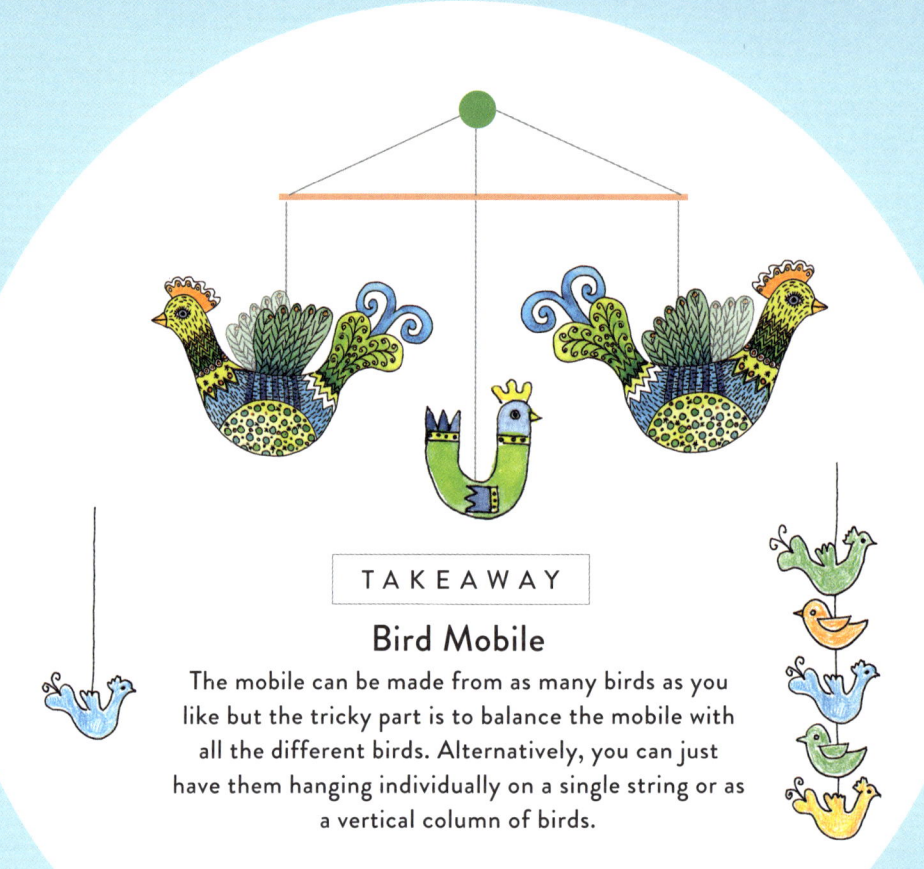

TAKEAWAY

Bird Mobile

The mobile can be made from as many birds as you like but the tricky part is to balance the mobile with all the different birds. Alternatively, you can just have them hanging individually on a single string or as a vertical column of birds.

Use the birds from the previous page and redraw them onto heavyweight paper (110–140 lb, 250–300 gsm). Create two mirror images for each of the bird shapes (see the opposite page for pieces you need to make). Cut them out and stick the two sides of the pieces together, sandwiching the string in the middle. Tie the birds onto the rod, then tie another thread at each end so you can hang the mobile. You will need to experiment with the position of the string and the rod to find the right balance and create a whole menagerie mobile.

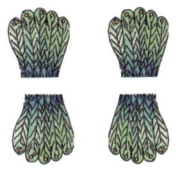

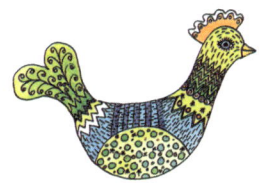

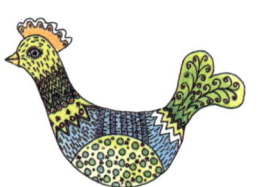

Thin wooden rod, about one foot long, and fine cotton or invisible thread.

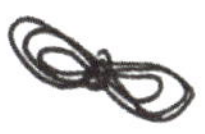

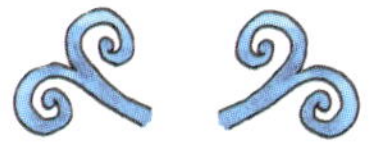

You will need
Paint two sets of mirrored wings, for the top and underside. To make it quicker you could just purchase plain or patterned colored paper for the underside of the wing (or paint it a flat color). Each wing is about 2 inches in length.

Two mirror images of your bird shapes. I drew these to be about 7 inches from beak to the end of the green tail.

Tail feathers, either two mirror painted or just one self-colored paper.

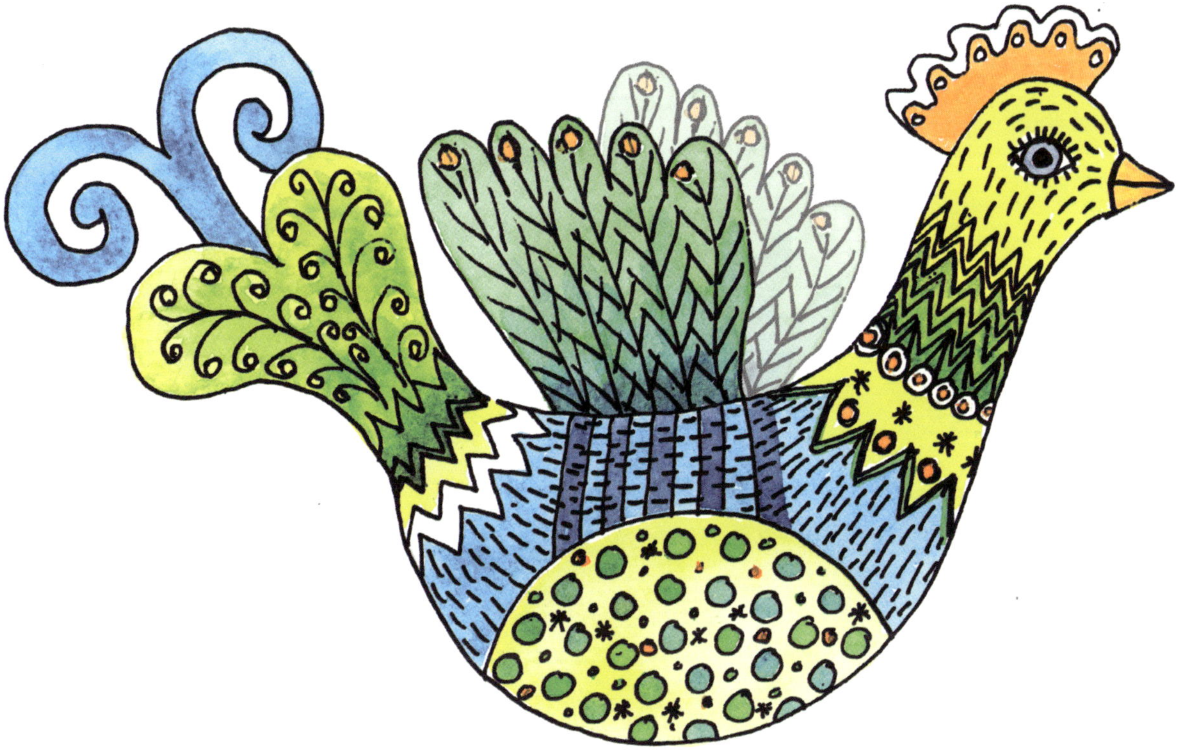

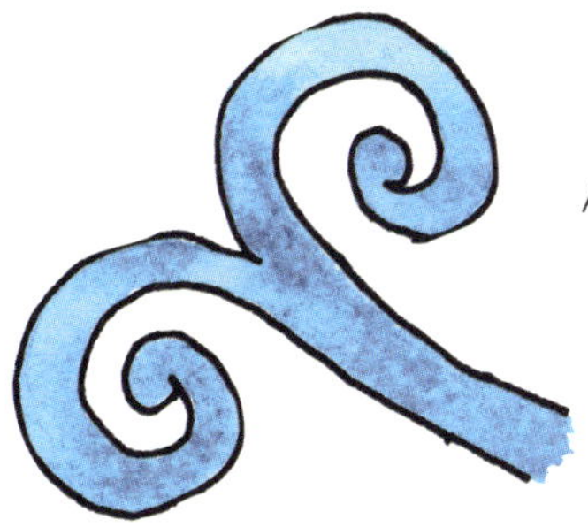

Allow a little extra at the bottom of the tail and each wing to stick into the paper sandwich.

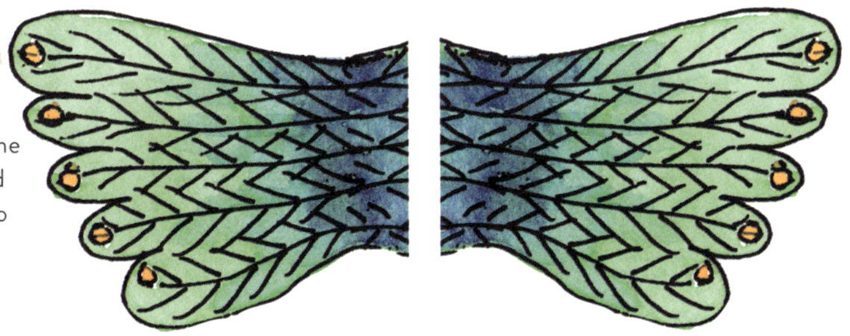

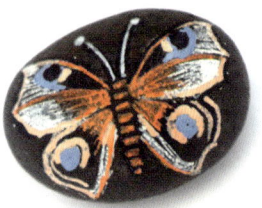
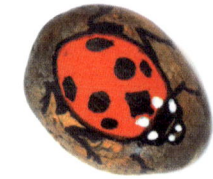
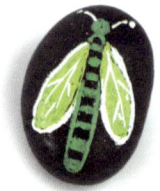

43

DRAWING ON PEBBLES

During the Covid-19 pandemic, I noticed someone placing pebbles with images and messages on steps, walls, and other visible ledges for people to enjoy. Drawing and painting on pebbles is popular, and looking online I found many great examples from the simplest to the most exquisite detail.

Just fun

The pebbles over the next four pages are a selection of starting-point ideas, however the most important thing is having fun, from collecting the pebbles on a river or beach, to working on the small precious "canvas."

Geometric patterns
Try sketching out the design on paper to ensure the size and number of triangles or checks will fit.

You need a pack of markers (generally acrylic paint pens) suitable for drawing on ceramics, glass, metal, and pebbles. Prepare your pebble by washing and drying it well, then apply a primer coat of white (PVA) glue. This makes the surface smoother and easier to draw on, and it also protects the tip of the pen. Once drawn, you can protect your finished design by coating it with a clear acrylic varnish.

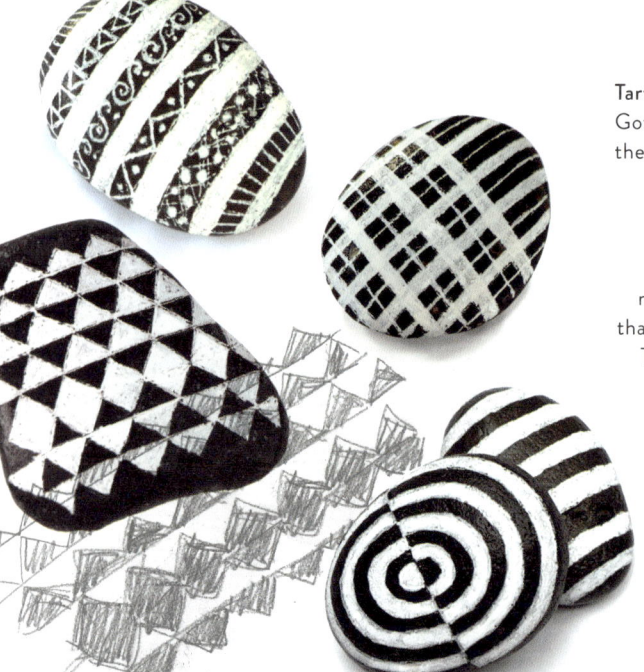

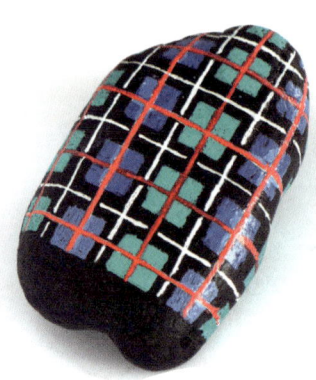

Tartan rocks
Got a Scottish friend? Perhaps they have a clan tartan.

Choose a black pebble and cut thin stripes of masking tape to block out black checks (much nicer to keep the pebble surface than to paint a black background). Then draw the wide blue and green stripes. Remove the tape and add in the thin red and white stripes.

The red tartan pebble uses a building brick that has been eroded down to a flat sliver.

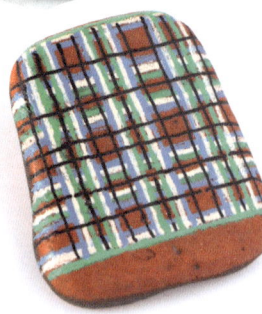

Flowers and leaves

The organic shapes work well to fit the curves of any shape pebble.

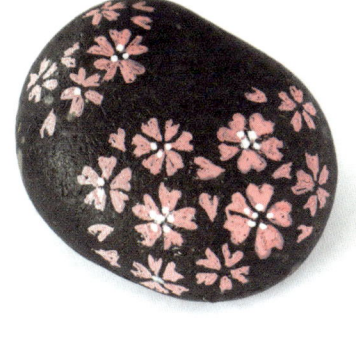

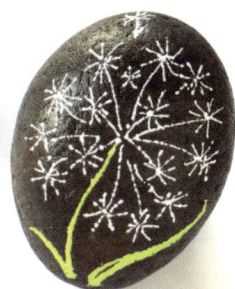

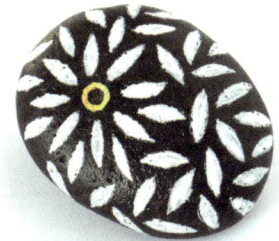

This little pebble had a hole in the surface, ideal for a flower center, or possibly a bird or animal eye.

A rough sketch first to check scale and position of the design.

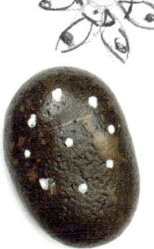

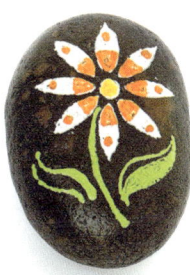

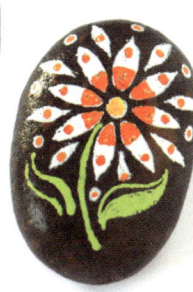

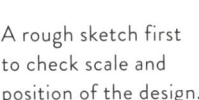

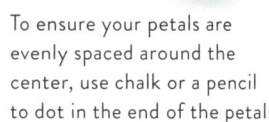

To ensure your petals are evenly spaced around the center, use chalk or a pencil to dot in the end of the petals.

Sometimes you will find a pebble that is just perfect for a particular motif, like this paisley pebble.

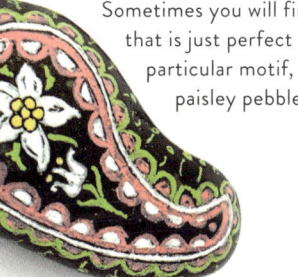

Paint half of the pebble with a color, this could be for design considerations or to conceal any blemish on the stone. Draw the motifs over the top, leaving some areas of the original surface visible to link it to the other half of the pebble.

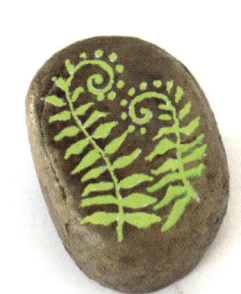

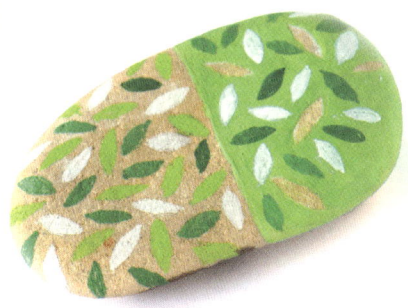

If the tone of your pebble is similar to the colors you are using in the drawing, outline the finished motif with white.

Pebble pet gift box

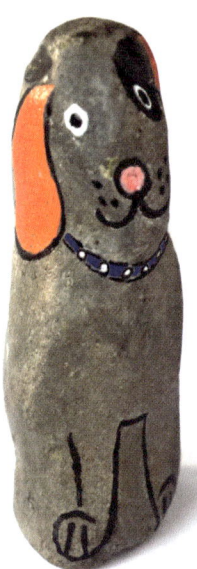

To create a miniature version of human's best friend, be it a dog or a cat, you need the right shaped pebble. Ideally one with a flat base so the animal can stand or sit upright, and enough room at the top for facial details like ears, a nose, or whiskers.

If you want to create a pet box (right) the faces need to be drawn nearer the top of the stone.

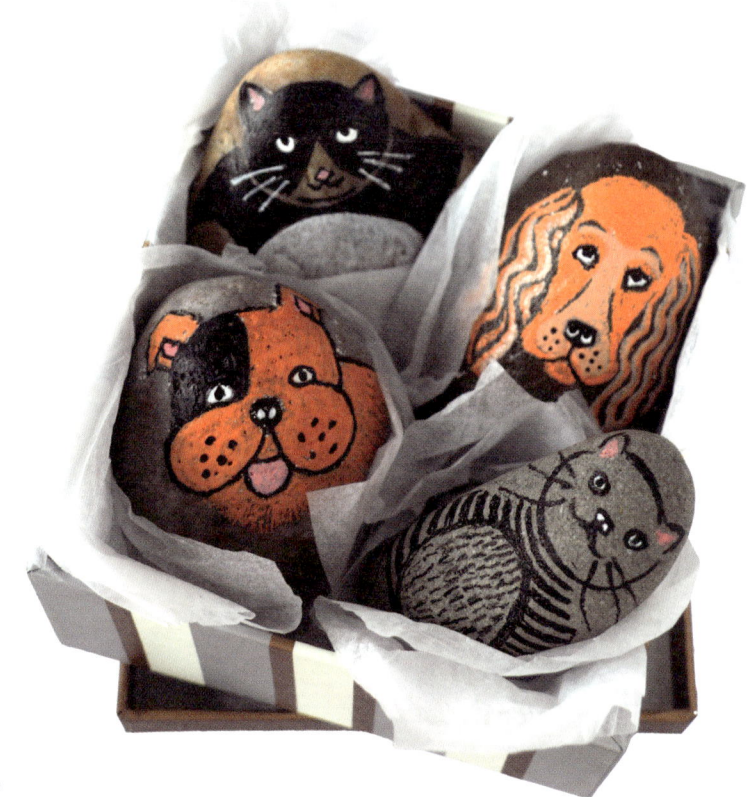

The pet puppy pebble was a perfect shape from all sides, and even had a dark mark for the eye patch.

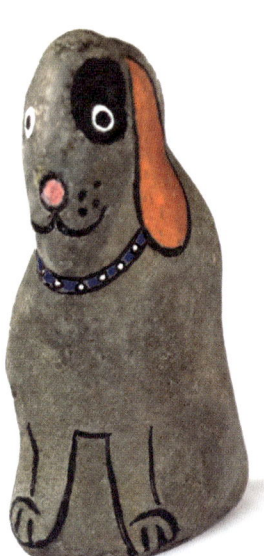

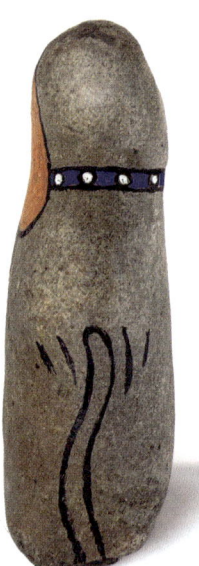

A seal shape stone and a little round stone—I haven't quite decided how to join them, perhaps some super glue, or drill a hole in each with a jewelry bit and join with a little rod.

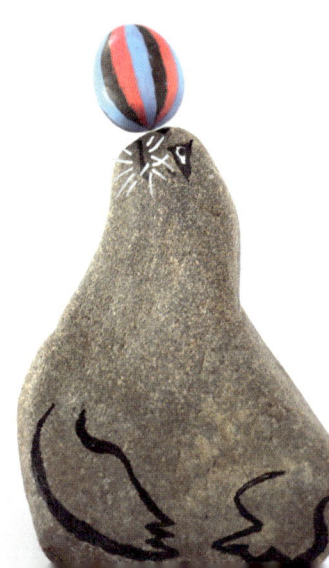

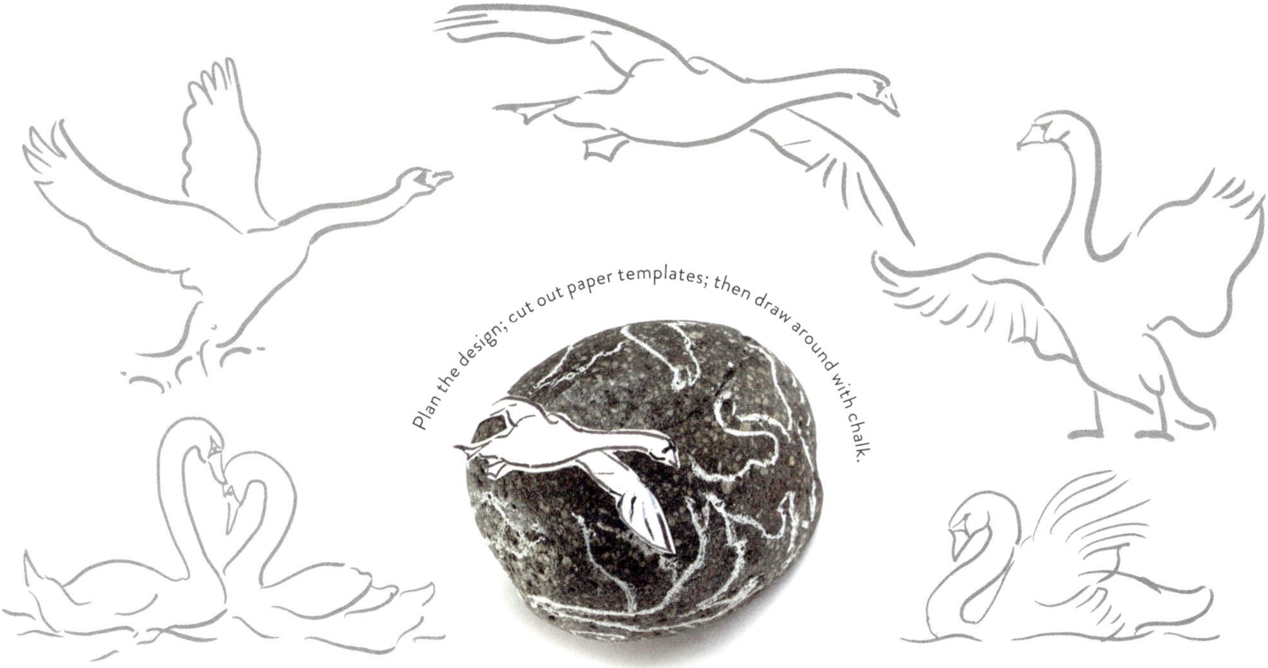

Plan the design; cut out paper templates; then draw around with chalk.

Swan stone globe

There are pebbles, or stones a little larger than the palm of your hand, that are split in half, creating a flat base with a domed top, like the shape of a snow globe. These are great for creating circular dioramas.

You could draw birds flying around the globe, like the swans here, or try with fish or butterflies. You can use any image or pattern motif and repeat in the round. A street scene or fantasy landscape would also wrap around well.

To plan the overall design, and make sure it all fits, make a rough sketch onto the pebble with chalk or pencil. Or, as above, experiment with paper templates to check size and position. Stick the templates to the surface of the pebble with either tiny pieces of tape or a "removable glue," and using a chalk or graphite pencil, draw around the templates to make a rough guide for your design. Finally, draw the swans with the acrylic markers.

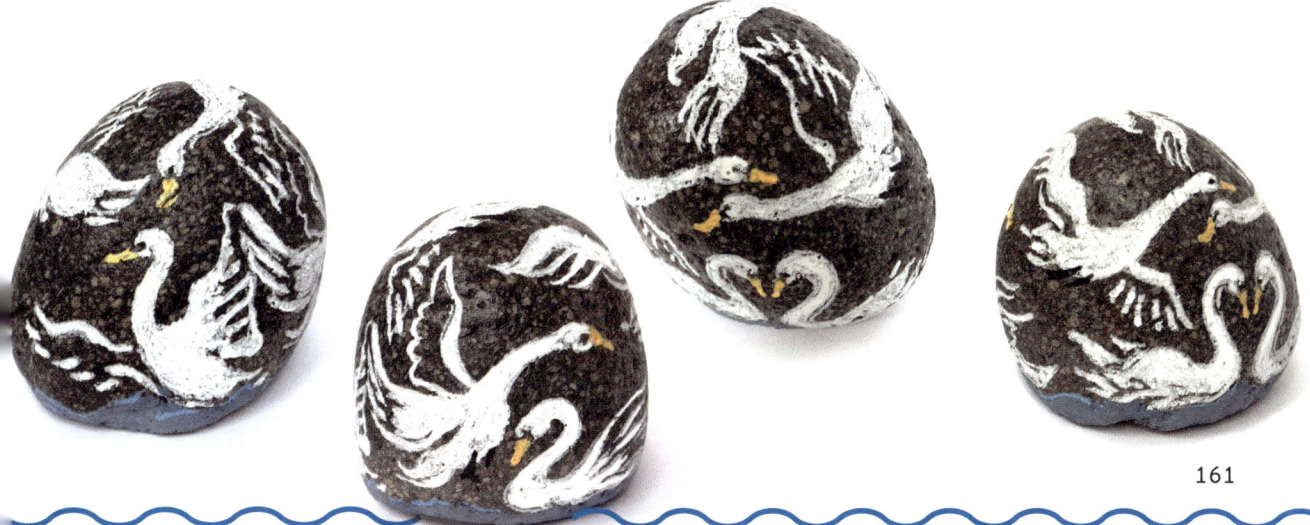

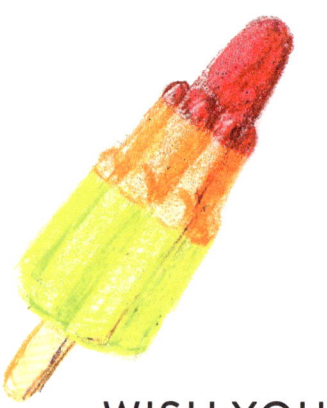

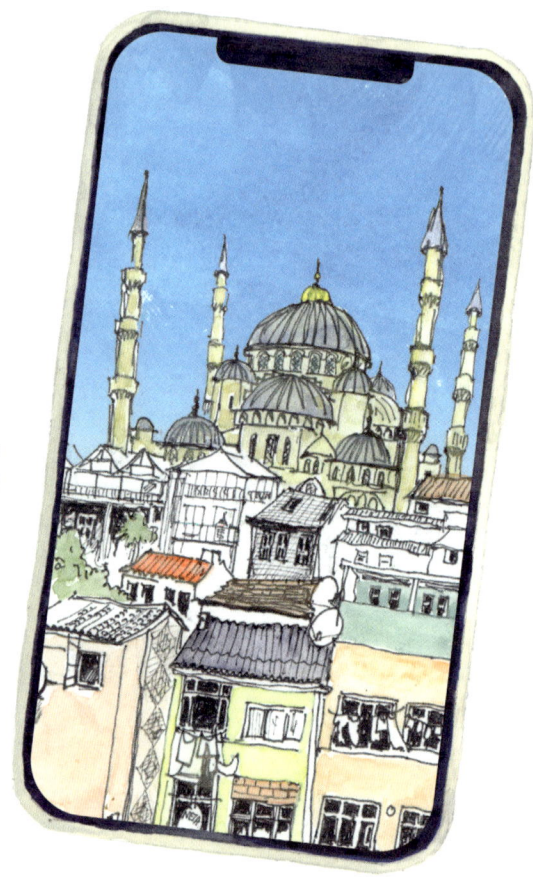

WISH YOU WERE HERE

Want to share with friends or remember your vacation in a unique way? Try drawing some of the experiences and send them as a traditional postcard, a cell phone photo, or upload your picture to social media.

If you think you might want to send a traditional postcard buy a pack of blank cards before you go. They are available in different papers depending on the media you use. If this is your first vacation sketch adventure, try to be realistic with your time. Keep it simple because on vacation you have family time to enjoy, sightseeing to do, plus relaxing time as well! Plan to set aside some drawing time, perhaps at your hotel or on the beach.

You might be lucky enough to have a great view from your hotel room, so you can snatch spare moments throughout the vacation to sketch.

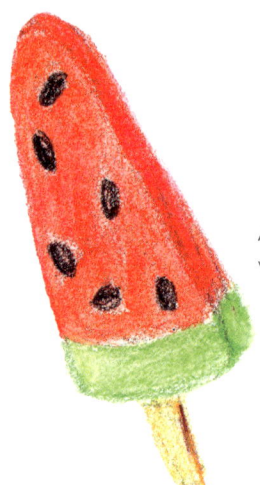

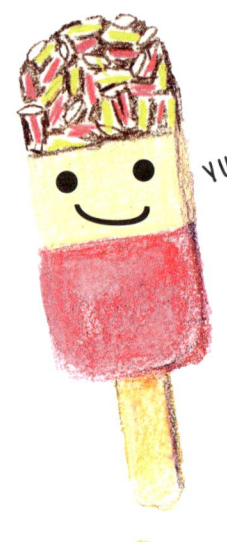

YUM YUM

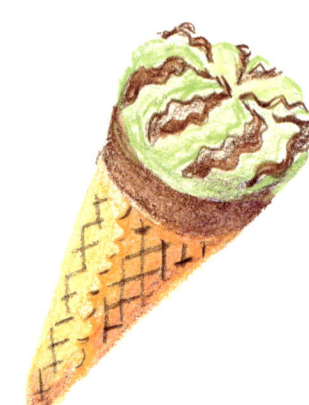

An ice cream a day? Either work very quickly, draw from memory, or take a photo. These ice creams were drawn with watercolor pencils.

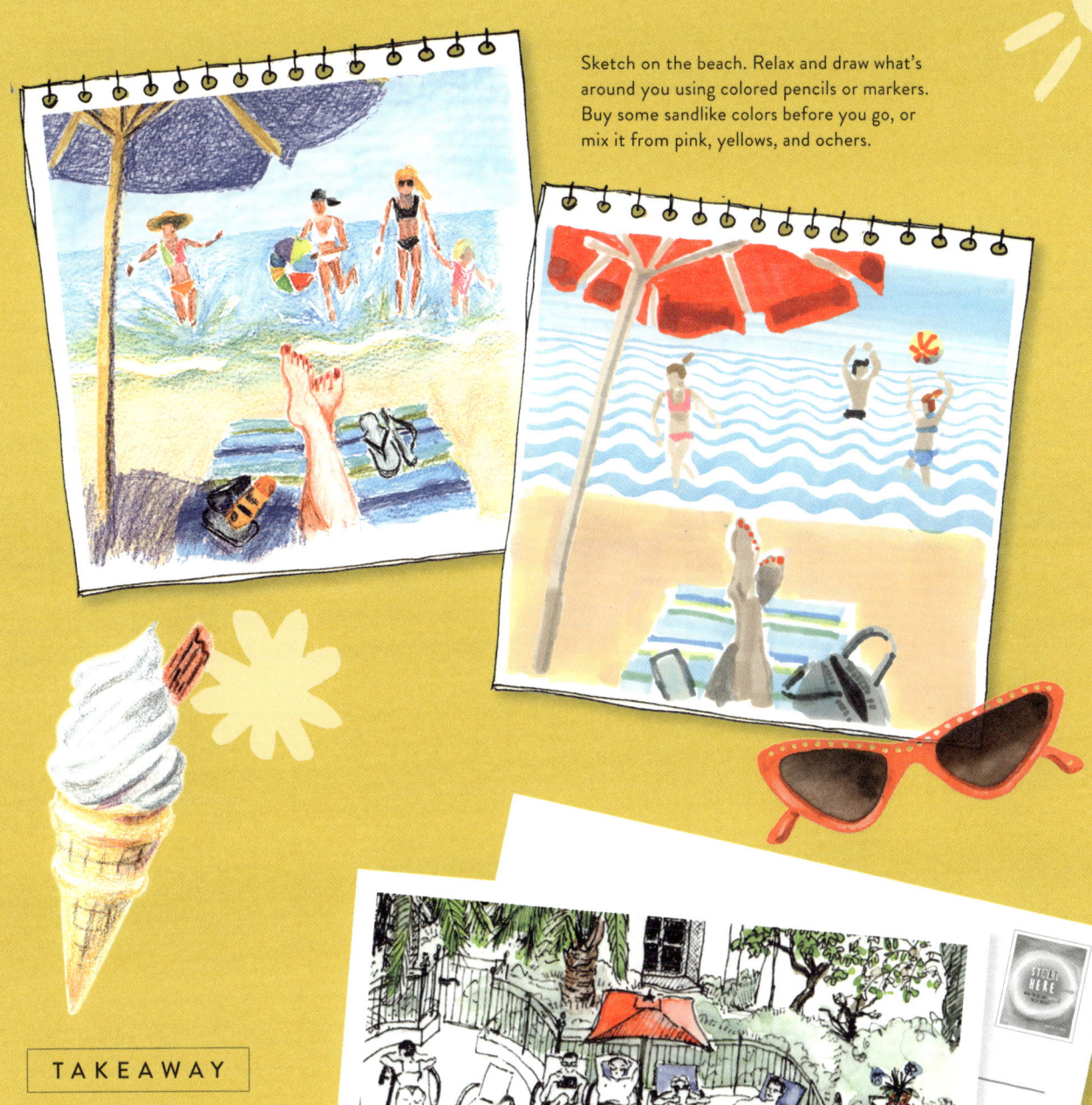

Sketch on the beach. Relax and draw what's around you using colored pencils or markers. Buy some sandlike colors before you go, or mix it from pink, yellows, and ochers.

TAKEAWAY

Send a postcard

For that special someone, you can send your art as a postcard. Paper manufacturers make packs of blank cards, or there might be a copy shop near your hotel if you needed to get several printed.

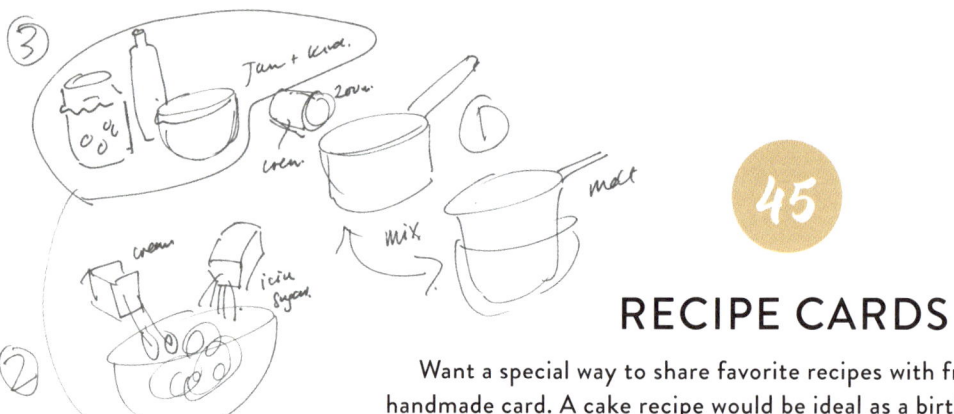

45

RECIPE CARDS

Want a special way to share favorite recipes with friends? Send it as a handmade card. A cake recipe would be ideal as a birthday card, or perhaps a celebratory cocktail!

Plan it

In the same way that you prepare to cook by chopping and weighing ingredients, plan the arrangement of your recipe card. Write out the recipe, breaking it into numbered stages (above, top left) that are interesting to draw (think stripy or glass bowls and nice packaging shapes and ingredients). Write the text out in short lines, because that tends to work better with the illustrations, and cut out the blocks of handwriting.

Draw rough sketches of the stages, cut them out, and arrange on a sheet of paper with the text (or you can scan and arrange both on a computer). When you are satisfied with the arrangement of the sketched elements, using the rough draft as a positional guide, draw the final images and handwrite the text in position on a sheet of letter paper (or you could make a collage). Scan it or take it to your local copy shop, to scan and print.

For a letter sheet, which is a little larger than this book, you could fit a couple more illustrations than on the opposite page, or make things bigger.

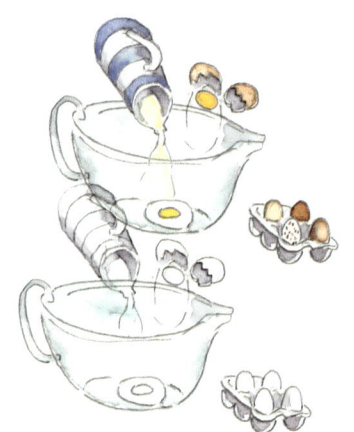

The recipe pictures can be painted with color or just drawn with monochrome tints added.

Try it in *kawaii*

If you want your recipe card to be really cute, try drawing in a *kawaii* style. Everything can be given a human persona.

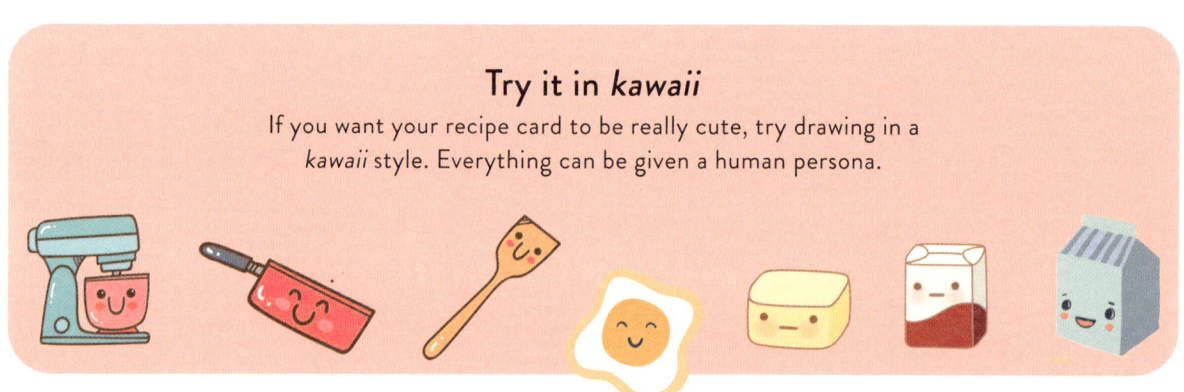

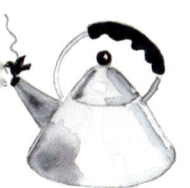

1 Boil some water

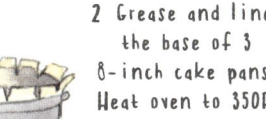

2 Grease and line the base of 3 8-inch cake pans. Heat oven to 350F.

Best chocolate cake ever

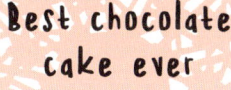

3/4 cup salted butter, plus some for greasing

7 oz bar dark chocolate, broken into pieces

1 3/4 cups all-purpose flour

1 3/4 cups granulated sugar

2 tbsp cocoa powder

1 tsp baking soda

2 medium eggs

3/4 cup buttermilk or natural yogurt

pinch of salt

1/2 cup boiled water

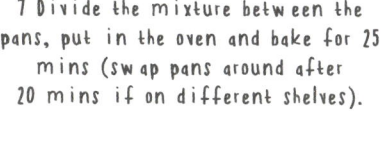

7 Divide the mixture between the pans, put in the oven and bake for 25 mins (swap pans around after 20 mins if on different shelves).

8 CHOCOLATE TOPPING

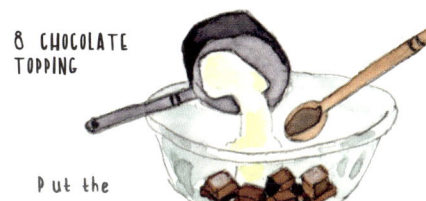

Put the remaining chocolate in a heatproof bowl. Place 1 cup of the cream into a saucepan, heat until just below simmering point. Pour over chocolate and stir until melted. Let it cool slightly until you can spread it.

3 CAKE MIX

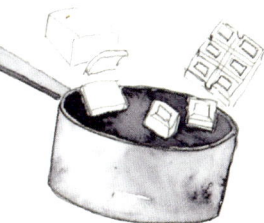

Put the butter and half the chocolate pieces in a small pan and gently heat, stirring until melted.

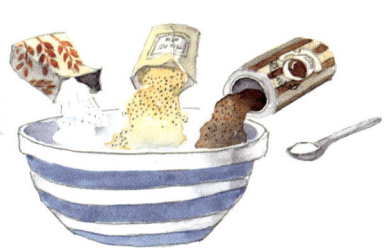

4 Mix together the dry ingredients of flour, sugar, cocoa, baking soda and a pinch of salt

TO ASSEMBLE

1 jar morello cherry jam

2 cups whipped cream

3 tbsp powdered sugar

Some fresh cherries/strawberries

9 CREAM FILLING

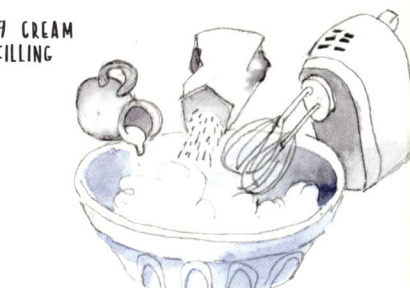

When the cakes are cool, whisk the remaining cream and powdered sugar together until softly whipped.

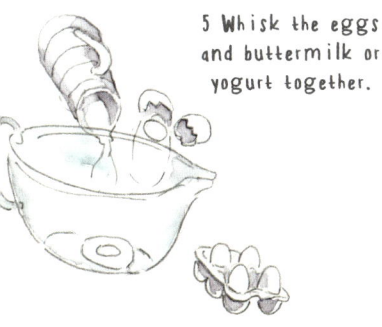

5 Whisk the eggs and buttermilk or yogurt together.

6 Combine melted chocolate mixture and egg mixture into the dry ingredients, then add 1/2 cup boiled water and whizz with an electric whisk until the cake batter is smooth.

HAPPY BIRTHDAY

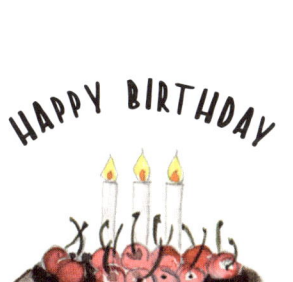

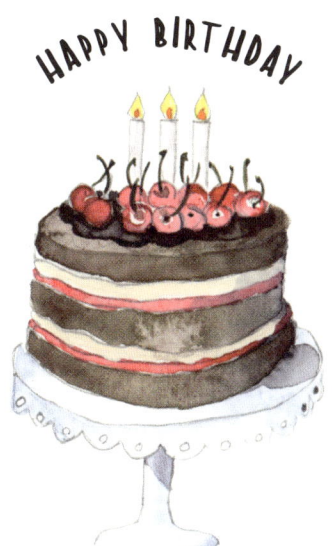

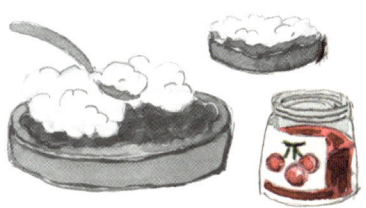

10 Spread the jam over two of the cakes. pile on the whipped cream and stack the two cakes.

11 Add the third cake, spread on the chocolate topping, and decorate with fresh cherries

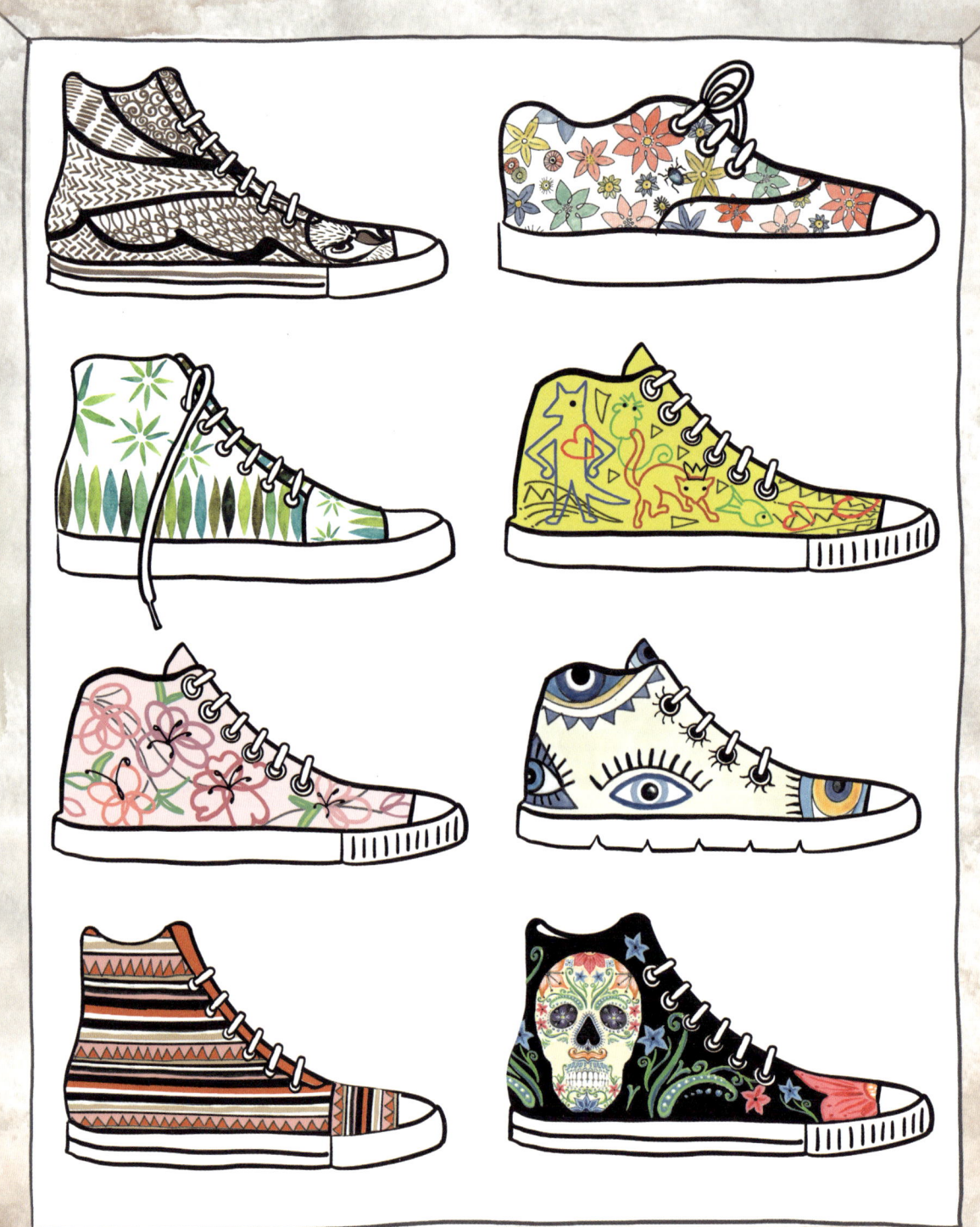

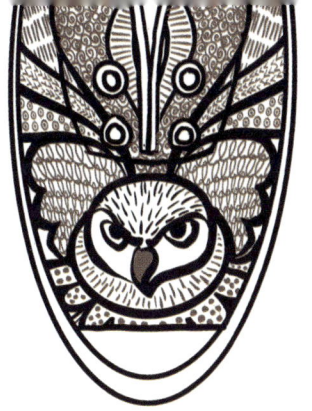

Front design
Here the owl from page 112 is placed as a central motif, with the pattern of wings extending around either side.

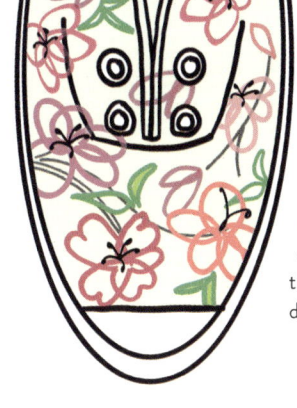

It could be a random scattered design as with these blossom flowers from page 34, or a mirror effect that meets on the front midline like the center flower design below.

46

SHARP SNEAKERS

Sneakers have evolved from being purely functional into cultural icons and art objects. Celebrate them with these takeaways.

Art shoes or wall art?

Use your sketches from this book as a starting point or draw something completely new. Make a wall art poster like on the previous page, or decorate a pair of canvas sneakers to wear, or even hang in a 3D frame on the wall. Check out some great examples online.

The sneakers you choose may have a better blank art space on the sides or at the front, so plan your design accordingly. Take measurements of the shoe and draw a rough outline template of each side, back, and front, including any seams or components of the shoe that may interfere with your drawing. Then sketch your designs on the template pieces, considering how these are going to merge on the shoe (I photocopied the templates so I could try a few different ideas). Next, make a light copy of your drawing onto the shoe, using a B or 2B pencil so you can erase if needed. Or, if you want, you can "just do it" and start drawing in color on the shoe straight away.

Use alcohol-based permanent markers, or pens sold as fabric markers. They both tend to be slightly transparent, so for more opacity apply a couple of layers. Acrylic markers are opaque, more permanent, and resilient. Depending on which marker used, you may have to seal with a clear protective coat.

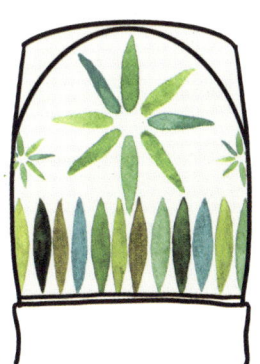

1

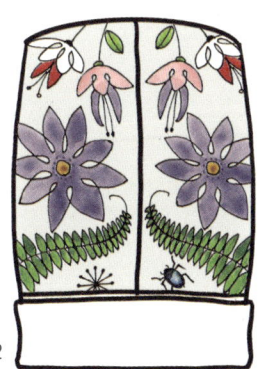

2

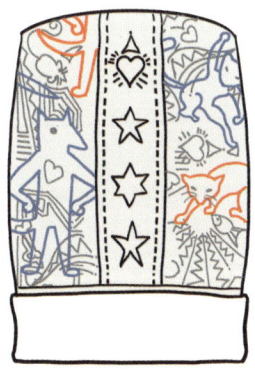

3

Back design
The sneakers will have some construction details to join the fabric and give it strength, and you can use these to inform your design.
1. Central motif on a wrap-around heel backstay.
2. Mirror design with a central seam.
3. Add simple motifs to the vertical seamed back panel.

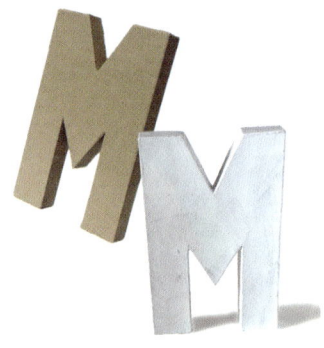

47

SEND A LETTER

You can buy blank 3D cardboard boxes, animals, letters, and more. Draw decorations to cover these three-dimensional blank canvases.

Initial gifts

Letters or numbers make great presents for friends. Prime the surface of the letter with an oil-based (not water based!) primer, such as one for MDF or plywood. Apply a couple of coats and sand between each if you want to achieve a really smooth surface. You can draw your motifs straight onto the primed surface, or as on the letters shown here, on a sheet of colored drawing paper. Trace around the shape of the letter, draw your motifs onto the shape, cut the paper letter out, and stick it to the surface of the cardboard.

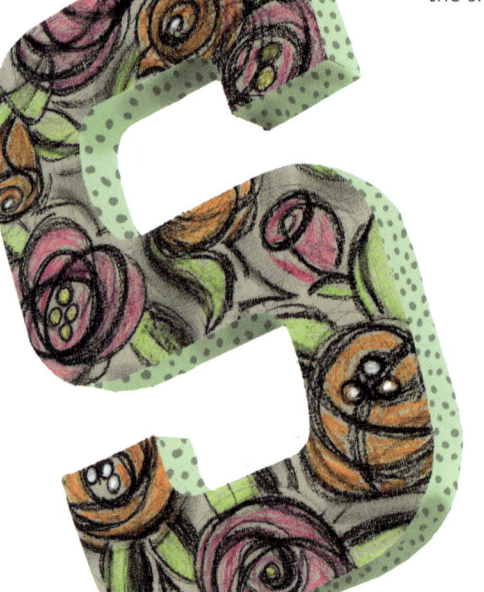

M

Using smooth yellow paper, draw the flower and leaf motif in a waterproof black fineliner pen, then add color with colored pencil. For the sides of the letter, use buff-colored paper with acrylic white marker wavy lines, and colored pencil dots in between.

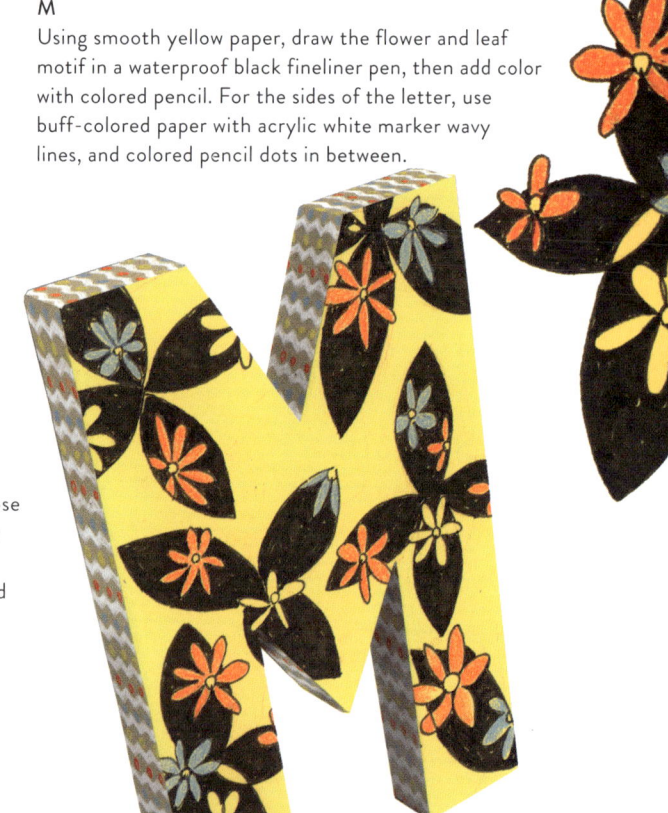

S

A fifties-style scribbly retro rose drawn on pastel paper. For the line's soft-edged effect, this is drawn in charcoal, then colored with colored or chalk pencil. The sides were made from a green pastel paper with gray felt-tip dots.

C

Dog-lover friend? Using pale-colored paper, lightly draw the pencil outlines to plan the position of the dog characters. You might like to draw some breaking out at the edges as if they are moving, or you may prefer to have complete dogs. Draw the final positions with a darker pencil line, or black fineliner, and then add colors and white with colored pencils. The sides were made from decoupage paper.

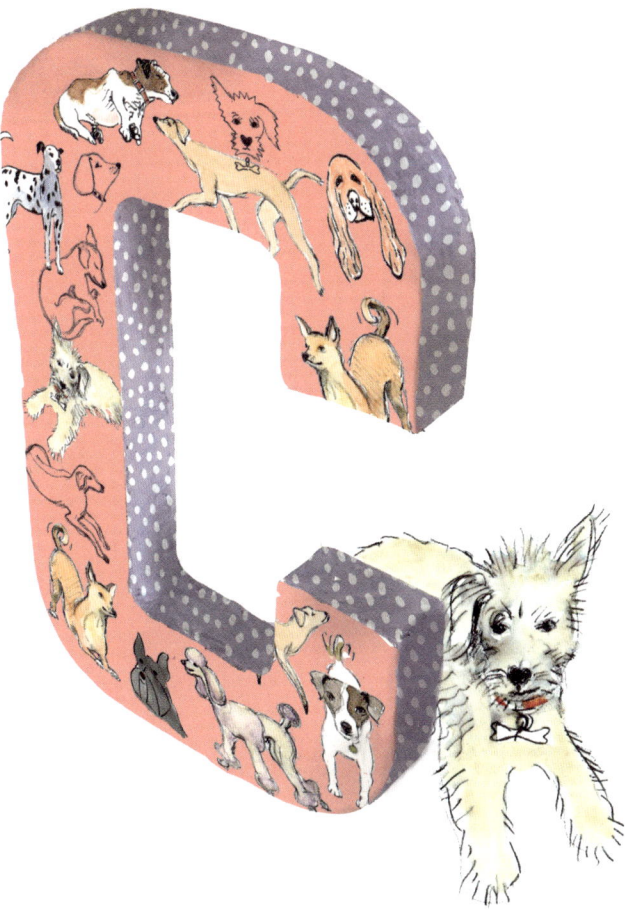

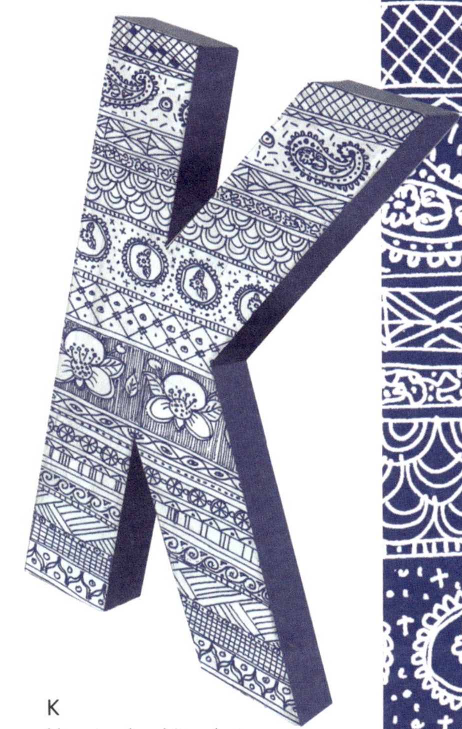

K

Use simple white photocopy paper and draw border patterns (see page 120). Add plain blue paper to fill the sides. Since I had a scan of this border pattern I reversed the colors and printed out the negative version for the back.

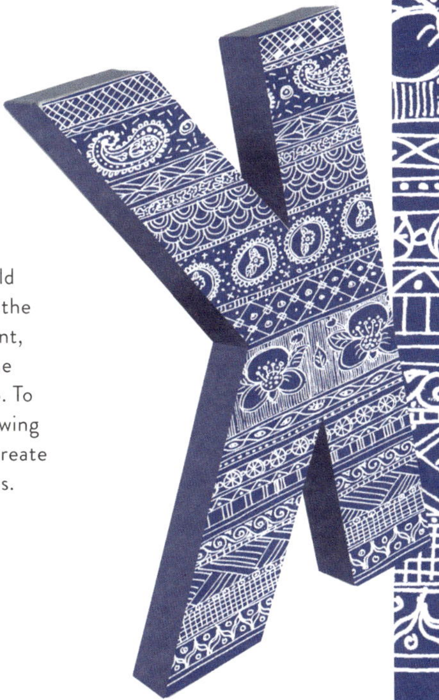

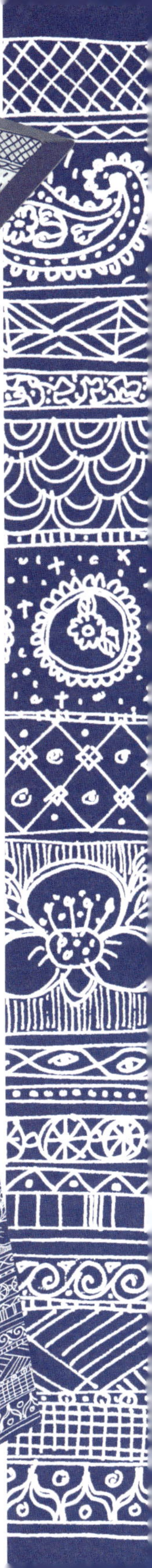

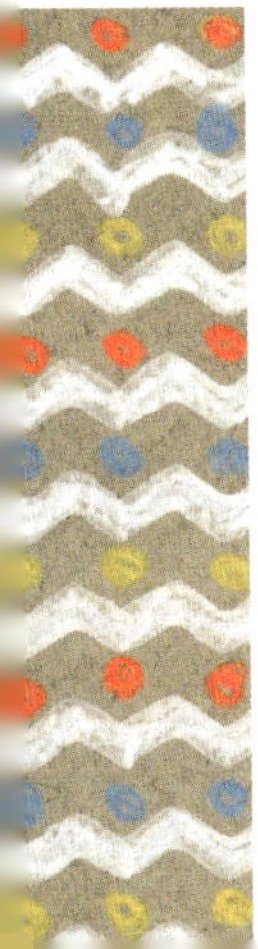

The sides

For the sides of all the letters, use a separate strip of paper, or you could paint them. If you are using paper, either cut a strip the exact width of the sides to wrap all the way around the letter, or, to achieve a seamless joint, cut the strip a centimeter wider on either side, fold and wrap around the front and back of the letter and then stick the main image over the top. To fold in curves and corners, some sewing or craft knowledge is helpful to create mitered corners or clipped curves.

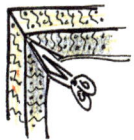
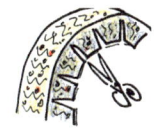

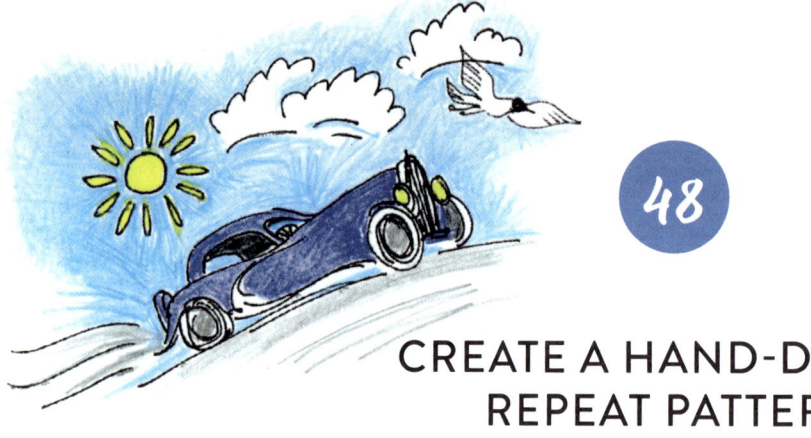

CREATE A HAND-DRAWN REPEAT PATTERN

A pattern repeat is from the point where a pattern starts and then starts again. It repeats evenly with equal spacing. Repeating a motif is eye-catching and sets up pleasing visual rhythms. For inspiration, look at the patterns on fabrics and wallpapers.

Create a simple pattern tile

A pattern repeat is also called a pattern tile. They can be arranged in many ways— in a grid pattern, staggered, flipped left to right or top to bottom, on the diagonal, or arranged in pairs. Some examples are shown below.

1-4

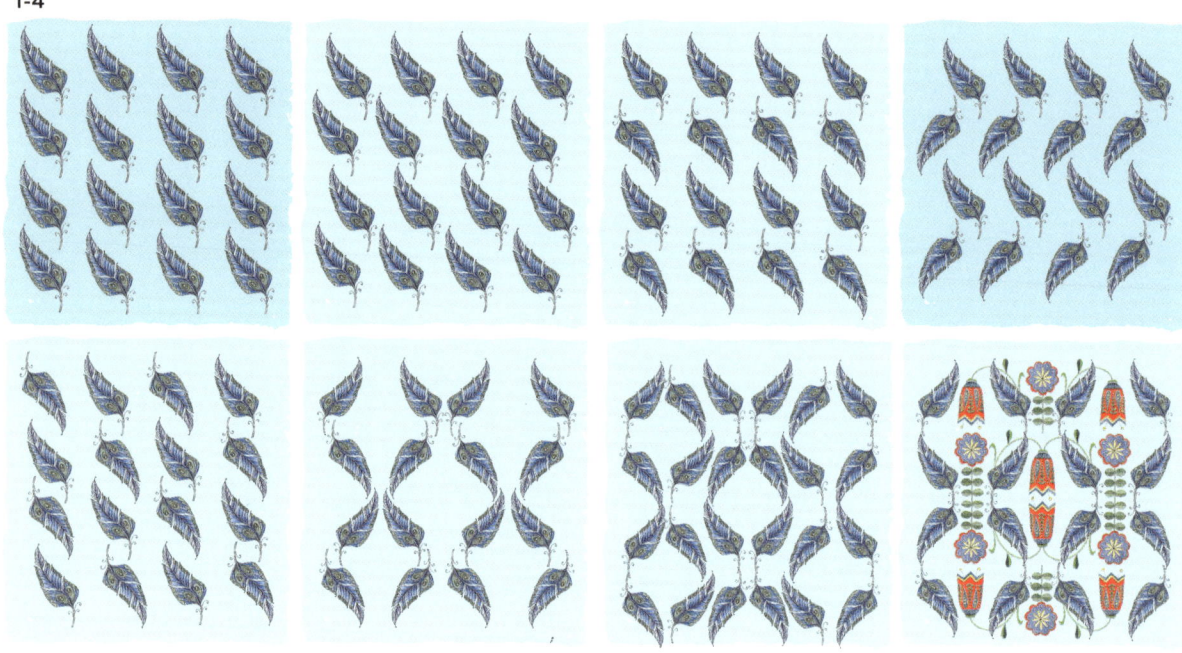

5-8

In a square, draw a **single** motif such as a flower sprig or a feather (from page 30). This is your tile. Now repeat it in different positions to create repeat patterns, as in the doodles above. Finally, try adding more motifs and colors to the design. The options are endless.

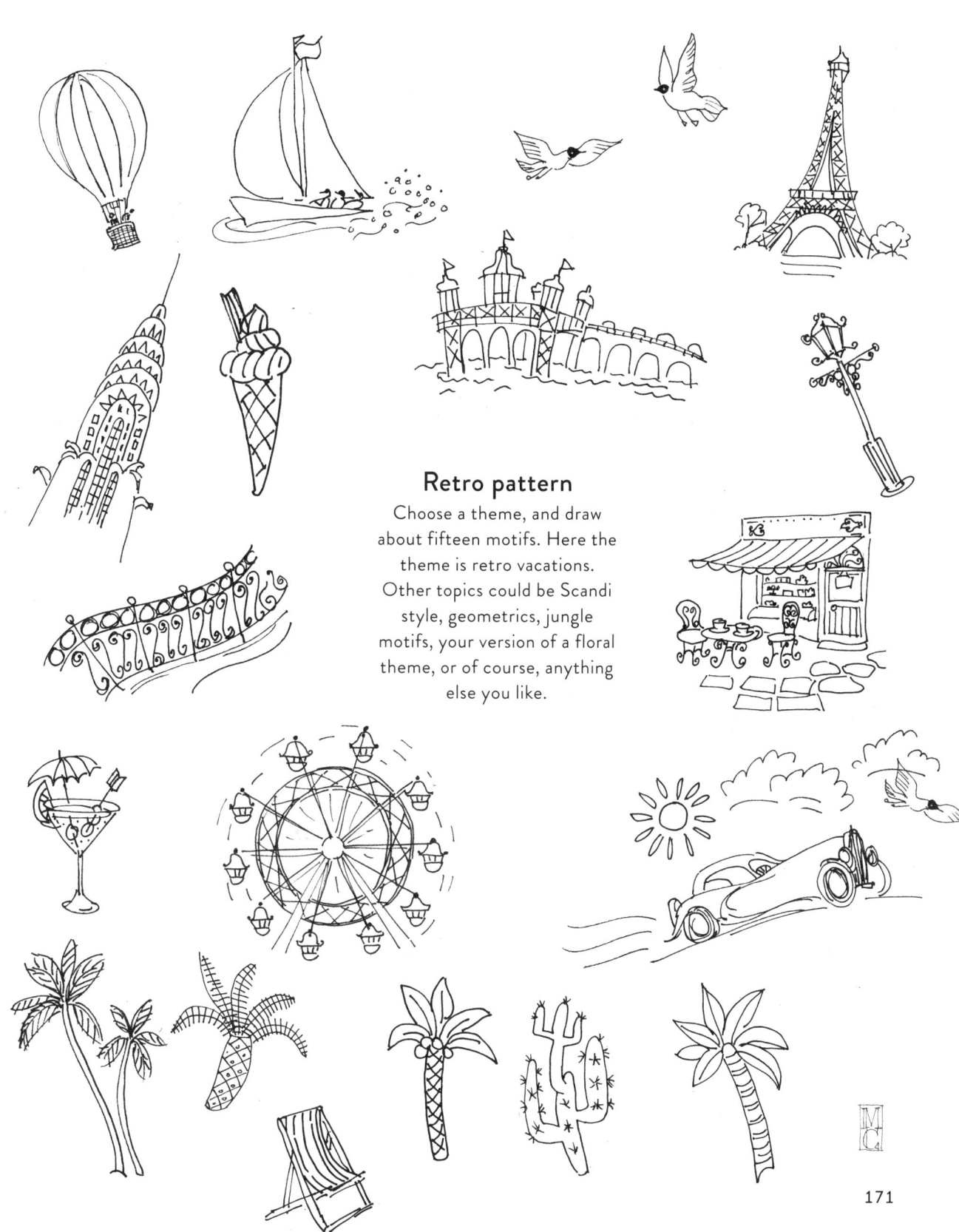

Retro pattern

Choose a theme, and draw about fifteen motifs. Here the theme is retro vacations. Other topics could be Scandi style, geometrics, jungle motifs, your version of a floral theme, or of course, anything else you like.

Single tile to repeat pattern

Combine your motifs to make your pattern tile, experimenting with the design to see what works. You probably will have to edit out some of your little drawings. When you have one you like, copy it onto tracing or thin paper so you can repeat it a couple of times to check they fit together well.

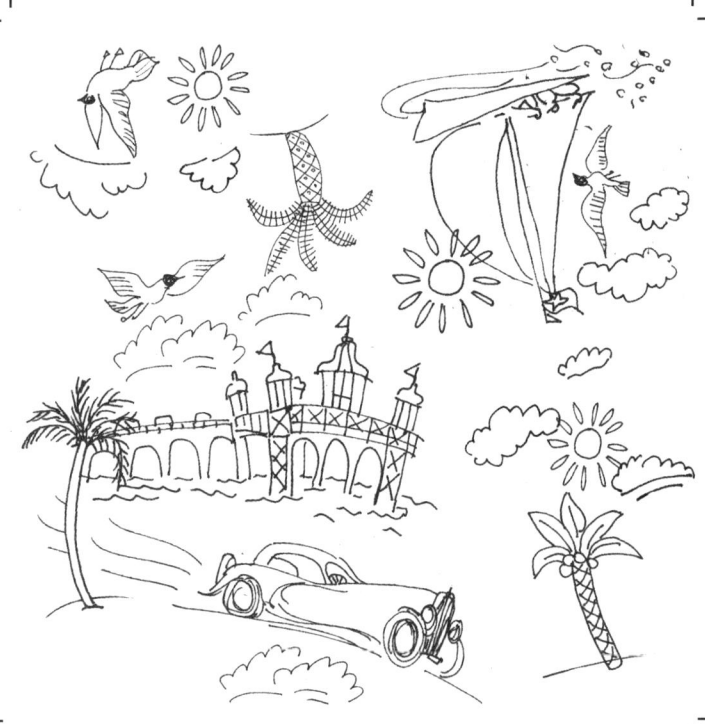

To position the tiles together accurately, add registration marks at the corners.

To make the finished pattern work from more than one viewpoint, position some of the motifs upside down.

Useful clouds

It is good to have a motif at the edges, that can act as a subtle link between each tile, such as the clouds that can be viewed from the top or bottom. You can see in the main tile above there are clouds positioned near the edges.

The process

When you have a design you like, use a black waterproof pen to copy the tile pattern. This design (right) uses repeat number **5** from the page 170.

There are a few methods

1. Draw a master tile with registration marks, then, using a light box, repeat the tile.
2. Using tracing paper, draw the line work before using the traced image as a master.
3. If its a simple design, you could draw the repeats freehand. Small differences between each tile would add to its hand-crafted nature.
4. If you have a computer or tablet you can digitally repeat the tile.

To add color, use normal colored pencils, or if you used a waterproof pen for the line then use watercolor pencils with a wash, or colored ink.

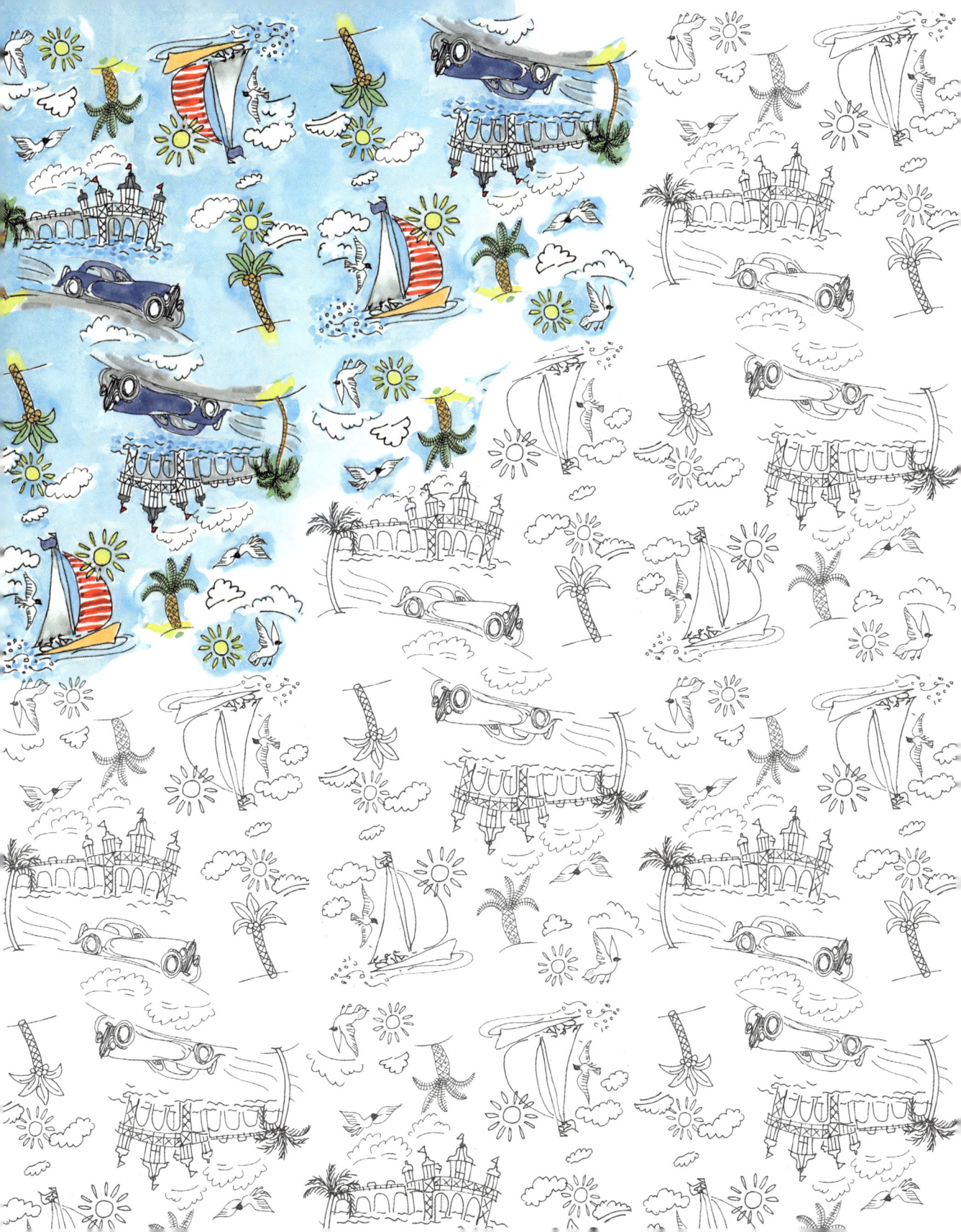

Scarf design

This scarf design has a radiating pattern. Use similar motifs to the previous page to plan your quarter-corner tile. I liked the idea of the Chrysler building and the Eiffel Tower creating a star around the Ferris wheel, while the yacht made a good triangular corner shape. Testing the four corners together with rough drawings, I could see there were some gaps so I added in the hot-air balloon, the car, seagulls, and clouds.

Repeat the corner
Draw your first corner, then copy for the other three corners. You could just draw the whole thing freehand and each corner might be slightly different or you could trace, rotate, and repeat (or scan, rotate, and repeat).

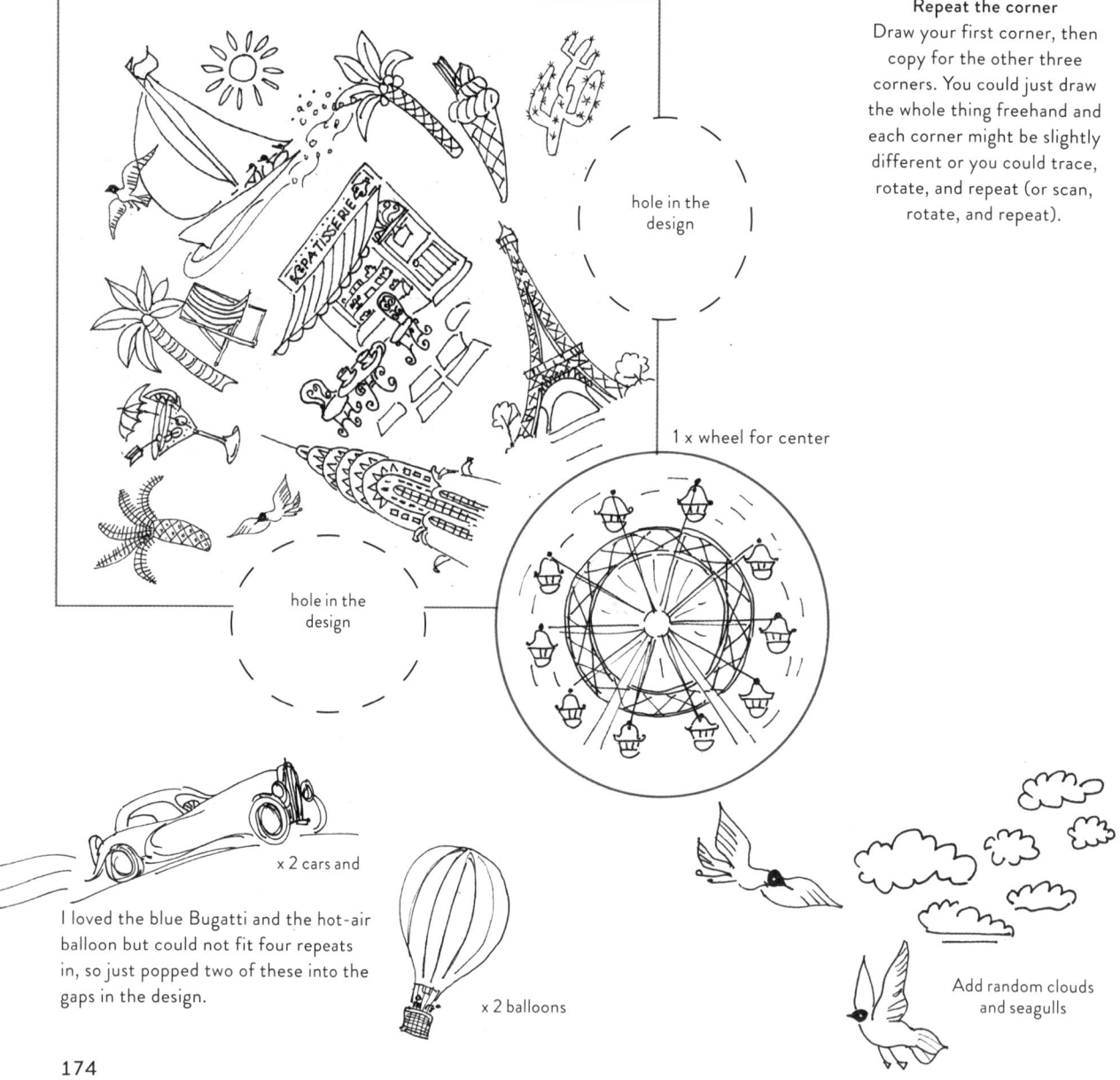

hole in the design

hole in the design

1 x wheel for center

x 2 cars and

I loved the blue Bugatti and the hot-air balloon but could not fit four repeats in, so just popped two of these into the gaps in the design.

x 2 balloons

Add random clouds and seagulls

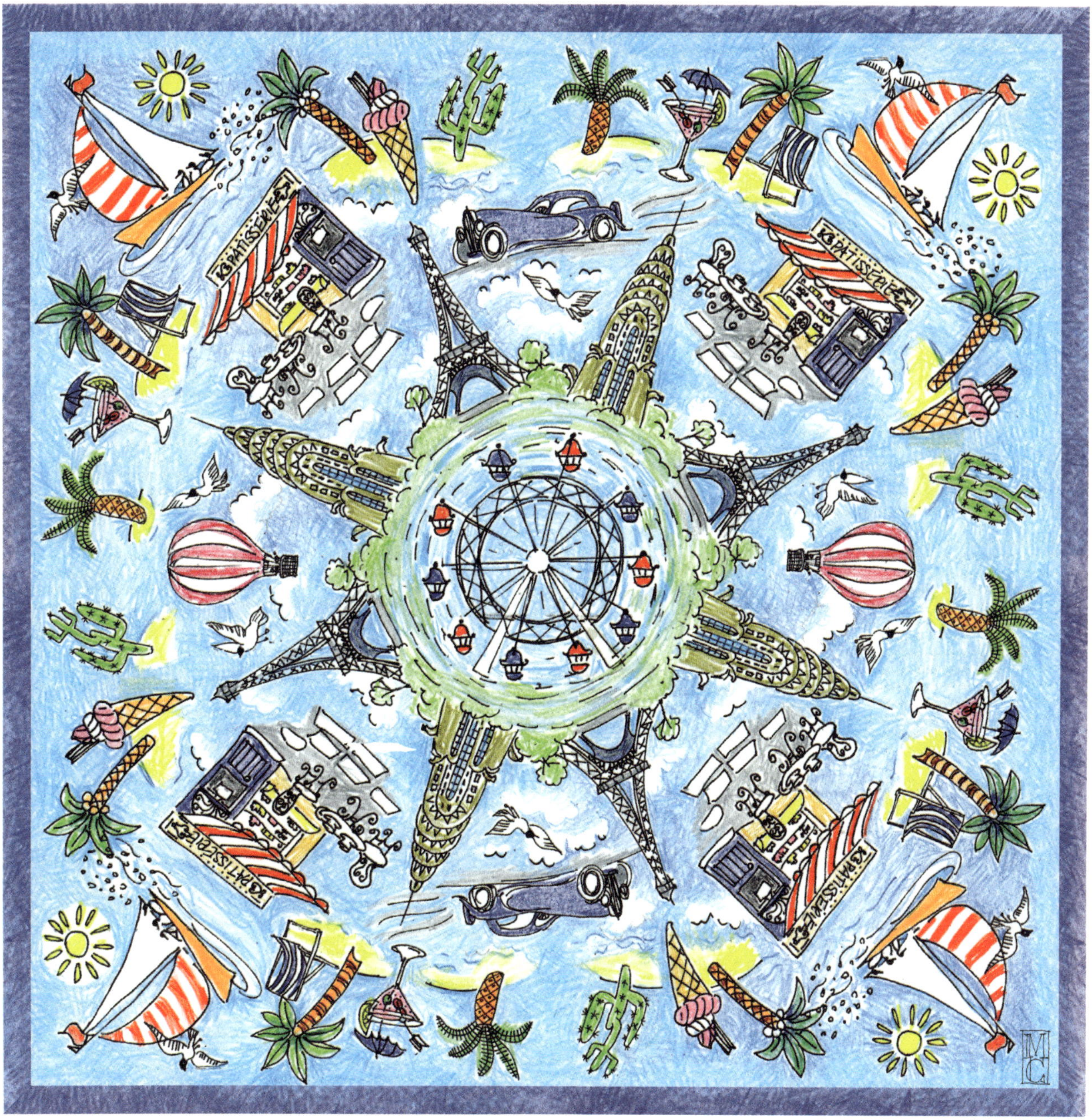

Add some color
I liked the scribbly texture of colored pencils, so decided to use them for the whole scarf design. There are websites that will print scarf designs. Who needs Hermès?

Add a border and your signature or monogram!

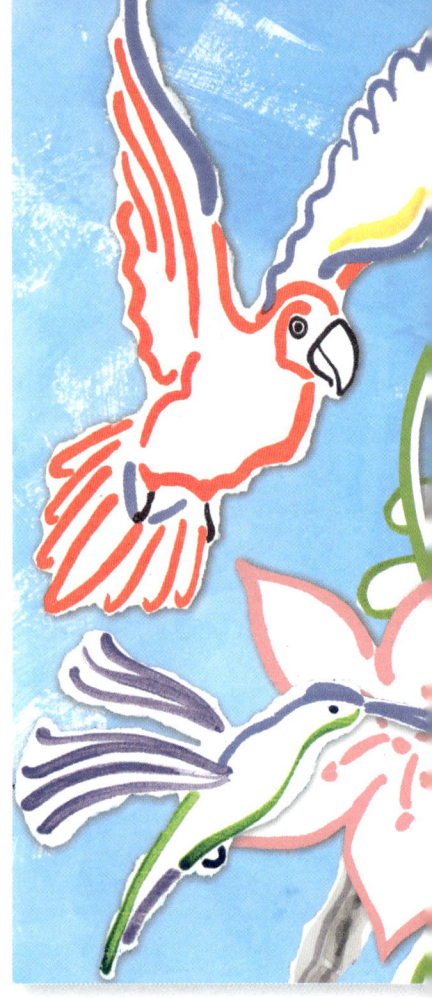

49 MAKE IT BIG

It is difficult to show you this idea in a little book! You can create something more imposing for a piece of wall art, or take an existing small drawing and recreate it larger. You may also want to reproduce the image for gifts. Printing out large pieces at your art or frame store can be expensive, so check out the cost of one large piece of art versus a triptych.

TAKEAWAY

Make a collage . . .

Most of the drawings in the book were done as elements that fit easily on an letter or poster-size sheet of paper. If you wanted to draw something much bigger you could buy a roll of paper or a larger canvas or you could collage individual drawings from smaller pages onto whatever size you want.

. . . or a triptych

Another idea would be to create a triptych. Again you can work to whatever size you wish. Plan how you are going to divide the composition into three parts. If it is collage you have some flexibility to make the final decisions when you are gluing the pieces in place.

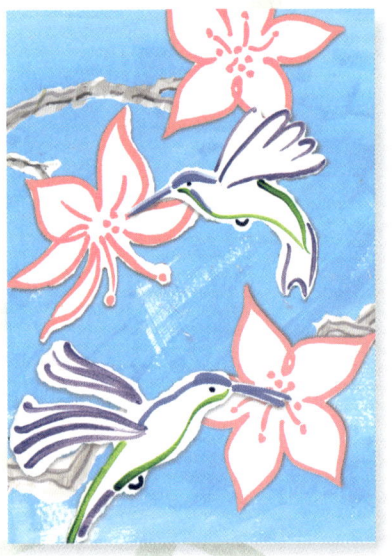
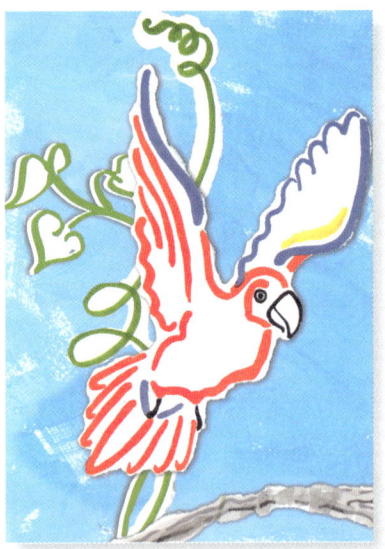
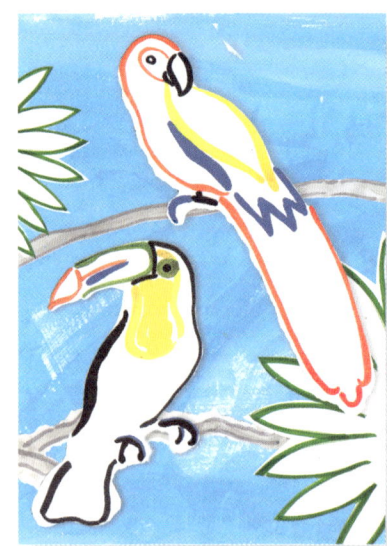

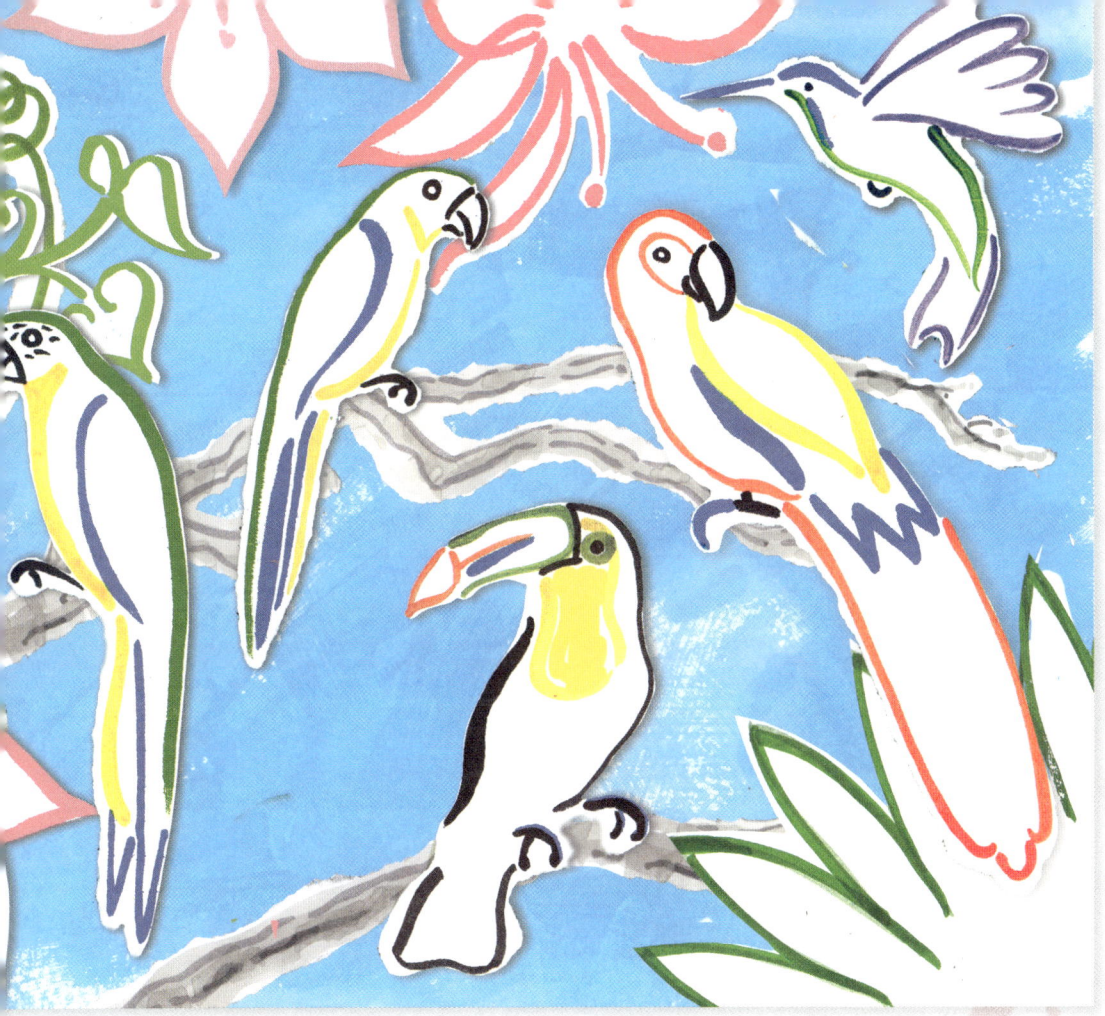

Collage method

Both the larger poster and the triptych use this method, with the brush-drawn birds on page 38 as an example of the process.

Work out the eventual size you want the wall art to be and make sure you have a background paper that size. You could buy colored paper, or as shown in these examples, you can paint your own background and make it lively and textured by leaving areas white or blending in another color.

Roughly plan the composition. Make a very rough sketch of the birds, then tear them out and check the positions. Draw the final birds and foliage in whatever medium you have chosen.

Tear or cut out both the birds and foliage drawings, some close to the line others not, then arrange the drawings on the background before sticking them down (see page 189 for adhesive). I liked the lively wobbly white torn edge of the paper so decided to keep some, others I cut out close to the drawn edge.

Paper for painted backgrounds

Use a heavyweight (160 lb, 350 gsm or thicker) paper to prevent it from buckling when you apply the color wash. Experiment with the amount of water—if you use less water the paper will buckle less, but if you want to use a "wet wash" then stretch it onto a board. There are lots of online demos showing you how to do this. Or you could paint acrylic on a thin piece of board.

50

HOW'S YOUR SKETCHBOOK?

As one of the final notes in the book, check the health of your sketchbook. Are you exercising it enough? Sometimes we get caught up with life and gradually fall out of the habit of sketching, a little like losing the routine of going to the gym, or some other form of exercise. Kick-start getting back into the habit of sketching. Once you get going again, you will wonder why you ever stopped. Family life can be chaotic so try to carve out some sketching time once a week. You could create a journal of your family playing, sleeping, or watching TV. If you take anything away from this book, then I hope it's the sketchbook habit.

Two for one

At the salon, a long train journey, waiting for an appointment, at the airport, or an outside event? Take your sketchbook. You never know what you might see.

At the hairdressers
The challenge was to capture the quick-moving hands, and the way they move around. Covid masks were a sign of the times. Six months later the hairdressers was a different place, but still the same challenge of capturing the moving arms.

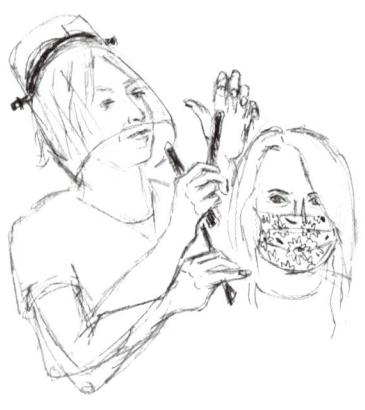

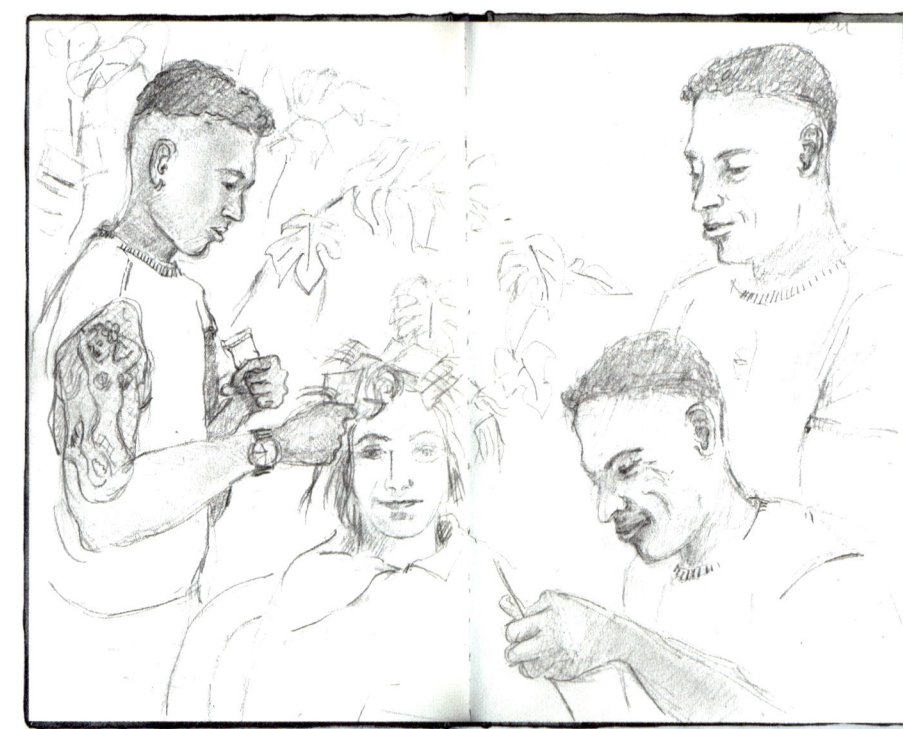

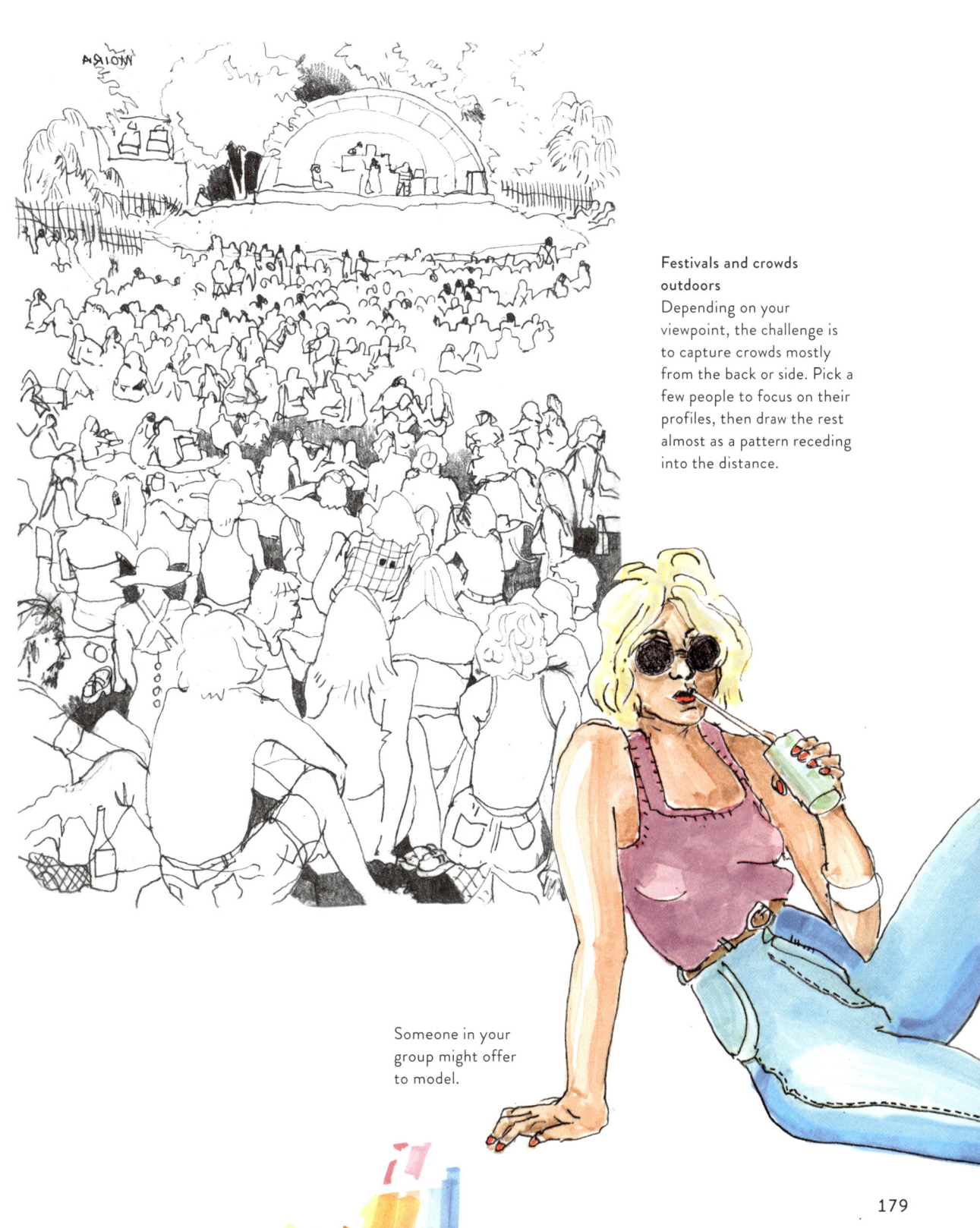

Festivals and crowds outdoors
Depending on your viewpoint, the challenge is to capture crowds mostly from the back or side. Pick a few people to focus on their profiles, then draw the rest almost as a pattern receding into the distance.

Someone in your group might offer to model.

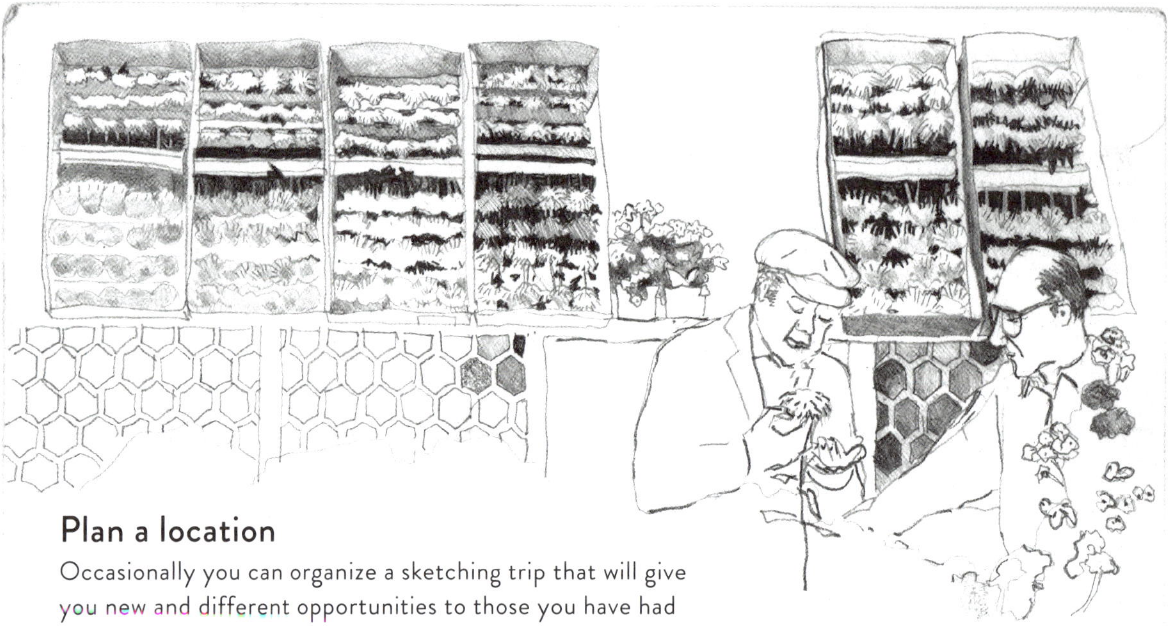

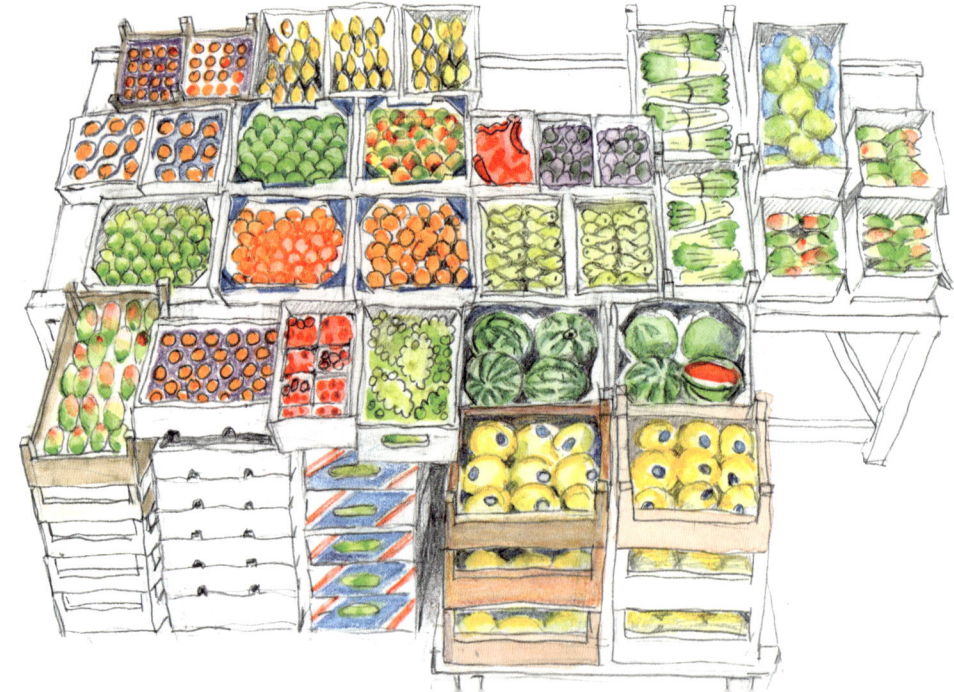

Plan a location

Occasionally you can organize a sketching trip that will give you new and different opportunities to those you have had before. These sketches were all done with easy-to-carry graphite pencils and some colored pencils.

At an early morning farmer's market where there are less crowds, try to capture the traders haggling over the price of flowers, or the repeat patterns created by boxes of fruit and veg. If you are not able to go to a market, a local store would be just as good. The fresh produce boxes below are drawn in three-point perspective (see page 62) using a pencil line and watercolor markers.

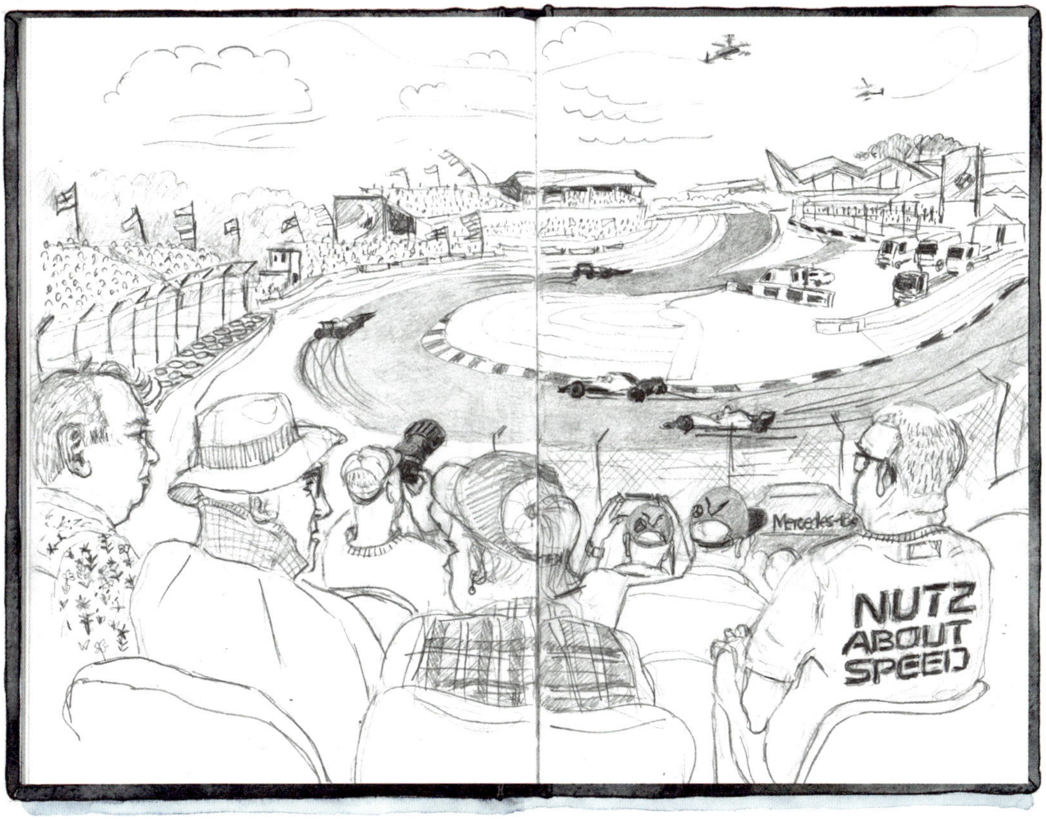

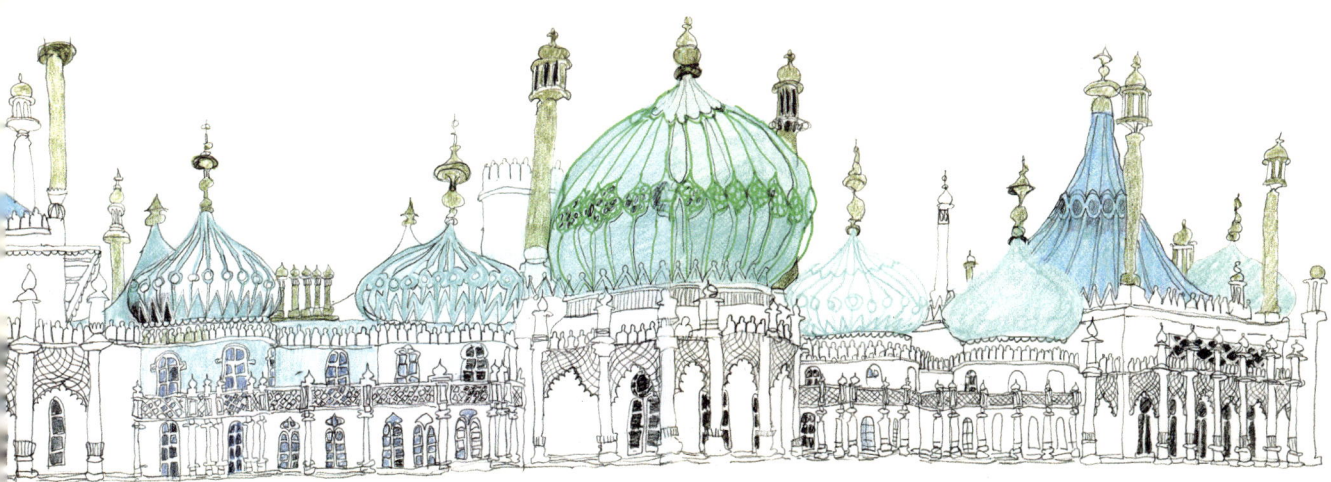

You might not be NUTZ ABOUT SPEED, but you might like to sketch the event.

Research if there are any unique buildings close to you. This is not an Indian palace (below), it is the Pavilion in Brighton, England, a seaside resort.

RESOURCES

Equipment advice, reproducing your work and printing it out, digital file size, and putting your work online.

VISIT THE ART STORE

It might seem odd to have this as a reminder prompt, however, once in a while take a trip to the art store. If you are new to art, or have worked through all or some of the ideas in the book, go and have a browse. It's easy to get into the habit of just replacing your equipment that has run out (I did) rather than being creative and trying something new.

Equipment

For most of the ideas in this book, the media is interchangeable, so if you prefer working in one, do (although it would increase your drawing skills to try a different media). The list below is a suggestion if you need to buy materials from scratch.

Pencils

The ideal staring point. We have all used them and they are great for half-imagined ideas that need to be quickly captured on paper before forgotten, or for planning and experimenting with the composition. Pencils are good used on their own to create drawings, and they can be erased and re-drawn until the image is just right.

Starter pack

Graphite pencils I would buy H or HB (these have a harder core, so make a lighter, scratchier mark), B or 2B (these are softer, so make mid-tone velvety marks), and 4B or 6B (these are very soft and make a dark tone and rich marks).

Black, fiber-tips pens The manufacturers make starter packs that generally have six different tips and are a great value.

Colored pencils or felt-tips markers If you are used to using one of these then continue with that. A set of eight to twelve colors would be a good starting point.

Paper To start, a letter-size drawing pad, and a pad of "CP" (cold-pressed) paper for the watercolor pencils or anything you are adding water to.

Pencils
Available in different grades to make different tones; from delicate and light to rich and dark.

H   B   6B   watercolor graphite

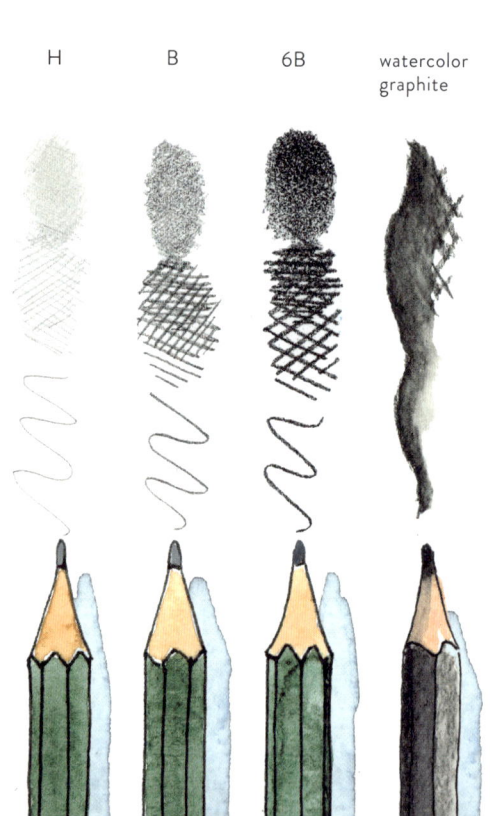

Colored pencils. Used for lines or areas of color. Waterproof (non-water-soluble): the colors are merged by drawing layers of dry colors. Water-soluble: the colors are merged by adding water. Soften the color with a brush and water or the water brush see page 189.

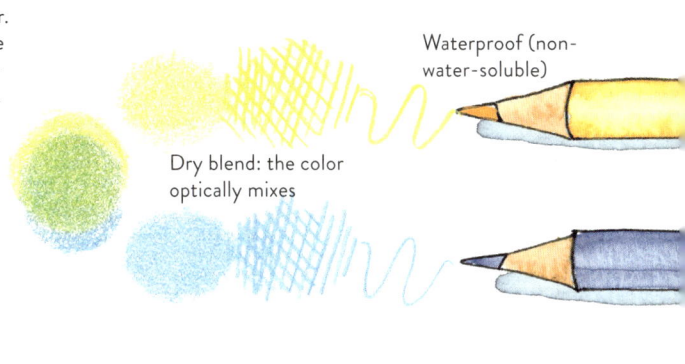

Waterproof (non-water-soluble)

Dry blend: the color optically mixes

Colored pencils

Available as water-soluble or waterproof, they are a good way to start working with color. Colors can be blended together to get soft transitions, either building up dry layers with waterproof pencils, where the pigment attaches on the paper surface to optically mix, or with water-soluble pencil, where the pigments actually mix to make a combined color. With water, the color can still be moved around on the paper. Manufacturers are constantly developing pencils to make the colors either more vivid or have different properties. I have recently discovered some ink-based pencils that can be used dry, or wet with water, and blended like watercolor pencils. However once dry, your initial drawing won't bleed more, so if desired you can overlay other drawn (and wetted) forms over the top. Experiment and see what you prefer.

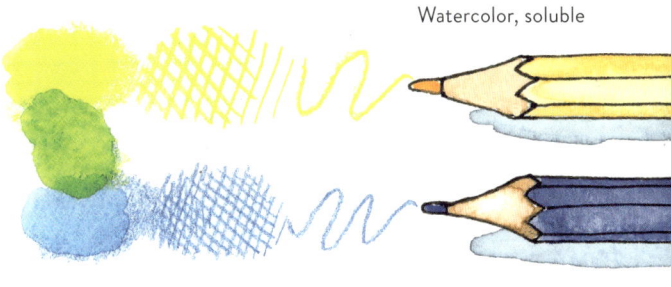

Watercolor, soluble

Chalk or pastel pencils

There are many types available, with slightly different compositions, making them either softer, chalkier, harder, waxier, and more. They are available as sticks or come encased in wood, like a pencil, which is a better choice for ease of transport, use, and budget. They are obtainable in many colors including the traditional black charcoal and the earth pigments. If you like the idea of using these (they are great for layering and textures, see page 50) start with chalk-pastel pencils, then move onto the sticks.

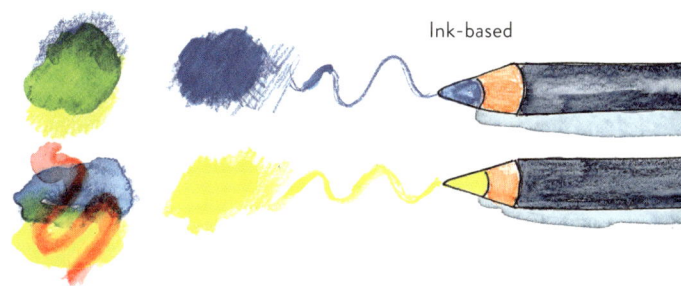

Ink-based

Chalk-pastel pencils. Great for working on colored paper, and can be blended together by drawing layers of color, rubbing with your finger, or with a paper tortillon, a rolled paper tool used for blending or smudging.

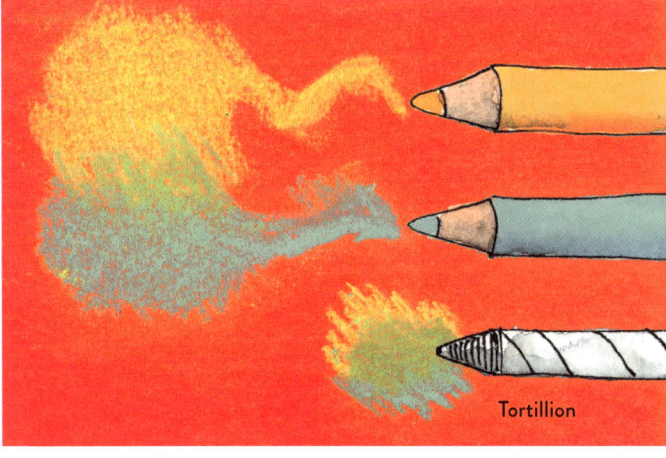

Chalk

Tortillion

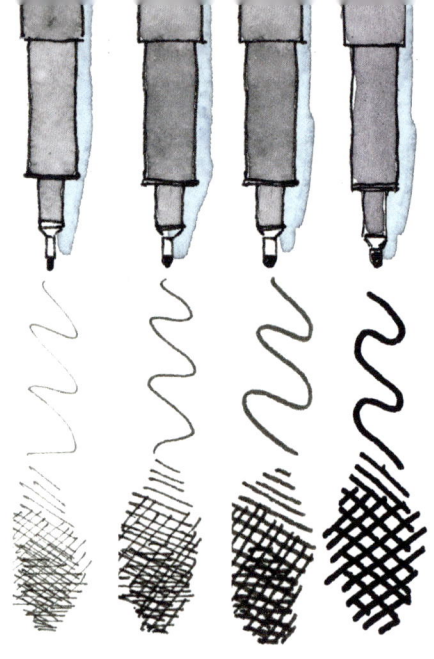

Fineliner pens (left) used for line drawing range from very fine 0.05 mm to 1.2 mm. Fineliner pens are generally water resilient.

0.05 mm   0.3 mm   0.8 mm   1.2 mm

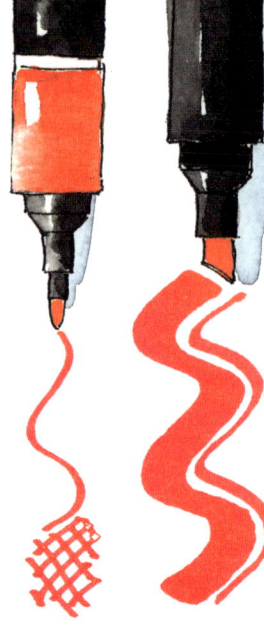

Alcohol-based marker pens (right) with a range of nibs

Bullet tip   Chisel tip has two edges

Fountain pen

Dip pen

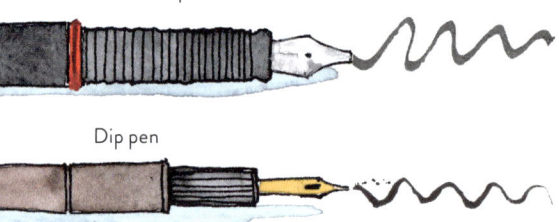

Traditional pens. Art cartridge pens/fountain pens (top) have constant ink flow and the nib gives a quirky character. The pasta drawing on page 79 was drawn with this pen.
A dip pen with bottle ink would give a finer line — a little unpredictable but that gives it charm.

Manufacturers make dual nib markers (center, below). Not only do you get two for the price of one, but the color match is guaranteed since the ink for both nibs is from the same reservoir. Depending on brand, the combination of tips vary.

Fiber, felt-tip pens, and markers

The names are used synonymously and confusingly to cover a wide variety of pens. Cheap to expensive, generally the latter will last longer, the color will be clearer, and it will be less problematic in the way it lays down a line on the paper.

Every artist should have a favorite black or dark color pen to draw with. The term fineliner is used by many companies to indicate a pen with a fine drawing nib, and mostly water-resistant ink.

Felt, fiber, and gel pens and markers generally have thicker tips for coloring, but can be used for strong line work. The best way to choose is to work out how you want to draw, then visit the art store or go online and ask for their advice on brands, and importantly, which paper surface to use.

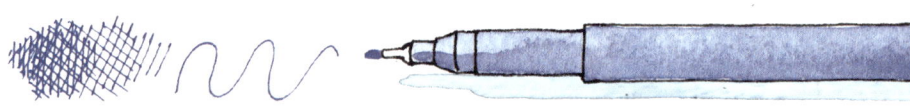

Fineliner tip.

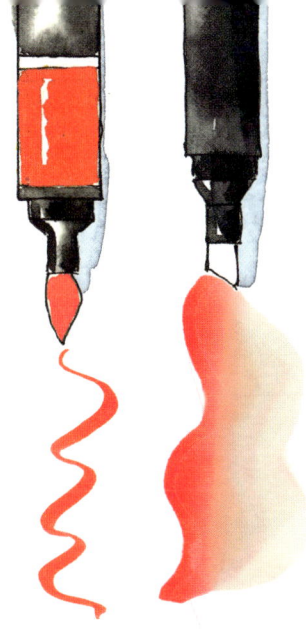

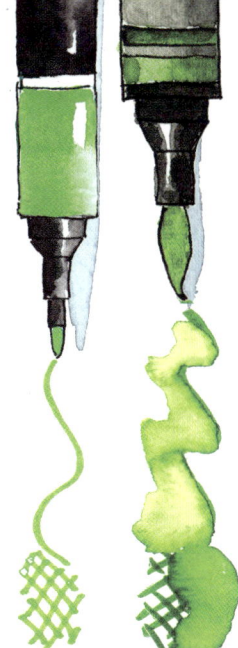

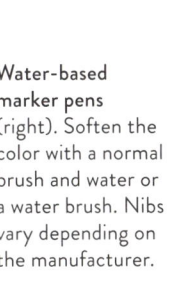

Water-based marker pens (right). Soften the color with a normal brush and water or a water brush. Nibs vary depending on the manufacturer.

Brush tip gives varied thicknesses

Solvent/alcohol color blender

The choices to consider are:

1. Which shape nib or tip?
2. Which type of ink or paint?
3. What color?

1. Nib or tip?

• For drawing and sketching—fineliners are best and there are about eight tip sizes (you will work out a couple that work for you).

• For a stronger, thicker line—or coloring in detail areas—try a fine, bullet tip or a normal bullet tip like on most felt-tip pens.

• For shading or coloring large areas—use the chisel tip or the brush tip.

• For flowing organic painting or calligraphic lines—try the brush tip.

• Another option for general line work or coloring in

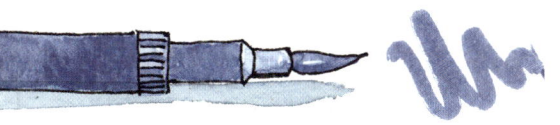

Brush tip.

details is the gel pen. This has a roller ball/ballpoint pen–type nib, available in thin, medium, or thick line weights.

2. Ink or Paint?

For inks and paints you have five main options:

• **Water-resistant.** You are probably most familiar with these, and it is in most standard felt-tip pens. Available in many colors and nib shapes, at all price ranges. (The cheaper ones are less waterproof.) Good to just draw with or for coloring in. Most fineliner pens use this ink so you can add a water wash color over without the line bleeding. Make sure to check, as there is nothing worse than applying water and the drawing disappearing!

• **Alcohol-based inks.** (Permanent, translucent) Colors can be laid down flat or blended. Most brands sell a blending tool. You need to use special marker paper (see page 186). Some brands have refillable reservoirs and you can replace the nibs when they become worn. More expensive brands claim better blending, no streaking, and longevity.

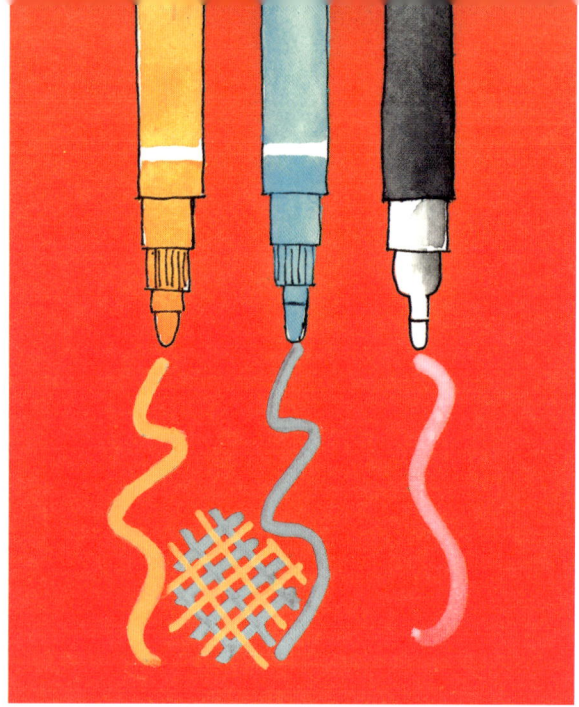

Acrylic markers with bullet nibs (left). When dry the paint is opaque and permanent.

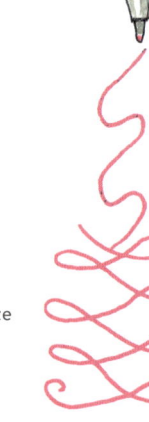

Gel pens (right) tip size range from 0.5 mm to 1.5 mm.

• **Water-based.** The opposite to water-resistant and has a more specific use. The drawn line is softened with clean water or merged with another color. "Tickle" the line to release the pigment with a brush or a water brush (see page 189).

• **Acrylic paint.** Great for drawing on unusual surfaces such as glass, ceramics, plastic, or canvas. Look online to see decorated bikes, shoes, and even furniture. The paint is thick, making it good for flat opaque areas. Acrylic can be blended with water when still wet and once dry another color can be drawn over the top. Since it is opaque it will retain its color. Most acrylic markers have a refillable reservoir, and a porous ceramic or plastic nib that can be taken out and cleaned, or replaced if needed.

• **Gel.** The ink, which can be either water-based or spirit-based, is suspended in the gel. It has a roller ball tip similar to a ballpoint pen. The pens are economical, come in a great range of colors (even glitter). Can be used for lettering, linework, and coloring.

3. Color pigments in pens
The ranges are amazing, from pastels to primaries, metallics to subtle grays. You can buy value packs, which are a great starting point, or more expensive professional markers sold individually or in limited palette ranges such as landscape tones.

Paper for drawing
General Drawing for most pencils, colored pencils, and fiber-tip pens use a good quality medium-weight paper (80 to 100 lb, 130 to 160 gsm) either as sheets or in a sketchbook. It will offer a nice surface to draw on and the pen or pencil will move easily. If you know you will never want to add a watercolor wash then use basic drawing paper, as it is cheaper.
Colored paper for drawing for use with colored pencils and the chalky pastel pencils. Some colored papers such as fine art paper have a textured surface, which remains attractively visible underneath the layers of color.
Alcohol markers require a special smooth surface, bleedproof paper. Like markers, the paper was

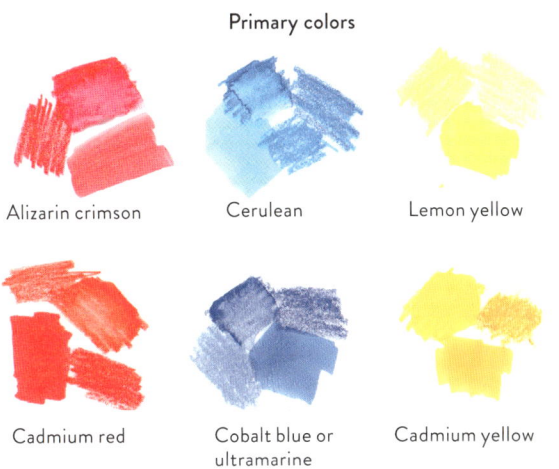

Primary colors

Alizarin crimson

Cerulean

Lemon yellow

Cadmium red

Cobalt blue or
ultramarine

Cadmium yellow

Secondary colors

Any mid green,
orange, violet

Adding paint color to black-and-white sketches The pigments can be expensive, but some manufacturers make quite reasonable pre-chosen sets at the same cost as two items if bought individually. If you need to buy colors individually, this selection (left), is a good start. Sometimes the names are the original pigment name as here, others are more evocative such as cornflower blue, or even a number. The art store will be able to help choose equivalents.

There are two of each primary colors here, as this give better color-mixing options.

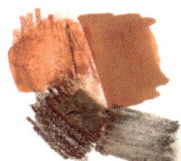

Extra colors If budget allows, add one or two earth colors, such as Venetian red and raw umber.

originally developed for professional visualizers such as architects and graphic designers to sketch rough concepts. It was not required to be archive quality, it was cheap and lightweight (20 lb, 70 gsm). The paper prevents the ink from bleeding through to anything underneath and the layers of marker color lay down better than on other papers. For something more permanent, use heavyweight marker paper (43 lb, 160 gsm) or Bristol board, with an ultra smooth surface (115 lb or 250 gsm).

Watercolor paper for watercolor pencils, markers, or adding watercolor wash to black waterproof line work. The paper will need to be a heavier weight so will not buckle (140 lb, 300gsm) There are three surfaces: hot pressed is very smooth, cold pressed has a slightly textured surface that gives watercolor its attractive character, and rough is a very textured surface. This can be too rough to draw with normal drawing media unless you are brush drawing.

Sketchbooks are available in all the paper types for all media, and in many binding styles.

Adding color

Aside from the pencils and markers shown on the previous page, you can add color to your drawings by using transparent paint. The quality of color washes is an attractive foil to line drawings.

Inks Unlike the other painting media, inks are made from dyes, not pigments, so colors tend to be brighter and cleaner. They are available in waterproof and non-waterproof versions, with the latter offering a more limited range of colors. They can both be diluted with water to make paler colors. Waterproof inks are made water-resistant with shellac. The shellac adds a glassy gloss to the dried ink surface, making the colors glow like stained glass. Waterproof ink cannot be moved or corrected, but can have transparent glazes of ink layers added over the top without moving underlayers. Unfortunately, it can clog/dry hard on brushes so always clean after use.

Watercolor Available in a vast range of colors and different qualities, and as little pans or larger expensive tubes. Watercolors work well with drawings, since they are transparent and can be applied over pencil, waterproof pen, or waterproof marker lines. Diluted with water to make paler colors, they are easy to mix together to make other colors (see right).

Brushes

Like other materials, there are many kinds of brushes to choose from. You can use the same brushes for brush drawing as for coloring your drawings.

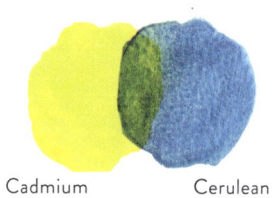

Cadmium yellow   Cerulean blue

Color-mixing paint
When layering two colors, the color underneath shows through and mixes visually to make another color, in this case a green. Try it with alizarin crimson and cobalt, or cadmium red and cadmium yellow.

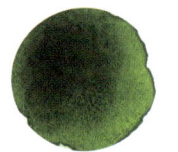

The same two colors mixed in a plastic palette prior to painting makes a lovely mossy green.

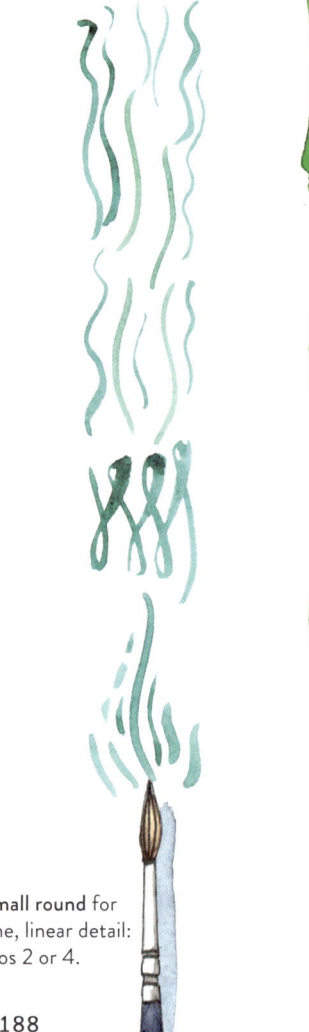

If you are buying your first brushes, and you have a total equipment budget, buy medium-priced brushes. Avoid cheap brushes since they can fall apart. Look after your brushes by cleaning and storing them correctly. (I have learned the hard way.)

See left for the brushes I would advise, they will be available in synthetic or animal hair. For watercolor and ink, the natural animal-hair brushes are best, but are more expensive. To start, try the synthetic sable or squirrel-hair brushes. When you have a bit of experience, buy a good-quality sable brush and note the difference. It may feel subtle but the way it holds and releases the paint combined with the way it reacts to the pressure you apply from the brush to the paper surface makes for a better technique.

Rounds A general "all-purpose" brush, they can be shaped to a soft point. The round body in the sizes above 3 hold a good amount of paint in relationship to each size. They can do most things, including linear work, washes, and flat areas of color.

Small round for fine, linear detail: Nos 2 or 4.

Round for linear strokes and color-wash areas: Nos. 6 or 8.

OTHER EQUIPMENT

Sharpener, a craft knife, or a scalpel is the best way to get a good point. Recently, I discovered a sharpener with a shavings collection box attached—it creates a good point and is great for location sketching since you can get rid of your shavings when you return home.

Eraser Never use the eraser on the end of a regular pencil—they are not good quality and will mark your paper. Get a good quality one from an art store. For erasing tiny areas or highlighting, there are proper pen erasers.

Water pots Keep replenishing so you have clean water for brighter colors and more accurate color mixing.

Water brush a great addition to the toolkit. Use with watercolor pencils, watercolor markers, or just paint. It's a convenient way to create a wash.

Palettes for getting your color ready, you can buy a cheap plastic one or just use some dishes from the kitchen.

Testing and scrap paper Keep a sheet or pad of cheap paper for testing your color mix before committing to your drawing. Sometimes you know you have too much paint on the brush for the area you want to paint, so lightly remove excess paint.

Hair dryer to speed up drying times, sometimes the phrase "watching paint dry" springs to mind.

For collage

Purchase papers in various colors, or color your own (see page 186). Use a glue stick or non-water-based glue, since they allow for a little correctional movement, and they don't buckle the papers (as water-based ones do). For a few of the collage projects in this book I have used a craft circle cutter.

A water brush is a great way to soften the lines and create a color wash from watercolor pencils or markers. Fill with clean water, and then brush. It's so easy for sketching on location, so take a couple.

Get the best point with a scalpel. Unless you have a particular reason you should always work with a fine point, because the drawings will look crisper.

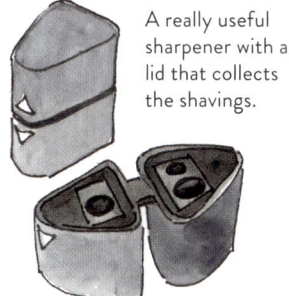

A really useful sharpener with a lid that collects the shavings.

Eraser pencil, for getting rid of tiny mistakes or creating highlights in areas of tone.

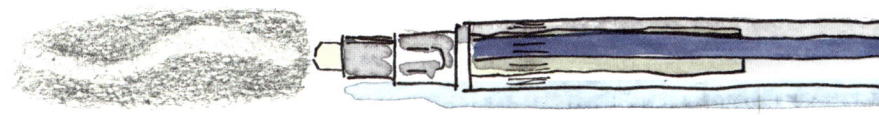

Travel stuff

When traveling by trains, boats, planes, or feet, take the minimum with you and be realistic with what you can achieve in the time available. It can feel defeating to carry a lot of items with you that go unused. If you travel by car, feel free to load up!

Electronics

Cell phone cameras, cameras, printers, scanners, tablets, and computers are all useful so that you can photograph your work, copy it, print it out, and give it as gifts. Drawing on your tablet works too.

FRAME OR SHARE ARTWORK

Some of the drawings would make great cards or presents for friends and family, others you may want to pop on a bare wall in your home. You can use the original drawing or reproduce it, so that you can gift it to many people.

Reproduce

You need to make a master digital image by photographing or scanning your art. Most of the recent cell phones, tablets, or ipads can produce good picture quality for general stationery-type

---

DIGITAL FILE SIZE TERMINOLOGY

You may have questions about sizing and digital specifications of the scan or photograph you want printed or put online. More importantly, if you are setting up and creating your art digitally, here are a few pointers:

PPI The size of the photo in pixels. This is how your camera sees/stores it. Pixels cannot overlap. Not the same as dpi.

DPI Dots per inch required for print machines. Think of four-color print in magazines. You can just see the cyan, magenta, yellow, and black dots, which overlap to create the image.

In both PPI and DPI a higher number means higher quality, which will contain more digital information, will take up more storage space, and will take longer to upload to the web.

If it looks good on screen, it does not guarantee it will print out well. If it looks pixelated on screen, then it will definitely print out poorly.

Which DPI?
- 72 dpi For web use only
- 150 dpi Simple ink jet or laser printers (you can user higher)
- 300 dpi For high-quality
- art prints.
- Your local copy store will be able to help you get the right scan quality if you are unsure.

Never take an existing digital file and try to enlarge the dpi in its profile. You are just stretching the information. There are software programs that can "guess" or interpolate which pixels to add, but it's best left to experts.

Size of the print out If you are reducing the size of your image

then having a low dpi might be okay (see below). You can see with 72 dpi the dots are spaced out, but if it is reduced dramatically the dots become closer. So the printout size of the image is always a consideration. To make it simpler: generally, if you have an image of 300 dpi it will be fine for all print methods, and only use 72 dpi for the web.

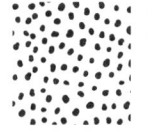

72 dpi

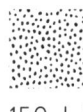

150 dpi

300 dpi

reproduction, but not if you wanted to make a large poster print for your wall. To do this you either need to photograph it or get the art scanned.

Photography There are lots of websites explaining how to photograph your work well. Make sure the artwork has no angle or tilt and is "square" in the frame; that it is evenly lit with no shadow to one side; and that the size of the digital file is large enough for the size you want to print out.

Scanner You may have a scanner function as part of a home photocopier/printer. If not, take it to your local copy shop. They can scan a piece of art up to poster size. The specific size of the scanned image will inform the quality of your printout.

Printing

A simple color print from your home copier could be all you need (use special heavier weight paper with a nicer surface rather than your standard copy paper). All copies will fade quite quickly. If you do take it to a copy shop, ask them if there are any issues of file size, color balance, or frame perspective before they print it out.

Putting your work online

Your work does not have to stay in the sketchbook or pinned to your wall. There are many ways you could get your work seen by a larger audience, such as social media to show your friends what you are up to, or for wider circulation. Dedicate an "art" Instagram, start a blog, or even a website. You could send drawings to an online agency to sell as multiples. If you have designed some patterns there are websites for this such as Redbubble and Zazzle.

As with printing your work out, the digital file size of the image needs to be considered.

For any commercial selling of your work, read up on and check out your copyright position.

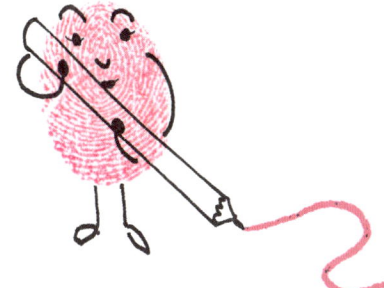

MAKE IT YOUR OWN

I hope you have enjoyed working your way through some or all of the ideas in this book. If you are able to draw once or twice a week you will gradually develop your own style or techniques.

Your technique is a bit like your finger print or signature: it will be unique to you. Initially you may copy other people's work, but it is something that will develop, and you will be influenced by things you observe. Going forward, it will become your way of expressing an idea or translating what you see onto paper. You can look at all the books and websites explaining "How to" techniques, and visit exhibitions and art galleries, but nothing beats finding subjects that YOU want to draw, and putting some lines or marks paper.

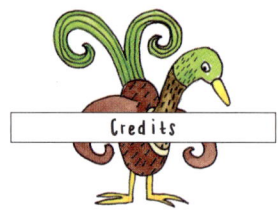

Credits

Quarto.com

First Published in North American in 2024 by Quarry Books, an imprint of The Quarto Group, 100 Cummings Center, Suite 265-D, Beverly, MA 01915, USA. T (978) 282-9590 F (978) 283-2742

Copyright © Elwin Street Productions 2024
Conceived and produced by Elwin Street Productions
10 Elwin Street, London E2 7BU

Text and Design by Moira Clinch

All images © Moira Clinch with the exception of:
© Anastasia Komarova, p. 149: Top right
© Anpannan, p. 164: Center right, right
© Lena Nikolaeva, p. 164: Center and far right
© Mhatzapa, p. 164: Far left, left, and center left
© Shutterstock, p. 148: Lower left, p. 164: Bottom panel

Quarry Books titles are also available at discount for retail, wholesale, promotional, and bulk purchase. For details, contact the Special Sales Manager by email at specialsales@quarto.com or by mail at The Quarto Group, Attn: Special Sales Manager, 100 Cummings Center, Suite 265-D, Beverly, MA 01915, USA.

ISBN 978-0-7603-9025-2

678910   54321

Printed in China

Library of Congress Control Number: 2023947421